921
JUNG
Hannah, Barbara 835032

Jung, his life and
work

# JUNG

## His Life and Work

# JUNG

## His Life and Work

### *A Biographical Memoir*

by

## Barbara Hannah

G. P. Putnam's Sons
New York

SNB: 399-11441-6

**Library of Congress Cataloging in Publication Data**

Hannah, Barbara.
  Jung, his life and work.

  Includes index.
  1. Jung, Carl Gustav, 1875–1961. I. Title.
BF173.J85H33 1976     150'.19'54  [B ]     76-13365
PRINTED IN THE UNITED STATES OF AMERICA

# CONTENTS

# PREFACE

This book is in no sense an official biography of C. G. Jung, but claims only to be a biographical memoir, showing his life as it appeared to me. It is too early for a detailed biography, such as Ernest Jones's *The Life and Work of Sigmund Freud*. Such a biography would require careful study of many documents which are at present held by the Jung family, and these are not yet accessible. Indeed, I knew that Jung's children were very much against anything biographical being written about their father, since they feel that all that is necessary has been said in his own *Memories, Dreams, Reflections*. I therefore did not inform any of them that I was writing this book. When it was finished, I gave it to them to read before publication, and they thoroughly disapproved.

This is not surprising when one thinks from what different standpoints we saw their father. I know little about Jung's family life, except that it was very happy and very meaningful to him. This book was written entirely from my own standpoint, the standpoint of those of his pupils who were privileged also to see him outside analysis.

In *Memories, Dreams, Reflections* Jung wrote almost entirely of his inner life, which was far more meaningful to him than any outer event. It was also of this inner side of his life that he almost always talked to me. I have tried to follow the course of his life chronologically, showing how he first lived his psychology and only much later formulated in words what he had lived.

Jung used to say that my common ground with him was my intense interest in psychological wholeness, in the process of individuation as he called it. I have therefore tried, throughout this book, to keep the spotlight on the development of this process in Jung himself. But the extraordinary degree of wholeness which he attained, and the thoroughness with which every possible aspect of his life was lived, make it impossible for any book about him, even if it ran into ten volumes, to portray more than a fraction of this fullness.

I have also tried to record information that would otherwise die with me. This was the motive that emboldened me to mention many things which it is perhaps too early to publish, including the facts, as I know them, of Jung's long friendship with Toni Wolff. There are such persistent and false rumors in circulation about this relationship that I felt I should present it in what seems to me its true perspective. I am probably one of the last people still alive who heard these facts from all three people concerned: Toni Wolff, Emma Jung, and Jung himself. This relationship has already been mentioned in a book by Paul Roazen on Freud and Tausk.*

For the same reason, I undertook the uncongenial task of going into detail concerning the ridiculous but strangely persistent rumor that Jung was a Nazi. I lived in Küsnacht and saw Jung frequently from the days of the first rise of the Nazis until their final downfall. It was one of the very few outer subjects which he often discussed with me. I therefore feel in a position to bear witness.

I have necessarily repeated a good deal, particularly in the early chapters, that is already available in *Memories, Dreams, Reflections*. These were the aspects of Jung's life which were important to him, of which, for the most part, I heard him speak long before he undertook the task of recording his memories. I have tried to convey many of these aspects from a slightly different standpoint, and—although I have done my best to make them intelligible as they stand—I have always given the references to more detail in *Memories*. That book has been very widely read, and will always remain the deepest and most authentic source concerning Jung.

My best thanks are due to the late Esther Harding for suggesting that I should write this book. Without her initiative I should never have thought of setting out on such a venture. The fact that I survived to finish the book, I owe to the wise care of Dr. Hugo Koch of Bad Ragaz. My thanks are also due to Peter Birkhäuser, who was kind enough to make inquiries for me at the Gymnasium and University of Basel and was very generous with information concerning his father-in-law, Albert Oeri, who was a lifelong friend of Jung. I am also grateful to Una Thomas, whose painstaking typing and retyping of almost the whole manuscript was of the greatest help.

Above all, I am indebted to Marie-Louise von Franz and Vernon Brooks. The former not only provided me with an excellent summary of Jung's article on synchronicity, but was indefatigable in assisting me in innumerable other ways. Vernon Brooks read the whole book twice during his summer holidays and undertook the enormous task of correcting it right through. He has a genius for improving language without altering the meaning, and the book owes a great deal to him.

B. H.

*Bollingen, 1974*

*Brother Animal*, Alfred A. Knopf, Inc., New York, 1969, p. 165.

# JUNG

## His Life and Work

# 1

# The Swiss Soil

Although Switzerland is probably the world's best-known tourist center, it is surprisingly little known in other ways. During the last years of his life Jung used to complain, with considerable amusement, that he had become a tourist attraction like the Bern bears! It was almost a part of a visit to Switzerland to want to see the famous old Jung, just as one should not miss the Matterhorn or the Jungfrau.

Although such intrusion on his privacy naturally had to be discouraged for obvious reasons, it was based on very sound instinct. Jung belonged organically to Switzerland, just as much as its famous mountains, and was just as much rooted in Swiss soil. In spite of his international reputation and his facility for seeing the point of view of all nationalities, of speaking their languages either literally or at least psychologically, he was and remained Swiss through and through. It would therefore be impossible to describe him without first presenting a brief survey of the less well-known characteristics of his country, particularly as they affected his growth and development.

James Joyce called Switzerland the last *"Naturpark des Geistes"* (National Park of the Spirit) and with considerable justification. To start with, it is truly a democracy and comparatively free from party politics. The Swiss, unlike the English, for example, do not elect the members of their parliament and then for several years place all political power in their hands, or worse, in their party's hands. If their government does not govern to suit them, all the English can do is grumble loudly, write letters to the newspapers, and demonstrate their disapproval in every by-election. It is very different in Switzerland. No Swiss government can decide any really important question without first appealing to the country; its citizens then settle that question for themselves by a direct vote: yes or no. And

11

since democracy, in the best sense of the word, is born and bred in the Swiss, for the most part they then accept the country's decision, however little they may like it, for it is the will of the majority and it would be bad form to make any further fuss. Of course, some individuals always think a particular decision deplorable, even disastrous.

In spite of tremendous demands on his time, Jung always fully accepted his duty as a voter, however little it suited him. Only at the end of his life did he request and obtain permission for his son to deliver his vote for him. Before then, when asked if he had had a nice weekend, he would very often reply rather sadly: "Oh, I couldn't go to Bollingen [his beloved holiday house], for you see I had to vote here."[1] The Swiss have a sense of responsibility that I have seldom or never seen equaled in any other country, and this has a considerable effect on their character. As schoolboys, they have already learned that there is no one to whom they can delegate the welfare of their nation, that it must always depend on the wise use of the individual vote.

Almost the majority of Swiss voters come from a peasant background and are still firmly rooted both in the soil and in their instincts. The fate of "daylight saving" in Switzerland illustrates this very well. It was hated by the farmers in every other country, for the cows naturally kept to sun time and it was difficult, if not impossible, for farmers to get their milk on the market in time for morning delivery. The rest of the population naturally reveled in the extra hour of daylight after work, and commercially it meant a considerable saving in electricity. In almost every nation the wishes of the latter won out, and the farmers and their cows had to cope as best they could. But in Switzerland, daylight saving lasted for only one summer, and then the country had to bow to natural facts, represented by the peasants and their cows.

In Switzerland, even today, there are far fewer large towns, with their uprooted urban population, than in the larger countries, and this was very much more marked in Jung's youth than it is now. Küsnacht, on the Lake of Zürich, for instance, was a small village when Jung moved there in 1909 from Zürich, by no means a large town itself at that time. The land he bought on the lake, where he built the house in which he lived for the rest of his life, was then completely in the country. Fortunately he bought enough land—it was very cheap in those days—to preserve his privacy by means of a large garden. But looking at the buildings which had sprung up like mushrooms all around his garden, he once said to me sadly: "When I look at all that, I feel I have outlived my age." Küsnacht, however, unlike most of the villages in the immediate neighborhood, has zealously guarded its independence and steadfastly refused to become part of metropolitan Zürich.

Of course, Switzerland has not wholly escaped the mass infections of the age. There are some Swiss Communists and there were before and during the last war a few Nazis. These, however, are and were a small minority which, so far at all events, is held well in check by the responsible common sense of the majority of the people, and strikes are practically unknown. Since I first came to live in Switzerland—over forty years ago—the big towns, especially Zürich, have indeed increased alarmingly in size and there are certain other signs of a considerable danger of infection from its large neighbors. Fortunately, however, the Swiss themselves are fully aware of the threat, and to be conscious of a danger is the best protection against it.

Another national characteristic which is seldom realized, even by otherwise well-informed people, is the vital importance of the Swiss army. The tendency is to think that because Switzerland is so small and has not engaged in a foreign war for hundreds of years its army must be an amateur sort of business, very dull for the poor Swiss who have to run it. Nothing could be further from the truth. It is only because the army is of vital interest to the entire male population, and everything is done to keep it efficient and up to date, that the country has been able to remain neutral for so long. Switzerland was not attacked during World War II only because the Germans reckoned that it would cost them a minimum of half a million men. It would probably have cost them much more, for the Swiss people would never have given in.

During World War II I lived in a hotel by the Lake of Zürich. Having already been there for some time, I knew the family to whom it belonged very well. The husband was mayor of the village, and when he was called up in the general mobilization just before war was actually declared, his wife said to me: "If the Germans come here [Zürich was not included in the main line of the Swiss defense], we will poison every German who eats here, *every one.*" I had no doubt whatever that that was exactly what she would do, and her spirit was shared by the vast majority of the nation. The Germans were well aware of this spirit; they were also aware of the modern equipment of the Swiss army. Although their troops were massed on the border at least twice, and probably at other times, during the war, they never risked attacking that "little armed hedgehog," as they called Switzerland.

As long as he was still of the required age, Jung was very enthusiastic about his military service. He used to say that during his "confrontation with the unconscious,"[2] when he often felt in doubt about everything, his anchors to his identity in normal life were the facts that he was a qualified doctor and a captain in the Swiss army. He would speak of his periods of service, particularly of the time on his beloved Gotthard Pass, as if they were most particularly happy recollections. And, though he was as a rule not musical, if someone began to sing an old military song, he would join in with the enthusiasm of a boy.

Another characteristic of Switzerland which played a large role in the development of Jung's psychology is the fact that his country ceased to fight other nations hundreds of years ago.

Speaking of the fatal human tendency to see the devil elsewhere than in one's own territory, Jung said on the Third Programme of the B.B.C. (Sunday, November 3, 1947):

If, for instance, the French-speaking Swiss should assume that the Alemanic Swiss were all devils, we in Switzerland could have the nicest civil war in no time, and we could also discover the most convincing economic reasons why such a war was inevitable. Well— we just don't, for we learned our lesson more than four hundred years ago. We came to the conclusion that it is better to avoid external wars, so we went home and took the strife with us. In Switzerland we have built up a so-called "perfect democracy" in which our warlike instincts spend themselves in the form of domestic quarrels called "political life." We fight each other within the limits of law and constitution, and we are inclined to think of democracy as a chronic state of mitigated civil war. We are far from being at peace with ourselves: on the contrary, we hate and fight each other, because we have succeeded in introverting war. Our peaceful outward manners merely serve to protect our internal dispute from foreign intruders who might disturb us. Thus far we have succeeded, but we are yet far from the ultimate goal. We still have enemies in the flesh, and we have not yet managed to introvert our political disharmonies into our personal selves. We still labour under the unwholesome conviction that we should be at peace within ourselves. Yet even our national mitigated state of war would come to an end if everybody could see his own shadow and begin the only struggle which is really worth while, the fight against the overwhelming power-drive of our own shadow. We have a tolerable social order in Switzerland because we fight among ourselves. Our order would be perfect if people could only take their lust of combat home into themselves. Unfortunately even our religious education prevents us from doing this, with its false promises of an immediate peace within. Peace may come in the end, but only when victory and defeat have lost their meaning. What did our Lord mean when He said: "I came not to send peace, but a sword"?[3]

It was left for Jung himself to take "the lust of combat" back into the individual, but we will return to this aspect later. The point is that Jung was born and bred in a country that had for hundreds of years "succeeded in introverting war," which means that it had already taken a vital step in the direction of seeing the conflict between the opposites at home and not abroad. When they learn the history of their country at school, the children of most nations are taught to see the mote in their neighboring country's eye and are not taught anything about the beam in their own (Matthew 7:3). From their very education therefore they have little chance of recognizing the importance of this most psychological of all Christ's sayings. Mote-and-beam psychology is clearest in such countries as France and Germany, which are next-door neighbors with conflicting interests, but the English National Anthem prays to God to "confound the politics" of its gracious sovereign's enemies and to "frustrate their knavish tricks," an extraordinarily naïve, not to say primitive, illustration of seeing the devil in other countries and not in one's own. It is not so far removed from the definition of good and evil as seen by some primitive tribes: "If you take my woman it is bad, but if I take yours it is good!"

But the boy Jung was not educated to think that any country was more sinful than his own. Naturally, the Swiss have their own private preferences for other countries, but it is the tradition of their country not only to have no national enemies but always to remain neutral in any quarrel or war between other nations. Jung often used to say that it is the fate of neutrals to be abused by both sides. One of the things for which Switzerland is often reproached is that when the Swiss clearly see an aggressor and even sometimes make little or no secret of this fact, they do not have the courage of their convictions to fight on the "right" side. No people have more courage than the Swiss; if this were not the case they would never have succeeded in protecting their tiny country all these years, for they are indeed a small David surrounded by Goliaths. But should they ever join in any war for any reason but defense against intruders, they would surrender their highest value: they have succeeded in introverting war and no longer see evil abroad instead of at home. The thing that shattered the Swiss most in World War II was the fact that they had their own fifth column, small as it was. No one who belonged to it has ever found their offense against Switzerland forgotten—they still have to pay the price for what they did. This is in striking contrast to some other countries where such derelictions seem, from the Swiss point of view, far too easily condoned.

It is well known that Jung rated wholeness much more highly than the "impossible" goal of perfection and, for the sake of wholeness, I must also speak of the negative qualities of the Swiss. I would say the chief of these is setting too high a value on money. When Switzerland decided against foreign wars more than four hundred years ago, there were still many Swiss soldiers who hired themselves out to fight for other countries. There is a French proverb, *"Pas d'argent, pas de Suisses"* (no money, no Swiss). A great deal of the best blood of the Swiss nation was thus lost for money. At the present time, moreover, it is undue respect for the claims of commerce that is endangering the highest Swiss values.

No one was more aware of this characteristic of his countrymen than Jung. He often quoted the French proverb and even said to me: "Money is always too strong for people, they can only know it." But there now seems to be an *unconscious* overvaluation of the claims of commerce that is very dangerous indeed to Switzerland and has already done it much harm.

Since nearly all the Swiss vacation resorts are in the mountains, Switzerland is usually thought of as consisting entirely of mountains. It is indeed mountainous, which has a lot to do with its national characteristics; there is very little soil, and most of it is so rocky and poor in quality that only exceptional energy and industry could have managed to wrest a living from it at all. But there are stretches of much flatter and more fertile land. One of the largest of these runs along the stretch of the Rhine that forms much of the northern boundary of Switzerland. From the place where the Rhine turns west and flows into Lake Constance, until it leaves Switzerland in Basel to form the boundary between Germany and France, it flows through very beautiful, undulating country where only occasional glimpses of the Alps can be caught in the distance. Except for these glimpses on exceptionally clear days, one could easily be in England or some other nonmountainous country. It was in this stretch of comparatively level land that Jung spent the first twenty-five years of his life, with the Alps as a sort of "unattainable land of dreams."[4] The first time he consciously saw the Alps was while his father was still vicar of Laufen, that is, before he was four years old. An aunt took him out to the road in front of the Vicarage and he saw the whole chain of the Alps bathed in the fiery red of the sunset. This made an indelible impression on him. The very next day when he heard that all the schoolchildren were going on an outing to the Uetliberg, near Zürich, he was terribly upset to learn that he was still too small to go. From then on Zürich was linked with the Alps in his mind, although it is actually in the foothills. Perhaps this had something to do with his move to Zürich as soon as he was a qualified doctor and free to work where he wished. At all events, he remained on the Lake of Zürich for the rest of his life.

Jung maintained that no child is born a *tabula rasa*. It is curious that, although this fact is well known and is now generally recognized in the innate "patterns of behavior" in animals, it still arouses strong opposition when it comes to human beings. Both Freud and Adler, for instance, regarded the unconscious as a kind of rubbish heap onto which all that is found inconvenient is thrown, and that it therefore consists of material that once was conscious. Jung fully recognized the existence of this layer, which he called the "personal unconscious," but one of his greatest discoveries was the so-called "collective unconscious," deep levels of the unconscious that are common to all mankind.

Jung once used a large colored diagram during a lecture to make the layers in the unconscious particularly clear. The lowest level of all he called "the central fire" (life itself), and a spark from this fire ascends through all intervening levels into every living creature. The next layer he called "animal ancestors in general," and this is also represented in all the higher forms of life. The next he called "primeval ancestors," a level present in all

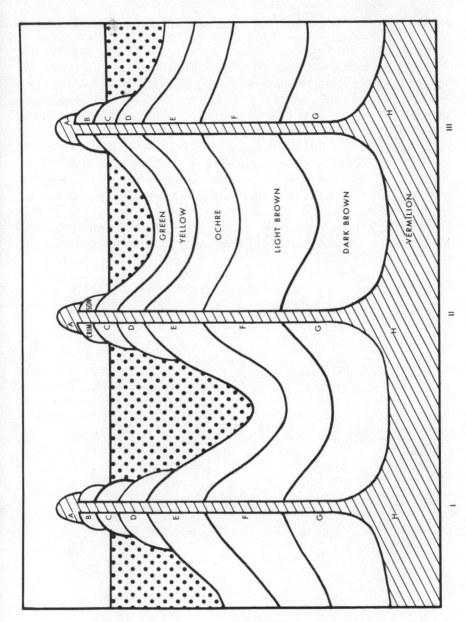

*Key to Diagram*

A. Individual (highest point)—Vermilion
B. Family—Crimson
C. Clan—Green
D. Nation—Yellow

E. Large group (*e.g.*, Europe)—Ochre
F. Primeval ancestors—Light Brown
G. Animal ancestors in general—Dark Brown
H. Central fire—Vermilion

mankind. In the next layer the latter began to split up into large groups, such as Western or Asiatic man.

Up to this level the foundation, although it supplies most of the archetypal images which form the human "pattern of behavior," is much the same in any individual belonging to the same large group; with the layer of the nation considerable differences appear. We need only look at the present state of the world to see how difficult it is for the peoples of the various nations to understand each other, and I have been struck, during my long experience of the many people of different nationalities who were drawn to Jung, and who still come to the C. G. Jung Institute in Zürich, by how necessary it is to have at least some knowledge of the national layers in order to understand the individual. I have therefore begun with some account of Switzerland. In the next chapter we will consider the last two layers beneath the individual: the clan and the immediate family. These top three layers color and modify the purely archetypal images which come from the deeper layers.

# 2

# Early Impressions
# 1875–1886

Carl Gustav Jung was born in Kesswil, a small village on Lake Constance, on July 26, 1875.[a] Although Kesswil is in the Canton of Thurgau, Jung was born a citizen of Basel because his father was a citizen of that city.[b]

The Rev. Paul Jung (1842–1896) was the son of Prof. Dr. Carl Gustav Jung (1795–1864). This Carl Gustav was born at Mannheim (where his father was also a well-known doctor) and seems from early life to have been independent and original in his outlook. He studied the natural sciences and medicine at Heidelberg and passed his final exams with considerable distinction, but he amused the whole of Heidelberg, while he was a student there, by keeping as a pet a small pig which he took on a lead for walks as if it were a dog.[c]

When he was only twenty-four he went to Berlin as surgical assistant to a well-known oculist and as lecturer to the Royal Military Academy. He seemed all set for a distinguished career in Germany and lived in Berlin, for part of the time at any rate, in the house of the publisher George Andreas Reimer, where he met an interesting circle of well-known people. He also

[a] The present vicar of Kesswil has had a stone let into the Vicarage wall on which is inscribed: "In this house was born Carl Gustav Jung, July 26, 1875-June 6, 1961, explorer of the human soul and its hidden depths."

[b] Citizenship is much more important in Switzerland than in the Anglo-Saxon countries. Children are born with the citizenship of their father and, even if they live their whole lives in another city or village, it requires quite a complicated procedure to change their citizenship. In Jung's case his mother was also a citizen of Basel, but this plays no role for the children. When I first came to live in Switzerland (1929), it was still quite difficult to explain to some Swiss officials why I was not legally attached to some place in the British Isles, but lately they ask only the nationality and are satisfied with the passport without asking for a "Heimatschein."

[c] I owe this story and several other details concerning Jung's grandparents to an appendix by Aniela Jaffé in the German edition of *Memories, Dreams, Reflections* (which does not appear in the English edition), p. 399 ff.

wrote at that time and some of his poems were published in the *Teutsches Liederbuch*. But the students in Germany in Carl Gustav senior's youth were full of political plans and were crying out for a "united Germany." August von Kotzebue (1761–1819), the German dramatist and politician, fell under their displeasure as a reactionary, and a theological student, Karl Ludwig Sand, murdered him in March, 1819. Sand was executed, but as the *Encyclopaedia Britannica* (1911) says: "The government made his crime an excuse for placing the universities under strict supervision." Many arrests were made, including C. G. Jung, who was known to have been friendly with Sand and was even unfortunate enough to possess a hammer for mineralogical research which Sand had given him. (This harmless hammer was always alluded to in the official reports as an ax!) He was kept in prison for a year, then released, but had to leave Prussia. He went to Paris, where he was able to work as a surgeon and to continue his studies.

At twenty-eight, through the influence of Baron von Humboldt,[d] he was called to a professor's chair in Basel. He found the university there at a very low ebb and did a great deal toward bringing it up to its present high standard. Above all, he was beloved in the town as a kindhearted and able doctor and even, interestingly enough, took a very early step toward assisting the mentally sick, founding the Institute of Good Hope for psychically disturbed children. In a lecture, which was later published anonymously, he said:

> In our age, when the attention of so many doctors is occupied with the psychic aspect of medical science to such an extent that special periodicals are being devoted to this subject, it would undoubtedly be greatly to the credit of any university to found an institution where it would be possible to study such cases objectively under the direction of a professor. I am not thinking of the usual type of mental hospital where, for the most part, all the cases are incurable but of a hospital that would take patients of all kinds and endeavor to heal them by psychic methods.[1]

This reveals amazing psychological insight, when one remembers that this Carl Gustav died in 1865, long before such pioneers as Janet and Freud had thrown light on the darkness and ignorance that prevailed in the psychiatric field of the nineteenth century.

[d]Alexander von Humboldt (1769–1859), German naturalist and traveler. The *Encyclopaedia Britannica* (1911) says of his exploratory journey in South America in 1802: "This memorable expedition laid the foundations in their larger bearings of the sciences of geography and meteorology," and even calls him a "colossal figure, not unworthy to take his place beside Goethe as the representative of the scientific side of the culture of his country." He always regarded Paris as his "true home" and it was while he was living there that he came across C. G. Jung. Later he received a summons to join his sovereign's court at Berlin. He obeyed and moved there, to his lasting regret.

Jung wrote of his grandfather:

> He was a striking and strong personality. A great organizer, extremely active, brilliant, witty and with a ready command of language. I myself still swam in his wake. One constantly heard in Basel: "Now, Prof. Jung, he was somebody." His children also were tremendously impressed by him, but they did not only respect him, they also feared him for he was a somewhat tyrannical father. For instance, after lunch he always had about a quarter of an hour's sleep, during which his large family had to remain quiet as mice sitting at the luncheon table.[2]

The later C. G. Jung's father was the earlier Carl Gustav's youngest son by his third marriage, to a daughter of an old Basel family, Frey. Dr. Franz Riklin, his great-grandson, told me that his exile from Germany was a great grief to him, particularly in his old age.

His grandfather, Sigmund Jung, who lived at the beginning of the eighteenth century and was Jung's great-great-grandfather, is the first authenticated member of the Jung family tree. He was a citizen of Mainz and the reason the family tree cannot be traced much farther back is due to the "fact that the municipal archives of Mainz were burned in the course of a siege during the War of the Spanish Succession."[3] It was his son, Jung's great-grandfather, who moved from Mainz to Mannheim. But it is known that an evidently learned doctor of medicine and of law called Carl Jung lived in Mainz in the early seventeenth century. Jung was always very much interested in this man, who was probably a direct ancestor, because he was a contemporary of two particularly interesting alchemists, Michael Maier and Gerardus Dorneus (Gerard Dorn), who were working in Frankfurt, quite close to Mainz. Although it can probably never be ascertained for certain, it would be noteworthy—in view of Jung's later great interest in alchemy—if his direct ancestor had been connected with these two famous alchemists. Jung thought that this early physician, Carl Jung, must at the very least have been familiar with the writings of Dorneus, who was the best known of Paracelsus's pupils, for the whole pharmacology of the day was still very much under the influence of Paracelsus.[4]

To return to the nineteenth century, the Rev. Paul Jung had married Emilie Preiswerk, a girl from an old Basel family, and was vicar of Kesswil when Carl Gustav junior was born. Emilie's father, Samuel Preiswerk (1799-1871), was *Antistes* of Basel. (Jung used to explain this title to me by saying: "You would have called him the Bishop of Basel.") He was said to have had second sight and to have carried on lively conversations with the dead. Jung said of this grandfather: "I did not know my maternal grandfather personally. [All Jung's grandparents died before he was born.] But, from everything I heard of him, his Old Testament name Samuel must have suited him very well. He still believed that Hebrew was the language spoken in heaven and therefore devoted himself with the greatest enthusiasm to the study of the Hebrew language. He was not only extremely learned but also poetically gifted. He was, however, a rather peculiar and original man who always believed himself to be surrounded with ghosts. My mother often told me how she had to sit behind him while he wrote his sermons because he could not bear ghosts to pass behind him while he was studying. The presence of a living human being at his back frightened them away!''

Jung's mother was the youngest child of his second marriage with a Würtemberg clergyman's daughter, Augusta Faber. Curiously enough, both Paul and Emilie were the youngest in families of thirteen children, although their son was an only son and for nine years an only child.

The rumor that the elder Carl Gustav Jung was a natural son of Goethe should be mentioned here. Jung spoke of this to me more than once, but I did not receive the impression that he took the rumor seriously. Rather, the existence of this singularly persistent idea—against all the external evidence—was exceedingly interesting to him in and for itself, taken in connection with the enormous impression that *Faust* had made upon him as a schoolboy,[5] and with all his subsequent realizations about Goethe's "main business," as he himself always referred to *Faust*.

One could say that Basel was the headquarters of the clan on both sides of the family, but Jung was four years old before his parents moved back to the neighborhood of Basel. He had no conscious recollections of Kesswil, for his family moved farther down the Rhine to the Falls[e] when he was only six months old. But he vividly remembered being taken to visit friends on Lake Constance when he was still a very small child and the impression it made upon him. He wrote:

> I could not be dragged away from the water. The waves from the steamer washed up to the shore, the sun glistened on the water, and the sand under the water had been curled into little ridges by the waves. The lake stretched away and away into the distance. This expanse of water was an inconceivable pleasure to me, an incomparable splendor. At that time the idea became fixed in my mind that I must live near a lake; without water, I thought, nobody could live at all.[6]

This may or may not have been the effect of being born on the shores of a large lake, but at all events the idea of living by a lake was so firmly fixed in his mind that he afterward not only built his house in Küsnacht by the lake

---

[e] The castle, church and Vicarage of Laufen are perched above the Falls on their left bank. All three stand more or less isolated today, as they did when the Jung family lived there, but, as the Falls have become a popular tourist attraction, there is a large parking lot and the castle has become a restaurant.

but in 1922 he also bought land on the upper Lake of Zürich at Bollingen, where he built his beloved Tower even closer to the water. The lake actually laps the walls of the courtyard at the Tower.

It is strange that Jung's insistence that the child is not born a *tabula rasa,* and the accompanying realization of the existence of the collective unconscious, should have aroused such strong and persistent resistances. After all, the Anglo-Saxon world has been accustomed for many decades to exactly the same idea in Wordsworth's "Intimations of Immortality from Recollections of Early Childhood." I have never heard anyone object to the idea expressed in this poem that:

> Not in entire forgetfulness,
> And not in utter nakedness,
> But trailing clouds of glory do we come.

In fact, most of those who reject the rest of Wordsworth as sentimental, moralistic, or banal will make an exception for this poem. I can only suppose that "trailing clouds of glory" can be dismissed as poetic license, so that no one has felt the need to take it seriously. Yet Wordsworth made it clear throughout the poem that he conceived the child's soul as perceiving a *very real* aspect of the world which unfortunately later becomes invisible, although he personally could remember a time when he lived in this aspect of the world. He even said, in a note,[f] that he believed that "everyone," if he could only look back, could "bear testimony" to this fact. How few, if one comes to think of it, have carried even this advice of the poet into their daily lives. Most people seem to prefer to identify with the "common day":

> At length the Man perceives it die away,
> And fade into the light of common day.

When one reads the first chapter of Jung's *Memories* attentively,[7] one realizes that his first recollections are not in themselves very different from those of the majority of serious children. Even the first childhood dreams are remembered by a surprising number of adults.[8] The striking thing is the difference in attitude toward these childhood memories, a difference that manifested itself before Jung was four. He was between three and four when he had the earliest dream he could remember. It was a dream that was not only to color his childhood but to preoccupy him during his whole life.

He dreamed that he suddenly discovered a "dark, rectangular, stone-

---

[f] Printed in "Everyman's" edition of *Wordsworth Poems,* Vol. 1, p. 240 f. Evidently, certain "good and pious people" took this poem as evidence that Wordsworth believed in actual rebirth, which he denied, adding "it is far too shadowy a notion to be recommended to faith, as more than an element in our instincts of immortality."

[8] Jung gave a seminar at the E.T.H. in Zürich, which lasted over several years, on children's dreams, almost all of which were given him by adults from their own childhood memories.

lined hole in the ground'' of a big meadow near his home. There was a stone stairway leading down into it. With considerable trepidation, he descended and found a sumptuous green curtain closing off an archway. He pushed it aside and found a large rectangular chamber, only dimly lighted. A red carpet ran from the entrance to a platform on which there was a magnificent golden throne. A huge thing, nearly touching the ceiling, was standing on this throne, which at first he thought was a tree trunk, but then he saw it was made of skin and naked flesh and that it ended in something very like a rounded, faceless head. "On the very top of the head was a single eye, gazing motionlessly upward." There was an aura of brightness above this head and, paralyzed with terror, he had "the feeling that it might at any moment crawl off the throne like a worm and creep toward me." Then he heard his mother's voice calling out: "Yes, just look at him. That is the man-eater!" Still more terrified, he woke up and was afraid to go to sleep again for many nights for fear of having another similar dream.[8]

This extraordinarily unchildlike dream anticipates the whole of Jung's life for, as he often pointed out, the earliest remembered dream as a rule contains the pattern of the future fate and personality. Indeed, Jung's life was impregnated throughout by the creative principle, which is represented here as a concealed principle of nature striving toward the light of consciousness. His fear that it would crawl after him anticipates what he afterward called the daimon of his creativity which haunted him all his life. Nearly eighty years after this dream, he wrote in the "Retrospect" to *Memories:*

> There was a daimon in me, and in the end its presence proved decisive. It overpowered me, and if I was at times ruthless it was because I was in the grip of this daimon. I could never stop at anything once attained. I had to hasten on to catch up with my vision. . . . I had to obey an inner law which was imposed on me and left me no freedom of choice.[9]

Toward the end of his life, Jung realized that this dream was initiating him into the secrets of the earth. It foretold a kind of burial in the earth, in the realm of darkness, where he had to pass many years in order that the greatest possible amount of light should be brought into the darkness. He even said that this dream was the beginning of his intellectual life.[10] But already at the time, when he was barely four years old, he knew that he had dreamed of a subterranean God and always thought of it involuntarily whenever he heard Jesus praised too emphatically. He realized very soon that this subterranean God was somehow connected with Jesus, was even his counterpart. This probably happened because a certain doubt of Jesus had already been sown by his daily life in the Vicarage.

To give an example: every evening he was taught to say a prayer to the

"Lord Jesus," asking him to *take* his child to himself, to prevent Satan from devouring it. That in itself was very comforting, and the child thought of Jesus as a "nice benevolent gentleman," like the squire at the castle, always ready to be mindful of little children in the dark. But the cemetery was very close to the Vicarage, and he found it most disturbing that people he was accustomed to see around the village suddenly disappeared. At the same time a hole appeared in the ground, and he was told that the missing person was being "buried and that Lord Jesus had *taken* them to himself.[11] This analogy had the unfortunate effect of causing the child to distrust Jesus long before other children usually lose their childlike faith, but it also laid the foundation to Jung's lifelong preoccupation with the paradoxical nature of God, which culminated over seventy years later in *Answer to Job*.[12]

Another event reinforced this very early distrust of Jesus. He overheard a conversation between his father and a visiting colleague about the Jesuits, in which he gathered that Jesuits were something specially dangerous, even for his father. He had no idea what a Jesuit was but immediately associated the word with Jesus. A few days later, meeting a Catholic priest in his cassock,[h] he once again made the connection with the Jesuits and Jesus and fled in panic. He could not remember afterward whether this occurred before or after his dream.

These very strong, highly emotional, early impressions had the result of fixing Jung's interest on the eternal preoccupations of man to such an extent that, unlike most growing boys, he never forgot them. As he grew older, his interest in this inner side of life increased and he was able, with one short exception when he was eleven or twelve, to do justice to it without neglecting the duties of his outer life.

Passing the most formative years of his life so close to the Rhine Falls undoubtedly had a considerable influence on Jung. Particularly when the river is full—as it often is, especially while the winter snow is melting in the mountains—it is very impressive. Jung says, however, that all around the Falls "lay a danger zone. People drowned and bodies were swept over the rocks."[13] When he was about three the fishermen pulled out one of the corpses below the Falls and asked permission to put it in the Vicarage washhouse. His mother sternly forbade him to go into the garden while it was there, but naturally, directly things had quieted down sufficiently for him to be unobserved, he slipped out. He tells us that he saw blood and water trickling out below the door, but instead of being frightened, he found this just "extraordinarily interesting!"[14]

Children brought up in the country, as Jung was, do start with a certain advantage over city children, in that they have every opportunity from an

[h] It does seem to be instinctively disturbing to meet a man in a skirt! I have been struck by the shock it seems to give our otherwise friendly and tolerant bulldog. He greets most visitors warmly, but he took a long time to accept a priest in a cassock or a woman in trousers.

early age to face up to life as it is, to its dark side as well as its light. Things did not change much in this respect when the family moved to Klein-Hüningen in 1879, for it was then a small village right in the country. Since then—like most of the larger cities in Switzerland—Basel has grown so much larger that Klein-Hüningen has been more or less absorbed into it, but in Jung's days—his father remained its vicar until his death in 1896—the town and village were still separated by a long country walk.

Nevertheless, the comparative nearness of Basel meant that the influence of the clan became much stronger in Jung's life. In those days, long before the invention of motorcars, Laufen was still quite a journey from Basel and visiting relations must have been a comparative rarity. But at Klein-Hüningen the families of both the Rev. Paul Jung and of his wife were close at hand. This influence was above all theological; two brothers of Jung's father were parsons, there were no fewer than six on his mother's side, and the head of her family was pastor of St. Albans, Basel, all of whose sons became theologians. It is true that it was much later before Jung first became consciously aware of the influence they were trying to exert on him, but as he said: "Children react much less to what grown-ups say than to the imponderables in the surrounding atmosphere."[15] From the beginning this atmosphere was full of preconceived opinions and also of secret doubts from the overwhelming theological influences in the Jung and Preiswerk clans, to say nothing as yet of the tragic fate in this respect that was lying in wait for his father. Jung told me more than once that he could never have analyzed me nor understood my dreams had he not been a parson's son himself, and probably it is my being a parson's daughter that gives me any understanding of this aspect of Jung's childhood and the "imponderables" in the atmosphere that surrounded it.

But there were other "imponderables" of a difficult nature still closer to Jung's early childhood. At Laufen there was already what he called "a temporary separation of my parents." His mother was away for several months, in a hospital in Basel, and "presumably her illness had something to do with the difficulty in the marriage."[16] Her absence "deeply troubled" him and he attributed the fact that he suffered for a time from a "general eczema" to this cause. Things do not seem to have improved between his parents when they reached Klein-Hüningen; before long they were sleeping apart and Jung was sleeping in his father's room.[17]

I have seen many marriages of this kind among the clergymen I have known (that of my parents Jung called "conventionally right and psychologically all wrong"). One of the most disturbing things for all clergymen who take their profession seriously, and for their growing families, is the attentive and critical eye which is turned by the congregation and acquaintances on everything they do and say. Something different is generally expected of them, and it is difficult to feel accepted as an ordinary human being. In fact, when I came to Zürich, I learned consciously for the first time that this was the reason for my early and strangely persistent feeling that I was somehow an outcast. Jung told me that at school and in the village no one ever called him Carl Jung but always "parson's Carl," which was naturally disagreeable to him.

This is, I think, at bottom the result of Christianity being a religion it is impossible to live up to, because it does not allow enough room for the dark side of man or, for that matter, for the dark side of God either. All practicing or even professing Christians suffer constantly from a bad conscience, because they feel they *should* be living a completely unattainable perfection. They naïvely hope that clergymen do know how to do this, hence their expectations. But, since such expectations will inevitably be disappointed, they console themselves with an unduly pleasurable sense of relief, even triumph, when they observe the shortcomings of the clergy and their immediate families.

I remember that once in a game of rounders[i] at a children's party, I ran inside a stick entirely by mistake—the sun was in my eyes. Our host, a militant military man, literally howled with triumph: "That's a nice thing, a Dean's daughter cheating, see if I don't tell your father!" I still recall the feeling of utter despair that invaded me: he *wanted* to believe I had done it on purpose, and there was nothing I could do about it. Several other children had done the same thing, yet he had merely mildly pointed out their mistakes or even overlooked them.

It is clear, with such surrounding expectations, that a particularly sharp eye is kept on the marriages of clergymen, that they are lived in the limelight so to speak. Both partners usually do their utmost to live up to the ideal of marriage that is expected of them and this is a terrible strain. Moreover, it is not only what is expected of them by other people but, far worse, what they expect of themselves. Jung said that both his "parents made great efforts to live devout lives, with the result that there were angry scenes between them only too frequently. These difficulties, understandably enough, later shattered my father's faith." [18] Later he said frankly: "My parents' marriage was not a happy one, but full of trials and difficulties and tests of patience. Both made the mistakes typical of many couples." [19]

It must be emphasized, however, that both seem to have been unusually valuable individuals. One gets an exceedingly positive impression in reading Jung's *Memories* and he always spoke of both—however much he criticized their mistakes—in terms that left no doubt as to his love and respect for them. He said of his mother, for example: "My mother was a very good mother to me. She had hearty animal warmth, cooked wonderfully, and was most companionable and pleasant." [20]

His father was indeed a tragic figure to him, although he did not realize

---

[i] This is an English game, a kind of primitive cricket, but instead of running straight between the wickets, there is a circle of sticks which must be run around.

this consciously until later, only thinking as a child that, whereas there was something unexpected, even alarming, about his mother, especially at night, his father was exceedingly reliable but unfortunately powerless. When he was six or seven he began to suffer from a "pseudo croup" which he saw as "a psychogenic factor: the atmosphere of the house was beginning to be unbreathable."[21]

He did not attribute these "imponderables" solely to his parents' marriage—although almost all psychologists agree that this is a decisive factor in the childhood of most children—but attributed a great deal to the growing religious doubts of his father. He said:

> The peculiar religious ideas that came to me even in my earliest childhood were spontaneous products which can be understood only as reactions to my parental environment and to the spirit of the age. The religious doubts to which my father was later to succumb naturally had to pass through a long period of incubation. Such a revolution of one's world, and of the world in general, threw its shadows ahead, and the shadows were all the longer, the more desperately my father's conscious mind resisted their power. It is not surprising that my father's forebodings put him in a state of unrest, which then communicated itself to me.[22]

Later he added:

> Looking back, I now see how much my development as a child anticipated future events and paved the way for modes of adaptation to my father's religious collapse as well as to the shattering revelation of the world as we see it today—a revelation which had not taken shape from one day to the next but had cast its shadows long in advance.[23]

Although there were alarming emanations from his mother *at night,* such as the "faintly luminous, indefinite figure" with a detachable head that he saw early in the Klein-Hüningen days coming from her room,[24] he felt the "peculiar religious ideas" as emanating only from his father. He said:

> I never had the impression that these influences emanated from my mother, for she was somehow rooted in deep, invisible ground, though it never appeared to me as confidence in her Christian faith. For me it was somehow connected with animals, trees, meadows, and running water, all of which contrasted most strangely with her Christian surface and her conventional assertions of faith. This background corresponded so well to my own attitude that it caused me no uneasiness; on the contrary, it gave me a sense of security and the

conviction that here was solid ground on which one could stand. It never occurred to me how "pagan" this foundation was.[25]

It also certainly did not occur to his mother either. She was never consistently conscious of this instinctive foundation which was nevertheless the greatest asset that Jung had as a child, a fertile soil which made it possible for him to develop as he did.

Not all the members of the two clans were theologians. Some were very deeply rooted in the soil and full of natural wisdom. Very early in my time in Zürich, I received a positive impression of Jung's uncles, for he very often quoted them or told stories about them that gave one the impression of a fund of natural wisdom and the feeling that they were exceedingly sound people.[j] These uncles certainly had more influence on him than the many theologians in the clan.

In the meantime, apart from the invisible "imponderables" in the situation, Jung grew up as a healthy country child, surrounded by the nature he loved all his life. He went to the village school soon after he was six, as is the custom with all Swiss children. This must have been a school of the good old style, built upon the idea of "spare the rod, spoil the child," for I remember that in a seminar Jung once described his first lessons at that school. The teacher put a letter or whatever he wanted to teach the children on the blackboard, then a whip lash was applied to their backs—swish— just to impress the lesson upon them! I was very much struck by the fact that this treatment left no resentment whatever. On the contrary, Jung seemed to think that it was the best *aide mémoire* in existence! (He pointed out more than once that Zen masters often use such methods with their pupils.)

Before going to school, Jung had been a lonely child, but he did not mind that at all, for he played alone and in his own way. He could not remember what he played while he was very small, only that he did not want to be disturbed and that he was deeply absorbed in these games and hated anyone watching or judging him.[26] This is confirmed by his oldest friend, Albert Oeri, long editor of the *Basler Nachrichten* and a well-known member of the Nationalrat.[k] In a few youthful reminiscences he contributed to the *Festschrift* for Jung's sixtieth birthday, Oeri wrote that his parents visited Jung's parents while the Jungs were still at Laufen, and took him along, since he was the same age as Carl Jung and both sets of parents wanted them to be friends and play together. "But," said Oeri ruefully, "there was no question of that. Carl sat in the middle of the living room engrossed in a game and did not take the slightest notice of me." He asked himself why he remembered this so vividly after more than half a century

[j] Swiss children usually call their first cousins once removed uncle and aunt, so that I am not sure whether all these uncles were actually brothers of his parents.

[k] The Swiss equivalent of the American Congress or the British Parliament.

and said that in all his life (he was three or four) he had never met such "an asocial monster." Oeri was one of a large family, all of whom played or fought together in their large nursery; whereas Carl was an only child at the time, and had never had anything to do with other children.[27]

Jung recalled that he liked going to school because, for one thing, he at last found the playmates he had lacked for so long. But he soon discovered that this was not an unmixed blessing; he found that being with all these children "alienated me from myself." He was different at school from what he was at home, and although he evidently got on well with his schoolfellows, joined in their pranks and even invented others for them, he realized very soon that this made him feel uncomfortable. "The influence of this wider world, which contained others beside my parents, seemed to me dubious if not altogether suspect and, in some obscure way, hostile."

This reaction is by no means unusual in children who are introverts, as Jung much later called this type. Although extraverted children usually enjoy the "influence of the outer world," this is by no means the case with introverted children, who always shrink from it in one way or another. Jung definitely reckoned himself an introvert and one can see this clearly in his childhood reaction to outer objects and people. At the same time his love for nature, where "the golden sunlight filters through green leaves," increased rapidly, but this contrasted with the world of shadows of which he had also become increasingly aware since his very early experiences at Laufen (his first remembered dream, Jesus "taking" the dead, the Jesuit, and so on). He said of his early days at school: "It was as if I sensed a splitting of myself, and feared it. My inner security was threatened."[28]

Soon after he went to the village school—when he was seven or eight—he began to remember the games he played by himself. Building with bricks became a passion.[l] Like most boys of his age, he equally enjoyed destroying what he had built by "earthquakes." He also drew rapturously at this time, particularly pictures of battles of all kinds,[m] and he

---

[l] It is interesting that this passion persisted even into his old age. Not only did he build a great deal of the original Tower at Bollingen with his own hands in 1923 but his chief relaxation every spring, right up to the year he died, was to make the most elaborate canals—with earth and stones—at the mouth of a small stream where it emptied itself into the lake on his own ground at Bollingen. He called this his "waterworks." The rising lake—with the melting of the winter snow—destroyed these fortifications every year, but that was a matter of indifference to him. He once told me that this work—or even staring at the water itself—was the best preparation he knew for his creative work, and for shaking off the extraversion of the semester. Ideas flowed to him from the unconscious far more freely there than in the house or when he was actually writing.

[m] Painting was another activity that persisted most of his life. At Bollingen there are some of his pictures, painted straight onto the walls. Toward the end of his life, however, he preferred stone as a medium. The battle scenes, of course, did not persist, but he once told me how thrilling it was to him when he was in Madeira (or the Canary Islands), about 1902, to see English troopships bringing back soldiers from a "real war" in South Africa. He explained ruefully that before 1914 he had often thought the world rather tame and dull!

even anticipated the Rorschach method by making blots in exercise books and then giving them fantastic interpretations.[29]

He met the insecurity implanted in him by school in two ways.[30] Jung's psychology was based throughout on his *actual experience* and a great deal of this experience came from his own childhood. He said of one of his experiences: "When I was a child I performed the ritual just as I have seen it done by the natives of Africa, they act first and do not know what they are doing. Only long afterward do they reflect on what they have done."[31] Of course, he did not yet know what he was doing, but he was already *living* the psychology that later made him famous. I realized soon after first getting to know him that, wonderful as his seminars and books were, the really convincing thing was Jung himself. *He was his own psychology* and this fact was anticipated even in early childhood. He wrote in the "Retrospect" to *Memories* that he did not know what started him off "perceiving the stream of life. Probably the unconscious itself. Or perhaps my early dreams. They determined my course from the beginning. Knowledge of processes in the background early shaped my relationship to the world. *Basically that relationship was the same in my childhood as it is to this day*."[32]

The first ritual he performed, when he felt this unpleasant feeling of being out of himself, was to sit on a large stone on the slope below the old garden wall at Klein-Hüningen Vicarage. He had "some secret relationship" with this stone and he would sit on it alone for hours and play an "imaginary game with it." He was sitting on the stone, which was plainly underneath him, yet the stone could also be thinking: "I am lying here on this slope and he is sitting on top of me." He identified so completely with this stone—it was *his* special stone—that he became puzzled over the question of whether he was the boy or the stone. He could never find an answer to this question, but his "uncertainty was accompanied by a feeling of curious and fascinating darkness."[33]

At this point in *Memories* Jung interpolated an experience which occurred thirty years later and which first adequately explained the matter of the boy and the stone to him. He was already a practicing psychiatrist, married, with children and "a head full of ideas and plans," but suddenly—as he revisited the Vicarage slope—his whole life in Zürich became remote and alien and he was again absorbed in the world of childhood. Then he realized, as a psychological fact that must be reckoned with in daily life, that the world of childhood is the *eternal* world, whereas his life in Zürich belonged to the world of time. Wordsworth recognized exactly the same thing and expressed it poetically, as vague evidence of the existence of immortality. The latter is an idea that is easily digested, for most people prefer the idea of immortality to the idea of death as an end. But Jung's realization confronts every one of us with the task of somehow reconciling two worlds which exist *within ourselves*. We are aware of one, the eternal, in childhood; later it fades in most people, who then become aware only of the external world of time; it can be a terrifying thought that something beyond it undoubtedly exists. We begin to understand why so many people fanatically hope—against all the real evidence—that every child *is* born a *tabula rasa*.

To return to the child Jung and his stone. The stone is infinitely more durable than the human being or any kind of animal life or vegetation. Since the oldest tree is the merest infant compared to a stone, the latter has been seen as a symbol of eternity since olden days! One can mention "the philosopher's stone" of the alchemists, and Christ as the "Rock of Ages" or as the cornerstone. When he puzzled over whether he was the boy sitting on the stone or the stone being sat upon, the child Jung was already unconsciously puzzling over what he called, nearly eighty years later, "the thorny problem of the relationship between eternal man" and the "earthly man in time and space." [34] He even said that the decisive question for man is: "Is he related to something infinite or not? That is the telling question of his life." [35] We shall see this "thorny problem" reappearing in many forms during the rest of his life.

The second way in which he met "this disunion in myself and uncertainty in the world at large" [36] he discovered only when he was nine, nearly three years after first going to the village school. It once again took the form of a symbol, and it can be called his first creative effort to meet the split between the two worlds, although at the time it naturally was "quite incomprehensible" to him. Like all schoolchildren at that time, Jung had a yellow varnished pencil box with a lock, which contained a ruler in addition to the pencils and other objects carried around by the child. He took this ruler and carefully carved a manikin at one end of it. Then he sawed off the ruler and bedded it down comfortably in the pencil box. The manikin had a "frock coat, top hat, and shiny black boots." He also provided it with a stone, a parallel to his own on the slope. This stone had long been a treasure carried about in his pocket, an oblong smooth stone from the Rhine, which he had carefully painted to look as if it were "divided into an upper and lower half." He then hid the box on a beam in the attic of his home and felt quite safe about his secret, for no one ever went to the attic because of the worm-eaten and unsafe floorboards. Now at last—when all this ritual was carefully performed—he felt secure, he lost the tormenting feeling of being at odds with himself. [37] Whenever he felt unhappy or in any way threatened, he would think of his carefully bedded down manikin with his stone, and he would feel comforted. Occasionally, when he could do so unobserved, he visited his cache; at such times he always took a written paper with him to put into the pencil box to serve as the manikin's library. When telling of this in *Memories,* he could no longer remember what had been written on the papers.

One must be conscious of the sense in which Jung used the word "symbol" in order to understand why this ritual gave him at last such a sense of security. The word is too often used to indicate a mere emblem, a sign or image to express a known fact, such as the winged wheel that the Swiss railroad men wear. But Jung never used it in this sense; he meant it always to represent the best expression obtainable at the time for *something that is essentially unknown*. The child, who made this manikin so carefully, had no idea what he was trying to express, but he did know that his very life might depend on keeping it an "inviolable secret." He had done all he could, and having made the tremendous effort of producing this symbol, he could be at peace. He remembered and visited it for about a year, then forgot about it until he was thirty-five years old and doing the preliminary reading for his book *The Psychology of the Unconscious,* revised many years later and republished as *Symbols of Transformation.*[38] Then he realized it was one of those "little cloaked gods of the ancient world," a Telesphoros[39] (one who helps to a goal or to special efficiency), so often connected with Aesculapius. This connection seems to me especially meaningful, because Jung never once thought as a schoolboy of becoming a doctor (which is in itself curious, since he heard so much of his Jung grandfather who, like his great-grandfather, was a well-known doctor), yet his unconscious was already bringing up an image related to Aesculapius when he was only nine years old. In general, the dwarf gods of antiquity—best known as the Cabiri, who appear again in Goethe's *Faust*—symbolize creative impulses; these impulses were to play a great role in Jung's life, as his many books bear witness.

It was when Jung, through his reading, remembered this manikin and recognized it as a universal symbol that he first realized that "there are archaic psychic components which have entered the individual psyche without any direct line of tradition," an idea that was to play such an enormous role in the further development of his psychology. This manikin was a content which rose from the lowest, completely collective layers (see the diagram on page 17) and was practically uncolored by country, clan, or family, although the two latter layers made a certain contribution in that they inclined the child Jung to an unusually serious and religious attitude. On the surface, indeed, he remained religious in the Christian sense, although he doubted from a very early age whether all the good and beautiful things were so certain as he was assured they were, for he never forgot the dark side that had impressed him so much, even before he was four. Not that he seems to have made any direct connection between his fear of the dark side of Jesus (and all the rest of those very early alarming realizations) and the manikin, for he said: "The dream of the ithyphallic god was my first great secret; the manikin was the second." He said of this motif: "This possession of a secret had a very powerful formative influence on my character; I consider it the essential feature of my boyhood."[40] And later, in "Retrospect," he wrote: "It is important to have a secret, a premonition of things unknown. It fills life with something impersonal, a *numinosum*. A man who has never experienced that has missed something important. . . . The unexpected and the incredible belong in this world. Only then is life whole. To me the world has from the beginning been infinite and ungraspable.'' [41]

Although at the time he did not recognize any association between his first uncanny realizations before he was four and the manikin, the symbolism shows how closely they were connected in the unconscious. The manikin was dressed exactly like the ''solemn men in long frock coats, unusually tall hats and shiny black boots,'' [42] who stood by the open graves in Laufen cemetery and had given him his first distrust of Jesus. There is also a secret connection between the phallus of his first dream and the manikin, for the antique god in the *kista* (a receptacle for sacred objects in the antique mysteries)—with which Jung compared him—was sometimes represented by a human figure and sometimes by a phallus. So that we definitely meet the same secret in the dream and the manikin, but in the latter the inhuman, terrifying phallus is replaced by a human figure, and has therefore become much more human and personal.

It was very fortunate that the child Jung made this tremendous effort to heal the split in himself, for while he still remembered and found comfort in the thought of the manikin and his stone, [43] like all Swiss children whose parents want them to have a good education, he was taken away from the village school in his eleventh year and sent to the gymnasium[n] in Basel, a far greater step into the wider world than the original step to the village school had been. Before we consider the Basel years, we need a clearer idea of what kind of boy it was who went from a small country school to the different atmosphere of a large town gymnasium, where his companions also changed radically. At Klein-Hüningen Jung's father was the vicar, one of the most important and cultured men of the village, and his son, however little he may have liked it, carried a certain prestige with him into the village school. Jung was also always top of his class. Most of his schoolfellows were the sons of parishioners of his father. At his Basel school he learned for the first time how poor his parents were, and soon realized that his new companions almost all came from much richer homes, that their fathers, reckoned by the prevailing worldly standard, were much more important men than a village pastor. This was reflected in their personal advantages, such as ample pocket money, good clothes and shoes, and being able to talk in familiar terms of the mountains and even of the sea, which were still in ''the unattainable land of dreams'' for the boy Jung.

He was an unusually serious boy who—even before he was four years old—allowed no sentimental wool to be pulled over his eyes, particularly in

[n] School for the second decade of life which prepares its pupils for the university. Jung entered the gymnasium in the spring of 1886.

regard to religious matters. He always took facts as he learned them comparing them with one another and drawing conclusions from these comparisons that faced him, at a very early age, with the opposites in human fate and nature. This gave him an extraordinarily empirical image of life as it is. Such realism was reinforced by the majority of his companions at the village school, for no one is more realistic or down to earth than the Swiss farmer and peasant. He knew the parents of many of his school-fellows well and was thus used from earliest youth to hearing a spade called a spade.

The insight thus gained into the background and character of the Swiss peasant benefited Jung all his life. He was on excellent terms with the inhabitants of the small village of Bollingen and with the surrounding farmers. Only recently a middle-aged farmer (unprovoked by any question) mentioned how well Jung had understood the children of Bollingen. He remembered vividly, for instance, how Professor Jung used to hide Easter eggs all along the lake on his ground and then turn the children loose to find them. In fact, just as Jung in his own boyhood in Basel had been accustomed to hear of his grandfather, "Now Professor Jung, he was somebody," so now one can hear the same remark made of the grandson any day of the week in the Bollingen neighborhood. This has nothing to do with his fame (I doubt if most of the peasants even realize that he is famous) but simply with his personality.

Local people talked extraordinarily freely to Jung and discussed things with him that they would never mention to other outsiders and it was the same wherever he went among the mountain and country population of Switzerland. It is striking how often his books are to be found in such homes, and not just as ornaments, for they have clearly been read again and again. These people, still in touch with the soil, seem to have an instinctive understanding that has too often been lost, for one usually hears that Jung's books are difficult. When such simple people from all over Switzerland came—as they often did—to Jung to ask questions about what they could not understand, he soon realized that they had often understood far more of the *essential* meaning of his books than is usually the case in academic circles. He was so impressed with how many such people there were and with their sincere search that, when he was over eighty, he asked a few of his pupils, particularly Marie-Louise von Franz, who had also received her first five years of education at a Swiss village school, to found a reading circle for them, where they could bring their questions twice a month. This circle is still functioning and is refreshingly sincere and unpretentious.

It was also through Jung's early contact with peasants that he learned to know and respect such products of nature as wood and stone. Until just before his death he cut all his own firewood at Bollingen, and one seldom saw him happier and more relaxed than when he was engaged in such tasks.

One still hears him spoken of with the greatest respect as a stonemason. The way he understood and handled the individual stone particularly roused the admiration of every expert stonemason.

But it was not only in the future that Jung benefited from his early experience of the realism of the Swiss peasant. As a boy it was already a very helpful influence in avoiding the illusions that polite society so often seems to favor. His reactions when he was nine years old to his sister's birth give us some idea of how this operated in his daily life. This event was a complete surprise to him, for although, like most children brought up in close touch with nature and animals, he had learned the facts of life easily and early, he had as yet noticed nothing to make him suspect that a baby was on the way. This seems odd at first sight, in such an observant boy, but it is really a typically masculine reaction. The male is mainly concerned with discrimination and *facts*, not primarily with relationship. A girl would probably have noticed that her mother was preoccupied and not so concerned with her as usual, but the interest of a healthy masculine boy is so occupied with his own concerns that he notices only really inescapable disturbances in relationship, such as his mother being away in the hospital, unable to cook, or something of that kind. But in those days practically all children were born at home and—though he afterward remembered that she had lain down oftener than usual—in between she most probably discharged all her household duties as usual until the last moment. However this may have been, the arrival of his sister took Jung entirely by surprise. His parents, who were conventional on the surface, told him the usual myth of the stork; he rejected it at once, for the peasants had never pretended any such fairy story, and anyway, how could a stork manage to carry a calf? He saw at once, however, that his parents were determined not to tell him exactly how that baby arrived and, as usual, he kept his thoughts to himself. Though he afterward learned to have a great respect for his sister's character, she had come too late for any common childhood life between them, and they both grew up more or less as if each was an only child.

On the surface Jung's mother made great efforts to improve her son's manners and to make him a well-brought-up, gentlemanly little boy, but her heart was not in these efforts. Her instinctive foundation was realistic and far more concerned with his growing up a healthy, manly boy, able to use his fists when necessary and to hold his own in every way. She was always giving this secret wish away to her son, although their conversation was mainly concerned with his manners and appearance, and he was often unfavorably compared with a few more elegant children of some of their relations and friends.

I remember his once telling me that when a particularly prinked-up little girl cousin was coming to tea his mother's injunctions were especially exact as to how nicely he must behave. Anything but pleased to see her, he nevertheless politely took her into the garden and intended to do his best to amuse her. But the garden had just been manured, and her attention could not be recalled from the smell and substance of the manure. He was then greatly amazed and even shocked to see her eat some of it with evident relish. He later told his mother triumphantly what his to-be-copied cousin had done, and for once she openly admitted that a child could be too well brought up. The cousin had just followed the principle of a dog who is kept in too unnatural and human a way; such a dog will usually roll in every horror he can find, as a compensation for his unnatural life.

Such occasional satisfactory admissions on his mother's part and, still more, the things she murmured under her breath—which he soon learned were unconscious and could not be discussed—made a satisfactory relationship between mother and son. On the surface he attended just enough to her constant admonitions concerning his appearance and manners, and in essentials—although he soon learned that though speech might be silver, silence was certainly gold—he really always felt free, even encouraged, to be himself. Thus he was, from all accounts, an exceedingly natural child. I remember when I first saw some of his own children, the thing that struck me most forcibly was that they were the most natural young people I had ever seen.

Although Jung grew up in this realistic milieu, in the Swiss village, it was by no means a materialistic environment. Quite apart from the emphasis on religion in his family and clan, he met with the certainty of the Swiss peasant concerning "events which overstepped the limited categories of space, time, and causality. Animals were known to sense beforehand storms and earthquakes. There were dreams which foresaw the death of certain persons, clocks which stopped at the moment of death, glasses which shattered at the critical moment. All these things had been taken for granted in the world of my childhood." [44] It was not until much later that Jung realized how unknown all this aspect of life was to the urban population of a town like Basel. By the time he left the village school, it had never occurred to him to doubt the empirical existence of irrational facts that were in no way bound by the "limited categories of space, time, and causality." He could therefore draw unlimited satisfaction and a complete sense of security from the existence of his carefully bedded down manikin in the attic, for there had been little or nothing in his village life to awake any doubt as to the efficacy of such symbols.

Although as a small child Jung's health seems to have been somewhat uncertain, it was not long before his natural robustness of constitution asserted itself and he began to enjoy the excellent health which charac-terized most of his life. He also became unusually strong. He told me that this was a great help to him all his school days for, being physically stronger than all the other boys in his class, he could always count on being let alone and winning their respect when it came to a fight of any kind. Although he went for many years first to the gymnasium and then to the university in Basel, he remained resident in Klein-Hüningen. This not only gave him a long country walk at least twice a day, but it also left his essential roots undisturbed. Therefore, although his image of the social world and the importance of his parents in it undoubtedly underwent a severe shock in his new school, he proved exceptionally well prepared *in all essentials* to meet whatever he found. One could say it was his first experience of one of the later cornerstones of his psychology: it is the individual that counts and not his outer circumstances.

# 3

# The Basel Gymnasium
## 1886–1895

The Jung family had been at Klein-Hüningen for about seven years when the time came for Jung to enter the Basel Gymnasium. Since many of his relations and family friends lived in Basel and since Klein-Hüningen was so close to it, he already knew the town quite well, but only as a visitor. When he went to the gymnasium, however, he entered the warp and woof of the city itself and became, as it were, a small part of it.

Although it is one of the most traditional of the Swiss cities, Basel is very close to the German border. As it stands today, you enter both Germany and France while still in the streets of the town, but France was farther away in those days because, since 1870, Alsace and Lorraine had been part of Germany. Nevertheless, only a few years before, it had been French, and Jung recorded that the town dwellers talked "a refined German and French."[1] High German is the official language of the Alemannic part of Switzerland and, as soon as they go to school, Swiss children, even in the lowest classes of the village schools, are forced, usually unwillingly, to speak High German. But in the village schools it is anything but "refined," keeping much closer to the children's own beloved language. So we may be sure that it was disagreeable to young Carl Jung to have to "refine" his language to the point demanded by the gymnasium. Even in Basel, Swiss German is the home language of every family, but people take more trouble to speak "refined German and French" when they have to than is the case in Zürich, for instance.

In the days before World War I—Jung had already been fourteen years on the Lake of Zürich in 1914—there were no passports required for traveling, except for a few rather remote countries, and although there were already customs duties on merchandise, the frontier was much less marked than it is today. Pedestrians walked over it quite freely and Jung very frequently used to go on long walks in the Black Forest. On clear days, when one can see it especially well from near Zürich, he would often point out its landmarks, as if they were old and valued acquaintances.

It is probably just because it is so near the large and powerful Germany that Basel is so traditional and Swiss. It has had to be especially Swiss or it would have been overrun. One sees this right through its history, and in the way it zealously preserves its old customs, such as Vogel Grvff.[a] Above all one sees it in the way *Fasnacht* (carnival) is celebrated every spring. The citizens are so strictly traditional and conventional that they need a complete contrast once a year, when all their sometimes cramping conventions, rules, and regulations are relaxed and even forgotten. Forgotten, and yet somehow Basel never goes too far. Once, many years ago in my earliest years in Switzerland, I had the good fortune to go to the Basel Fasnacht with Jung and about twenty members of the Zürich Psychological Club, and we were most impressed by the unique Basel spirit. We all circulated freely among the masked people in the streets, and though frequently spoken to by complete strangers—something totally new to me, for in England there is nothing like carnival—yet never once were the essential rules of good taste forgotten, and a genuine and rare sense of humor governed the most critical and open remarks, so that one was forced to laugh and never felt uncomfortable. But when we returned to Zürich, in the early hours, and I walked through the streets to get my car, it was a totally different thing. It was also carnival in Zürich, and the masks also spoke to one, but totally differently, with none of the indefinable something that governs the Basel carnival. Jung often used to quote Schopenhauer, who said: "A sense of humor is the only divine quality of man." That divine quality is a real ingrained characteristic of the

[a] The history of Vogel Gryff is typical of Basel. In order to defend themselves, the inhabitants of Klein-Basel, soon after the city was founded, formed three companies whose members had the important task of guarding and defending the town. As is usual in Switzerland, these companies or guilds were formed of the various trades. One of these guilds had the "Vogel Gryff," a fantastic great bird with an animal's tail and human feet, depicted in its coat of arms, another the "Leu" (lion), and the third the "Wilde Mann" (wild man). In the Middle Ages there was still a military review every year when each of the companies was led by a man disguised as the Vogel Gryff, the Leu, and the Wilde Mann. In the course of the centuries, the companies were relieved of their military duties, but the Vogel Gryff, the Leu, and the Wilde Mann continued to march through the town every year, delighting the inhabitants with their fantastic dances.

This ceremony still takes place every January. The Wilde Mann comes down the Rhine, accompanied by drums and shots, dancing his wild dance on the raft. He lands just below the "middle bridge," where he is joined by the Vogel Gryff and the Leu. All three then dance their way through the streets. About 1932, Jung once took just a few of us to see this ceremony and I have seldom enjoyed a day more. As the raft approached down the Rhine, one seemed to lose all sense of time and to be quite uncertain if one was living now or in the Middle Ages. Jung pointed out to us that—thrilling as it was to visit—the weight of the past could be very oppressive when living in Basel, a thing I understood well from having also lived for many years in the old English city of Chichester. The details of the history of Vogel Gryff were kindly supplied by a citizen of Basel, the late Erhard Jacoby.

inhabitants of Basel. Jung had more sense of humor than anyone I ever knew, and whatever difficulties and disadvantages he met with in Basel, he certainly owed much of the foundation of this "divine quality" to his early years in that city.

The first few months at his Basel school opened up a different world to Jung. As mentioned before, there are large circles of the Swiss population who have exceedingly materialistic values and, being very clever businessmen as a rule, the Swiss often become rich. Instead of the preponderance of simple peasant children, as in his village school, he now found that the majority of his new schoolfellows were the sons of wealthy men. They came from large houses and gardens, and their fathers possessed many magnificent horses. It was still the age of horses, and a carriage and pair could be a much more impressive sight than the most shining Rolls-Royce of today.

At first such novelties—being invited to these houses and the setup of his new school—were exciting to Jung, but it was not long before it began to bore him in a way he never seems to have been bored in his village school. It was not that he could not keep up with the other children. He always had good marks. But certain classes were particularly disagreeable to him, and he felt great resistance to what and how he was taught in them. He hated gymnastics, for instance, for he "could not endure having others tell him how to move."[2] And, though unusually gifted in drawing and painting, he could draw only something that stirred his imagination and failed completely with the soulless copying that is—or was at that time—demanded by so many drawing teachers. Far worse than these, however, were the mathematics classes he hated so much that within a year or so they ruined school altogether for him.

We get an interesting light on Jung at school from his old friend Albert Oeri. When they were very small boys at Laufen, the friendship did not begin auspiciously. Their parents tried again when they were both a bit older, and this time it was a different story. On the first visit Jung hailed Oeri as an ally, because he was a real boy and not a dressed-up little gentleman, like a cousin he detested, and after that Oeri's parents took him often to Klein-Hüningen Vicarage on Sunday afternoons.

Since they were both born in 1875, they attended the gymnasium at the same time. Although they did not remain in the same class and studied different subjects at the university, they still saw a good deal of each other and remained friends until the end of their lives. We owe the account of several incidents from Jung's youth to the paper Oeri contributed to the *Festschrift* on the occasion of Jung's sixtieth birthday, incidents that would certainly otherwise have been forgotten. Jung was rather ruefully amused that such incidents were recalled after so many years—and as a birthday present!—but did not deny any of them. Even when he was well over eighty, when Jung was really amused he had a natural and infectious laugh, which seemed to come from his whole being and was hardly a whisper. Oeri related that he had exactly the same laugh from early boyhood, and that he loved to organize pranks that would give him a chance to be genuinely amused and then to let loose these peals of laughter. So their first renewal of acquaintance in Klein-Hüningen was characterized by Jung's triumphant laughter because he had succeeded in placing his refined cousin on a bench where an old drunkard had just been sitting and his elegant clothes smelled of alcohol. Another time, he organized a solemn duel between two of his schoolfellows in the Vicarage garden, only, so Oeri said, because he wanted to laugh at them afterward. But his amusement quickly turned to genuine concern when the combatants took the duel a bit too seriously and one wounded the other in the hand. His father was still more concerned, for in his own boyhood the father of the boy whose hand was bleeding freely had been dangerously wounded while fencing and had been brought to their home for his own father's medical attention. The boys were most concerned of all, however, with the terrible row that they regarded as certain when the story was known in the gymnasium. But since there were no serious consequences, the old rector, Fritz Burckhardt, took it calmly, merely remarking to the two combatants with a mild smile: "Oh, so you thought you would play with foils!"

Although Jung was already original and gifted in most subjects, according to Oeri this did not apply to mathematics; in fact, he was "a mathematical dunce." But, he added:

He was really not responsible for his defect in mathematics. It had been an inherited family weakness for at least three generations. His grandfather (Carl Gustav Jung senior) wrote in his diary for October 26, 1859, after having attended a lecture about a photometric instrument: "I really did not understand a word. If a subject has even the remotest connection to mathematics, it finishes me right off at once. Really no one can blame my boys for their stupidity in this subject. They inherited it from me."[3]

It was not that Jung was unable to calculate—to "add two and two"—but that the assertions, the playful inconsistencies, of algebra, for instance, roused his resistance to such an extent that they "finished him right off," like his grandfather, and contributed a great deal to the fact that, after a year or two, he came to hate going to school. This, and his longing to be more alone in the woods and fields and to have time again to steep himself in the mysteries of nature, led him into another secret, but this time one that he bitterly regretted.

As he stood in his beloved Cathedral Square one morning, another boy made a sudden unprovoked attack on him, and he fell, hitting his head on the curbstone. This was the beginning of a series of fainting spells which led to his being taken away from school and allowed to run wild for more than six months. No doctor could find out what was the matter with him and his parents were nearly in despair. He was delighted to have escaped from school and would have been as happy as the day is long, had it not been for an increasingly uneasy "conscience and an obscure feeling that he was running away" [4] from himself.

The fits of fainting ended suddenly and dramatically when he overheard his father telling a friend how dreadful it would be if his boy proved incurable, for he had lost what little money he had inherited and what could he do for the boy if he were unable to earn his own living? Jung had felt vaguely sorry for his father ever since he went to the gymnasium; he had seen that he had many cares and worries that the parents of his richer schoolfellows were spared. But, absorbed like all boys of his age in his own interests, it had never occurred to him that there was anything that he could do about it.

We can see the integrity and sense of responsibility, which were perhaps his most striking characteristics later as a doctor, in the way this boy of twelve took the shock of overhearing this conversation. Drawing the immediate conclusion that he must get back to work, he set about overcoming the fainting spells that had attacked him, ever since his fall many months before, whenever he so much as touched a school book. His efforts were so successful that he was able to return to school in a few weeks. There was never any relapse, and he worked more conscientiously, never getting up later than five, often much earlier, in order to study before going to school at seven o'clock. He used his good visual memory to memorize mathematics and to get good marks even in that subject, his most hated of all.

The most striking thing to me, however, was the way he faced the matter of ethical responsibility for what had happened. Far from blaming anyone else—such as the boy who hit him—he slowly but surely faced the painful fact that it was his own doing from start to finish. He remembered thinking as he felt the blow: "Now you won't have to go to school any more," [5] and also, although he was dazed by his fall, that he had not got up as soon as he might have. During his illness he had forgotten all this completely, and it must have taken the utmost courage and endurance to recall it and to realize that his illness had been a flight from his boredom with, and resistance to, school. He later revealed that it was this experience that first taught him what a neurosis is.

Because of the enormous importance of what Jung learned from this neurotic illness, it is worthwhile to look more closely at what actually happened. For a moment, as the totally unexpected blow from behind felled him, he saw plainly that here was his chance to escape school. *If he had kept this thought in mind,* there would have been no neurosis and no illness, for he was far too honest a boy to play such a trick *consciously*. He might (and did) lie on the ground a bit longer than was necessary, mainly to punish the boy who had hit him, but he could never have pretended week after week to be ill. To attain his goal, the illness had to be completely genuine and beyond his control. So involuntarily and, as he realized painfully later, also somewhat on purpose, he completely forgot for many months his original thought of escaping from school. The most important point that Jung learned from this early experience was that while his scheme remained unconscious he was really ill, but as soon as he remembered it and faced the pain of having brought about the whole thing himself, he recovered completely and permanently.

The first results of his realization were anything but pleasant. He could not know then what a valuable lesson he had learned about the cause of and remedy for many cases of neurosis, and he felt deadly ashamed of himself as he realized all that his parents had suffered through what he now felt to be his own fault. It was another thing that he could not talk to anyone about. The thought of his manikin in the attic had helped him over many hurdles at the very beginning of his years at the gymnasium; but unfortunately he had forgotten all about it at the time of his fall, so he no longer had this security to turn to. Moreover, as we know from Oeri, his long illness and absence from school had led—as it always does in Swiss schools—to his falling behind and thus losing his former classmates, including Oeri, and having to start once again with a new set of companions. There was indeed no outer stigma attached to this, for everyone except himself believed that he had been genuinely ill and that it was his misfortune and not his fault.

About this time—I do not know for certain if it was before or after his illness—he had another experience[6] which, I have often heard him say, marked the end of his childhood. One morning, as he was taking the usual long walk from his home to the gymnasium, he was astonished to find himself suddenly, as it were, walking out of a thick cloud into a place where he instantly knew: *"Now I am myself."* It was not a foggy morning, yet there seemed to be a dense wall of mist behind him, in which he had indeed existed but only passively, for every previous event had just happened *to* him. It was as if he had been willed to do everything while in the fog, but now he himself could will. This made an overwhelming impression upon him, for suddenly he had a sense of authority. This led to another problem later, but the first result was a new interest in God. Although Jung had remained religious in the Christian sense,[7] Jesus had become an increasingly problematic figure for him ever since the funerals in Laufen churchyard; now, as he became conscious of himself, "the unity, the greatness, and the superhuman majesty of God" began to haunt his imagination.[8]

One must keep in mind how much God mattered to him at that time in order to understand the agony he went through in the next experience he recorded. He reported this in detail himself,[9] but, as he told me more than once, since the attitude which he gained through this painful experience remained with him all his life, we must also consider it briefly here.

It was in Cathedral Square again, this time on a day of radiant sunshine, when the thought of God, the maker of all this beauty, shot through his mind. He imagined Him seated on a golden throne, high up in the sky, above the sparkling, newly tiled roof of the cathedral. But then he was suddenly brought up short by "a great hole in his thoughts and a choking sensation" and knew that to think his thought to the end would be to commit "the most frightful of sins," the sin against the Holy Ghost which can never be forgiven. He could not sleep for two nights, and the days were sheer torture, but the thought—though he kept it just at bay—unremittingly tried to force its way into his consciousness. If we return to the diagram on page 17, we can see particularly clearly that this thought was an "archaic psychic component" trying to enter "his individual psyche without any direct line of tradition" from the lowest depths of the collective unconscious. The thought of the "little god of the ancient world," the Telesphoros, had entered his mind much more gently, as a creative hunch which expressed itself in the symbol of the manikin. But this new thought, which seemed to him the sin against the Holy Ghost, was evidently far more explosive and strange, and moreover it was clearly going to express itself much more terrifyingly than in the earlier case.

On the third night, however, the torment became unbearable and he felt his resistance weakening. At all events, he decided he must not yield until he had thought it all out beforehand. *Who* wanted to force him to think something that he neither knew nor wanted to know? To answer this question he instinctively went back through the ancestral steps that he recognized so many decades later as the layers of the unconscious. First he wondered if his parents could be forcing him to think this thought, but found the idea "utterly absurd." His grandparents? He had known them only from their portraits, and from all he had heard of them he knew it was also absolutely impossible. Then he "mentally ran through the long procession of unknown ancestors until he finally arrived at Adam and Eve." That was the deepest layer he could think of at that time, the first parents of Christian and Jewish tradition. They were newly created by God, who must have made them as He wanted them to be, that is, He could have made them incapable of sin, but He did not. Therefore *it was God's intention that they should sin.*

The idea that God intended Adam and Eve to sin, and the similar idea of the *felix culpa*, the blessed sin which brings about redemption, had already appeared in the early Gnostics and had reappeared fairly frequently down the centuries. But it had never become part of Christian tradition, which, on the contrary, emphasized the idea of original sin; that is, of an entirely reprehensible act of disobedience to God's will. Protestants particularly always stressed the latter aspect; so it is unlikely that Jung had ever heard of the former. Nevertheless, it carried instant conviction and liberated him from his worst torment, for now he knew beyond doubt that God *intended* him to suffer this conflict. But he still had no idea which alternative he should choose: to think the thought or to go on resisting? At last he came to the conclusion that probably God also wanted him to have the courage to think the dreaded thought.

Once again he saw the same scene in the sky above the cathedral, but this time he let the thought continue and saw an enormous turd fall from beneath the throne, shattering the sparkling new roof and breaking the walls of the cathedral asunder. Instead of the expected damnation, however, he felt an "indescribable relief " and "an unutterable feeling of bliss" such as he had never known before. This highly blasphemous thought, from the traditional point of view, gave him his first experience of "the miracle of grace which heals all and makes all comprehensible." He realized at once that this was the result of his obedience to the inexorable demand of God, who evidently refused to abide by any tradition, no matter how sacred it might be; he realized also that the only thing in life which really matters is fulfilling God's will.[10]

This shattering experience had a double effect on the boy. On the one hand, many things that had been puzzling him for years were at last explained. Above all he understood for the first time the depression and irritability of his father. Evidently his father did not know "the immediate living God who stands, omnipotent and free, above His Bible and His Church." In other words: had the father been in the same situation as the son, he would have kept to the traditional idea of right and wrong *at all costs,* because he believed (or tried to believe) in "God as the Bible prescribed and as his forefathers had taught him" and this for the "best reasons and out of the deepest faith." Nevertheless, he thus saw only one side, and in consequence cut himself off from the living God and from the miracle of grace. The boy realized this completely, and felt compassion for his father as he never had before. On the other hand, the traditional standpoint—as Jung used so often to point out in later years—is not just a matter of personal education but is, as it were, written in the blood of us all. This side in the boy was deeply shocked by this thought from the deepest unconscious, for which there was not only no direct line of tradition but also, as far as I know, no parallels. In later years he found a so-called context—other ideas of the same kind in different times and places—for almost all his childhood experiences (the phallic dream, the manikin, the stone, and so on), but never, as far as I know, for this idea of God destroying His cathedral in such a way. He was forced to the conclusion that God could be terrible and terrifying, and that he himself must be "infinitely depraved," a devil or a swine, to have seen such a thing belonging to God's dark side. On the one hand, because of his experience of the miracle of grace, he was sure he knew much more about the living God than his father or the many clergymen in his environment. He felt this "as a kind of distinction," and yet actually it was at the same time "a shaming experience," because of the enormity and blasphemy of the thought, seen from his own traditional side. He thus painfully learned to know the opposites—which were later to play such a leading role in his psychology—in actual daily experience and as part of himself.

The opposites made themselves felt in another way at this period, shortly after he walked out of the mist of childhood and felt a "sense of authority" for the first time.[11] He went to stay with friends of the family on the Lake of Lucerne and was sharply rebuked for disobedience by the master of the house. To his great surprise, he had a double reaction to this occurrence: on the one side, he completely acknowledged the justice of the rebuke, but on the other, he was irrationally seized by rage that such "a fat ignorant boor" should dare to insult *him*. He knew he was only a schoolboy of barely twelve years, and that his host was a rich and powerful man; yet he could not help *also* feeling that somewhere he was someone important himself, even "an old man, an object of awe and respect!" To his intense confusion, it occurred to him that he must actually be two different persons, the one an unimportant schoolboy, far from certain of himself, and the other an important old man who lived in the eighteenth century.

As is well known, Jung later discovered that, whereas the center of consciousness is the ego, consciousness represents only a fraction of the whole psyche. "Self and ego" represent a modern formulation for an age-old fact that Saint Paul formulated as "I live, yet not I but Christ liveth in me" (Galatians 2:20). The East has used the term "Self" for the center of the wider personality since olden days; for instance, the Brihadâranyaka Upanishad states that:

> He who dwells in the seed, and within the seed, whom the seed does not know, whose body the seed is, and who pulls (rules) the seed within, he is the Self, the puller (ruler) within, the immortal; unseen, but seeing; unheard, but hearing; unperceived, but perceiving; unknown, but knowing. There is no other seer but he, there is no other hearer but he, there is no other perceiver but he, there is no other knower but he. This is thy Self, the ruler within, the immortal. Everything else is of evil.[12]

Jung took the term "Self" from this Eastern use of it. Those few critics of his *Memories, Dreams, Reflections* who took these two persons in Jung as an indication of a case of split personality, even as a schizophrenic split, were exposing their own ignorance. On the contrary, these two figures are present in every normal human being, only, as the Upanishad puts it, the Self is usually "unseen" (although it sees), "unheard" (although it hears), "unperceived" (although it perceives), "unknown" (although it knows) by the limited, conscious ego. But Jung, at the age of twelve, to his own great consternation, did see, hear, perceive, and know this figure.

I do not know why this first intuition of Jung's concerning the Self and the ego began with the idea of the former as an old man from the eighteenth century. I have often heard him wonder why that century seemed to be familiar. A great many things from that time were apparently *déjà vu* to him, like the old green carriage from the Black Forest and the shoes which he mentioned in *Memories*.[13] He would sometimes remark that people who believed in reincarnation would say that he had last lived at that time, but he himself never felt that he was "in a position to assert a definite opinion" on "the problem of reincarnation."[14]

Be this as it may, there is certainly endless evidence that someone or something exists in the human being that knows a great deal more than the person himself ever knew or experienced. We find evidence for this phenomenon since olden days all over the world. Jung, as a boy of twelve, naturally knew nothing of this; he just experienced the phenomenon afresh (and as if there were two people in him, different in age and importance) and found it disturbing. He had already experienced the same thing in a different form when he sat on the stone and wondered whether he was the boy or the stone, and then again in the symbol of the carved manikin. He did not forget the former, even sitting on the stone from time to time during his years at the Basel Gymnasium and finding it "strangely reassuring and calming."[15] The manikin, however, was entirely forgotten for many years.

But the feeling of being two different persons was much more confusing and also more persistent, so that eventually for "his own private use"[16] he took to thinking of them as two separate personalities in himself: No. 1 and No. 2.[b] The schoolboy was No. 1 and the other part of him "that lives in the centuries" was No. 2. While he was a boy, of course, he did not see this as consistently or as clearly as he did later. He would sometimes even claim the realm of No. 2 as "his own personal world," although he always really knew somewhere that "something other than myself was involved."[17] There were even times when he thought that any idea of an "other person must be sheer nonsense,"[18] but he still could not deny him for long. When he was on the verge of leaving the gymnasium, he had a dream which showed him clearly that No. 2 must be left behind while he went out into the world as No. 1, but even then he was still convinced that No. 2 must never on any account be declared invalid.[19]

We see here clearly the difference between Jung and his contemporaries

---

[b] As far as I know, Jung first used the *actual* terms—No. 1 and No. 2—when he was trying to make this curious phenomenon clear to the reader of *Memories*, although I had often heard him speak of the phenomenon itself, even many years earlier. He often used to discuss the formulations most likely to be understood for such things during the time he was writing the first three chapters of the book.

and the reason he so often felt isolated. The students at the gymnasium naturally followed the pattern described by Wordsworth in his "Intimations of Immortality." The "shades of the prison house" had begun to close on the growing boys, had even already closed on many of them. By something like a miracle, these prison walls failed to imprison Jung, and he still saw "the clouds of glory" far more clearly than his fellow schoolboys. Even at the university—where most, if not all, of his fellow students had lost "the splendid vision" altogether, for it had long since died away into "the light of common day"—Jung still remembered it and, however isolated it made him, knew that he must never forget or deny it.

But the dream which authorized Jung to leave his No. 2 personality for a time was still several years in the future and all through those years he had to cope with the confusion as best he could. He said that at least he had the merit of carrying this burden by himself and he never spoke to anyone about it. The only person he ever seems to have been seriously tempted to tell was his mother, for he soon realized that she also had a No. 2 personality, one who said things that rejoiced his heart. But he soon learned that although his mother said these things, she could not be asked about them. Reluctantly, he therefore decided he could not confide in her either and kept this whole problem to himself. Nearly seventy years later in "Retrospect," he came to the conclusion that such secrets are of the utmost value and importance in a human life, but naturally at the time he felt his situation as a painful loneliness.

Some of the masters at the gymnasium, such as Oeri's father and the Latin teacher, seem to have had the highest opinion of the boy, but occasionally there was one who disliked him beyond reason. There are always some masters in big schools who seem to hate any sign of originality in their pupils and who do their utmost to nip it in the bud. At the time, all this struck Jung as exceedingly unfair, especially when one of these masters went so far as to accuse him of cribbing, simply on the grounds that his essay was too good for him to have written it himself![20] Such an unfounded accusation is all the more extraordinary when we know that Oeri mentioned how original and interesting Jung's essays at school were. He found them such a pleasure that they tempted him to creep into his father's study when the essays were lying on his table to be corrected, in order to read them secretly.[21]

Rage, especially when based on well-founded indignation, was often a difficulty for Jung and, after this piece of flagrant injustice about his essay, his "grief and rage threatened to get out of control." Then the experienced old man in him must have taken over, for he felt—and not for the first time—a "sudden inner silence" and found himself looking at the whole thing differently. Calmly and objectively he saw that the master was just an idiot who did not (and could not) understand his nature, so naturally he was mistrustful—just as Jung often mistrusted himself. At the time, he made no connection between this understanding and his previous recognition of the old man within, but it must have been somehow visible in him, for some months after this incident his schoolfellows began calling him "Father Abraham"! He could not at all understand why he had earned such a nickname and "thought it silly and ridiculous. Yet somewhere in the background I felt the name had hit the mark."[22]

He made a lot of good friends at school, particularly among "shy boys of simple origin."[23] His love of animals and nature increased; he found them "dear and faithful, unchanging and trustworthy,"[24] and at times he trusted them more than people. He even said, in reference to such incidents as his essay; "People I now distrusted more than ever." He could distrust people without bitterness because he also distrusted himself; it was the dark side of human nature itself he suspected. As he got to know it better, he learned how evenly the opposites are balanced within it and that it can *also* be trusted. I remember being enormously impressed in one of his seminars by his explanation that people always make the mistake of thinking they can expect one opposite from their friends all the time. If someone does something really nice for them one day, they think they can expect something even better the next. But he knew that was not possible. The pendulum was bound to swing in the other direction, and that if someone had been especially positive one day, you must expect something negative the next.

Of course, such an amazing understanding of human nature was still far in the future when Jung was a schoolboy and, just as he had painfully realized the dark side of Jesus and later of God, so now he had to realize the dark side of human nature in other people, but above all in himself. This also had the advantage of giving him many joyful surprises. For example, when his mother once said to him, "You have always been a good boy," he could hardly believe his ears, so sure was he that he was a "corrupt and inferior person."[25]

His dream of the phallus when he was not yet four years old, and his later vision of God destroying His cathedral in an unheard-of way, had already made the boy Jung feel "corrupt and inferior" (with the inevitable opposite of feeling correspondingly superior). Especially they made him feel most painfully isolated. Nevertheless, he kept a certain sense of union with the Church and his familiar home religious world until he was fifteen. Then the time came for his confirmation,[26] for which he was prepared by his father. This event showed him, far more clearly than anything had yet done, that his father never allowed himself to *think* about anything to do with his profession but tried valiantly to swallow it whole, so to speak, and to *believe* the whole Christian creed. Naturally, the wide-awake mind of the boy, which always wanted to think out everything, was bored to death by this kind of instruction. But he made a last and sincere effort to accept the point of view of his father, that is, "to believe without understanding," and to prepare himself honestly for his first communion.

Jung seems from the beginning to have been attracted and fascinated by paradoxes, much as Tertullian must have been when he said: "And the Son of God is dead, which is worthy of belief because it is absurd. And when buried He rose again, which is certain because it is impossible." So the boy felt fascinated by the idea of the Trinity: how could a oneness be simultaneously a threeness? When his father passed over the whole subject with the remark "We come now to the Trinity, but we'll skip that for I really understand nothing of it myself," it was a bitter disappointment to his son, although he admired his father's honesty. And, in preparing for his first communion, he felt there must be a great mystery behind "so preposterous an impossibility" as ordinary bread becoming the body of Christ and ordinary wine the blood, so that clearly we were meant to incorporate Him into ourselves. How could that be? He set his last hopes on being able to experience something—he hardly knew what—when he took part in this mystery, which he regarded as "the pinnacle of religious initiation" into the Church.

The day was marked by a new black suit and hat, more grown-up than ever before, which in themselves gave him a feeling of being "accepted into the society of men." Jung mentioned only old men at the service. An old wheelwright, whom he liked and had often observed admiringly at his work, was his sponsor, and he watched the faces of all these men in suspense for signs of "the vast despair, the overpowering elation and outpouring of grace which constituted the essence of God" for him. But there was nothing of the kind to be seen or felt, only the impression that, as usual in church, everything was being conscientiously performed in the "traditionally correct manner." He hardly knew how he felt on the day itself, but slowly he came to "understand that this communion had been a fatal experience. It had proved hollow, more than that, it had proved to be a total loss," and he knew he could never participate in this ceremony again. For him God was in no way present in His Church, which seemed to him to be a place of death, not of life. He must keep as far away from it as he could in future.

This was not just the customary revolt of the parson's son against too much church. Jung's father seems to have been unusually liberal in this respect. Jung once told me that he had never been *made* to go to church, as had been my own dismal experience, but that, before his confirmation, he had usually gone of his own free will. "One just did," he said. And his father never took him to task for not going to communion service again, or for the fact that afterward he very often stayed away from church. The whole experience went very deep, for the Church had somehow meant much more to Jung than it usually does to the parson's child, and after the disaster of his first communion he felt more of an outcast than ever. He wrote:

> My sense of union with the Church and with the human world, so far as I knew it, was shattered. I had, so it seemed to me, suffered the greatest defeat of my life. The religious outlook which I imagined constituted my sole meaningful relation with the universe had disintegrated; I could no longer participate in the general faith, but found myself involved in something inexpressible, in my secret, which
> I began to ponder: What must one think of God? I had not invented that thought about God and the cathedral, still less the dream that had
> i began to ponder: What must one think of God? I had not invented that thought about God and the cathedral, still less the dream thathad befallen me at the age of three. A stronger will than mine had imposed both on me. Had nature been responsible? But nature was nothing other than the will of the Creator. Nor did it help to accuse the devil, for he too was a creature of God. God alone was real—an annihilating fire and an indescribable grace.
> What about the failure of Communion to affect me? Was that my own failure? I had prepared for it in all earnestness, and hoped for an experience of grace and illumination, and nothing had happened. God had been absent. For God's sake I now found myself cut off from the Church and from my father's and everybody else's faith. Insofar as they all represented the Christian religion, I was an outsider. This knowledge filled me with a sadness which was to overshadow all the years until the time I entered the university.[27]

Isolated as he was by all these experiences, he turned to books in order to find out "what was known about God." His search began in his father's library, in which he seems mainly to have read books on theology.[28] He read a great many of these, including a long work by Biedermann on Christian dogma. But he was again disappointed; nothing was really thought out, and basically he met just the same demand to "believe without understanding," to believe, for instance, in God as the highest good with no explanation of his creation, in spite of its sublime beauty, being "so imperfect, so corrupt, so pitiable." His reading might well have ended in disaster like his first communion had not his mother, or rather her No. 2 personality, intervened about this time.[29] "Suddenly and without preamble she said: 'You must read Goethe's *Faust* one of these days.' "

These side remarks of his mother's, which she seems to have dropped quite unconsciously, were often full of wisdom. Her son evidently took her advice at once, and the book poured into his soul like a "miraculous balm." This was probably his first experience of a phenomenon that was to be of the greatest value to him all his life: that is, when the strangeness of his ideas made him feel "an outsider," he would suddenly meet with the same or similar ideas in his reading. Through this, he realized with the greatest relief that there were, or at least had been, people who were preoccupied with the same problems, had even reached much the same conclusions as his own. I remember vividly once hearing him describe his joy when he found that many of his own ideas had already been thought by the old Gnostics: "I felt as if I had at last found a circle of friends who understood me."

The fact that he had found someone else who "saw evil and its universal power and—more important—the mysterious role that it played in delivering man from darkness and suffering" was a tremendous comfort to him when he first read *Faust*. (He must have been about sixteen at the time; therefore it was quite a few years after his own experience when the agony of the blasphemous thought was followed by the miracle of grace.) In this respect, Goethe "became a prophet" in his eyes. Even at that early age, Jung already showed a lifelong characteristic: the ability to be enthusiastic about people, and yet critical, at one and the same time. Faust, he saw immediately, was "a bit of a windbag" and added: "The real problem, it seemed to me, lay with Mephistopheles, whose whole figure made the deepest impression on me, and who, I vaguely sensed, had a relationship to the mystery of the Mothers. At any rate Mephistopheles and the great initiation at the end remained for me a wonderful and mysterious experience on the fringes of my conscious world." It was therefore a great disappointment to him when Goethe allowed this powerful and intelligent figure to be cheated of Faust's soul by those "silly little angels," thus showing that, after all, he, like the theologians, had fallen for the dangerous fallacy that evil can be rendered innocuous by a trick.

The fact that Faust had originally been a philosopher, though he left philosophy, and that this had apparently given him "a certain receptivity to the truth" opened up a new hope to Jung: he must read the philosophers and see whether they could shed any light on the problems that troubled him. But this was not so easy. His father disapproved of philosophers— they *thought*!—so Jung found in his father's library only Krug's *General Dictionary of the Philosophical Sciences*.[30] This did not help him at all. In fact, he gathered from it that philosophers were even worse than theologians, for apparently the former knew of God only as an idea or by hearsay, whereas the latter were at least certain He existed. There was evidently a gap in time—I am not sure how long—before he found a very different "introduction to the history of philosophy" which gave him "a bird's-eye view of everything that had been thought in this field."[31] Here again he found a comforting mitigation of his loneliness, for he discovered historical parallels for many of his ideas and intuitions.

Since Jung wrote that this interest in reading the philosophers lasted from his seventeenth year until well into the time of his medical studies, it is difficult to know just when he read what. We know for certain only that he had read both Schopenhauer and Kant some time before he left school, because he tells us that he was suspected of *pretending* to know something about them *before* he had "taken them at school." Schopenhauer, like *Faust*, was a revelation because of his great preoccupation with the "suffering of the world." Jung said:

> Here at last was a philosopher who had the courage to see that all was not for the best in the fundaments of the universe. He spoke neither of the all-good and all-wise providence of a Creator, nor of the harmony of the cosmos, but stated bluntly that a fundamental flaw underlay the sorrowful course of human history and the cruelty of nature: the blindness of world-creating Will. . . . Schopenhauer's somber picture of the world had my undivided approval, but not his solution of the problem.[32]

Undoubtedly Schopenhauer really meant God, the creator, by the "Will." He was therefore accusing God of blindness. This did not shock the boy at all, for he knew from his own experience that God was not offended by—could even insist on—blasphemy. But he was bitterly disappointed by Schopenhauer's "theory that the intellect need only confront the blind Will with its image as it were in a mirror in order to cause it to reverse itself," and he was "very puzzled" by Schopenhauer's being "satisfied with such an inadequate answer." This is the same critical reaction in the midst of enthusiasm that he had to "the cheated devil" in *Faust* and was to have again to Freud in the first long interview. We already see, by just three examples out of a lifetime, how characteristic this reaction was of Jung.

After the fiasco of his first communion, with his father's teaching during the preparation for confirmation still fresh in his mind, Jung realized fully that their totally different attitudes toward God and religion had opened an abyss between them that was infinite in extent. He knew at the time that discussion was useless, the abyss was too wide to bridge.[33] Indeed, he even then felt an infinite compassion for his father and saw the tragedy of his fate as never before. As time went on, when Jung was about seventeen, things went even more wrong with his father. He became more and more depressed and irritable, and his son's concern increased.[34] Moreover, his father's irritability got on his nerves and, though he realized his mother was right in avoiding discussion, he could not always keep his own temper in check. The natural optimism of his disposition then reasserted itself and he began to hope against hope that he could help his father in his crushing despair, for he became more and more convinced that it was a matter of religious doubts. The Rev. Paul Jung, however, was hopelessly trapped in the Church and its theological teaching and had thus blocked off every possibility of a direct experience of God. Now, too late, at the end of his life, he evidently saw—though did not admit—the hollowness of everything secondhand which was only "believed" and not experienced.[c]

Faced with his father's misery, but against his own better judgment, Jung tried again and again over a period of nearly two years to have "a constructive talk" with his father. He naturally cherished "the secret hope of being able to let him know about the miracle of grace, and thereby help to mitigate his pangs of conscience."[35] But he found it impossible to tell him about his own experience, for his father showed no signs of being "capable of understanding the direct experience of God."[36] Thus, they never even came within sight of this problem. Undoubtedly they were partly hindered by type: at this time of his life, at all events, Jung was certainly predominantly a thinking type—he was always concerned with what things could *mean*—whereas thinking was obviously his father's inferior function: what things meant was always taboo, their *value* must never be questioned. Had these discussions taken place after Jung had discovered and understood his four types, they might well have been successful, for he would then have known enough to speak his father's language. But, as it was, almost everything Jung said was like a red rag to a bull, and he was totally unable at that time to understand how a "perfectly rational argument could meet with such emotional resistance." In fact, these conversations led nowhere for, as Jung realized years afterward, he set about them "in a very unpsychological and intellectual way and did everything possible to avoid the emotional aspects." These "fruitless discussions" exasperated them both and, a year or two before his father's death, they were given up by mutual consent, but they left "each burdened with his own specific feeling of inferiority." They had one positive result, however, for Jung himself. When he saw how imprisoned his father was in the traditional teaching of the Church, and how those walls cut him off from experiencing the living God, he understood better than ever before why in his vision God had destroyed the walls of his own cathedral.

During these years the question of what profession Jung was to adopt became more and more acute. His father said of him: "The boy is interested in everything imaginable, but he does not know what he wants."[37] The boy could only sadly admit that his father was right. However, at least he knew what he did *not* want, and that was to study theology. In this respect his father came right out into the open. If he could not admit his own mistake, at least he was determined to prevent his son

---

[c] When he was over eighty, my own father admitted to me that he was in despair for, faced with death, he realized that he did not really believe anything he had taught in over fifty years as a clergyman. I can testify from my own experience how shattering it is to watch such a development. But I was nearly forty at the time and Jung was still in his teens. Moreover, the Rev. Paul Jung never admitted his doubts but went on defending to the end what was for him a hopeless position.

from repeating it. He told him he might be anything he liked but, if his advice was wanted, then it would be better to keep away from theology: "Be anything you like except a theologian," he declared emphatically.[38] This at least was a point on which father and son were in complete agreement.

Jung's relations were not all of the same opinion. While he was at the gymnasium, he lunched every Thursday with one of his many clerical uncles, the head of his mother's family who was the vicar of St. Alban's in Basel. At first he enjoyed this and listened eagerly to the conversation at lunch, which was often about religious subjects, for all the sons of the house were also theologians. He originally placed great hopes on these conversations, expecting to hear something more substantial than he had ever heard from his own father, for were not all these people in "close touch with the dizzy heights of the university"?[39] But he was soon disillusioned, for he never got the impression that any of them knew anything about a real religious *experience;* on the contrary, all their discussions centered on "doctrinal opinions." Moreover, they all seemed to be wrapped in "a world of social and spiritual security," far removed from his own experience of God. As the choice of a profession became an urgent problem, he noticed that this uncle—on account of the interest with which he had followed such conversations—was beginning to push him, gently but firmly, in the direction of studying theology. This distressed him, because he knew it would be quite hopeless to make his uncle understand his point of view, and he began to dread these luncheons as much as he had formerly looked forward to them.

As the time for his matriculation examination approached, he was obliged at least to decide in which faculty to register at the university. But that was just the difficulty for, as he reported, his No. 1 personality was all for science, his No. 2 for the humanities. Now, presumably for the first time, this important *outer* question was decided by dreams. Two dreams led to his choice,[40] but the most decisive dream that he had at this time caused him to leave his No. 2 personality for many years.

He dreamed that he was walking slowly in the pitch dark against a strong wind, sheltering a tiny light with his hands. Everything depended on his keeping this light alive against almost impossible odds. At the same time he was terrified to realize that a "gigantic black figure" was following him. As soon as he woke, he associated this figure with the "specter of the Brocken," i.e., to his own shadow on the swirling mist, cast by the little light of his consciousness. (The reader can find full details in *Memories.*[41]) Jung regarded the dream as a parallel to Adam leaving Paradise. What had been full of light, his No. 2 personality, had now become dark and spectral, and Jung's own "path led irrevocably outward, into the limitations and darkness of three-dimensionality." The vital thing was to keep the light of his consciousness burning in the outer world. He could no longer identify with his No. 2 personality, yet he was obligated never to forget it or deny its existence. Although No. 2 had become a specter, or perhaps on that very account, he was "a spirit who could hold his own against a world of darkness." No one is likely to deny—now, some seventy-five years later, in the present dark state of the world—the vital necessity of never denying a spirit who is able to hold its own in all of the darkness, including our own.

Jung reported all of the steps in his choice of a profession in considerable detail in *Memories*.[42] But one gets the impression that it was his *fate* to become a doctor, that he had little if any choice in the matter, and that he tried to escape an inexorable fate by thinking of *other* professions rather than that he really started "life with a compromise," as he regretfully stated in *Memories*.[43] He went even further, when he was asked in a 1959 interview on the B.B.C. why he had become a doctor. His answer was: "Opportunism." In writing of the process of individuation (becoming whole) in *Psychology and Alchemy*, he used the simile of how this process catches us in its pattern like the framework of a crystal and went so far as to say:

Indeed, it seems as if all the personal entanglements and dramatic changes of fortune that go to make up the intensity of life were nothing but hesitations, timid shrinkings, almost like petty complications and meticulous excuses manufactured to avoid facing the finality of this strange or uncanny process of crystallization. Often one has the impression that the personal psyche is running round this central point like a shy animal, at once fascinated and frightened, always in flight and yet steadily drawing nearer.[44]

Therefore, I venture the hypothesis that this was exactly what happened to him during the "choice" of his profession, although I bring only two pieces of psychological evidence that it must have been so: (1) the fact that his unconscious brought up the idea of Aesculapius[d] when he was only nine years old: his carefully treasured manikin which is clearly a parallel to the Telesphoros of Aesculapius and (2) his vision during his illness in 1944 when the doctor appeared in his primal form as *basileus* of Kos to recall Jung to earth.[45] He said in *Memories* only that he was presumably also in his "primal form" but after his illness he told me that, to his great surprise, he learned then that he was also a "basileus of Kos".[e]

It is evident, from the way he wrote and from the way he spoke on the

[d] See above, page 33.

[e] There was an Asclepion at Kos which was nearly as well known as Epidaurus itself, but Kos is most famous by reason of Hippocrates (termed the "Father of Medicine"), who was born there about 460 B.C. He studied at the Asclepion and subsequently made its school of medicine the greatest in the ancient world. Hippocrates was the first Basileus of Kos (which came to mean prince of medicine). This title was then given to the greatest doctors, who were thought to be divinely appointed.

B.B.C. interview, when he was over eighty, that it was difficult indeed for his ego to realize what a great doctor he was or that, from the beginning, he had really had no choice but to follow his vocation, which was just as "divinely appointed" as that of any "basileus of Kos." Jung's genuine and innate modesty—which had no trace of a sense of inferiority, at least not in the years I knew him—was one of his most endearing qualities.

Certainly, in later years, he fully realized that being a doctor was the most important outer fact in his life. This fact always took precedence over every other claim. I can still hear him saying, in his most reproachful voice: "But my dear lady, you forget I am a doctor." Jung called his friends or pupils "dear sir" or "dear lady" only when he was really disgusted with them.

Jung's irrevocable decision to study medicine, in spite of his disagreeable feeling that he was starting life with a compromise, also brought him a feeling of considerable relief. But, as is well known, medicine is one of the most expensive and longest courses of study. Since his father could raise only a part of the sum required, he applied for, and obtained, a stipend from the university for his son. The fact that he got this seems to have been a major shock to Jung, for he had been secretly convinced that the "top people" thought little of him and were therefore "ill disposed" toward him. He could only suppose that he owed it entirely to the reputation of his father, "who was a good and uncomplicated person."[46]

After roughly nine years spent at the gymnasium, Jung looked forward to the end of his school days and to going to the university, where at last he would learn something *real*.[47] He also reported that his time at the gymnasium was the only period in his life that he was ever bored.[48] Undoubtedly a great many, if not all, of the classes at the gymnasium did bore him to death, and the same long walk every day must also have been wearisome. In addition, the change from country to urban standards was certainly anything but congenial. Nevertheless, it is doubtful whether those nine years were unhappy years. Jung had a faculty, if not a genius, for enjoying life which really never failed him, and I remember when I once asked him if he had been unhappy as a boy, he emphatically denied it. In *Memories* he wrote that, although his mother told him afterward that he was often depressed during his years at the gymnasium, this was not really the case. He was, rather, "brooding on the secret" (the secret that became much more acute through the experience of being forced by God to think the blasphemous thought) but that, even at such times, he was reassured and calmed when he went to sit on his stone.[49]

His secret—which began with the ithyphallic dream at Laufen—would almost certainly weigh more heavily upon him at the gymnasium than it had in his village school. Not that he told anyone about it even there, but the whole rural atmosphere of his childhood took the irrational for granted,[50] whereas the atmosphere of Basel was far more rational and one-sided. He soon learned at the gymnasium to avoid all mention of the irrational side of life, and this naturally led him into much greater isolation. He tells us that "the more familiar I became with city life, the stronger grew my impression that what I was now getting to know as reality belonged to an order of things different from the view of the world I had grown up with in the country."[51] He was hardly at the university, however, before he was obliged to deal with this "different world" in a way he could not have achieved had he not learned to know it really well during his long years at the gymnasium, however boring and uncongenial he may have found them.

Learning to know the reality of city life made him value his country world still more highly. He spoke of having grown up "among rivers and woods, among men and animals in a small village bathed in sunlight, with the winds and the clouds moving over it, and encompassed by dark night in which uncertain things happened. It was no mere locality on the map but 'God's world,' so ordered by Him and filled with secret meaning." Then he regretted that men and even animals have somehow lost the senses to perceive this, and that the former only make use of everything they can, but do not see that they swell "in a unified cosmos, in God's world, in an eternity where everything is already born and everything has already died."[52]

It is really remarkable, if one comes to think about it, that he remained so completely true to his own nature at a time of life when boys usually want to fit into the school atmosphere and be like the other boys at all costs. It was not that he had no desire to fit in or to be ordinary. I have heard him say that in his youth he badly wanted not to be different from other boys, but his interests were totally different, and from the beginning he saw far more than his companions did. So, whether he liked it or not, this made him what he was. During these nine years, he matured enormously, and, as a result of the experience of bringing a neurosis on himself, he developed a high sense of responsibility which was to be invaluable to him in the next phase of his life.

These years also contained great pleasures. Because of poverty, Jung usually spent his vacations with his mother and sister in Klein-Hüningen, but because of his increasing love of "God's world," which also included some of his reading, this was anything but a hardship. Both the Black Forest and the Jura mountains can easily be reached from Basel and he explored them both endlessly. Moreover, as his interest in science awoke, he searched unceasingly, also in the Rhineland plain, for fossils, minerals, bones, and the like, in which the country seemed to be rich.[53] His few vacations away from home were prized all the more for their rarity.

The expedition which filled him with the greatest joy of all took place when he was fourteen, when his father took him to Lucerne and at last he approached the "unattainable land of dreams," the mountains. The steamer on the lake, with which they went from Lucerne to Vitznau, was joy enough, but his happiness knew no bounds when his father pressed a ticket into his hand and told him he could go up to the summit of the Rigi by himself. Sixty years later, for a year or two, Jung was very much drawn to the Rigi and spent several short holidays at Rigi-Staffel. On one of these, I happened to go up in the same funicular from Vitznau, and he told me about his first ascent, which he also described later in *Memories*.[54] He was still deeply touched by his father's kindness, for his father could not possibly afford two tickets—funiculars were very expensive in those days.[f] The trip represented a sort of summit in his experience of "God's world for, as he said, he felt that world was "physically present" up there. He added that "this was the best and most precious gift my father had ever given me," adding that the impression was so profound that "his memories of everything that happened afterward in 'God's world' were blotted out," But his No. 1 personality, the schoolboy, also had a wonderful time on this trip and he felt "a world traveler" with his bamboo cane and English jockey cap.

The Rev. Paul Jung spent his summer holidays at Sachseln[g] and one year, when he was about fifteen or sixteen, Jung was allowed to visit him there. Perhaps the first idea for his Tower at Bollingen was born there, when he visited the Hermitage of Brother Niklaus, which still stands, much as Brother Klaus left it when he died in 1487, in a deep valley behind Sachseln. Certainly that place is in "God's world" and it made a deep impression on the boy. As he was walking away from it, he had his first glimpse of the anima.[h] He met a pretty girl in the local *Tracht* (costume), which was worn much more generally at that time, and found himself walking to Sachseln with her as if they "belonged together."[55] This was practically the first girl he had ever met, except his cousins, and he felt strangely moved and embarrassed and even wondered whether the girl could be his fate. But, as he thought over all the subjects that interested him, none seemed suitable to talk to her about, and besides, since they were in the Catholic part of Switzerland, he could not even tell her that he was the son of a Protestant clergyman; consequently they could speak only of the merest superficialities. He never saw her again and recorded: "Outwardly this encounter was completely meaningless. But, seen from within, it was so weighty that it not only occupied my thoughts for days but has remained forever in my memory, like a shrine by the wayside." He could not know it

[f] Even in 1911, twenty-two years later than Jung's trip, when I first went up the Rigi with my father, it was far more of an outlay than it is now.

[g] A small village on the way up to the Brünig Pass from Lucerne. It is famous as the home village of the Swiss saint Niklaus von der Flüe.

[h] Jung called the feminine figure in men the "anima." Many years later, partly from wondering what happened to the feminine genes that are also in every male fetus and partly from observations of the feminine reactions which are often to be seen even in the most masculine of men as well as from the fact that man's soul has always been thought of as feminine, he postulated this figure of the anima.

then, but it was his first experience of how this numinous and fascinating figure of the inner anima can project[i] herself into an outer girl or woman and remain there just for a moment, sometimes for much longer, even for a whole lifetime. Goethe was describing this experience when he said: "Were you not in a previous existence my sister or my bride."

The only other projection of the anima during his school days was of a different aspect. The mother of a school friend, who lived in a large country house near or in Klein-Hüningen, also fascinated him strangely, so that he put up with her boring son in order to be invited to the house. Although she was very good looking, her eyes were slightly crossed. He told me he thought this was the reason for the projection of the anima: one eye looking outward into the visible world and one inward into the unconscious.

This period of his life finally came to an end when, after creditably passing his matriculation examinations, he entered the university as a medical student in the spring of 1895. He was then nineteen and was twenty after his first semester. This is about the usual age in Switzerland, although, if he had not lost a year on account of his illness, he would have passed this examination at an unusually young age, when he was eighteen.

---

[i] "Projection" is a Jungian term that is often misunderstood. We do not *make* projections, but meet parts of our own psyche, which we do not know, projected into another human being where we get our first chance of seeing them at all. Such projected contents always have an unusually strong attraction for us, whether positive or negative.

# 4

# Basel University
# 1895–1900

In 1895 the university at Basel was in a flourishing state, largely owing to the efforts of Jung's own grandfather. Jung's relief at leaving school stemmed not only from the fact that it marked the end of the only period of his life that ever bored him and from his consequent anticipation of at last learning something *real,* but it must also have come from feeling more free than ever before to live as his contemporaries were doing. Despite the dream[a] that showed him that he must no longer identify with his No. 2 personality, but must concentrate on keeping the light of consciousness burning in the outer world and thus for the time live only in his No. 1 personality, he could not forget or deny the existence of the No. 2. Nevertheless, for many years he was spared the worst confusion of double reaction.[b] This enabled him to make many friends at the university and to take part wholeheartedly in student life.

The first semester was particularly carefree, but soon his father's health began to cast a shadow on his life at home. Before this anxious period began, Jung was full of enthusiasm as he saw "the golden gates to the *universitas litterarum* and to academic freedom opening wide." His father's participation in an outing of the "color-wearing fraternity" to which he had belonged and his son was now admitted soon taught the son how short-lived such enthusiasm can be. On the one hand, he was delighted to see his father seized once more by "the gay spirit of his own student days" and to hear him deliver a very apt speech, but on the other, he realized in a flash that his father's life had come to a standstill at his graduation. Once he had been an enthusiastic freshman, as his son was

[a] See above, page 156.
[b] See above, page 147.

now, and had evidently lived life as he should have. Then—his son wondered painfully why—everything had gone wrong, had changed into frustration and bitterness.[1]

That cheerful evening with his son's contemporaries was his last chance to enjoy life even in retrospect, for early in the next semester the elder Jung became too ill to get up. He had always been an active man and one can imagine what a trial it must have been to him when his son had to carry him about like "a sack full of bones," as he told his old friend, Albert Oeri's father.[2] He had evidently been feeling ill for a long time. It was even more difficult in those days to recognize internal cancers than it is now, but his bedridden sufferings were mercifully short, for he died early in 1896.

His death was a great grief to his son, for in spite of their differences of opinion Jung had been devoted to his father. The No. 2 personality of his mother made it more difficult by announcing that "he died just at the right time *for you*." The words "for you" hit him hard; they must have reactivated the feeling of inferiority with which his fruitless religious discussions with his father had ended. He told me many years later that at the time he had no doubt that his father had died because he could not solve his religious dilemma. He even thought that at least a contributory cause to cancer was probably the patient's inability to solve a problem. Then, he said, for many years, indeed for most of his life, his medical training taught him to assume that it was a purely physical disease with an unknown but undoubtedly physical cause. At the end of his life he reopened the question, because he had seen many deaths from cancer where the patient struggled with an unresolved conflict. I do not think he ever made up his mind on the subject, nor did he, as far as I know, ever mention it in writing or in any kind of public speech. Yet I think it should be recorded—in the event it should turn out in the future to be a fact—that Jung thought it possible that cancer was at least partly caused by an unsolved problem, though not necessarily one which its owner was able to solve.

Jung must have gone through an especially difficult period immediately following his father's death. Instead of having been able to help his father from his own conviction, based on experience, of the reality of God, he had even needed his father's death—according to the ruthless opinion of his mother's No. 2 personality—in order to be free to develop his own ideas, based always on experience and never on tradition or dogma. To make matters worse, his father was anything but gifted with regard to money, and he died leaving his family a hopelessly inadequate income. Jung thus found himself at the age of twenty confronted with the responsibility of looking after his mother and sister and somehow or other of paying his own expenses at the university. Many of his mother's relatives advised him to give up his medical studies and to find a paid job at once. He knew this was not the solution, that he must somehow find a way to continue his studies and obtain enough money for his mother and sister to be able to live without hardship.

I have often heard him speak of that time and of how up against it he was. When, almost in despair, he went to ask the uncle whom he trusted most for advice and poured out his whole problem to him, he confidently expected at least some advice as to what to do. His uncle just looked at him, however, took his pipe out of his mouth, and said: "Well, that is how one learns to be a man, my boy." At first he was furious and stalked angrily out of his uncle's house. But since Jung's furies were almost always followed by an extraordinary calm in which he could see far more clearly than usual, he stopped short before he got home and thought: "Why, that is the best advice he could possibly have given." It met an unusual fate for advice: it was taken. And it was at that time that the boy Jung learned to be a man.

It was, however, a hard struggle, for his mother was quite unable to economize and was unpractical about money. He had to keep everything in his own hands, giving her the housekeeping money every week. Even so, she could do things he found hard to understand. For instance, one day when she was going into Basel, he asked her to get enough muslin to make about a hundred bags to save their grapes from the wasps that were devouring them. She came back with a hundred dusters instead! The shop did not have the right muslin for their purpose and the salesman had told her that the dusters were such exceptionally good value! "But a hundred?" asked her exasperated son. "Well, *you* said a hundred," she replied. I remember that he used this example once in a seminar to illustrate unadulterated animus thinking, but the incident occurred many years before Jung recognized that there was any such thing as an anima or an animus. At the time it merely reflected the kind of difficulties that confronted him on the domestic front. Except for such amazing unpracticality, with its inroads on their narrow budget, his mother remained a warm, companionable woman who cooked superbly and kept house for her student son and schoolgirl daughter most adequately. Oeri told that whenever possible Jung used to pick her a bunch of wildflowers on the way home, as a peace offering, when he was late.

The Jungs did get some financial aid from their relations. His mother's youngest brother helped her as much as he could, and a brother of his father lent him some money so that he could continue his studies. He earned all the rest by working as a junior assistant and by selling a large collection of antiques for an aged aunt, for which he received a welcome commission. This experience forced him to develop the business ability which his father had lacked so sadly. In fact, all the experiences of this time—hard as they were—were a great help to his patients later, because they opened his understanding for a side of life that too many analysts have never experienced and taught him to value the little pleasures of life in a way that he never lost. It was at this time that he realized that happiness is in no way dependent on income: rich people are often unhappy and the poor frequently enjoy life to the full.

Another way he earned money, though this was late in his medical studies, was by taking over the practice of Dr. Heinrich Pestalozzi in the village of Männedorf during Dr. Pestalozzi's vacation.[c] I think this was Jung's first experience of life on the Lake of Zürich. It was a widespread country practice and involved a lot of walking[d] to outlying farms and cottages. Jung always loved the Swiss peasant and, although tremendous responsibility was involved and he often found himself faced with problems beyond his knowledge and experience at the time, he much enjoyed his rural practice and felt that life as a general practitioner in the country would be interesting and rewarding.

Dr. Pestalozzi's son wrote Adolf Jacob that, when he was sixteen and ill in bed, he was attended by Jung and was greatly impressed by his personality, his imposing size, and his self-reliance. His mother had once remarked that she had thought Jung too self-confident and also somewhat uncanny!

We hear a great deal more of Jung as a student than as a schoolboy from his old friend Oeri, in spite of their being in different faculties. They belonged, however, to the same fraternity, the Zofingia.[e] From the beginning Jung was exceedingly active in the discussions and lectures of this fraternity and was its president in the year 1897–98. Oeri reported that when Jung spoke he could hold fifty or sixty students, from all the faculties of the university, spellbound with interest, for he spoke of what was an unknown wonderland to almost all of them. The titles of some of his lectures recorded by Oeri were: "Concerning the Boundaries of the Exact Sciences," "Reflections on the Attitudes to Christianity, with Special Reference to Albrecht Ritschl," "The Value of Speculative Exploration," and "Some Reflections on Psychology." Oeri, who was responsible for the

[c] I owe this information to the kindness of Adolf Jacob of Lörrach, near Basel, whose wife is a granddaughter of Dr. Pestalozzi. He also obtained a photostat copy of the visitors' book at the time with a poem of Jung's which he wrote after his stay in Männedorf.

[d] He may possibly already have had a bicycle. Jung got about on a bicycle for many years, using it both for work and pleasure, often going for long bicycle tours during the holidays. He only very reluctantly bought a car in the spring of 1929, almost thirty years after qualifying as a doctor.

[e] Another paper on Jung as an undergraduate, mainly as he was in the Zofingia, appeared in the *Basler Stadtbuch,* 1965. It is by Gustav Steiner, who had joined the Zofingia a year later than Jung. Dr. Steiner evidently wrote Jung on December 18, 1957, to ask him to contribute an autobiographical paper on his early life in Basel to the *Basler Stadtbuch.* Steiner printed the exact text of Jung's handwritten reply, dated December 30, 1957. Jung regretfully refused the request, since he was already engaged in writing the first three chapters of *Memories.* This is a very interesting letter and appears in Vol. III of the German edition of Jung's letters; it is included in Vol. II of the English edition. Dr. Steiner's article appeared as a reaction to the publication of *Memories, Dreams, Reflections.*

protocol of this last-cited lecture, told that he recorded no fewer than thirty contributions to the discussion which followed it. He pointed out how amazing this was, in the last half of the 1890s, when the realm of medicine and science were governed by unadulterated materialism, and a haughty skepticism was preserved toward anything having to do with psychology.

Oeri also related that the fraternity nicknames—still used when they were sixty by their oldest friends—were the *Walze* (steam roller) for Jung and *Es* (it) for Oeri. Only once, he told, did the *Walze* fail to interest his audience. There was no lecture scheduled for that evening and no theme for discussion. Most of the fraternity wanted just a social evening and began it with what wine they could afford. When Jung was feeling somewhat elated by the wine, he maintained that they could just as well discuss *all* the philosophical questions that had remained unanswered! Before anyone could stop him, he sprang to his feet, and *"schwadronierte"* (chattered) on and on into the blue. This was duly recorded in the protocol and read at the next meeting. Jung objected only to the word *"schwadronierte,"* as being too subjective, and insisted on its being replaced by *"redete"* (spoke).

Oeri spoke with particular admiration of the way Jung as a student championed the despised realm of occultism. He insisted that it was downright stupid to dismiss it as nonsense, just because it was still an unknown field which no one understood; it should rather be explored and discussed in a scientific spirit. Jung did explore it most conscientiously and, although at the time no idea of being a psychiatrist had entered his head, he was, even then, a pioneer in making occultism the object of scientific study. When we remember how carefully he had avoided speaking of such unknown things as a schoolboy and how he dreaded the isolation that even the suspicion of such interests entailed, we can see how much more secure he must have felt as a student and how his earlier experiences must have given him firm enough ground to defend such an unpopular theme successfully with such skeptical and outspoken beings as his fellow undergraduates. Oeri's testimony is particularly valuable here, for he frankly admitted his own preference for a purely rational point of view.

After the death of her husband, Jung's mother had moved to Binningen, then a village in the immediate neighborhood of Basel. The walk to that house from the town led through a wood which had an eerie reputation, in spite of its peaceful name, "the nightingale wood of Bottmingermühle." When Jung was late at the Zofingia fraternity meetings, he did not care for the walk through that wood alone; he would therefore start some particularly interesting conversation, and then one or more of his friends would become so enthralled that they walked home with him without noticing where they were going in spite of the fact that Jung liked to point out the exact spot in the wood where a Dr. Götz had been murdered. Oeri related that at his own front door Jung then always kindly offered the use of his revolver for the return walk, but that, as far as he (Oeri) was concerned, he found Jung's revolver in his pocket far more alarming than the ghost of Dr. Götz or any living malefactor. He admitted frankly that he was not gifted in such things and never knew whether the revolver was cocked or not, thus expecting it to go off at any moment.

Jung had been at Basel University nearly four years when two strange things happened within a fortnight of each other and for which it was impossible to find any rational explanation. These challenged him to the depths of his being by proving beyond doubt that things could happen, even in the very citadel of matter, which no one could understand or explain. It is a peculiar but widespread human characteristic—and one which Jung always found difficult to understand—that, when it proves impossible to deny an irrational fact, people will often do their utmost to ignore its existence. Jung, on the other hand, although he always did his best to find a rational explanation (he was not *at all* credulous or willing to accept anything but proved *facts*), when this turned out to be *really* impossible, as it did in these two early instances, always felt under an obligation to do all he could to understand, or at least to accept, the inexplicable. There is a detailed account of these events in *Memories*.[3] I will briefly mention that suddenly, with no warning, the family's seventy-year-old round dining table, made of seasoned walnut wood and very solid, split, with a loud report, from the rim to beyond the center. A fortnight later there was another deafening report; a bread knife made of flawless steel had broken into several pieces.[f] On the first occasion Jung was studying in the adjoining room with the door open and his mother was quietly knitting within a yard of the table. On the second, he came home about 6 P.M. to find his mother, his fourteen-year-old sister (who had been absent on the first occasion), and their maid terribly upset because they had all been startled by a report but could find no cause for it. They could only say that it came from the direction of the sideboard. In a more careful search, Jung found the shattered bread knife in the heavy nineteenth-century cupboard. The knife had been used shortly before and put away as usual.

Jung felt completely baffled by these two undeniable, yet almost incredible events. His rational side longed to deny that he was profoundly impressed, but he found it impossible to do so. For some weeks, however, he could find nothing that could be even remotely connected with these phenomena. Then he heard of a table turning, an event that led to séances that certain relatives of his had been holding with a fifteen-and-a-half-year-old medium who was also related to him. I do not think he knew her, at least not well. There had, however, been some talk in the group of inviting him to attend the séances. He immediately found himself wondering if this

[f] Jung once showed me the remnants of this knife.

medium could have had anything to do with the strange manifestations in his own home.

Jung had already, after his second semester at the university, in the spring of 1896, read an account of the beginning of spiritualism by a theologian which had interested him enormously, for the material reported was much the same as the stories he had heard again and again in the area where he had lived since his childhood.[4] The data were certainly authentic, but in no way answered the burning question of whether a spiritualist manifestation was *physically* true. He wrote: "The observations of the spiritualists, weird and questionable as they seemed to me, were the first accounts I had seen of objective psychic phenomena. . . . But with regard to this cardinal question—the objective nature of the psyche—I could find out absolutely nothing, except what the philosophers said."[g]

But the book opened his eyes to the fact that the *same* phenomena appear in all places and times, and he got perhaps his first glimpse of what he afterward called the "collective unconscious" and of the deep layers that exist in the objective psyche and which are the same in all mankind.[h] It was no doubt owing to the fact that he had already given a lot of thought to spiritualistic phenomena that he immediately saw that there might be some connection between a circle of his relatives who were holding séances and the amazing happenings that had autonomously broken into his intimate home life and shattered two particularly durable objects that were used several times a day when the family had their meals. He cannot have much liked thus being forced to extend his field of interest in just this direction, for the Zofingia fraternity and all the friends he made at the university were very important to him. They had rescued him from the loneliness that troubled him so much as a schoolboy and he already knew that anything to do with the occult would be treated not only with "derision and disbelief " by his fellow students but also with a sort of "anxious defensiveness." This last puzzled him deeply, for although this whole field also appeared to him to be "weird and questionable," he could not understand his friends being *afraid* of it and scoffing at it as impossible. It seemed to him just as indefensible to assert that anything unexplainable was *impossible* as to be

---

[g] It is strange that, although everybody speaks glibly of "psychology," which means the science of the psyche, many people are confused as to the meaning of the word "psyche" or vaguely equate it with the word "soul." Yet "psyche" has a much wider meaning than "soul," the latter used, as it generally is, in the Christian sense of the word. Roughly, "psyche" refers to everything *inside,* in contradistinction to the *outside* world. Formerly the inner human being was always equated with the conscious ego, but research during the last seventy or eighty years has predicated the existence of the unconscious, i.e., that a great deal exists *in* us that the ego does not know, hence the "objective nature of the psyche," which Jung speaks of here. Perforce we take everything in by means of the psyche, so that strictly speaking we can never be *sure* that our impressions of people or things correspond to outer reality, so that we can ultimately only say, "They seem *to me* to be like this or like that."

[h] See above, page 16 ff.

so annoyingly credulous and uncritical as many of the spiritualists were. How could one *know* one way or the other, until far more scientific investigation had been undertaken? He found unexplained and unknown things "extremely interesting and attractive"; therefore he decided to attend these séances regularly, although there was a great deal about them which he found uncongenial.

We see here in the young Jung the attitude that led to most of his discoveries about the unknown realm of the collective unconscious. He always investigated and explored the unknown realm of the occult, however tempted he was, by its uncongenial character, to dismiss certain of its phenomena as too remote or as nonsense. Jung had a strong rational side; he was certainly mainly a thinking type in those days, and his time at Basel University coincided with the most materialistic years of our era. So the temptation, to which his great contemporaries, Sigmund Freud and Alfred Adler largely succumbed, to stop short at personal and rational explanations was almost overwhelming. But Jung never allowed himself a cheap way out. *Facts*—such as the splitting of that table and knife— although they led into a totally unknown and exceedingly unpopular realm, *must* be accepted and investigated in every possible way, even if, as was often the case for many years and in some cases even for his whole life, he had to leave them as open questions which he was unable to understand.

It was nearly twenty years later that Jung had the dream that finally taught him that all application of self-will ("where there is a will, there is a way") not only obscures the search for truth but also imposes disastrous limits to the natural development of life which can lead to the worst catastrophes. (He described this in *Memories* in the chapter "Confrontation with the Unconscious"[5] in an unusually dramatic way.) But even in his student days he saw this great truth partially, and constantly sacrificed his own way, such as his longing for rational explanations, as he did now when he risked losing his friends by turning his full attention to the only possibility he saw of explaining an incomprehensible event. We have already seen, in the admiration expressed by Oeri for Jung's courage in championing the despised realm of "occultism," that he did not lose the best among his friends. But undoubtedly, as indeed was apt to happen all his life, it weeded away many with less integrity than Oeri.

Jung attended the séances regularly for some time exactly at the turn of the century. He was twenty-five at the time and had already had nearly five years' experience in assuming responsibility for being the man of the house. He made no secret of the fact, in the circle that was holding these séances, that his only purpose in attending was to prove whether the phenomena were genuine or not, and if they were, to investigate them as scientifically as possible. Two or three years later he took this case as the main theme of his doctor's thesis,[6] but at the time he had no idea of doing so, for his decision to become a psychiatrist was made only on the eve of his final examinations, shortly *after* the séances themselves. It was sheer interest in an unknown realm that prompted him to keep a detailed diary of each séance.

The séances started with table turning, but the medium soon began having visions and reporting conversations with her control spirits, or more exactly, she allowed them to speak through her. In the first weeks (Jung said that "the whole process reached its climax within four to eight weeks"[7]) two strongly marked personalities emerged: one, whom the medium at first identified with her deceased clergyman grandfather; and the other, a tiresome, superficial chatterer who called himself Ulrich von Gerbenstein. At the same time, two characters became marked in the medium herself: the rather silly schoolgirl that she was and a far more mature and interesting feminine personality whom she called Ivenes. Whether her grandfather was his own ghost, or an autonomous figure in the medium herself, is a question that Jung left open all his life. Shortly before his death, he wrote that, although he admitted there were well-documented cases pointing in the direction of the dead being able to manifest themselves, "the question remains whether the ghost or the voice is really identical with the dead person or is a psychic projection, and whether the things said really derive from the deceased or from knowledge which may be present in the unconscious."[8]

Certainly in this case a quaternion is clear in the medium's own unconscious: the two feminine figures, Self and ego, and two main animus figures, positive and negative. At the time—through his still earlier experience of his own and his mother's No. 1 and No. 2 personalities—he was already familiar with the idea of an eternal and a temporal figure in each of us which, many years later, he named the Self and ego, but he was still far from the recognition of animus (male) figures in women and anima (female) figures in men. After the first months of the séances they slowly but steadily decreased in interest, and Jung left them before his final examinations. The most interesting discovery—as he related in *Memories*—was that he "had learned from this example how a No. 2 personality is formed, how it enters into a child's consciousness and finally integrates it into itself."[9] He did not mention, and I never heard him say, whether these sessions explained in any way the incomprehensible shattering of objects in his house, but he did say that there was no doubt that the psychic phenomena at the séances were completely genuine. Although there was little change in the conscious, schoolgirl personality of the medium, she later became an unusually good dressmaker, and in *Memories* he reported: "I saw her once again, when she was twenty-four, and received a lasting impression of the independence and maturity of her character." She died of tuberculosis at the age of twenty-six, so, as Jung said, she "was one of those precociously matured personalities." He heard from her family after her death that "during the last months of her life her character disintegrated bit by bit, and that ultimately she returned to the state of a two-year-old child, in which condition she fell into her last sleep." [10, i]

Not long after the sessions, Jung had to take his final examinations. Curiously enough, in spite of his strong interest in the "occult realm," no idea of becoming a psychiatrist had entered his head. Before his exams he was offered a tempting post in Munich as assistant to Friedrich von Müller, who had just accepted an appointment there. Von Müller was a man of keen intellect, who seems to have impressed Jung more than any of his other teachers; the post was, therefore, an extremely enviable one for a young doctor only just fully fledged. Jung still did not know to which branch of medicine he wanted to devote himself, but the question would have been decided for internal medicine had he chosen to go to Munich. Somehow he still hesitated to accept von Müller's offer. Then—he once told me it was the evening before he had to take his exam in psychiatry—he at last, at the eleventh hour, overcame his resistance sufficiently at least to read Krafft-Ebing's psychiatric textbook. [11]

His resistance is understandable, for psychiatry at the turn of the century was the most despised branch of medicine. Almost no one knew or cared anything about it, except to label the various mental diseases with long names that usually meant nothing. The lectures at Basel University and the clinical demonstrations had made no impression at all except "boredom and disgust." Jung recorded that Krafft-Ebing's book "did not differ essentially from other books of the kind." Nevertheless, the time was evidently ripe, for it jolted him like a bolt of lightning; he knew before he had read a page that psychiatry was "the only possible goal for him." In it his two fields of interest could at last unite. If it had been difficult to stick to his interest in the "occult" in the face of the attitude of all his friends, that was a mere pinprick in comparison with the difficulties that confronted him now in openly deciding for the most despised branch of medicine and refusing an enviable post in Munich, with a recognized and respectable goal attached to it. In *Memories* [12] he alluded to what agony this decision cost him, for he knew he was alienating the sympathy of everyone he cared about. In those days no one could understand anyone becoming a psychiatrist, especially someone like Jung who was being freely offered the first rung of the reputable ladder of internal medicine. However, there was

---

[i] This information was given to Jung by her family just after her death. More than sixty years later her niece wrote a biographical study of her aunt but, in her enthusiasm to make her a heroine, completely misrepresented the situation. Stefanie Zumstein-Preiswerk, *C. G. Jung's Medium* (Munich: Kindler Verlag, 1975).

never any doubt in his mind after that memorable evening, and, in spite of the violence he felt he was doing to his feeling relationships, he was carried through his examinations on a mighty stream, where all his interests had united. He passed them with flying colors.

He became an assistant at Burghölzli, the chief mental hospital in Zürich, and entered his new duties on December 10, 1900, nearly six years after he had begun his studies at Basel University. I have often heard him describe his reasons for leaving Basel (he also presented them briefly in *Memories*) and how difficult it was for him to get away. He was still grateful to those few people who had encouraged the step he made, and said they had helped him more than they knew, whereas, every time he was reproached for doing so, he was pulled a bit back and had to fight the battle over again. His mother—though naturally it hit her hard—saw that it was a necessary step for him and took it very well. But in a way that made it more difficult, for when all his relations and friends reproached him for his cruelty to her, he probably felt worse than if she had behaved badly.

Although his mother behaved well over his leaving Basel, he had learned earlier that, like every young man of his age, he must win the battle with the hampering influence that every mother exerts willingly or unwillingly, consciously or unconsciously, over her children. He described once in a seminar the way he woke up to this fact. His mother came into his room one day where there were a lot of diagrams pinned up on the wall. She looked at them disparagingly and remarked: "I suppose you think those are something." She shattered her son by this contempt, for he had poured a lot of creative energy into them and he felt that they had thrown some light onto a dark question. For two or three days, he told us, he was totally unable to work, utterly lamed in the vital sphere of his creativeness. Then he pulled himself together and thought: "She knows nothing about it and I shall not let her interfere whatever it leads to, whatever it costs her." Immediately his creativeness was freed and he was able to continue with his diagrams and thus to clarify his problem.

It is in just this way that the necessary battles are fought out between mother and son and enable him to become a man. If Jung had lost this battle and allowed his creative energy to be lamed, he would have remained an eternal boy caught in his mother complex, as unfortunately many are in our day. Perhaps Jung's clearest, and his last description of this problem is in the beginning of his book *Aion*, first published in German in 1951.[13] It is a young man's most difficult and persistent problem—especially when he is really fond of his mother, as Jung always was—and is never won in one battle. It is fatally easy to regress without noticing it, especially if the man regards the battle as won. Jung was therefore always against young people remaining too long in the home nest. Because of his father's death when he was twenty, and the economic problem, Jung took all his medical training in Basel, and thus lived at home until he was twenty-five, but then he knew beyond doubt he must go, however unhappy it made his mother. It was not only the home situation but also the terrible pull of the centuries that is always present in an age-old, highly cultured city like Basel. Zürich is mainly a commercial city, much less cultured than Basel. It relates to the world through its commerce, and Jung often pointed out that its air was free. There was far less pull back into tradition than in Basel.

It was therefore an absolutely necessary step for Jung to do his practical work in some place other than Basel, and Zürich had held an attraction for him ever since he was four. It was equally necessary to leave his mother in Basel. They never lived under one roof again, although years later, when Jung was married and had children going to school, he found his mother and sister a house not far from his own in Küsnacht on the Lake of Zürich.

As a matter of fact, his mother had no reason to feel slighted at not being taken to Zürich, for Jung lived right inside the hospital, partly to study his subject as thoroughly as possible, partly to spend as little of his salary as was practicable. He still helped his mother financially and owed a debt of three thousand francs to the uncle who had lent him the money to enable him to continue his studies. He was anxious to pay this off as soon as possible. The split with Basel was complete. He always retained a nostalgic love for it, but never returned, in spite of the prophecies of his family and friends that he would never be able to stay away. He settled instead on the Lake of Zürich and lived there for just over sixty years, from December, 1900, to his death in June, 1961.

At the end of the first three chapters of *Memories*, which he wrote entirely himself, he described the treat he gave himself after his final examinations. He went for the first time in his life to the opera (Bizet's *Carmen*) and went for a few days both to Munich and Stuttgart, where an enchanting old aunt was still living in the past. Such fleeting visits to remnants of a bygone age are important for young people, for they tend to preserve an unbroken line of life. Jung said: "This visit was a final farewell to the nostalgias of my childhood."[14]

In spite of the great difficulties Jung met during his undergraduate years, or rather, probably because of them, they were a happy period of his life, and he looked back on them with far more pleasure than he did on his school days. This was largely because it was a much freer life: those lectures and demonstrations he found uncongenial could to some extent be cut, so he was not forced to build up resistance to a subject or a teacher, as sometimes happened at the gymnasium, where all classes were compulsory. Moreover, he found his studies infinitely more interesting.

Jung often used to deplore the fact that the Christian religion had a fatal tendency to leave its adherents childish. The strong emphasis that it lays on the weakness of man, who can hope to achieve anything only by relying entirely on Christ, has undoubtedly encouraged a universal but fatal human tendency to remain infantile. In later years Jung often used to point out that the totalitarian state could never have gained its almighty power had not the majority of people *preferred* to leave the responsibility for the major problems of life to someone else. One could say that an analysis with Jung largely consisted in shedding the childishness of which one had been unconscious but which became deplorably evident in the course of the analysis.

One of Jung's most striking characteristics was the fact that he never asked anything of other people that he had not first asked of himself, and he told me once, when he was nearly sixty, that he could say his whole life had been spent in eliminating his own childishness. He added ruefully, with that uncompromising honesty that was so convincing, that he was afraid there was still quite a bit left. No time of his life was more fruitful in eliminating childishness than his six years at the university. From the introverted point of view Jung was singularly adult even in his childhood. He faced the *inner* facts and problems that confronted him with an amazingly adult thoughtfulness and sense of responsibility, but as regards the extraverted point of view, that is, dealing with the outer world and the problems it confronted him with, he was still rather helpless and young when he left school.

It is true that he had realized vividly at the end of his "neurosis" that it was much more difficult for his father to meet the expenses of his education than was the case with most of his schoolfellows. He felt that put him under an obligation, always scrupulously honored, to work hard at his lessons. But he had nothing to do with the financial side. Because of the fact that clergymen in general (and the Rev. Paul Jung in particular) feel under an obligation to value the spiritual more highly than the material, the latter is too often repressed and becomes surrounded with an unspoken taboo. This can have an adverse effect on parsonage children. Especially, sex and money are felt to be somehow demonic and therefore better avoided. Jung's country upbringing protected him most efficiently as regards sex, but he felt the full impact in respect to money, and he never quite got over it. When he was well over sixty, he told me that, although one could teach oneself *never* to shirk anything to do with money and to deal efficiently with it, he did not think it was possible to free it entirely from its early taboo, for it always somehow remained connected with an uncomfortable feeling. "Even now," he said ruefully, "I dislike it when someone who comes for a single consultation asks me how much he owes me, and I experience pleasurable relief when he gives me his address and asks me to send him a bill."

This gives us some idea of how almost unbearably difficult it must have been for him when his father's death, during his second semester, pitchforked him suddenly into full responsibility for the family finances. As we have seen, his mother was anything but a help, and his most trusted uncle just pointed out that it was his chance to grow up. He took the opportunity, intensely disagreeable as it was to him. He gave his mother an allowance for the housekeeping and generally managed their expenditures. He also took every opportunity to earn money, both in his profession and outside.

Probably the piece of work that went furthest toward curing his original childishness about money was selling his old aunt's collection of antiques on commission. Antique dealers are usually experienced businessmen, with a natural determination to buy their wares as cheaply and sell them as expensively as possible. Jung, with no business experience whatever, was forced to take his aunt's pieces to such a market, to get over his repugnance at the idea of bargaining, and then to get the best possible price for each item separately. He learned quickly and, when the collection was disposed of, he was told by experts that he had got an amazingly good price for it as a whole. He learned unusual efficiency in money matters but not to enjoy dealing, for he told me that it was a great relief to him at Burghölzli to get his salary handed him every month in an envelope as though it had nothing directly to do with the business of earning his living. But what he had learned as an undergraduate naturally was of the greatest use to him later when it came to his private practice. His charges were always reasonable. Even when he was a famous man and could have asked what he liked, people were always amazed at the modesty of his fees, in comparison with Freudian analysts in America, for instance, and also, unfortunately, with some of his own pupils.

It was not only in regard to money but in many other ways that Jung had to face the outside world in those years. At school he had always had a tendency to feel an outsider, because his interests were so different from those of his companions, but at the university he learned to stand up for those interests with his fellow undergraduates. He did this so successfully that he attracted them in spite of themselves. He learned to be far more sure of himself in those years, so that he was able to risk all he had gained in order to follow what he then fully recognized as his vocation, even though this entailed devoting himself to the most unpopular field of medicine in existence at that date. He did this with his eyes wide open, for he tells us that in the face of the "amazement and disappointment" of his respected teacher, von Müller, and of all his friends, his "old wound, the feeling of being an outsider and of alienating others began to ache again. But now I understood why."[15]

This understanding "why" was always the most important thing to Jung. I have often heard him say that the only unbearable torture is the torture of not understanding. And this above all was the gain of his years at the university: he learned to understand a great deal at that time, but more important still, he learned that understanding follows only if you always face this "unbearable torture" and never turn your back on it. This insight was to be of the greatest use to him in the next phase of his life.

# 5

# Burghölzli Psychiatric Hospital
# 1900–1909

Jung had no sooner arrived at Burghölzli and taken stock of his work there than he found himself exposed as never before to "the unbearable torture of not understanding." It was not that Burghölzli was any worse than other such hospitals; on the contrary, it was a good deal better, particularly as regards its building and site. It was regarded as the best of all Swiss hospitals at that time, a model of what a psychiatric hospital should be. When Jung went there in December, 1900, it had been in existence only a few years and was not only a fine building, equipped with every facility known at the time, but was also situated on the edge of the town, almost in the country. It is difficult to realize how enormously Zürich has grown since the First World War, for Burghölzli is now situated far within the limits of the town. Dr. Franz Riklin Jr. told me that it had one disadvantage from the beginning: it should and could have been built with a magnificent view of the lake and the mountains, but in those days it was thought dangerous to let psychiatric patients see the lake, because the sight of water might give rise to the idea of suicide.

It was not only the building that was far above the average at Burghölzli. Jung's chief there, Prof. Eugen Bleuler Sr., was unusually broad-minded, willing to allow his young assistants more freedom than was then usual. The subject of Jung's inaugural dissertation was *Occult Phenomena*. It is mentioned on the 1902 title page that this "dissertation was approved on the motion of Professor Eugen Bleuler" while Jung was his "First Assistant." This was really remarkable at that date.

But in spite of all these advantages, it was a melancholy fact that psychiatric knowledge was almost nonexistent at the turn of the century, that is, empirical and psychiatric knowledge that could appeal to a mind like Jung's and give him substantial help in how to treat the individual

77

patients whom he found entrusted to his care at the hospital. There was indeed plenty of theory with which to diagnose and label the patients, but terms and theory never appealed to Jung except as a temporary aid. Speaking of the terms he himself gave to various aspects of the human psyche, he wrote, in his last long book, *Mysterium Coniunctionis* (published in 1955): "If such concepts provisionally serve to put the empirical material in order, they will have fulfilled their purpose."[1] He used to deplore the tendency of too many of his pupils to make dogma of such concepts, and once in exasperation remarked: "Thank God, I am Jung, and not a Jungian!"

This attitude was no late acquisition; it was with him from the beginning of his practice. It was the *individual* patient that counted. Did the theory and the name stand up to that test or not? When he began his work at Burghölzli he found such tools woefully inadequate. At first he assumed it was his own ignorance that was at fault and in order to overcome this handicap read everything that had been published on the subject, including all fifty volumes of the *Allgemeine Zeitschrift für Psychiatrie.*[2]

It was not that there had been no inquiring minds at work on these subjects before Jung, but their books had not been accepted in the hospitals and were still difficult for the young psychiatrist to obtain. Moreover, when he did obtain them, he found himself ostracized by his colleagues for reading such nonsense and still more for taking it seriously. This last applied especially to the writings of Freud.

I often heard Jung speak of these first years at Burghölzli and of his horror when he found he had adopted a profession of which, as he expressed it, "I understood nothing at all." Most of his colleagues seemed quite happy and to be performing their duties conscientiously to their own satisfaction. At first he thought that there must be some recognized knowledge that had somehow escaped him. It did not take him long to realize that his colleagues' results were no better than his own and that for the most part they never questioned their results. They were satisfied that they had done all that could possibly be expected of them, and therefore they could enjoy their time off duty with a good conscience. I remember Jung telling me that in those first years he had a constant bad conscience about his patients which effectually temporarily extinguished his usual *joie de vivre* and that during the first six months he spent *all* his free time struggling in every way he knew, mainly by reading, to cope with his ignorance and insufficiency.

In the winter of 1902–03, he made a further effort to increase his knowledge by spending a few months in Paris to study with Pierrre Janet. When Janet, as an old man, lectured once at Zürich University, I saw Jung greet him with the warmest affection and respect.

One supposes it was this early bad conscience, and no doubt the disastrous and destructive results of overindulgence in alcohol that must have been evident in many of his patients at the hospital, that made him become a teetotaler for a number of years. Oeri rightly attributed this to the influence of Bleuler, (who was a fanatical teetotaler) and that when he (Oeri) returned to Switzerland after a long absence abroad and met Jung again the glances the latter cast at his glass of wine turned it to vinegar on the spot!

Oeri visited his old friend while he was an assistant at Burghölzli, but from his description it must have been after Jung was finding his feet in his profession. Oeri said that, although he had missed whatever steps there were that led Jung to choose psych      , there could be no doubt, after seeing him among his patients, of his enthusiasm for his work. Oeri gave an amusing description of a personally conducted tour around Jung's wards with which he was honored during his visit to the hospital. In one of these wards, which housed the worst patients, the more restless were lying on their beds or standing around. Jung engaged some of them in conversation that could show where their trouble lay. Oeri found this so fascinating that he joined in the conversation himself, until a recumbent and apparently quiet patient suddenly leaped up in his bed and aimed a terrific blow at him from behind. Far from showing any concern at his friend's fright, Jung remarked with some pride that the man could indeed deliver real knockout blows if one did not look out. He laughed so wholeheartedly that Oeri felt himself back in the Klein-Hüningen Vicarage garden where he had first heard the small schoolboy Jung laugh in exactly the same way.[3]

Jung always found it difficult to realize the healing, "whole-making" effect that his personality—even when unaided by understanding of the material—had on his patients, in fact sometimes even on people who came little into personal contact with him. Since to him the "torture of not understanding was the only unbearable torture," he assumed for many years that all thoughtful people felt the same way. Even in later years, therefore, when it happened that he did not understand the dreams of a patient, he always told him so and even advised him to try to find another analyst who would. It was always a surprise to him when such a patient replied that he was perfectly satisfied and absolutely refused to change. I remember one case he mentioned of a patient who had been born and lived as a small child in the East. Jung was quite in despair at not being able to understand her dreams at all, though it did not disturb the patient in the least. Then Arthur Avalon's *Serpent Power* with its description of Kundalini Yoga fell into his hands. Immediately the dreams were clear to him, for apparently this whole Eastern process had entered her unconscious as a tiny child, through her *Ayah* or the environment, had lain dormant there for some thirty years, and then come to the surface in her dreams.

This example, although it must have occurred at least twenty years later than the time we are considering, gives us the key to the reason he felt so bad in his first years at Burghölzli. At that time he lacked the knowledge to *understand* the material of his patients, although even then he realized that it had meaning and that the individual, not the ward in general, was the only thing that mattered and was where the answers could be found. Writing his thesis, which was published in Leipzig in 1902, must have helped to clarify his mind and to reveal some of the background of his cases, but probably the first real light came with the use of the association experiment.

This test was originated by the German doctor and philosopher Wilhelm Wundt (1832–1920), and was developed by several others. However, it was used in those days only to explore conscious lines of thought. Although Jung had undoubtedly read about it before, it first appeared to him as a practical possibility for his own work about 1904, when Franz Riklin Sr. came back from Germany, where he had been working on the association test with Gustav Aschaffenburg. His son, Franz Riklin Jr. once described how this came about. His father was greatly interested in his work with Aschaffenburg and would have liked to remain longer in Germany, but financial considerations brought him back to Switzerland to take his final medical examinations. The same considerations made him take a post at Burghölzli in order to earn something, even during the exams. He arrived in Zürich late one evening and, to his pleasurable surprise, found that his future chief, Professor Bleuler, had come to the station to meet his new assistant. On the way to Burghölzli, Bleuler spoke enthusiastically of his First Assistant, C. G. Jung, and, late though it was, Jung was called from his apartment and the three spent some hours discussing the association experiment and planning how to put it to practical use in the hospital.

The test had previously been used only on conscious lines of thought, and the reason it is so often associated with Jung (I have even heard it stated that he began it) is that he was the first to inquire into the *disturbances* in reaction, thus making it a valuable method for investigating the deeper roots of mental illnesses. This led Jung to a recognition of the existence of the complexes and thus, independently of Freud, to the discovery of the unconscious. At first, like Freud and Adler, he discovered what he later called the personal unconscious, but he soon found many psychic contents which obviously reached far beyond the personal sphere. (The contents of the lower levels as depicted in the diagram on page 17 often appeared in the results of the association experiment and also in dreams.) This realization forced him to dig deeper and thus to discover the collective unconscious.

Without attempting to describe the association experiment, for such descriptions can be found in many other sources,[a] I will just mention that it consists in the test person responding to a long list of words with the first word that comes into his head. It struck Jung that the difficulties in

[a] Especially the second volume of the *Collected Works, Experimental Researches*, where a great many of the papers deal with the association experiment.

supplying the word (no notice of these disturbances had been taken before) were the really interesting aspects of the test, because they would lead straight to the unconscious disturbance in the test person. The method yielded amazing and fruitful results, particularly during the time Jung was at Burghölzli, though he gave it up in his practice soon after, because he found—as his knowledge of the psyche, and particularly of dreams, increased—that it was no longer necessary to him. For some time later, however, he continued to use it whenever he was asked by the Swiss courts for his advice in criminal cases. In addition, he went on drawing it to the attention of young lay psychologists and also of doctors who had had little or no previous experience of the unconscious. In 1935, for instance, when he gave a course of five lectures to about two hundred doctors at the Tavistock Clinic in London, he devoted quite a lot of time to explaining it carefully.[4] He also made it a compulsory examination subject at the C. G. Jung Institute, Zürich, when the statutes were drawn up in 1948.

It was the association test that primarily drew Jung's attention to the complexes that exist in everyone. To define the term "complex" briefly, one might say that it is an unconscious or half-conscious cluster of representations, laden with emotion. A complex consists of a nucleus and a surrounding field of associations. A complex can be acquired by personal experience or its nucleus can be formed by an archetypal content. When the emotion involved is acute, the complex can lead to every kind of neurotic, even pathological, disturbance. This emotion is naturally revealed by the test words that relate to it, and here Jung must have been much helped by his own experience as a boy of the neurosis that he brought on himself by forgetting his original thought. The reader will remember that when the boy attacked him from behind in Cathedral Square and knocked him down, the thought shot through his mind: "Now I won't have to go to school anymore." As long as he forgot this motive, he was genuinely ill, but as soon as he remembered and faced the pain and shame of his trick he recovered entirely with no relapse.[b]

If we return again for a moment to this simple example, we can see exactly how a complex can start. If the boy Jung had never faced up to having brought his illness on himself, by forgetting its origin and purpose, he would not only have continued in his neurosis but the forgotten incident would have formed the nucleus of a complex. All similar later experiences would have clustered around it; then any word that recalled his forgotten guilt would provoke a disturbed reaction. But he had learned once and for all that to remember and know one's guilt, whatever it costs in pain, is the most essential element in being able to live and breathe freely.

It can only really have been the knowledge and certainty this experience gave him that provided him with the courage to act on the information he

[b] See above, page 42 ff.

gathered from the association test and from questioning his patients about their past lives. Whenever it was possible, he faced them with the truth, and wherever they had the courage to face whatever they had done or whatever had happened to them, it was always with beneficial results. He risked this, in his early years at Burghölzli, in a case that proved to be a milestone in his practice and which in later years he spoke of more frequently than any other of his early cases.[5] The case involved a mother who had to face the guilt of having murdered her favorite child.

As a young girl this woman had been in love with a wealthy young man whom she believed was too much above her ever to propose to her, and in despair she had married another. Five years afterward a friend of the first man told her that he had been inconsolable when he heard of her marriage. Shortly afterward she was bathing her two children in water that she knew was not drinking water, yet she allowed the girl to suck the sponge and even gave the boy a glass of the infected water to drink. She was acting from an *unconscious* wish to destroy all trace of her present marriage so that she should once more be free for the man of her choice. The little girl contracted typhoid fever and died. The mother's depression, which had started when she learned the truth about the man she had loved, became so acute after the girl's death that she had to be sent to Burghölzli where, after conscientious examination, she was labeled "dementia praecox" with a poor chance of recovery.

It was with this label and with nothing known of her history except the death of her child that Jung found himself responsible for her. At first he did not dare question the diagnosis; but when her dreams, the association test, and careful questioning revealed the story, he found himself in a terrible conflict, for he knew from his own experience that she would not recover unless she was told and faced the truth, and yet he was uncertain about whether or not she had the necessary courage. He was forced to act entirely on his own responsibility; he knew very well that his colleagues would have been dead set against such a course. At last he made up his mind to tell her outright that she had murdered her child, although he knew that if she could not accept the fact it might well mean the end of his own career.

She was evidently a brave woman because after an outbreak of despair she faced the truth, with the result that in three weeks she could leave the hospital. Jung was able to trace her for many years; there was no relapse. Of course, it had not been a premeditated murder, for which she could have been held legally responsible. Yet she had known that the water was infected, so that somehow she had known the truth from the beginning, just as Jung had known he was escaping from school. This case made a tremendous impression on the young doctor, but he kept the reason for her recovery entirely to himself. He felt that the woman was already bearing an almost intolerable burden, in the loss of the child and the guilt of what she had done, and he could not risk anyone speaking of it or even possibly raising a legal question.

He was, however, confirmed in his previous convictions: the paramount importance of the individual and of hearing what he can tell of his past life and of treating each case differently in the way that suits its psychology. Although it now sounds almost incredible, until Freud and Jung saw the importance of the individual story and individual psychology, no one in psychiatry had dreamed of taking these elements seriously. Jung always gave Freud the full credit of having been the first to introduce psychology into psychiatry, although the latter was himself a neurologist, not a psychiatrist. As Jung read his books, they more and more seemed to point "the way to a closer investigation and understanding of individual cases."[6]

It was not only in his profession but also in his private life that Jung found his roots during the years at Burghölzli. Several years before, while he was a young medical student at Basel, Jung had had an indelible experience that now bore fruit. He was going on an expedition with a friend to Schaffhausen when his mother asked him to visit an old family friend, Frau Rauschenbach. He was probably quite willing to do so, for one of his earliest memories concerned this very Frau Rauschenbach. He remembered vividly that while he was still living at Laufen—certainly before he was five years old—he was led by a "young, very pretty and charming girl" on a "blue autumn day along the Rhine below the falls." The sun was shining through the leaves, in a way which he always especially loved, and there were "a lot of yellow leaves on the ground."[7] As a girl Frau Rauschenbach had had a great admiration for his father, but then she had married and lived at Schaffhausen, so that Jung probably never saw her again until sent to call on her by his mother when he was twenty-one.

During this visit he saw a young girl, still in her teens, go up the stairs and knew in a flash, beyond all doubt, that he was looking at his future wife. He was rash enough to confide this conviction to the friend he was with and was well laughed at for his pains. Emma Rauschenbach was still only a child—barely fourteen—and belonged to a rich industrial family. Jung was not only a young student, just two years into the long medical course, but, a year or so after his father's death, at the lowest ebb of the family fortunes. No ridicule or rational considerations changed Jung's inner conviction, however, although he probably fully realized that he must wait for years before he could prove to his friend or anyone else that his conviction was based on fact.

I do not know if he saw Emma Rauschenbach again while he was still a student but, since he married her after a not altogether rapid courtship in his third year at Burghölzli (1903), he must have approached her soon after he found himself in an independent position. Inwardly he certainly knew even then that he was destined to go far in his profession, but his circumstances at the time he married cannot have been inviting for a girl brought up as Emma Rauschenbach had been. Her father was a successful businessman and from all she told me later of her girlhood, she grew up at Schaffhausen within a traditional Swiss social pattern. Psychiatry was still the most despised branch of medicine and, although they had their own separate and attractive flat, Jung's work obliged them to live at Burghölzli for the first six years of their marriage. Moreover, through all the early years of his professional life, his chief worldly ambition was to become a professor, with leisure for study and congenial colleagues. It was not until many years later that he finally sacrificed this dream, for he learned, through his "confrontation with the unconscious," that it was incompatible with his real task.[8] When he was made a professor in 1935, his wife, according to Swiss usage, was from then on always addressed as "Frau Professor," and she told me then, with great disgust, that it was the title she disliked the most of any and that, as a young girl, she had always been determined never to marry a Herr Professor! Yet she must have known, when she married the young Dr. Jung, how likely it was that this fate would befall her. It is therefore not surprising, as Jung reported,[9] that she refused him at first. But the relationship between them was far too fateful and "meant" for any outer considerations to hold it up for long, and Emma Rauschenbach's "No" soon became a "Yes."

During his nine years at Burghölzli Jung learned a great deal in his work and his knowledge of the human psyche was deeply increased. As he was to comprehend later, the symbolism in which the unconscious expresses itself is much the same in the insane and the sane, the great difference being that in the former consciousness is entirely submerged, whereas it maintains its position in the latter. Naturally, this symbolism pours in much more freely where there are no defenses, so that Jung really had a much better opportunity to observe it than any doctor or psychologist who has not been a psychiatrist. Before Freud and Jung, however, it had not struck any psychiatrist that the strange ideas and fantasies of the insane could mean anything at all. Confusing and bewildering as Jung also found them at first, he never doubted that there was some meaning behind them and that it was the doctor's deficiency if he did not understand. Why did one patient have one kind of fantasy and another a totally different kind? Even at the beginning of his work at Burghölzli, it struck him as amazing that his colleagues were content to classify all cases of those who thought anybody had evil designs on them as patients suffering from ideas of persecution, with no regard or interest in the content of their fantasies or in the great difference in the kind or class of people who were regarded as the persecutors. Another thing that struck him early in his work was the importance of the doctor's knowledge of himself. He soon realized that the doctor could do little or nothing unless he also risked himself, and for that he must know himself. To repeat, a simple example of this is the case of the mother who had to be told that she had murdered her child. Unless Jung had known that he himself could also face guilt, and that doing so had cured his neurosis, what he said to this woman would not have carried conviction, even if—which is unlikely—he had realized the importance of saying it. If he himself had never recognized his own trick, he and his patient would have shared a common blind spot, and the healing result would not have taken place. Of course, it took him many years and long experience to be able to eliminate his blind spots sufficiently to meet every patient as completely as this one. I have laid such stress upon this one case only because we happen to know just how he first learned the necessity of knowing and facing his own guilt, and because we also know that his therapy had a permanently healing effect on this woman.

Soon after the senior Franz Riklin's return from Germany, Jung set up a laboratory for experimental psychopathology at the Burghölzli Psychiatric Clinic with Riklin as his chief collaborator. In 1905, Jung became the senior physician of Burghölzli, and in the same year he was made lecturer in psychiatry at the University of Zürich. The association experiment was used a great deal in the clinic and a large group of young doctors participated in this work, including two Americans, Jung's first contact, as far as I know, with Anglo-Saxons. Soon a number of patients were coming to him from the United States. Later he was to pay many visits there, and in some ways one can say that the Americans were the first to recognize the extraordinary quality of his psychology. They have a certain instinctive feeling for the absolutely genuine thing, which is unsurpassed in other nationalities.

When I went to the States to lecture in 1952, I remember Jung telling me how different it would be from lecturing, for instance, in England. In England, he said, one must be careful not to make any uneducated mistakes, but that did not matter at all in the United States. There the one important thing was never to say anything which one was not certain was genuine through and through. The Americans have a kind of sixth sense, he said, for detecting the real thing and for recognizing any pretenses and untested imitations. Jung spoke English as fluently as his own language and, although he never quite lost his Swiss accent, we used often to admit ruefully that he really knew our language better than we did ourselves. This was partly because, in contrast to most foreigners who speak English fluently, he was always grateful if one pointed out a mistake and, what is more, he seldom made it a second time. He had, it is true, a few pet mistakes that one could correct again and again without success. For years, for instance, he insisted on being "remembered" of things, instead of "reminded." When he was given a doctor's degree at Oxford, he returned home enthusiastic about the whole ceremony and about Oxford University, and he even remarked that he was now practically an Englishman himself. A few minutes later, however, he was as usual "remembered" of something. I remarked in an unfeeling way that if he was now an Englishman there was no escape from being "reminded" of things. He looked sad for a minute, but I never heard him make that mistake again.

While he was at Burghölzli, during the first years of the Psychiatric Clinic, Jung used hypnosis rather freely. He also lectured on it at the university during his first years there. But he was considerably upset by one spectacular cure of a lame woman through hypnosis, a case in which he had no idea what it was that had happened.[10] Since Jung hated working in the dark ("the unbearable torture of not understanding"), this one case discouraged him, in spite of its apparently positive result. As his experience in the hospital, and also in private practice, increased, he very soon gave up hypnosis altogether. This was for several reasons: first, not understanding how it worked; second, a great dislike of telling the patient what he ought to do, for he saw more and more that the patient should be left to follow his natural bent; third, that one never knew how long a cure by hypnosis would last; and fourth, with increasing experience, he found that the unconscious itself resented it. About this time he began to find himself in agreement with Freud, that understanding dreams is the *via regia* (the royal road) in therapy, and he consequently used dream analysis more and more in his treatments.[11]

Freud was still *persona non grata* in academic and medical circles; nevertheless, Jung stood up for him openly and lectured on his books at the university. His defense, not only in his lectures but also at congresses and in publications, went so far he was warned by professors that he was endangering his promising academic career. He replied: "If what Freud says is the truth I am with him. I don't give a damn for a career if it has to be based on the premise of restricting research and concealing the truth." [12] He took this stand in spite of being still greatly attracted by an academic life and in spite of the fact that he already had considerable doubts as to the exclusively sexual interpretations of Freud; even then it was "*if* what Freud says is the truth."

Although the final break with Freud did not come for a few more years, and toward the end of the friendship, Freud stayed more than once with the Jungs in their house by the lake at Küsnacht, by far the most important part of the Freud chapter in Jung's life took place while he was still at Burghölzli, so this seems the right place to mention it. I did not know Jung in those days, but I often heard him speak about the break. It was, however, already in the past, a completely digested experience, in which there was no longer any emotion.

In spite of the reservations he had from the beginning Freud undoubtedly meant a great deal to Jung during his years at Burghölzli. He had a great respect for him and always acknowledged his debt to him. As he has frequently said and written, he regarded him as a superior personality and projected the father onto him,[13] but I do not think he ever felt, even from the first long meeting in 1907, that their paths would run parallel for more than a limited time. In 1909, two years after they first met, they went to America together, since each had been independently invited to lecture at Clark University. Already the relationship was becoming problematic to Jung. His trust in Freud was shaken again and again by limitations in Freud's objective observation. Jung felt more and more that Freud put other things, such as his authority, his pet theories, and his passionate attachment to an exclusively sexual explanation of everything above the search for truth. While they were in the United States they analyzed each other's dreams, an activity which revealed these characteristics of Freud far more clearly than ever before. Nevertheless, Jung felt a strong affection for Freud, and he suffered a great deal when he began to see that a parting of the ways was inevitable.

A dream Jung had while he was in America,[14] a dream that led to his writing the book that is now *Symbols of Transformation,*[15] was the message from the unconscious itself that showed Jung he could no longer remain on Freud's path but must somehow find his own way in a completely unknown realm. Freud interpreted this dream (the whole text is given in *Memories*[16] and in *Man and His Symbols*[17]) entirely reductively, on the personal level, and did not seem to have had any idea of how inadequate this was. Jung had already been deeply disappointed when Freud refused to provide the necessary details from his private life as associations to one of his own dreams because, as he said with "a curious look" at Jung, "I cannot risk my authority." Jung added, "At that moment he lost it altogether."[18] I should perhaps explain that it is impossible for any honest analyst, Freudian, Jungian, or whatever he may be, to analyze any dream adequately if associations are withheld, a fact that was, of course, perfectly well known to Freud.

When in addition to refusing to provide personal associations for his own dream, Freud insisted on taking the archetypal dream of Jung's on the purely personal level, Jung was faced with a probable break with Freud if he "stuck to his guns," so to speak. He saw this clearly, even at the time, but he could not yet bear the idea of losing Freud's friendship. He therefore decided to humor him, to answer his inquiries for personal associations with an invented association. In *Man and His Symbols* he candidly admitted that he told Freud a lie.[19] It would be easy to misunderstand Jung here. Jung never told an easy, unconscious lie, but when he decided, as in this instance, that there was a still more important issue at stake, he could go against traditional morality and do something—like telling a lie—for which the traditional moralist could condemn him. But the big difference between *ordinary* lying and *conscious* lying is that in the latter case you *know* you have done it, and you *suffer* for it by knowing that you have done something below your standards and can no longer pride yourself on your upright character. Jung used to say that consciousness is widened by such actions but that it is also darkened: it is no longer all white, so to speak, and it is really unethical if one maintains or even thinks that it is.

Although admittedly Jung "pulled the wool" over Freud's eyes in giving an association that was not genuine, one is still surprised that Freud did not notice that he was failing to live up to Jung's standard. According to Ernest Jones's biography of Freud, he actually noticed nothing wrong in the relationship until two or three years later. In fact, at the time of the trip to America, it was Jones himself whom Freud feared would fail to remain his "close adherent." Jones said that in America "Freud formed an exaggerated idea of my independence," which led him to make "the special gesture of coming to the station to see me off to Toronto at the end of the stay and expressing the warm hope that I would keep together with them. His last words were: 'You will find it worth while.' "[20] Ernest Jones was indeed one of his most faithful adherents to the end of his life, so that the whole account of the time in America, among many other examples in Jones's biography, gives one a strange idea of Freud's ability to judge character.

But it was not until the following year (1910), in Vienna, that Jung became aware of the exact area in which Freud could stand no other opinion. From the beginning of the acquaintance, Jung dimly suspected that Freud's religious feeling was projected into his sexual theory. That Freud rejected religion entirely is well known. Confronted with the totally unexpected death of his daughter, Sophie, in 1920, he wrote to Sandor Ferenczi: "Since I am *profoundly irreligious* there is no one I can accuse and I *know* there is nowhere to which any complaint could be addressed."[21] But, as Nietzsche found to his cost, no human being can afford to announce that "God is dead." Someone or something inside him will take revenge. Jung was more and more impressed by the way in which Freud spoke of sexuality. He wrote:

> There was no mistaking the fact that Freud was emotionally involved in his sexual theory to an extraordinary degree. When he spoke of it, his tone became urgent, almost anxious, and all signs of his normally critical and skeptical manner vanished. A strange, deeply moved expression came over his face, the cause of which I was at a loss to understand. I had a strong intuition that for him sexuality was a sort of *numinosum*.[22]

He went on to say that his intuition was confirmed by a conversation in 1910 when Freud suddenly said to him: "My dear Jung, promise me never to abandon the sexual theory. That is the most essential thing of all. You see, we must make a dogma of it, an unshakable bulwark." Jung, in spite of his previous intuition, was *amazed*, for no one wants to make a dogma except "to suppress doubts once and for all. But that no longer has anything to do with scientific judgement; only with a personal power drive." It took Jung some years to understand fully that what he had "observed in Freud" was "the eruption of unconscious religious factors."[23] Freud, who always made so much of having no religion, had now constructed another compelling image, in the place of the jealous God, Yahweh, whom he had lost. Jung said that the

> advantage of this transformation for Freud was, apparently, that he was able to regard the new numinous principle as scientifically irreproachable and free from all religious taint. At bottom, however, the numinosity, that is, the psychological qualities of the two rationally incommensurable opposites—Yahweh and sexuality—remained the same. The name alone had changed, and with it, of course, the point of view: the lost god had now to be sought below, not above. But what difference does it make, ultimately, to the stronger agency if it is called now by one name and now by another?[24]

It was interesting to me, when reading Jones's biography of Freud, to find that in almost every case of Freud's many friendships that ended in hopeless misunderstandings, sexuality was the bone of contention. Jones often emphasized Freud's tolerance, but one can clearly see that this came to an end when the sexual theory was involved. To Freud—and probably also to Jones himself—it was impossible to desert this theory *except* from sheer cowardice, or opportunism. Freud even wrote to Jones concerning Jung: "Anyone who promises mankind liberation from the hardship of sex will be hailed as a hero, let him talk whatever nonsense he chooses."[25] Certainly, Jung never promised mankind anything of the kind. In certain individual cases, in which sex was really the basic problem, he even emphasized it as much as Freud, but he saw more and more clearly that no general rule could be made, for it is *not* the only urge. Only a fanatic can ever believe that his truth is the *only* truth. But to Freud his sexual theory was the *one* ultimate truth and—as the old Jews would risk and sacrifice everything for Yahweh—so Freud would risk and sacrifice everything for his convictions regarding sexuality.

Ernest Jones pointed out some superficial analogies between what he called Otto Rank's "defection" from Freud and Jung's. He was, however, honest enough to end this comparison with the following words: "The outstanding difference in the two cases is of course that Jung was not afflicted by any of the mental trouble that wrecked Rank and so was able to pursue an unusually fruitful and productive life."[26] It seems to me that Jones would have found a far more interesting parallel if he had chosen Josef Breuer instead of Rank as a comparison. The roles were indeed reversed, since Breuer was a much older man than Freud, but there are really interesting analogies to the necessary break in each case. Jones even said that Breuer's "attitude had been most satisfactory so long as Freud was a young son in need of help, but he seemed to grudge his growing independence as many fathers do with their children."[27] I need hardly add that it was Breuer's refusal to accept Freud's totalitarian claim with regard to sexuality that led to the final break after twenty years of friendship.

Be all this as it may, Jung had already realized in America that if he was to explore adequately the field that was opening up before him, he would not be able to go on pretending to agree with Freud's pet theories. He went back to the United States almost every year until the outbreak of the 1914 war, to lecture or to give consultations. Probably the American sixth sense for detecting the real thing strengthened, or rather reinforced, Jung's own innate sense that facts are far more important than theories, but it was not until he came to write the book (now *Symbols of Transformation*) that he realized fully how unpalatable these facts would be to Freud.

Emma Jung was more hopeful here than her husband; she thought that Freud would magnanimously accept the facts. Nevertheless, as she once told me, she had her own doubts of Freud by this time. He told her on one occasion that one of his daughters had disturbingly many dreams. Mrs. Jung said confidently, "You analyze them, of course, or at least understand them yourself?" But Freud replied, "My dear lady, I must use all my time attending to the dreams of my patients, so that my daughter can go on dreaming."[28] This gave Emma Jung as great a shock as any her husband suffered in other fields. She took it for granted that Jung would give his full attention to any important dream a family member had, and the fact that this was not the case with Freud shattered her faith in him as probably nothing else could have done. Nevertheless, she also was sad when it became clear that her husband was to lose this friendship. The fact that many men were able to go only a certain distance with Jung was always a great grief to Emma Jung. Women take more easily to psychology, for ideas are not as important to them and they can therefore accept something new in the realm of ideas much more readily than men. It is the realm of relationship which is all important to women, as we see in Emma Jung's shock over Freud's attitude to his daughter's dreams, which would have been unlikely to disturb a man seriously.

If one reads Jung's "Retrospect"[29] carefully (this was one of the last things he wrote), it is easy to see what it was that made the break between these two psychologists inevitable. The most important thing in Jung's life was his creative spirit, which in "Retrospect" he called his daimon and which revealed ever new truths to him. He said that he could never stop at anything once attained, but always had to hasten on to try to keep up with his creative daimon. When people no longer understood him—as Freud was unable to understand the facts and ideas in *Symbols of Transformation*—Jung still had to move on. He wrote that he often felt as if he were on a battlefield, saying: "Now you have fallen, my good comrade, but I must go on. . . . I am fond of you, indeed I love you, but I cannot stay." That was just it; he was fond of Freud, he even loved him, and it tore his heart to leave him, yet he *could not* stay. He had to follow his creative daimon and somehow make his own peace with the new ideas that were crowding in on him, just as, when the battle is still raging, the officer or soldier *cannot* stay with his wounded or even with his dying friend. One wonders whether Freud ever understood why Jung had to leave him, or whether he himself ever really saw that Jung had to go his own way against the father, just as he himself had had to go against Breuer, whom he had known much longer and from whom he had even accepted money, both as gifts and loans.[30] Since in both cases the bone of contention was Freud's unacknowledged religious conviction concerning sexuality, it does not seem likely. It was (so it seems to me) a temperamental difference between the two men: Jung could *not* stay with what he had attained, his creative daimon urged him onward; whereas Freud did stay, the whole of his life, with his attainment of the sexual theory, never able to bring himself to question its eternal truth but standing by it and defending it until the end, although he was quite willing to revise other parts of his theory.[c]

The later years at Burghölzli were a time when life opened out more and more for Jung. Not only was he beginning to feel more confident in his profession, but it was also a time when life beyond the borders of Switzerland opened up increasingly. There were congresses in Germany and elsewhere, at which he met a great many people who were working in his own field, with the opportunity to exchange ideas, which he always found stimulating. His attitude to congresses was always rather an ambivalent one, for there is usually a good deal of narrow-mindedness and condemnation of new ideas, and too many of the participants are more moved by personal ambition than by the search for truth for its own sake that was by far the most important thing to Jung. In later years I attended many congresses in which Jung took part; I witnessed his enormous pleasure at conversations that really interested him, and his disappointment and impatience with the inevitably stupid and petty aspects of such meetings. He often used to say in later years: "If our civilization is destroyed and disappears, it will be mostly due to stupidity and only in the second place to evil." All his life, like Saint Paul, he found it difficult "to suffer fools gladly." He found it particularly hard to suffer the blindness

[c] Readers who want more information about the difference between the Jungian and Freudian point of view are recommended to read *From Freud to Jung* by Liliane Frey-Rohn (New York: C. G. Jung Foundation and G. P. Putnam's Sons, 1974).

and prejudice with which new possibilities were met in academic and medical circles, for these prevent otherwise intelligent people from being open to a free exchange of ideas and cause them to react to life far more stupidly than is really necessary.

Probably the most exciting of his journeys to lecture during these years was the first to America, in 1909, which lasted for seven weeks including the voyage each way. Some letters to his wife[31] give a good idea of the impact made on him by the "New World." For an introverted Swiss, the open-door extraversion of America is the greatest contrast that can be imagined. The Swiss, although they are hospitable and exceedingly friendly once they feel they really know someone, take a very long time to open their doors to strangers. An invitation takes a long time to mature, and months, if not years, usually elapse between the first "you must come to see us" and the invitation to come on a definite date. The Americans, on the other hand, keep open house. Jung used to say that every door was wide open in America and that it was all but impossible to get five minutes alone. Once he found himself in a spare room with a door open to the double room occupied by his host and hostess, and any attempt to shut it during his toilet was immediately frustrated. "They evidently regarded me as their baby and felt they had every right to look after me all the time, in fact they clearly regarded it as their sacred duty!"

Clark University bestowed the degree of Doctor of Law *honoris causa* on both Jung and Freud during this visit. This was the first of many honorary degrees in the next decades, but from the beginning until the end such gestures made little impression on Jung. He appreciated them, for they made a welcome contrast to the lack of recognition in other academic circles, in fact to the almost fanatical opposition his psychology aroused. He always had an adequate reaction to both recognition and censure, but neither made any difference to his essential standpoint, which was founded on inner conviction, unshaken by either excessive praise or blame.

Much as he enjoyed the contrast of America, particularly the beautiful countryside, like many Europeans he found it tiring and in the end was glad to board his ship and find peace and solitude once more on the Atlantic Ocean. Jung always loved the sea and was an excellent sailor, able to enjoy his food when most of the other passengers were laid low. America finally put an end to his time as a teetotaler, which had evidently begun to wear on him. He now wrote to his wife that he was "honorably withdrawing from his various teetotal societies." Jung had the best attitude to wine of anyone I ever knew: he enjoyed it thoroughly, knew a great deal about it, could at times drink a good deal, but never for a moment did he lose his objectivity toward it. It is therefore difficult for anyone who knew him well in later years to imagine him as a teetotaler. He wrote to his wife from the return voyage: "Only the forbidden attracts. I think I must not forbid myself too much." Certainly, he was most successful in permitting himself alcohol, and one is amused to think how pleased his friend Oeri must have been when he found Jung's teetotal stage was at an end.

The year 1909 was a fateful year for Jung, for he then left Burghölzli and settled in the house he had built on the lake at Küsnacht. Emma Jung told me that during the last years at Burghölzli they often spoke of how much they would like to build a house of their own, but that it took some time to find the right site. One recalls Jung's early resolution, made when he was a small child, on the shore of Lake Constance, to live beside a lake, for even then he thought, "Without water, nobody could live at all." [d] He could not even see the lake in the distance from his flat in Burghölzli, so naturally his house could not be built until he found the right site by the lake. Mrs. Jung told me that they finally found this more or less by chance. They were out for a Sunday walk along the lake when, between the villages of Erlenbach and Küsnacht, they unexpectedly came on some land for sale. Her eyes still shone as she described the joy and excitement this aroused in them both. It was an unusually attractive site, for the land there is broad between the lake and the main road that runs along the entire length of the lake. Of course, it was only a quiet road in those days; it has since developed heavy traffic, and many otherwise wholly satisfactory houses by the lake have been ruined by constant noise where the land between road and lake is too narrow. Fortunately, the Jungs bought a deep piece of land and thus built their house far enough from the road not to be at all seriously disturbed as the traffic increased year by year. At first the ground they bought had only a rather narrow front on the lake, but they were able later to increase this considerably.

Jung said in *Memories* that he left Burghölzli because his private practice had become too large and as a sacrifice to Freud, so that he could devote more time to all the things Freud wanted him to undertake.[32] In those days the doctors at Burghölzli were allowed to take private patients in addition to their work in the hospital, and Jung could no longer cope with all he had to do. He cherished the illusion that by retiring he would not only be freed from his hospital work but that his private patients would also find other doctors at Burghölzli and he would at last find himself free for research and an academic career. Thus he went on with his lectures at the University for several more years, and he built his house without a waiting room for patients. There was a chamber that could be used as a satisfactory waiting room next to his library on the second floor, and the library itself had a small separate room which eventually became an adequate consulting room. But the waiting room had been built as a linen room and was entirely lined with cupboards and—as Mrs. Jung pointed out to me—it was unsatisfactory from a household point of view to have access to those

[d] See above, page 22.

cupboards only when there happened to be no patients in the waiting room.

Unlike his Tower at Bollingen, which was added to frequently, the house at Küsnacht was built almost as it stands today. There was only one structural alteration of any consequence made in 1925 while Jung was in Africa. He was to live in this Küsnacht house for over fifty years.

Jung called the nine years he spent at Burghölzli "my years of apprenticeship."[33] Since his resolve to become a psychiatrist was taken only on the eve of his final examination, he went to Burghölzli with practically no knowledge of the subject, for his medical studies had all been concentrated on the physical body. This naturally made him very uncertain, until he had read everything he could find on the subject. Even then he only changed one kind of uncertainty for another, for his reading and experience with other psychiatrists convinced him that the profession itself still had everything to learn.

Difficulties were always a challenge to Jung, seldom or never a discouragement, so that, in spite of his early uncertainty and feeling of complete ignorance, his enthusiasm for his chosen profession increased rapidly. I do not think that he ever regretted his choice for a moment. He also rapidly increased his knowledge and with it his feeling of security, although indeed the great struggle—the "confrontation with the unconscious"—was, when he left Burghölzli, still a few years in the future. He had, however, already served his apprenticeship and was as secure as any really conscientious psychiatrist could be at that time. He was still often exposed to the "only unbearable torture, the torture of not understanding," but the years at Burghölzli, even more than his time at Basel University, had taught him to face this torture and never to turn his back on it. Moreover, he had learned that if he brought his integrity and everything he was and knew at the time into his dealings with his patients, the results could be unexpectedly good, and he had to admit great improvements, even complete cures, when he had no idea how or why they had taken place.

In later years, indeed, such cures still occurred in his practice, but by that time he had learned that they can indeed be constellated by the physician but can be brought about only through the patient's own unconscious. During the years at Burghölzli he, like Freud and Adler, had discovered only the personal unconscious. He suspected that there were depths in the human psyche that were completely unknown, but it was not until he began to study mythology, and above all to experiment with his own unconscious, that he became aware of the collective unconscious as an empirical, verifiable fact. He was indeed experiencing it daily in fantasies of his patients and, unlike the great majority of his contemporaries, he believed these fantasies to be meaningful, but he was still far from having the key that could unlock the mystery. Even more than in his student days, he had to face daily his own particular hell: the torture of not understanding; but he could do so by this time without feelings of inferiority and without being lamed in doing everything he could for his patients.

When Jung went to Burghölzli, he was a young man of twenty-five and still unmarried. When he left it he was a married man of thirty-four with two small daughters and a baby son. (His two younger daughters were born after the move to Küsnacht.) He was, then, close to what he afterward called the middle point of life, which he placed at about thirty-five. He often pointed out that the task of the first half of life is to establish one's roots in *outer life*. With the building of the house at Küsnacht, Jung had accomplished this task: he had made a name for himself in his profession, both in Europe and America, he had married and had a growing family, and he now had his own house and land in which to establish his roots finally. Indeed, he went to Küsnacht with the firm intention of leaving the *outer* practice of his profession and of devoting himself to research.

The direction changes, Jung used to say, after the middle point of life is passed; then the task becomes to establish one's inner roots. The goal is no longer directed out into the world, but is rather a widening of the personality and its consolidation. After all, the goal of the latter part of life is no longer the world but ultimately the inevitability of death. The latter is a meaningful goal, although in our materialistic age this fact is usually ignored. This does not mean that we have no obligations to life in its second half; we need no longer *seek* the world, so to speak, but when it comes to us we are still obliged to deal with its claims. Indeed, Jung himself, though he no longer *sought* the tasks of his profession, always accepted them when they came to him. So, when it proved to be an illusion that he could leave his practice behind him in Burghölzli, he fully accepted this unwelcome fact and began his lifelong task of dividing his time and energy between the two apparently conflicting tasks of an ever growing practice and research into the forgotten knowledge of the past, his new ideas, and his writing.

The dream at the end of Jung's school days taught him that he must leave his No. 2 personality behind and go out into the world exclusively in his No. 1 personality. He could never deny the existence of his No. 2 personality nor of the latter's eternal world, but during the whole of his time at Basel University and during the nine years at Burghölzli he gave his full attention to No. 1 and its world: the outer, everyday world that is all most people know. As we have seen, he fulfilled the task of the first half of life successfully, making firm, enduring roots in the outer world.

It must be emphasized that Jung never succeeded, even in his old age, in leaving his practice behind, nor did he later wish to do more than reduce it. But moving to his quiet house on the lake and the garden he loved so well gave him a great deal more freedom: for example, he could set his own working hours and his own holidays. Presumably, what had happened was that he had fulfilled the demand made on him by his dream:[e] he had gone out into the world in his No. 1 personality; he had kept his lamp burning in all the storms and difficulties of finding his way into the outer world; and now he had come to the time when he must turn around once more and face his No. 2 personality and its inner world.

[e] See above, page 56.

# 6

# The First Years in Küsnacht
## 1909–1914

It was fortunate that Jung and his wife were so pleased with their new house in Küsnacht and that at last his lifelong wish to live by a lake had been fulfilled, for the first years there were difficult ones for Jung. The dream he had had in America made an indelible impression upon him and he knew that he must now face all its implications. In the beginning of this dream, reported in detail in *Memories*,[1] he was in an unknown house, which was yet "his house," in the upper story, furnished with fine old furniture in rococo style and valuable old paintings. With surprise he remembered that he had never been on the lower floor. Descending, he found that both building and contents dated from the fifteenth and sixteenth centuries. Going through a heavy door, he found a stone stairway that led down to a fine old vaulted cellar with walls that undoubtedly dated from Roman times, and below that, to a low cave with remains, including two human skulls, obviously belonging to a primitive culture. Incredible as it seems now, Freud had tried to interpret this dream entirely from the personal level; Jung now faced the task of finding out the real meaning of the dream for himself.

Even in 1909 in America, soon after he had the dream, Jung realized that it referred to layers of the unconscious that lie below the consciousness of man. Now that he was back in Switzerland and with some leisure, he knew he must explore these levels. But once again—as at the beginning of his work at Burghölzli—he was faced with the dark and with the "only unbearable torture, the torture of not understanding."

The longing to live beside a large sheet of water that had seized him by Lake Constance when he was a very small child was no light, childish fantasy. It was a life need, something that was to be more help and support to him during the later decades of his life than anything else. Although he certainly did not know it as a child, and I am rather doubtful that he knew it even when he bought his land by the lake, water is the symbol *par excellence* for the unconscious. Although it is, of course, only an outer image, it helps more than anything else when one is faced with ignorance about the unconscious; from 1909 until the end of his life, Jung was always able to take his "unbearable torture" to the edge of the lake. So it is interesting that his dream faced him with the unknown depths in the unconscious during the same year that he went to live by the water.

While he was still at the gymnasium in Basel, trying to make up his mind about his profession, he was powerfully attracted by archaeology. In fact, it was lack of funds alone that made him give up the goal of becoming an archaeologist. The first effect of his dream was to revive his old interest. After his return home he read a book on Babylonian excavations, then devoured endless books on mythology and the old Gnostics, altogether accumulating a mountain of knowledge. But at the end he found himself just as perplexed as he had been when he started his work at Burghölzli. Then he came across an American girl's fantasies. He never met Miss Miller, but her fantasies were a godsend to him, since they worked like a catalyst on the mountain of material he had accumulated and on his stored-up but still confused ideas about it.

These fantasies had been published by Jung's old friend, Théodore Flournoy of Geneva. I often heard Jung speak of Flournoy with the greatest affection and respect; in the German edition of *Memories* there are two pages of appreciation that do not appear in the English edition.[2] Unfortunately, Flournoy was already an old man when they first met, at the time Jung was leaving Burghölzli, so there were only a few years left before Flournoy's death. Jung spoke, however, in the warmest terms of his debt to this old doctor who was also a professor of psychology and philosophy. Flournoy was a great support, particularly during the years of the separation from Freud, the first years at Küsnacht. Jung said that Flournoy spoke most intelligently of Freud, pointing out Freud's adherence to the antireligious age of enlightenment, which explained a great deal, particularly his one-sided attitude. Jung would often go to Geneva to see Flournoy during those years, and found he could discuss a far wider range of subjects with him than he ever could with Freud. Flournoy had an objective and scientific, yet warmhearted, approach not only to his patients but to every subject. Jung could speak freely to him of his interest in such themes as somnambulism, parapsychology, and the psychology of religion. Jung related that after the break with Freud he still felt too young and inexperienced to stand alone and that Flournoy was a helpful bridge to his later independence. It was a great pleasure to Jung that Flournoy agreed warmly with his analysis of Miss Miller's fantasies.

Throughout his life Jung was inclined to have a bad time with his creative daimon *before* writing a new book. This daimon urged him on when it was time for him to write another book and gave him no peace until it was started. Although most of his books were produced under great pressure and tired him considerably, he enjoyed the actual writing and found great satisfaction in it. *Symbols of Transformation* was an exception to this rule. When I once told him, early in my acquaintance with him, that whereas most of his books filled me with new hope and a feeling of at last understanding things I had never understood before, *Symbols of Transformation* (then admittedly badly translated into English and published under the title *The Psychology of the Unconscious*) had had exactly the contrary effect, he exclaimed: "How extraordinary, for I was in a bad depression myself all the time I was writing it."

This depression undoubtedly came largely from his increasing conviction that if he wrote the book as he felt he must it would cost him his friendship with Freud. But there was also a deeper reason. If we return to the dream he had in America, the immediate cause of this whole development, we will recall that its exposition (beginning scene) stressed that the unknown house of the dream was *his own*. The dream continued with his exploration of the house and his discovery that there were three stories below the one in which the dream began; he even then interpreted the "upper" story as representing his consciousness. Now, in order to understand dreams at all it is necessary to find a context, that is, personal associations when any exist and, if there are none, parallels from the general human store: history, mythology, and so on. Therefore, all the research Jung had done before writing *Symbols of Transformation* and the actual writing of the book were absolutely indispensable first steps. He could never have understood his dream without a wide knowledge of the world's mythology, for example, and even writing the book was only a preliminary step. It was only the "confrontation with the unconscious," his own unconscious, that revealed the real meaning of the dream, and that step—even the knowledge that there was such a step—still lay in the future. Therefore the cause for Jung's depression continuing through the writing of the book, and of his experiencing none of the satisfaction that writing usually gave him, was undoubtedly that he did not see at the time that the full meaning of the dream could be discovered only after he had realized that it was also subjectively his own inner problem.

In 1925 Jung gave a seminar to a few of his pupils and patients in Zürich in which, for the first time, he spoke of the development of his psychology from his own experience. This seminar was in English and was transcribed by several members of the class. Cary de Angulo—who later married Dr. Godwin Baynes and became well known as a translator of Jung's books under her later name of Cary Baynes—took the leading role in editing the transcription of this seminar and in having it multigraphed for the use of the class. These lectures were distributed only to a few people, all of whom he knew well. Therefore they offer some aspects of the time we are considering that are not so clear in *Memories*.

When Jung's patients and pupils were having difficulty in facing the unconscious, he would often speak of the time he was writing *Symbols of Transformation*. He was haunted by bad dreams, and it still took him a few years to see that the book *Symbols of Transformation* could be taken as *himself*, as a picture of his own psychic condition, and that an analysis of the book, even at the time, would have led to an analysis of his own unconscious processes. He used to explain that the two kinds of thinking (with which the book opens) could be defined as intellectual or directed thinking and fantastic thinking. At the time he felt the latter to be completely impure, almost a kind of incestuous intercourse with the unconscious that was immoral from an intellectual point of view.

When he was writing the book, permitting fantasy in himself would have had much the same effect on him as it would on a carpenter if he went one morning into his workshop and found all his tools flying about, doing things independently of his intentions. In other words, he would have been so profoundly shocked that the only way his conscious could get him to recognize fantastic thinking at all was by projecting his own inner material.

At the time such thinking seemed to him a weak and perverted thing, such as he had often seen in his patients at Burghölzli. He could handle it only in the fantasies of such a woman as Miss Miller. This gives us a foretaste of the agony his later confrontation with his own unconscious was to cost him and a clue to his great depression as he wrote the book.

From all one knows of how new ideas came into Jung's consciousness, one may be sure that in these years that directly preceded the "confrontation with the unconscious," he already had at least a dim feeling that the adequate answer to his dream would have to be a great deal more subjective than any book in order to be complete. As mentioned before, although it was still unknown, it was *his own house* in the dream, a fact that certainly did not escape him.

Even though one can be sure that this deeper subjective reason had a great deal to do with his depression, I do not want to minimize the outer reason, of which he was certainly more conscious at the time. Jung was a most faithful friend, especially when he felt strong gratitude toward the friend, which he certainly did toward Freud, and he tells us that as he was working on the book and "approaching the end of the chapter 'The Sacrifice,' I knew in advance that its publication would cost me my friendship with Freud. . . . To me incest signified a personal complication only in the rarest cases. Usually incest has a highly religious aspect, for which reason the incest theme plays a decisive part in almost all cosmogonies and in numerous myths. But Freud clung to the literal interpretation of it and could not grasp the spiritual significance of incest as a symbol. I knew he would never be able to accept any of my ideas on this subject."[3]

Jung was so tormented by this conflict that for two months he was unable to touch his pen. To lose Freud's friendship and to seem ungrateful to him at that time was a sacrifice almost beyond bearing. During those two months he seriously considered "keeping his thoughts to himself " and not publishing the book, but in the end he decided "to go ahead with the writing." Just as he sacrificed his academic career for Freud—"I don't give a damn for a career if it has to be based on the premise of restricting research and concealing the truth"—so now he sacrificed Freud's friendship for exactly the same reason.

It is clear in reading Ernest Jones's biography of Freud that the latter had no idea of the pain and conflict which the sacrifice of the friendship cost Jung. To Freud and his close adherents *the* one and only truth had already been discovered and anyone who doubted it was simply a traitor and a coward, moved by the basest motives. At the end of his life Jung realized that, ironically enough, he was at that time devoting his research to pursuing just "the two problems which most interested Freud: the problem of 'archaic vestiges,' and that of sexuality." It is a great mistake, and a widespread one, to think that Jung failed to see the value of sexuality. But he could not stop short at "its personal significance and biological function," as Freud did. He also saw and gave full value to "its spiritual aspect and its numinous meaning." This was indeed the *numinosum* by which Freud was completely fascinated but which he was unable to recognize. Jung said "Sexuality is of the greatest importance as the expression of the chthonic spirit. That spirit is the 'other face of God,' the dark side of the God-image."[4] He went on to say that his interest in this dark side of the God-image was basically awakened in him by the 1910 conversation with Freud, which mystified him so much at the time, when Freud asked him to promise never to abandon the sexual theory but to help him "make a dogma of it, an unshakable bulwark." It was the terrific emotion by which Freud was evidently gripped, and the religious ardor which he showed whenever he spoke of sexuality, that first opened Jung's eyes to the fact that sexuality is not just what it seems but has another, far deeper meaning.

This fact has been realized in the East for thousands of years. Eastern religions are full of the religious side of sexuality—one need think only of the sculptures in many Eastern temples. When Jung was in India in 1938 he asked a learned Indian, who accompanied him on his visit to the temple at Konarak, why the sculptures were so unabashedly obscene. The Pundit replied: "But see how interested the people are." Jung objected that they were probably far too much interested in sex already. "That is how it should be," the Pundit answered, "otherwise they keep out of life and then how could they live their right karma through? Let them be stupid, promise them every kind of treat, that is how they are meant to be." Jung used to say that this was a point of view that would well repay meditation.

There were traces of a similar insight in the early and even in the medieval Church, and above all in alchemy, which, as Jung often said, more and more picked up and lived the side of totality that the Church ignored and even condemned. In pointing out the rich sexual symbolism in alchemy, especially the theme of incest, Jung indicated that this also fell into oblivion as alchemy died out and was picked up again at the end of the nineteenth century by Freud. There was reason enough for Freud's religious preoccupation with sexuality, if only his conception of it had not been so narrow and exclusively biological. Jung knew little of the Eastern religions, and nothing as yet of alchemy, when he was writing *Symbols of Transformation*. Nevertheless, his researches were quite enough to convince him that sexuality had a "spiritual aspect" and a "numinous meaning" which were far richer and more interesting than the continual emphasis on its personal and biological aspects. Of course, these aspects cannot be minimized or overlooked—they certainly have a vital place in the problem of sexuality as a whole—but, dragged out of their place and continually harped on, they become hopelessly inadequate, even tasteless in the extreme.

Although the friendship with Freud continued during the first years at Küsnacht (Freud stayed with Jung for four days just before the Weimar congress in September, 1911), it was naturally overshadowed by Jung's certainty that Freud would not accept his new ideas. He could not talk nearly as freely with Freud as he had earlier. Moreover, Freud increasingly pressed Jung into playing a central role in the psychoanalytic group—he was made editor of the *Jahrbuch* and president of the International Association—often alluding to him as "the crown prince," a role Jung had no wish whatever to play. Ernest Jones said

He [Jung] was to be the liaison officer between the various societies, advising and helping wherever necessary, and supervising the various administrative work of congresses, editorial work and so on. Freud would in this way be relieved from the active central position for which he had no taste. Unfortunately neither had Jung. Jung often said he was by nature a heretic, which was why he was drawn at first to Freud's heretical work. But he performed best alone and had none of the special talent needed for cooperative or supervisory effort with other colleagues. Nor had he much taste for business details, including regular correspondence. In short he was unsuited to the position Freud had planned for him as President of the Association and leader of the movement."[5]

When we realize that these congresses (Nuremberg, 1910; Weimar,

1911; Munich, 1913) all occurred during the time that Jung's whole interest was pouring into research, in the first years in his house by the lake, we can surmise that he undertook such distasteful duties only because he wanted to oblige Freud. He was painfully aware that his new ideas were going to disoblige him to an extreme degree, so naturally—as he was still fond of him and bound to him by ties of gratitude for having helped him to an absolutely new approach to psychiatry—he did everything he could to please Freud wherever it was still possible to do so. But Freud was also beginning to have doubts; even in 1909 Jung's reception of his "glad tidings" that he was appointing him as his "successor and crown prince" disappointed him. Still, he went on feeling sure that Jung was the chosen man for this role. Ernest Jones pointed out that Freud had "the strongest motives for turning a blind eye to" any signs of a future rift between himself and Jung,[6] but in 1912, Jones said, "the clouds began to darken." In fact, even before then Jung's "intense absorption with his researches" began to alarm Freud; he felt they were "interfering with the presidential duties he had assigned to him." One cannot help doubting Freud's ability to judge character when one realizes how long he kept the illusion that Jung, an introvert, could become the organizer, which is above all an extraverted job, that Freud wanted him to be.

*Symbols of Transformation* originally appeared in two parts in the *Jahrbuch der Psychoanalyse*. Freud was more or less able to accept the first part (1911), which he had seen in draft in 1910, although, according to Ernest Jones, Mrs. Jung remarked that when Freud stayed with them at Küsnacht in the summer of 1910 he seemed "very reserved on the subject."[7] It was the second part (1912) that contained the ideas which led to the final break. According to Jones, it was this part that contained the (for Freud and his close adherents hopelessly heretical) idea that "incest was no longer to be taken literally but as a 'symbol' of higher ideas." The year 1912 saw the end of the friendship; although the two men met once more (at the Munich congress in November, 1913), it was no longer possible for them to reach any mutual understanding. Freud was now afraid that Jung (through his editorship of the *Jahrbuch* and his presidency of the International Association, into both of which he had pushed Jung against his natural bent) would keep the power in his hands and put Freud and his inner group in a difficult position. Jung had no wish whatever for that sort of power and, to Freud's great surprise and relief, resigned the editorship of the *Jahrbuch* in October, 1913, and the presidency of the International Association in April, 1914.

It was in 1911—when Jung already knew that his friendship with Freud was doomed—that a new friendship, destined later to play a great role in his life, first dawned on his horizon. Not that it seemed important at first, just a new patient among the many who found their way to him. Early that year, Toni Wolff's mother brought her to Jung, because Toni was suffering from depression and disorientation much accentuated by the death of her father. She was an unusually intelligent girl of twenty-three. Jung, immediately recognizing that she needed a new goal to reawaken her interest in life (which had been shattered by her beloved father's sudden death), got her to do some of the research work that was still needed for his then uncompleted book. Her interest was immediately stimulated by the material, with the best results on her depression and disorientation. She appears in the photograph of the Weimar congress in September, 1911, looking very much at home; indeed, she had already found a new and interesting circle of friends in the psychological group. That in itself was life-giving to Toni, for she came from an old Zürich family whose circle was too restricted in its interests and too steeped in tradition for a girl of her unusual intelligence to be able to find sufficient nourishment. This friendship with Toni Wolff is an example of how the unconscious itself seems to compensate one loss with a gain, and in the most unexpected way. Anyone who knew Frau Wolff, a charming but conventional woman, cannot help wondering what induced her to go outside the tradition of her circle and take her daughter to such an original young doctor who, moreover, was still publicly championing Freud, a physician rejected by conventional Zürich at that time.[a]

To return to the deeper, subjective reason for Jung's depression while writing *Symbols of Transformation*, he knew that he had found the key to mythology while writing the book, but then the awkward idea occurred to him that he had explained only the myths of the *past*. Was Christianity still a living myth? And above all, did he himself still live in that myth?[8] He could answer that question only in the negative; then evidently the subjective side of his dream in America broke in on his consciousness most painfully. Again—worse than ever before—he was confronted with the "unbearable torture of not understanding." And this time it meant an exploration of a territory, not only unknown but whose existence was passionately denied, to find the answer.

Jung often told me how completely alone he felt after the break with Freud. It is true that most of the Swiss group were on his side. For a long time they had also doubted an exclusively literal explanation of incest; but almost all of them were equally opposed to its having a spiritual symbolic side. Most of his patients, moreover, preferred to stay with the more easily comprehensible Freudian approach, and for the only time in his practice, he found himself with a comparatively empty waiting room. But this was a great blessing, for it allowed him more time for the most difficult task of his life: the confrontation with his own unconscious.

The outer work on the myths of the past was done and the book written,

[a] Frau Erna Naeff-Wolff, Toni's sister, informed me that Frau Wolff took Toni to Jung because a friend of hers had warmly recommended him. He had treated a son of this friend very successfully. Frau Naeff thinks it unlikely that her mother realized the general prejudice against analysis at that time.

but now Jung was confronted with a much more difficult and exacting task: finding out what all this meant to himself. He began having more dreams. At the time he was unable to understand them, impressive though they were to him, although later he saw that they were right to the point in his task. He reported two of these dreams in detail in *Memories*.[9] These opened his eyes to the fact that the vestiges of old experiences that Freud had already recognized in the unconscious were *not* dead, outmoded forms, but were still full of life and "belong to our living being." Since he was still depressed, and even felt completely disoriented, he set himself to explore his own unconscious. He entered on this task in the only way he knew then, going into the details of his whole life with special attention to his childhood. He went right through this material *twice*, hoping to find the cause of the disturbance, but this led only to a fresh acknowledgment of his own ignorance. Since he had learned the value of facing such ignorance squarely, even though it represented for him the only unbearable torture, he did so again. He admitted his own ignorance fully: "Since I know nothing at all, I shall simply do whatever occurs to me. Thus I unconsciously submitted myself to the impulses of the unconscious."[10]

The first such impulse led him into an activity he found hard to accept, but it also taught him that the vestiges of old experiences, both racial and personal, which Freud had regarded as mere remnants of the past, could still be full of life, emotion, and energy. When he was nine or ten, he had had a great enthusiasm for building; now he discovered that this activity was still full of life and emotion. To realize that, in the painful darkness of his ignorance of how to proceed, the only thing that occurred to him was to play a childish game was almost more than he could stand. Very few people would have had the courage to draw the logical conclusion and actually to start building again on the shore of the lake in his garden. (Although it was his private garden, anyone in a boat on the lake could see what he was doing.) This, however, was the essence of Jung's character: if no way opened except one that most people would despise and dismiss as childish and unworthy of them, then he went that way and let everyone around him think as he liked. Even if they said it just showed his mental instability or the frivolity of his outlook, he still followed his creative impulse wherever it led him. It was only this extraordinary tenacity and willingness to appear a childish fool that led Jung to find the way to the riches of the unconscious. Before this time, the unconscious had been regarded as a rubbish heap, upon which everything one did not like was discarded, but he pressed on, by following every creative impulse, until he discovered the unknown realm of the collective unconscious.

Many old civilizations have known that play is the necessary *rite d'entrée* to the creative spirit of man, but I do not think Jung knew this at the time, or he would not have had such difficulty in accepting it. Play was regarded as vitally important, for example, in ancient China, Egypt, and

Sumeria, where the dead were even thought to be occupied with various board games.[11] When Jung realized that it was this building game that had proved the *rite d'entrée* that made it possible for him to face and get through the blank wall that confronted him after his book was completed and the foreseen break with Freud had taken place, he incorporated similar activities into his life whenever he was faced with another blank wall. He painted a picture, hewed stone, even played with the canalization of the stream that emptied itself into the lake on his grounds at Bollingen. He always found that he had thus overcome the obstacle which threatened to jeopardize his acceptance of the way chosen by his creative daimon. He even said—and indeed I witnessed this at the time—that it was only his preoccupation with hewing stone that enabled him to overcome the violent shock of his wife's death after fifty-two years of companionship and marriage.[12] Almost every time I went to see him in those months, he was occupied with his stone, and he often continued working on it all the time I was there.

All these discoveries still lay in the future. At the time he could only overcome his resistance and play his childish game wholeheartedly. This he succeeded in doing, and every hour in which he was free of patients and the weather permitted he spent in his garden or walking along the lake looking for suitable stones for a complete village he was building. He said that once he had overcome his pride he found himself greatly enjoying the game, a fact of which he was secretly rather ashamed. As he played, he found himself more and more interested in the fantasies his patients told him, and before long he began to observe similar fantasies in himself. Meanwhile the pressure from the unconscious reached an almost unbearable degree.

These years coincided with a tremendous general pressure from the unconscious all over Europe. Although no one believed that there *could* be a war in our enlightened age, it was undeniable that the German emperor was behaving in a warlike way. He was much distrusted in England, and one *often* heard people there croaking: "Oh, if only there isn't a war." But even in England one did not really *seriously* believe in such a barbarous possibility. On the Continent Wilhelm II was generally thought much more harmless, was even rather admired, and wars and rumors of wars were almost nonexistent. But that only made the pressure from the unconscious greater. By the autumn of 1913 Jung felt that this pressure, which had been distressing him so much inwardly, "seemed to be moving outward, as though there were something in the air. The atmosphere actually seemed to me darker than it had been. It was as though the sense of oppression no longer sprang exclusively from a psychic situation, but from concrete reality. This feeling grew more and more intense."[13]

In October, 1913, Jung had his first—what one may call—prophetic vision of the war which was then lurking so close in the unconscious. I must mention here that one of the characteristics which make it most difficult to understand dreams and autonomous fantasies that break into consciousness while one is awake is that there is either no dimension of time in the unconscious or a totally different time from our own. So it is common for dreams and fantasies to contain clear premonitions of future events, even images of the future events themselves, and there is nothing to distinguish such images from the ordinary contents of dreams. This is what happened to Jung. He saw an image of the coming war, which broke out nine months later. He gave the details of this vision in *Memories*.[14] He was alone on a train journey when he suddenly saw in a vision a monstrous flood full of bodies flow over Europe, later turning into blood. The Alps grew higher and higher to protect Switzerland, but in his account he did not say, although he emphasized it when he first told me the vision, that it was exactly the countries covered by the flood that were later involved in the war; the countries that were able to remain neutral, such as Holland, Denmark, and Scandinavia, were not affected. A fortnight later the vision recurred; that time the blood was more emphasized, and an inner voice declared: "Look at it well, it is wholly real and it will be so. You cannot doubt it." Later, when he had had more experience of the unconscious, he would have known that the vision was mainly to be taken objectively, i.e., that probably some awful danger threatened just those countries. Even at the time he wondered vaguely if it could point to revolutions where rivers of blood would flow, but he never once thought of the possibility of a war.

Since the revolution idea did not seem real to him and since Jung always took dreams and fantasies subjectively—that is, as referring to the dreamer's own unconscious—unless there were very good reasons for a purely objective approach, he decided this terrible vision referred to himself. He even came to the conclusion that he was menaced by a psychosis. This must have represented the deepest point of his depression, for a psychiatrist is especially well aware of what it means when the waves of the unconscious submerge consciousness. He had yet to learn by experience how totally different it is when you *see* the danger and when it overwhelms you unaware. But I do not think that at the time we are considering he had yet had enough experience even to know that the contents of the unconscious, and the images that it uses, are exactly the same in the insane and sane, and that everything depends on the attitude and strength of consciousness of the individual.

When Jung came to the conclusion, therefore, that the fantasy was subjective, he was faced with the worst anxiety that can assail any human being: the fear of going mad. He met it in a characteristic way. He thought if indeed this fate were inevitable, at least he would keep an exact record of everything that happened to him until the last moment in which he could write or think clearly. He was sure that such a record would be of great use to his successors and he would at least be able to make a valuable contribution to science. There were no signs in his practice or life that his mind was in any way slipping, but he evidently thought the flood might come suddenly when he least expected it, for the fear did not leave him during the nine months that elapsed between the vision and the outbreak of war.

In these nine months Jung was at first terribly troubled by floods of fantasies that had now been released, accompanied by corresponding floods of emotion. He managed to carry on his outer life successfully, but was also increasingly worrried by the fantasies of his patients which he felt he did not understand. He wrote down all his own fantasies as well as he could. This was sufficient for him to realize that there were always images hidden behind every emotion, and that whenever he succeeded in translating emotions into images, he was "inwardly calmed and re-assured." This experiment on himself taught him that therapeutically it is extraordinarily helpful to find the particular image behind every emotion. Or, to put it another way, instead of *yielding* to an emotion—when it would soon possess consciousness—you *objectify* an emotion and thus get it to change its form by producing an image, or even induce it to *tell* you what it wants. In a fit of rage, for instance, instead of losing control over your temper, you stop and say: "Why am I so angry? What can this anger really want of me?"

This helped Jung a lot, both with his own emotional reactions and in assisting his patients with theirs. Still, he felt that something more was needed, and just about two months after the alarming European flood fantasy, he decided to take a further step. In order to objectify emotion one has to sink down into it to some extent; he now decided to sink down into a fantasy.[15] Such an action has the result of concentrating the attention on that *one* fantasy, so that it can continue meaningfully, and preventing the whole energy being wasted in a flood of unconnected fantasies. In this chapter of *Memories* Jung described exactly how he came to discover the method of "active imagination," which was to play such a large role in his psychology later, although some years were to pass before he gave it that name. But the whole of what he discovered at this time can be seen in the term "*active* imagination," because in it the ego plays an *active* role—it makes a conscious decision to drop down into the fantasy and then plays an *active* role in the subsequent development. Before Jung made this experiment in December, 1913, he was just an observer of "*passive* imagina-tion," that is, he watched fantasy after fantasy, as helpless to have any influence on it as the spectator in a cinema. But once he learned to take an active role in it himself, he found that he could have an influence on its development and that he was no longer a passive spectator at an unending flood of fantasies. Not that consciousness can have its own way with the unconscious and enforce its own will. A dream soon shattered this illusion, if indeed Jung had ever harbored it. He learned in this dream that Siegfried, who represented the heroic "where there is a will there is a way" attitude, must be sacrificed whatever the cost.[16] The whole idea is an *Auseinandersetzung* between conscious and unconscious. This untranslatable German word means having it out with a thorough discussion of every aspect, airing all the pros and cons, always with a hint of eventually coming to terms.

An *Auseinandersetzung* is a demanding undertaking, even now, and unfortunately only a few of Jung's pupils saw its real value and were willing to make the great, but in the end rewarding, effort. It is the one way that I know by which people who take the unconscious seriously can become independent of analysis and keep *their own balance* between conscious and unconscious. Jung even said later that it was the touchstone by which to know the people who genuinely wanted to become independent from those who meant to shirk. But if it is so difficult and demanding even now, what must it have been for Jung in those years when he was the pioneer in the unknown unconscious? Everyone told him he was crazy to think such a thing was real and, after his fantasy of Europe bathed in blood, he was inclined to agree with them.

Jung used to say in later years that his tormenting doubts as to his own sanity should have been allayed by the amount of success he was having at the same time in the outer world, especially in America, where his realization that sexuality could not be taken only concretely met with immediate sympathy. Not only was he constantly asked to lecture there after his first 1909 visit, but he was also sent for in consultations and, in 1910, went to Chicago for such a consultation, although he could remain only seven days in the States.[17] In 1913 a fabulously rich American, daughter of a multimillionaire and wife of an unusually rich man, made up her mind that she needed an analysis. She calmly informed Jung that a far better house than his own was being bought for him in America and that all the arrangements were being made to bring his family over from Europe! She could hardly believe her ears when Jung flatly refused her offer, remarking that he analyzed in Switzerland and that if she wanted an analysis she must come there. She had to recognize, like Mohammed, that, since the mountain so unreasonably refused to move to her, she must go to the mountain. This was the first of a series of shocks that she had to undergo, for she was so convinced that there was nothing that money would not buy that it had entirely divorced her from reality. This alienation from ordinary reality is a common phenomenon with millionaires, because they have been able to buy their way out of difficult situations too often. In fact, when the money is inherited, as it was in this case, they have never come up against the struggle for existence that so much matured the student Jung, for example.

In such a case, by far the most effective therapy is to let the millionaire learn for him or herself. To give one amusing example of how this therapy worked out: This American lady had slight agoraphobia and one of its symptoms was not being able to travel by train. To overcome this, Jung suggested that she should constantly travel along the Lake of Zürich, where, on the right bank, the trains were slow and stopped at every station. Her chauffeur could wait with the Rolls-Royce at each station, giving her the opportunity of leaving the train when she could no longer stand it. Slowly she progressed, going a little farther each day, until at last she arrived triumphantly at Feldbach, the last station before Rapperswil at the end of the lake. Now Feldbach station is in an unusually beautiful situation, with a lovely view of the whole lake and the picturesque old town of Rapperswil with the mountains behind. She made up her mind that here, and here alone, was the ideal site for the house she was thinking of building. When she informed Jung of her plan, he told her that the railroad would never consent to sell. She refused to believe him, saying that he had no idea how much money they would receive as compensation. He then saw another ideal opportunity to bring her up against reality, so he said no more. Indeed she spared no effort; she engaged five lawyers to persuade the railroad officials; she had plans worked out as to how the railroad could be diverted, which she would naturally pay for; she raised the sum of money for compensation higher and higher. But all to no avail. It was impossible to tempt those obstinate, and obviously wicked, Swiss to give in, and at last she once more had to admit herself beaten.

I mention this one example among many to show how far Jung's therapy reached beyond the walls of his consulting room. He soon gave up the Freudian rule that the analyst never sees patients outside anlaysis. It was outside analysis that he often learned the most about his patients; moreover, it was in life itself that his patients learned the most about themselves. This is particularly true for people in the first half of life, or those who have not yet found their roots in outer life. A young girl who had been analyzing conscientiously for some years with one of Jung's colleagues, and who was sent to him for one consultation because the analysis seemed rather stuck, learned this dramatically. Jung immediately discovered that she was engaged, and his inquiries soon unearthed the fact that it was a love match, satisfactory in every way. "Then why on earth don't you get married?" asked Jung. She replied: "Oh, you see, I must finish my analysis, I have an obligation to do that first." Jung positively thundered at her: "Who told you you had an obligation to analysis? Your obligation is to life!"

In 1913, during this time of inner disorientation and outer success, Jung decided to withdraw from his lectures at Zürich University, where he had been a *Privatdozent*[b] since 1905. He himself said: "It would be unfair to continue teaching young students when my own intellectual situation was nothing but a mass of doubts."[18] He once told me that the last straw which led to this decision was overhearing a conversation between two students when they were all leaving the university after his lecture. One girl said to another, "Did you understand what he was saying today?" "Oh, no," replied the other, "not a word, but he must be right because he is so healthy!"

Although he withdrew from regular lecturing at the university, he usually accepted invitations, particularly for single lectures, which came to him from outside Zürich University. When his disorientation was at its worst and he was seriously reckoning with the possibility of a psychosis, he was asked by the British Medical Association to give a lecture, "On the Importance of the Unconscious in Psychopathology," at a congress in Aberdeen at the end of July, 1914. He later said: "In my state of mind just then, with the fears that were pursuing me, it seemed fateful to me that I should have to talk on the importance of the unconscious at such a time."[19] So it happened that when the First World War broke out, Jung found himself far from home in the north of Scotland. Shocked and horrified at the news as he was, he was completely and for always relieved of his fears about his own sanity, for he then recognized the vision for what it was: a singularly clear premonition of what had now befallen Europe. It must be difficult for younger people, who have lived all their lives during war or in post-war conditions, and to whom fear of another war is always present, to realize how completely by surprise the 1914 war took us all. Even in England, where if we had only listened we could have heard a few voices, including the young Winston Churchill's, raised in warning, it was a bolt from the blue. One can imagine how little Jung had expected to be cut off in Scotland from his home by the outbreak of war, although his fateful dreams had prepared him for the fact that *something* might happen.

One evening after supper in his Tower at Bollingen—he was well over eighty at the time—something must have reminded him of that adventurous journey home, well over forty years before, and he described it in detail.[c] He saw at once that it would be impossible, even for a neutral, to get home the direct way through France, for the Germans were sweeping through Belgium and it was clear they were aiming at Paris. So he made his way across to Holland with the greatest difficulty, for the British rail system was disorganized by the mobilization, and civilian communication with the Continent had almost ceased. Moreover, there were a great many neutral summer tourists eager to snap up what little transportation to Holland there

[b] *Privatdozent* is a professor without a salary. They receive just the fees paid by the audience at their own lectures.
[c] Ruth Bailey, Marie-Louise von Franz, and I were present.

was. At last, however, Jung managed to get an uncomfortable passage and finally found himself on Dutch soil. Although Holland was and managed to remain neutral in the First World War, the Dutch also were in an unparalleled state of excitement. The fate of Belgium left them in no doubt as to their own danger should it happen to suit Germany to invade Holland. It was only the fact that the country was clearly not on Germany's way to Paris that kept panic in check. Therefore, traveling through Holland to the German border was by far the easiest part of the journey for Jung, in spite of overcrowded trains and the overanxiety of everyone around him.

While in Holland, Jung took the best advice he could get as to his further route home. The only possible way was through Germany, keeping down the Rhine. He had joined up with some other Swiss men who were making their way home to join in the general mobilization of the Swiss army, which had been ordered as soon as war became inevitable. (During a war, although Switzerland is through and through neutral, the frontiers are always strongly defended in case of attack.) But haste was impossible. The few trains that started were incredibly overfilled. Jung told us that he spent several nights standing in the corridors, even in the toilets, and an incredible number of hours shunted onto sidings while the troop trains rushed through to the front.

What struck him most, however, was the state of mind of the German civilians. Refreshments of all kinds were given away in the stations, everyone refused payment, and the people seemed in a peculiar kind of ecstasy. He said the whole thing struck him as a kind of feast of love! It was impressive, and he was still much struck and not a little puzzled by it forty years later. He used to say that the Germans have a lower threshold between consciousness and the unconscious than the people of other nations, which is the reason they so easily fall victim to ideas that appeal to the masses. At last, about a month after he had started his journey, Jung found himself over the border in his well-known Basel. He told us that it seemed almost incredible to be able at last to telephone home, to find a normal train service and the usual amenities of civilization. For once mobilization is complete, and rationing in hand, the Swiss are capable of living a normal life, even when, as in 1940, they think it probable that they will be attacked any moment.

When war broke out, Jung had only just begun his fateful "confrontation with the unconscious"; moreover, he had been much handicapped by a certain doubt concerning how much he was blinded or misled by his fear of a lurking psychosis. By far the greater part of the struggle to find himself was still ahead of him and took place during the war years.

# 7

# The First World War
# 1914–1918

Although Jung was profoundly moved by the suffering and terror that had broken over Europe, he was naturally much relieved when he got back to his home on the lake after his difficult journey because the fear concerning his own sanity had been cast off. This fear, of course, had hampered him in his task of exploring the unconscious, but as he said: "Now my task was clear: I had to try to understand what had happened and to what extent my own experience coincided with that of mankind in general. *Therefore my first obligation was to probe the depths of my own psyche.* . . . This work took precedence over everything else." [1]

It will probably be difficult for those who have had no experience of the "depths of their own psyche" to understand what a perilous adventure this represents. To return to the diagram on page 17, Jung was now engaged in exploring the lower levels common to all mankind. Although he was by no means the first to enter these layers, they had not yet been taken into account by contemporary psychology, which at that time had stopped short at the first layer under consciousness, the layer Jung afterward called the "personal unconscious." He did not know it at that time, but a well-known compatriot of his, Paracelsus, had already explored those layers nearly four hundred years before.

Almost thirty years after the time we are considering, Jung gave two lectures on Paracelsus on the occasion of the four-hundredth anniversary of the death in 1541 of this famous Swiss doctor and alchemist. In the second of these, delivered to a crowded hall in Einsiedeln on the evening of October 5, 1941, he said:

I do not know how many or how few people today can imagine what "coming to terms with the unconscious" means. I fear they are only

113

too few. But perhaps it will be conceded that the second part of Goethe's *Faust* presents only incidentally and in doubtful degree an aesthetic problem, but primarily and in far greater degree a human one. It was a preoccupation that accompanied the poet right into old age, an alchemical encounter with the unconscious, comparable to the *labor Sophiae* of Paracelsus. It is on the one hand an endeavour to understand the archetypal world of the psyche, on the other hand a struggle against the sanity-threatening danger of fascination by the measureless heights and depths and paradoxes of psychic truth. The denser, concretistic, daytime mind here reaches its limits. . . . Here the human mind is confronted with its origins, the archetypes, the finite consciousness with its archaic foundations; the mortal ego, with the immortal Self, Anthropos, purusha, atman, or whatever else be the names that human speculation has given to that collective precon-scious state from which the individual ego arose. Kinsman and stranger at once, it recognizes and yet does not recognize that unknown brother who steps towards it, intangible yet real. . . . Here we must feel our way with Paracelsus into a question that was never openly asked before in our culture, and was never clearly put, partly from sheer unconsciousness, partly from holy dread. Moreover, the secret doctorine of the Anthropos was dangerous because it had nothing to do with the teachings of the Church, since from that point of view Christ was a reflection—and only a reflection—of the inner Anthropos. Hence there were a hundred good reasons for disguising this figure in indecipherable secret names.[2, a]

At the time, however, when Jung was exploring the depths of his own psyche, the only parallel journey that he knew of those mentioned in this excerpt was Goethe's *Faust*. We know that he had read this great drama from beginning to end while he was still at school and that it had poured into his soul "like a miraculous balm." But I do not know whether it was ever in his mind during his own "confrontation with the unconscious." I never heard him say that it was, and so far no one whom I have asked did either. I think it is more probable that he realized that the second part of *Faust* is such a confrontation only *after* he had studied alchemy, which he did not do until nearly twenty years after the time we are considering. At all events, he told me more than once that the *first* parallels he found to his own experience were in the Gnostic texts, that is, those reported in the *Elenchos* of Hippolytus.[b]

Before the outbreak of war—in that terribly dark time—Jung had written

---

[a] The "indecipherable secret names" refers to the "thousand names" given by the alchemists (including Paracelsus) to their central mystery.

[b] Although Hippolytus was a Church Father and supposedly writing *against* the Gnostics, we owe to him much, if not the majority, of our information about them.

down his fantasies and learned to hold onto one fantasy and gradually to take an active part in his fantasies himself. Now he made the further discovery that he could talk to the figures he encountered and find out what they wanted to tell him or what they wanted of him. He told me that at this time he made it a rule never to let a figure or figures that he encountered leave until they had told him *why* they had appeared to him. This requires a tremendous effort, for figures in fantasies are like autonomous figures in dreams and will disappear or change into something else with the utmost ease. But if consciousness concentrates on them sufficiently it is possible to hold them fast.

There is a classical example of how this can be done in the fourth book of Homer's *Odyssey*.[3] Telemachus, wearied of his home by the outrageous behavior of the suitors of his mother, Penelope, goes out to search for his father, Ulysses, who has not yet returned from Troy. The second place at which he inquires is Sparta, the home of Menelaus. The latter says that he will tell Telemachus without "concealment or reserve every word I heard myself from the infallible lips of the Old Man of the Sea" (Proteus). He then tells him that he (Menelaus) left Troy too quickly, without making the due sacrifices to the gods, so that he found himself becalmed on the island of Pharos, off the mouth of the Nile. Food was short, and Menelaus, knowing only that he "had offended the immortals," was entirely at a loss how to make reparation. One day while walking on the sands he met a beautiful woman, Eidothee, the daughter of Proteus, the Old Man of the Sea. After chiding him for his inaction, she promised to tell him all he needed to know.

She then informed him that the island was the haunt of Proteus, "who owes allegiance to Poseidon and knows the sea in all its depths," and who could tell him just how he could surmount all his difficulties. But Proteus would have to be *forced* to do so. Eidothee then explained how this could be done and promised to help Menelaus (thus revealing herself as a most helpful anima figure). Every day at high noon Proteus emerged from "his native salt" and took a midday sleep in the shelter of a cave, having first counted his seals as a shepherd counts his sheep. Menelaus must meet her there with his three best men the next morning, and she then enlightened him as to how to deal with her father.

The next morning they met the goddess at dawn. After having scooped out lairs for them in the sand, she covered each with the skin of a freshly flayed seal and gave them sweet-smelling ambrosia to enable them to endure the intolerable stench! Soon the seals came up thick and fast from the sea and lay down all around them. At midday Proteus himself emerged, and after unsuspiciously counting them with the rest of his seals, he lay down to sleep. Following Eidothee's directions, they first woke him with a shout, then the four strong men held him fast. As the goddess had foreseen, he immediately began a series of transformations: he changed rapidly into a lion, then into a snake, a panther, a giant boar. He even changed into running water and a great tree in leaf. But at last he grew tired of his "magic repertory" and, resuming his original shape, broke into speech. This was the moment for which the goddess had told them to wait, because now at last he was willing to answer questions. He not only told Menelaus to return to Egypt and how then to propitiate the angry gods with the sacrifices he had omitted before (so that he could then sail home with a favorable breeze), but most interesting of all to Telemachus, he unwillingly told him the fate of his countrymen still in Troy, when he himself left so hurriedly with Helen. The first two he spoke of (including Agamemnon, Menelaus's brother) had met with disaster, to the great grief of Menelaus. But the third, Odysseus, the father of Telemachus, was still alive, captive on the island of the nymph Calypso.

This story shows us most plastically how to deal with the figures we meet on our "confrontation with the unconscious"—almost exactly the method Jung discovered for himself. He told me, for example, that one day at this time, his fantasy led him into a remote valley, evidently inhabited by primitive people. A tall and rather impressive medicine man figure was silently beside him, watching his every step and movement. Jung came on some writing carved on a rock, which he wanted to read, but found that it was in a language quite unknown to him. Since it was also rather illegible, he took a chisel and hammer and began carefully deepening the letters in the stone. The medicine man came close, watching him even more intently, until he suddenly complained that a splinter of stone had got into his eye. He commanded Jung to take it out, but the latter, seeing his opportunity, refused to do so until the medicine man had read and translated the inscription for him! The man was unwilling to do so, but Jung held onto him and waited, just as Menelaus and his companions had done, until at last he read the text of the whole inscription. Then the fantasy ended and everything disappeared. However, Jung could remember and write down the inscription, which was evidently the point of the whole fantasy.

Jung had no doubt read the *Odyssey*, for he learned Greek as well as Latin at the Basel Gymnasium, but he had evidently not noticed the analogy to his own experience. He was, at all events, much struck and interested when Marie-Louise von Franz called his attention to this classical example as a parallel to active imagination. I mention it here because, in my lectures on active imagination, I have found that it helps greatly to show how such figures can be dealt with, and I hope it might also help the reader to get some idea of what Jung was up against in his exploration of the unconscious.

One of his first attempts to talk to such figures was with an old man and a girl who surprised him by telling him that they were Elijah and Salome. Jung thought it the strangest combination, but Elijah assured him that they had belonged together through all eternity. Later he found other examples of such couples in many myths: Klingsor and Kundry, Lao tzu and the dancing girl, the Gnostic tradition of Simon Magus, who was always with a young girl he had picked up in a brothel who was said to be a reincarnation of Helen of Troy, and many others. Elijah and Salome were accompanied by a large black snake that took a great fancy to Jung. Elijah seemed to Jung the most reasonable and intelligent of the three. This trio was with him for some time and gradually the figure of Philemon developed from Elijah. (We will return later to Philemon, the most important figure in all Jung's exploration.)

This pair—the young girl with the old man—was destined to have a far-reaching effect on Jung's fate, for—at much the same time as the fantasy—he made the extraordinary discovery that of all his friends and acquaintances only one young girl was able to follow his extraordinary experiences and to accompany him intrepidly on his Nekyia to the underworld. Toni Wolff was actually only thirteen years younger than Jung. He was only about forty at the time, but, as we know, his schoolfellows at the gymnasium had already called him "Father Abraham," and I think anyone who knew them both well, and often saw them together, would agree that, while he seemed the prototype of the wise old man, she had a quality of eternal youth. It was anything but easy at first for him to find a *modus vivendi* by which she could give him her extraordinary gift—it would not be an exaggeration to call it her genius—for companionship in the "confrontation with the unconscious."

As we saw in the preceding chapter, Toni Wolff was brought by her mother to Jung because of her depression, accentuated after the sudden death of her father. There had been no preparation for this event, for Herr Wolff was taken ill at his club, was brought home, and died a few hours later. I do not know exactly how long the analysis lasted but I think about three years. It was followed by a period during which they did not see each other at all. Jung had already realized her amazing gift, and now he found that his feeling for Toni added to rather than diminished his affection and devotion for his wife and family. The reality of his family and home were an absolute necessity to him, especially during this time of facing the unconscious, and we must remember that his problem of how to include Toni Wolff in his life fell within the same period. He said on the subject of his family:

> It was most essential for me to have a normal life in the real world as a counterpoise to that strange inner world. My family and my profession remained the base to which I could always return, assuring me that I was an actually existing, ordinary person. The unconscious contents could have driven me out of my wits . . . [but family and profession ] were actualities which made demands on me and proved to

me again and again that I really existed, that I was not a blank page whirling about in the winds of the spirit, like Nietzsche. Nietzsche had lost the ground under his feet because he possessed nothing more than the inner world of his thoughts—which incidentally possessed him more than he it. He was uprooted and hovered above the earth, and therefore he succumbed to exaggeration and irreality. For me, such irreality was the quintessence of horror, for I aimed, after all, at *this* world and *this* life. No matter how deeply absorbed and how blown about I was, I always knew that everything I was experiencing was ultimately directed at this real life of mine. I meant to meet its obligations and fulfill its meanings. My watchword was *Hic Rhodos, hic salta!* Thus my family and my profession always remained a joyful reality, and a guarantee that I also had a normal existence.[4]

It seems hard that, just at the time he was tried to the uttermost by his "confrontation with the unconscious," Jung had also to deal with perhaps the most difficult problem a married man ever has to face: the fact that he can love his wife and another woman simultaneously. But the one problem belonged to the other and they were really two facets of the same problem. Although he had not yet recognized the archetype of the anima, this figure is the nearest to a man of all the inner figures and she is above all the bridge to, and the mediator between, the man and his unconscious. Jung also did not yet know that the anima frequently projects herself into a real woman and that this projection endows that woman with the whole numinous quality of the unconscious—yes, she even has the fascination of a goddess. We have already seen a first appearance of the anima, when Jung was still a boy, in the girl he met near Sachseln on his way back from visiting the hermitage of Niklaus von der Flüe.[c] Although that encounter was only a mild foretaste, yet it had made an indelible impression upon him. It is interesting that on that occasion there was also a connection between the wise old man, Brother Klaus, whose cell he had just visited, and the young girl whom he met immediately afterward.

Toni Wolff was perhaps—of all the "anima types" I have ever known—the most fitted to carry the projection of this figure. She was not beautiful in the strictly classical sense, but she could look far more than beautiful, more like a goddess than a mortal woman. She had an extraordinary genius for accompanying men—and some women too, in a different way—whose destiny it was to enter the unconscious. Indeed, she learned of this gift through her relation to Jung, but she afterward showed the same gift when she became an analyst; in fact, it was her most valuable quality as an analyst. Curiously enough, she did not ever enter the

[c] See above, page 60 ff.

unconscious on her own account. Many years afterward—during Jung's long illness in 1944—she asked me if I could teach her how to do active imagination, because she had never really done it at all! (I was amazed, for I knew she had helped many people with the method and as a rule it is quite impossible to do this unless one has already gone through the experience oneself.) But I soon found out that not only had she no ability to do active imagination, she had not the slightest wish (except for a dim feeling that she really *ought* to) to experience the unconscious at first hand. She had no doubt whatever of its objective existence, but no inclination to go into it herself. She could unhesitatingly accept whatever genuine experiences other people had there, and give them the firmest support by her calm attitude toward the most irrational, even incredibly strange, phenomenon. I have never seen anyone else in the least like her in this respect, but then, people with a touch of genius are usually unique.

During the time of separation, Toni fell back into her original depression, not so badly, but unmistakably. Jung still hesitated to see more of her outside analysis, however, for he knew how drawn he was to her and he was most reluctant to inflict any suffering on his wife and family. He once told Marie-Louise von Franz and me that, curiously enough, it was his family that had given him the final impetus to seek a *modus vivendi*, whatever it might cost. He knew from his practice how necessary this was, for he had already seen all too often the untold damage that fathers can do to their daughters by not living the whole of their erotic life, which is seldom completely contained in marriage, and the father's unlived life is then *unconsciously* displaced onto the daughters. He told us that this fear had kept him awake a whole night, a night during which he slowly realized that if he refused to live the outside attraction that had come to him entirely from the unconscious against his will, he would inevitably ruin his daughters' eros. That he succeeded in his endeavor is witnessed by the fact that all of his four daughters married young, which is exceedingly rare when the father is an outstanding personality.

Jung was able to succeed in his effort to build his friendship with Toni into his life primarily because of his own scrupulous fairness to all parties. Of course there were the most painful difficulties for everyone concerned, especially before a *modus vivendi* was reached. Jealousy is a human quality that is never missing in any complete human being, but, as Jung often said: "The kernel of all jealousy is lack of love." [5] What saved the situation was that there was no "lack of love" in any of the three. Jung was able to give both his wife and Toni a most satisfactory amount, and *both* women *really* loved him. Therefore, although for a long while they were at times most painfully jealous of each other, love always won out in the end and prevented any destructive action on either side. Emma Jung even said years later: "You see, he never took anything from me to give to Toni, but the more he gave her, the more he seemed able to give me." Of course, this amazing insight was not reached easily or without suffering, but that it was reached at all is the amazing thing when one thinks of the possessive attitude of most wives. Toni also overcame the besetting sin of so many single women, the desire somehow to destroy the marriage and marry the man herself. Toni told me once it had cost her more than anything in her life to learn that she must *not* give way to this almost universal feminine instinct. It was a characteristic of Toni to learn *facts* slowly—she was an intuitive type—but once she had learned them, she knew them forever and never wavered again. She also realized later that Jung's unswerving loyalty to his marriage gave her more than she could possibly have had without it.

It was of the greatest possible help to Jung to have the companionship of Toni, with her unfailing sympathy and understanding, during the greater part of his "confrontation with the unconscious." He once told me years afterward that even if—as was far from being the case—she had never done anything more for him, he could *never* forget what she did for him then. He said: "Either she did not love me and was indifferent concerning my fate, or she loved me—as she certainly did—and then it was nothing short of heroism. Such things stand forever, and I shall be grateful to her in all eternity." I think he was doubtful that he could have survived this most difficult of all journeys had he been entirely alone in it. At all events, in the comparatively few cases when a patient of his evidently had a vocation for having it out with the unconscious and he advised him to attempt the journey into it in active imagination, he always made it a condition of the venture that he have a firm relationship with someone who would understand. (This role is often but not always taken by the analyst.) It is far too dangerous without such a relationship and must never be attempted.

Jung's own account of his "confrontation with the unconscious" can be read in the chapter of that title in *Memories*, but I should like to remind the reader of a few especially important points. The reader will recall the extraordinary events that occurred in Jung's home while he was still at Basel University when the seventy-year-old walnut dining table suddenly split, with a loud report, from the rim to beyond the center, and when a fortnight later the flawless steel bread knife shattered. In 1916 (most of his work on his own unconscious was done in the year before and during World War I) some events of the same kind started taking place in his house at Küsnacht.[6] Blankets were suddenly snatched away, one of his daughters saw a white figure passing through her room and so on. The series culminated one Sunday afternoon when the whole family and the two maids heard the front-door bell ringing frantically. Jung not only heard it but saw the bell moving. But although they investigated while the bell was still ringing violently, there was no one there. No longer able to stand the impossibly thick atmosphere of the house (felt by everyone in it), Jung went to his study and allowed the unconscious to express itself through his pen. In three evenings the strange document *Septem Sermones ad Mortuos*[d] was produced. He said "As soon as I took up the pen, the whole ghostly assemblage evaporated. The room quieted and the atmosphere cleared. The haunting was over."[7]

This was, I believe, the first time he experienced the fact that such parapsychological phenomena often take place when there is something in the unconscious that is striving, as it were, to become conscious. Later, Jung often experienced such phenomena (loud reports in the furniture, for example) as a pre-stage to a creative effort (usually they occurred *before* he realized what he was going to write). This is also probably the reason why parapsychological phenomena (in the form of poltergeists) are particularly frequent in the neighborhood of adolescents who have not yet become conscious of the great change that is taking place in them. One wonders whether the particularly violent phenomena (table and knife) during his time as an undergraduate had anything to do with the fact that he was not yet conscious of his destiny as a psychiatrist and "an explorer of the human soul and its hidden depths."[e]

The fact that the whole uncanny phenomena and thick atmosphere in the house vanished the moment he took up his pen made an enormous impression on Jung. It was a great encouragement in continuing the work on the unconscious, for he saw that any neglect of this affected his whole environment adversely. It was at bottom the same incentive as that which had led him finally to face all the difficulties of his friendship with Toni Wolff: not to accept the promptings of the unconscious had a negative effect on his surroundings. Not that he ever obeyed these blindly, but he learned always to take them seriously and to come to terms with them, taking the point of view of both conscious and unconscious into account.

Many years later, but a considerable time before Jung went to India, a highly cultivated Indian told him that his own guru was Shankaracharya, the commentator on the Vedas who died centuries ago. Jung then discovered that, although most Indians have a living guru, there are always some who have a spirit for their teacher. This was one of those confirmations of his own experience during the years of his "confrontation with the unconscious" which were always so welcome to Jung: when you have experiences that most Europeans condemn right away as "mystical" or even as crazy, it is an enormous comfort to find other people who,

[d] This was printed privately and given to a few close friends. Jung consented only unwillingly to its being published as an appendix to *MDR* (pp. 378–90). It is stated there that later "he described it as a sin of his youth and regretted it." This regret, of course, refers only to having *published* it, even privately. Afterward he felt strongly that it should only have been written in the Red Book, like his other fantasies and conversations with inner figures.

[e] In the words of the inscription on the wall of the house in which Jung was born. See above, page 19, footnote a.

entirely independently, have had exactly the same experience, and in this case even to find that in cultured Indian circles it is, or was then in the early thirties, regarded as just as natural to have a spirit teacher as to be the pupil of a living guru.

This had been Jung's experience exactly. He would have been only too glad to have a living guide to the unconscious. He had clung long to the hope that Freud would be such a guide—this was perhaps the real reason he had such difficulty in sacrificing the relationship—but from the beginning Freud's "attitude toward the spirit seemed highly questionable." [8] As he slowly learned that there was nothing to be done about this one-sided attitude,[9] he was forced to turn to the unconscious itself and to find guidance in it. (Indispensable as Toni Wolff's never-failing sympathy and understanding were to him, she had, of course, neither the experience nor the knowledge to be in any way a *guide*.) He found this guidance in a figure he called Philemon, who slowly developed out of the original figure of Elijah and who taught him far more about the unconscious than any of the other figures he encountered. Philemon was, in short, a spiritual guru, exactly similar to those found in India, but at least fifteen years before Jung had any idea of the existence of the latter.

The main thing Philemon taught him, which really gave him the key to his whole psychology, was the *reality of the psyche*. He did this in a very plastic way. He told him that he (Jung) regarded his own thoughts as if he had made them himself (which is indeed the usual Western prejudice). But Philemon said that to him thoughts were much more like animals in the forest or people in a room and added: "If you should see people in a room, you would not think that you had made those people, or that you were responsible for them." [10] It was through Philemon that Jung learned the objectivity and reality of the psyche, its absolutely independent existence. We can explore it, but we can influence it only in an exceedingly limited degree, in fact often not at all. I think this is a crucial point, for it is just here that most of the misunderstandings regarding Jungian psychology arise. Investigations of the unconscious are exactly like any other science; *you can investigate only what is there*, the particular animals that appear in your forest, to borrow Philemon's illustration. But just as many people walk through forests unaware of the animals that are there (often watching them intently), so many people—even, alas, the great majority—never see or hear anything from the unconscious. It is a general human characteristic for people to assert that what they cannot sense does not exist, so they deny the objective existence of the unconscious. Then they think themselves justified in calling statements of these *facts*, which they do not see, "mystical," "esoteric," anything but the scientific statements they really are.

Another vitally important discovery Jung made at this time was the figure of the anima in men. He had long wondered what became of the female genes in a man and the masculine genes in a woman,[f] and of course he knew that the soul of man was usually regarded as feminine. But he first learned practically of the existence of this figure by a sudden interference in his work on the unconscious by a voice asserting that what he was doing was art.[11] (He painted a great deal of what he saw, as well as keeping a careful written account. He had considerable innate talent for painting, as anyone who has seen some of his paintings will agree, so a more credulous man might easily have believed this insinuation.) He knew at once beyond doubt that the voice came from a woman, and also immediately wondered if the unconscious was forming a personality in him—not his conscious ego—who wanted to express herself. Unlike the male figures he encountered, this woman seemed to have difficulty in expressing herself—beyond her repeated assertion that it was art—so Jung had to offer her the use of his own means of expression and she immediately took advantage of the offer. Jung said:

> I was greatly intrigued by the fact that a woman should interfere with me from within. My conclusion was that she must be the "soul," in the primitive sense, and I began to speculate on the reasons why the name "anima." The corresponding figure in the unconscious of woman I Later I came to see that this inner feminine figure plays a typical, or archetypal, role in the unconscious of a man, and I called her the "anima." The corresponding figure in the unconscious of woman I called the "animus." At first it was the negative aspect of the anima that most impressed me. I felt a little awed by her. It was like the feeling of an invisible presence in the room.

As a rule it is the negative aspect of the anima or animus that first makes itself felt, usually as a real opposition to what one wants in the conscious. Emma Jung once gave me an example from her own girlhood, before she knew her husband and many years before he discovered either anima or animus. (She also gave me permission to quote this example in my lectures on the animus.) When she was a girl in her teens, her family moved into a new house and for the first time she had a room of her own. She was proud of this room, furnished it with the greatest care, and was especially proud of her toilet set.[g] She was so afraid of something being broken that she allowed no maid in the room but did all the cleaning herself. Then one morning she dropped and broke the jug belonging to her cherished set. Her mother tried to console her by promising an exact replacement, but she was inconsola-

---

[f] It is a matter of common knowledge that the sex of an embryo is decided by the majority of male or female genes that enter into it, and that this is often only a majority of one.

[g] In those days there was no running water in bedrooms and there were always large porcelain jugs, basins, and so on, on the so-called washstand. In larger houses the maids put cans of hot water in the basins before meals.

ble for, as she told me, she now knew beyond all doubt that there was something *in herself* that worked *against* and not *for* her. This experience must have helped her to realize the objectivity of the unconscious many years later, for as a sensation type Emma Jung found it especially difficult to accept anything she had not experienced.

Jung who also always needed experience before he could accept anything, had this in mind when he made his much quoted remark: "I don't believe, I know." John Freeman had asked him (in the B.B.C. television interview in 1959) whether he believed in God. Jung answered with that famous remark, which aroused a veritable storm of comment at the time. But this was exactly how it was: as a child he had naturally been told what to believe; he tried very hard but, like most honest children who have been much connected with the Church, failed entirely; then he *experienced* God[h] and then of course *he knew*. So when Philemon told him of the objectivity of the unconscious—that all he had thought about it was more like seeing animals in a forest than any invention of his own—he was able to accept it at once, for it was a plastic description of exactly what he had *experienced* even before his confrontation with the unconscious.

Nothing had been more unexpected, more completely removed from being any invention of his own, than this sudden interference of the anima trying to persuade him that everything he was so carefully recording was art. It is interesting that he tells us that he recognized the voice "as the voice of a patient, a talented psychopath who had a strong transference to me. She had become a living figure within my mind."[12] As far as I know, this was the first time Jung became aware of the phenomenon of projection, and of withdrawing it. Projection is a term that—like the objectivity of the psyche—is commonly misunderstood. People are always inclined to think that we project actively, even consciously. Nothing could be farther from the truth, as the term is used in Jungian psychology. Things we do not see in ourselves *project themselves* wherever they can find a suitable hook, i.e., a certain resemblance between the person or thing into which they project themselves and the inner content that has not yet been seen. In the case we are considering, for example, Jung was still unaware of the figure of the anima within himself, so she projected herself into this woman, as it were, and used her voice. Jung was thus able to recognize that something he had so far seen in this woman really belonged to an inner figure in himself. The projected element is clear, for he said later that the patient herself, an aesthetic lady, "stubbornly maintained that the fantasies arising from my unconscious had artistic value and should be considered art."[13] If he had believed any such thing, he would have gone right off the track, as this very anima figure would later have delighted in telling him! The man who believes such insinuations of the negative aspect of the anima becomes

[h] See above, page 45 ff.

anima possessed. Just as the anima can be most positive as a function or bridge between the man and his unconscious, so she is always negative if she interferes between the man and his conscious world, and when she acts—instead of the man himself—we speak of "anima possession."

Of course the positive aspect of the anima was also largely projected into Toni Wolff during the earlier stages of the "confrontation with the unconscious." Later, when he saw the figure of the anima as an inner figure, both in her positive and negative aspects, more and more clearly, he became less dependent on the mediation of the outer woman in the unconscious and was able to face it entirely alone. But taking back projections and becoming less dependent does *not* mean becoming less related. On the contrary, real individual relationship—in its highest sense—is possible only when projections are seen as such; for, naturally, projections of bits that really belong to ourselves blind us to seeing the other persons as they really are, and dependence prevents us from granting the other persons their freedom.[14] Therefore, as Jung saw the inner anima and made the tremendous effort to come to terms with her, so he was set free more and more for real individual relationships. It also enabled him to see his women patients as they really were and is the secret of his unparalleled genius as an analyst. Seeing and coming to terms with the anima is the hardest task a man ever meets, even harder than that of a woman with her animus. Jung once explained this fact by saying that since the beginning of recorded history man has had to deal with the outer world. In the primitive camp man had to stand on the earthworks around the camp and watch the surrounding country intently for the slightest sign of the approach of an enemy. Woman, on the other hand, was protected in the camp, looking after the fire, the cooking, and the children. She could therefore afford fantasies; men could not, which makes it much more difficult for man to realize his inner figures, for there is a strong primeval instinct which forbids him to do so.

I remember once when Jung was angry with the anima-possessed behavior of one of his men assistants, I tried to ask if he was not being overly severe. He replied that was quite true, but did I admit that he (Jung) had managed to come to terms with his own anima? Of course, I admitted it wholeheartedly, for I *knew* it to be the truth. "Well," retorted Jung, "then I have a right to be angry with these young men who don't even try, or I have to say that in coming to terms with my anima I achieved something impossible and then I can be sorry for them! But I will not be so presumptuous as to think anything I have done was impossible." I have often wondered since then, when I have seen how few men succeed in this task, which is the truth. Anyway, we can see what a tremendous achievement it was when Jung faced up to this task during his "confrontation with the unconscious."

Toward the end of the war most of the work on the unconscious was done and never had to be repeated. Then another symbol came up, the most important of all. Throughout the war Jung repeatedly had periods of military service, which he performed with great enthusiasm. To him one of the drawbacks of getting old was that he was over the age for military service in World War II, although he was still quite well and active enough until his severe illness in 1944. In World War I he was often stationed on the Gotthard Pass, for which he always retained a peculiarly warm feeling. He said once that he wrote his paper *The Transcendent Function*[i] during one of these periods of military services on the Gotthard.

In 1917–18 Jung had a long period of military service in Château-d'Oex as commandant of the British internees. When prisoners of war escaped and made their way into Switzerland, as a neutral country she accepted them but was bound to intern them so that they could not make their way back to their own country and fight again. By the end of the war there were quite a large number of these escaped prisoners collected into camps of different nationalities. Jung was in charge of the British and always spoke warmly of this time, during which he was joined at Château-d'Oex by most of his family. It was during this period—after he had emerged from the dark of the unconscious—that the new vitally important symbol engrossed his attention.

I must explain to the reader who is not familiar with mandalas why they represent the crown of all symbols, so to speak. All over the world and in all ages, when people have tried to find a symbol for the totality of man, they have used either a circular or a square form as the most satisfying expression they could find for a totality that stretched far beyond their own comprehension. Such symbols have reached their highest flowering in India, where in Sanskrit they are called mandalas, a term Jung borrowed. Just as the people of early ages—the Mayan culture, for instance—used this form instinctively, without troubling about what it meant, so Jung had already often used it in his paintings, without thinking much about its possible meaning. But in Château-d'Oex he found himself moved every morning to sketch a new circular drawing in a small notebook which seemed to correspond to his "inner situation at the time."[15] At the same time he felt a great need to understand mandala drawings. If he got upset, or out of himself, the mandala drawing showed signs of disturbance; in extreme cases, the periphery even burst open and its symmetry was destroyed. He said: "Only gradually did I discover what the mandala really is: 'Formation, Transformation, Eternal Mind's eternal recreation.' "[16] And that is the Self, the wholeness of the personality, which if all goes well is harmonious, but which cannot tolerate self-deception.

[i] This paper remained unpublished for many years but he showed me the original manuscript in 1951, which already had all the essential material, since he thought it would help me in my lectures on active imagination, as indeed it did. It is now printed in *Collected Works,* Vol. 8, par. 131-193.

The archetype of the totality—which really contains all the other archetypes—was the crown and culmination of Jung's whole "confrontation with the unconscious." He said of this time between 1918 and 1920 that he

began to understand that the goal of psychic development is the Self. There is no linear evolution; there is only a circumambulation of the Self. Uniform development exists, at most, only at the beginning; later, everything points toward the center. This insight gave me stability, and gradually my inner peace returned. I knew that in finding the mandala as an expression of the Self I had attained what was for me the ultimate. Perhaps someone else knows more, but not I.[17]

Jung wrote of this whole period:

The years when I was pursuing my inner images were the most important in my life—in them everything essential was decided. It all began then; the later details are only supplements and clarifications of the material that burst forth from the unconscious, and at first swamped me. It was the *prima materia* for a lifetime's work.[18]

We see here the tremendous importance that Jung gave to his inner life during these years while he was exploring the unconscious. I often heard him say that it was incomparably the hardest task he ever undertook. If in later years he was hard pressed by anything, he might say that it reminded him of the years he was struggling with his work on the unconscious, but he would always add: "But that was worse, far worse." He also used to tell his students and patients, when their inner lives were difficult for them, that once they had really touched rock bottom they would find stability because they would know nothing could ever be worse. Usually, if they suggested that such a time had now come for them, he would say kindly but firmly: "Now I wonder what makes you think that!" Only a few know what it is to experience the depths where Jung at last touched rock bottom and eventually found the crowning symbol: "the mandala as an expression of the Self " which restores "inner peace."

Because of its vital crowning importance in Jung's life and because he gave it "precedence over anything else" during the war, I also have put his inner situation first and foremost during these years. But perhaps it is difficult for many Western readers to realize the paramount importance of Jung's inner life (also to his patients and the people around him) when the outer world was in the throes and agonies of the war. Richard Wilhelm, who became a great friend of Jung, brought back the story of an experience of his own in China that Jung used to think explained this phenomenon better to Western ears than anything else. He even advised me never to give a course of lectures without relating it.

Richard Wilhelm was in a remote Chinese village which was suffering from a most unusually prolonged drought. Everything had been done to put an end to it, and every kind of prayer and charm had been used, but all to no avail. So the elders of the village told Wilhelm that the only thing to do was to send for a rainmaker from a distance. This interested him enormously and he was careful to be present when the rainmaker arrived. He came in a covered cart, a small, wizened old man. He got out of the cart, sniffed the air in distaste, then asked for a cottage on the outskirts of the village. He made the condition that no one should disturb him and that his food should be put down outside the door. Nothing was heard of him for three days, then everyone woke up to a downpour of rain. It even snowed, which was unknown at that time of year.

Wilhelm was greatly impressed and sought out the rainmaker, who had now come out of his seclusion. Wilhelm asked him in wonder: "So you can make rain?" The old man scoffed at the very idea and said *of course* he could not. "But there was the most persistent drought until you came," Wilhelm retorted, "and then—within three days—it rains?" "Oh," replied the old man, "that was something quite different. You see, I come from a region where everything is in order, it rains when it should and is fine when that is needed, and the people also are in order and in themselves. But that was not the case with the people here, they were all out of Tao and out of themselves. I was at once infected when I arrived, so I had to be quite alone until I was once more in Tao and then naturally it rained!"[j]

This story well repays the most careful consideration, different as it is in standpoint from our modern, rational, Western notions. In the Middle Ages there were people in Europe who thought in a similar way. For example, the people in her environment were all convinced that Saint Gertrude of Magdeburg could influence the weather by her prayers. And, if we come to think of it, the first necessity of praying the right prayer is to be in oneself, in Tao as the Chinese call it. In our own rational age, however, I hardly dare even point out that Jung's own inner peace was restored at the same time as peace came in the First World War! He himself, as far as I know, never noticed this "coincidence" and I admit I have only just recently noticed it myself. But if one can think synchronistically[19] for a moment instead of causally, it becomes clear that this had to be: it was the moment in time when the archetype of peace was constellated and therefore, naturally, peace came to Jung and to the world at one and the same time. As mentioned earlier, Jung had wondered, before he resumed his work on the depths of his own psyche after war broke out, how far his own experience

---

[j] Jung told this story frequently, even at one of the very last Christmas dinners he attended at the Psychological Club.

(in his encounter with the unconscious) "coincided with that of mankind in general." He never mentioned this question again but I think perhaps we may assume—from the fact that both ordeals ended at the same time—that they probably coincided considerably.

One of the most impressive things I ever heard Jung say was much along the lines of his favorite rainmaker story. About 1954 he was asked at a discussion in the Zürich Psychological Club, whether he thought there would be an atomic war and if so what would happen. He replied: "I think it depends on how many people can stand the tension of the opposites in themselves.[k] If enough can do so, I think the situation will *just* hold, and we shall be able to creep around innumerable threats and thus avoid the worst catastrophe of all: the final clash of opposites in an atomic war. But if there are not enough and such a war should break out, I am afraid it would inevitably mean the end of our civilization as so many civilizations have ended in the past but on a smaller scale." What a meaning and dignity this suggestion of Jung's gives to every individual! He can try to face the opposites in the depths of his own psyche, and thus perhaps place a grain on the scales of fate.

Although his inner struggle took precedence over everything else in these years of the First World War, Jung in no way neglected his outer life. In fact, it was his conviction that he could not help his patients with the fantasies they were bringing him without first knowing where his own were leading which was often his strongest motive for persevering with his inner work. How could he ask them to do something he did not dare to do himself? And he realized then that all he had to help them with were "a few theoretical prejudices of dubious value." He added: "This idea—that I was committing myself to a dangerous enterprise not for myself alone, but also for the sake of my patients—helped me over several critical phases."[20]

The welfare of his pupils and patients worried Jung in another way. He felt that particularly the foreigners among them were much too isolated and had little or no opportunity to meet other people with the same interests. Though there were, of course, fewer foreigners than in peacetime, when the frontiers were open and traveling was comparatively easier, until the United States entered the war quite a few Americans risked the journey in spite of the many difficulties, and there were a few foreigners who stayed in Switzerland right through the war. But Jung's Swiss pupils and patients— although they were not uprooted like the foreigners—also felt a great need to meet people who shared their interest in psychology. Although the Swiss as a whole were probably the last nation to recognize the life-giving quality of Jungian psychology ("a prophet is not without honor save in his own

[k] The mandala is a perfect expression of opposites being held together, since two conflicting pairs of opposites are reconciled within its square or round form.

country" remains eternally true), yet there were always individuals who were more discerning, and Jung's practice increased steadily throughout the war.

As the group around him increased, it became a problem how to give it some corporate life. For the most part the individuals of the group did not even know each other. They were mainly, though not entirely, pupils and patients of Jung, but they naturally never met, except occasionally in his waiting room. Nevertheless, they were joined together in the unconscious by their common interest in psychology. Jung increasingly felt that they needed a social group as a *reality* basis for what they were learning in psychology. He did not agree with the Freudian analysts who—at least at that time—avoided all social contact with their patients outside analysis, and he began to feel the need for opportunities to get to know his patients and their reactions in a setting nearer to outer life than the consulting room and the analytical hour. He often felt that he could learn much more about certain aspects of his patients by seeing them in a group than by what they told him during their hours. To prevent misunderstanding, it must be emphasized, however, that Jung always *strongly* disapproved of *any* form of "group analysis." Analysis is essentially an individual thing and has no meaning except in the individual. The need to find some kind of social group or life for his patients was entirely in order to prevent them from getting too isolated or cut off from life. He always said later: "You cannot individuate[1] on Mt. Everest!" The people in analysis badly needed a place where they were not alone but could meet other people with the same interests, where they could exchange views and find companionship. He also arranged for lectures on psychology and kindred subjects and encouraged his pupils and patients to try out their own ability to lecture.

These were the main reasons which led Jung to found the Psychological Club in 1916. He was greatly assisted in this enterprise by Mrs. Harold McCormick, an American who was in Zürich, analyzing with Jung and studying philosophy with Emil Abegg during the whole war, in fact from 1913 to 1923. Edith McCormick, besides being the wife of a rich man (Harold McCormick was also helpful in founding the club and both he and his wife were founder members), was the daughter of John D. Rockefeller, Sr. and so was in a position to endow the club at the beginning with a considerable fortune. In fact, Toni Wolff told me it started off on too luxurious lines, rather like an American club, and thus its restaurant and rooms proved too expensive for anyone to be able to use them! But this slightly unreal start, in the most expensive site in the center of Zürich, was soon given up and a comparatively modest house was bought in the Gemeindestrasse, a much quieter but also more pleasant part of the town. The club

---

[1] Individuation is the general term that Jung gave to the process of getting to know the totality of the psyche, and to yielding the central place to the "Self" instead of usurping it with the ego.

was accommodated on the ground floor, with a large room for lectures and parties and three or four smaller rooms for the library and other social purposes, while the upper floors were let as residential apartments. This building still stands, practically unchanged, with the club still on the ground floor and the C. G. Jung Institute now on the upper.

Although Jung was necessarily the central figure and inspiration of the club, he steadily refused the role of president or to play any leading part in its management, leaving this side entirely to the other members. Both Emma Jung and Toni Wolff told me many lively stories of the early days of the club, which were anything but smooth, but full of life and conflict. As Jung had known when he founded the club, the majority of the founder members, being his pupils and patients, were used to seeing him alone, with his whole attention fixed on them, as it must be in analysis, and were anything but pleased to learn to share him with a group of other such people. It did just what he had hoped; it confronted them with reality and with unexpected sides of themselves. *Unconscious* jealousy is one of the most destructive forces that exist, whereas jealousy that is realized, known, and suffered from becomes relatively harmless. This was only one of such unrealized aspects of the various members that came to light in the early days of the club, and only the hopelessly *un*-self-critical failed to learn a great deal, especially as Jung was always ready to discuss such experiences with them in their next analytical hour. It gradually grew into a highly valuable community and for many years, in spite of the most lively conflicts, did everything Jung had hoped for when he founded it.

If Jung was the spiritual center of the Club, Toni Wolff was certainly its greatest support. As an extreme introvert, she found the club difficult at first, but as the years went on she gave more and more of her energy to it and was by far the best president the club ever had. The club also owes more to her than to anyone except Jung himself. She was devoted to it and always thought of new activities for it; in short, the Psychological Club owes its most flourishing years, and the support and companionship it gave to many lonely people, almost as much to Toni as to Jung.

During the Second World War, the sympathy of the Swiss people throughout Switzerland, with the exception of a very small fifth column, was with the Allies and strongly anti-German. But in the First World War, I am told, it was much more divided. German Switzerland was inclined to sympathize with its next-door neighbor, Germany, and French Switzerland with its own neighbor, France. I once asked Jung how he had felt in the 1914 war. He replied that his sympathies were divided—he was sorry for the Germans but he never wanted them to win. At the time he wrote a letter in which he said that he hoped the Germans would not win, because it was their soul that was precious and that should not get lost. In fact, in the First World War his sympathies were almost as neutral as is the four-hundred-year-old tradition of his country, whereas in the Second, although he and all his countrymen were wholly against Switzerland taking an active part in the war, he and they never for a moment wavered in their whole-hearted sympathy with the Allies.

He once told me of a very curious experience he had had in the middle of the First World War (it must have been about 1916). He had a whole series of dreams in which he tried to persuade the German Kaiser to make peace! But the Kaiser always refused, and at last—as Jung said—the unconscious gave up the attempt. He said the dreams felt strangely objective and he had sometimes wondered whether the unconscious had made any similar attempt with the Kaiser himself. He might, for instance, have dreamed that an unknown man was attempting to persuade him to give up his ambitious schemes and make the best peace he still could. With his patients, and other people with whom Jung could discuss dreams, he did check on such things, sometimes with interesting and unexpected results.

Jung not only faced the unconscious during the First World War, but he was also deeply preoccupied with the problem of types. In the Foreword to the first German edition of *Psychological Types* (dated spring 1920) he wrote:

> This book is the fruit of nearly twenty years' work in the domain of practical psychology. It is a gradual intellectual structure, equally compounded of numberless impressions and experiences in the practice of psychiatry and nervous maladies, and of intercourse with men of all social levels; it is a product, therefore, of my personal dealings with friend and with foe; and finally it has a further source in the criticism of my own psychological particularity.[21]

Jung here dates his first experiences which taught him that human beings are different in type from one another to the beginning of his work at Burghölzli in 1900. But the problem became acute only when he began comparing the psychologies of Freud and Adler. The final break between these two took place in 1911,[22] but it had been in preparation for some time. Freud explained every case by sexuality, whereas Adler found power to be the guiding force of everyone. Jung quickly found that some of his cases fitted into the one category, others into the other. The mistake on each side was making its principle the one and only and applying it to *every* case.

When—soon after Freud's break with Adler if not before—Jung saw that his own break with Freud was inevitable, the problem of types became still more acute; Jung was scrupulously honest in criticizing himself and he wondered whether a difference in type was not responsible for the fact that he had been unable to make his discovery of the collective unconscious palatable to Freud. (We saw that types must also have played a role in the religious discussions with his own father,[m] although at that time he had as yet no inkling of the problem of types.) But, as mentioned in the excerpt from the spring 1920 Foreword of *Psychological Types*, he regarded the book as the outcome of his own "personal dealings with friend and with foe," and the criticism of his own "psychological particularity." He always taught his pupils that their own mistakes were their chief concern. I remember him once saying to me when I was telling him about a dispute I had had with a friend: "Look here, even if it is ninety percent his fault, and ten percent your own, you will have nothing from considering the ninety percent, because you cannot do a thing about it, whereas you will be able to learn most valuable things from your own ten percent." And, as mentioned before, Jung's most convincing characteristic was never to ask anything of other people that he had not first asked of himself. I think that this was one of the main reasons for the confidence, respect, and even devotion he inspired in so many people. So we may be certain that his own shortcomings were one of, if not the main, reason for the volume on typology.

Later, after he had written *Psychological Types* and had considerably more experience of people, Jung was able to speak the "language" of every type. Just as he took a lot of trouble to learn the languages of his patients (English, French, and so on), so he learned to put things into the language of the psychological type to whom he was talking. Not that people can be classified in sharply defined types, but if someone is always concerned with what a thing means (thinking) he just does not understand if you speak in terms of values (feeling), for example. Long before, when Jung had had the discussions on religion with his father, he naturally had talked in the language of his then prevailing type (thinking), whereas the meaning of anything was taboo to his father! If Jung had then been able to speak in terms of values (feeling) he *might* have been able to convey his own conviction of the immediate experience of God to his father, as he so urgently longed to do. But it seems to me that, even if he had already had sufficient knowledge to speak Freud's "language" instead of his own, he could probably have made no headway against Freud's *idée fixe*: that *everything* must be explained by his own theory of sexuality.

Jung often said that he wrote the book in order to *understand* the dissensions in Freud's circle. By the time he had written it, the pain of the separation with Freud was already overcome and wholly accepted. I do not think he ever regretted the separation in later years. He saw it as absolutely inevitable, for, though he always acknowledged his debt to Freud, he also saw their friendship as a transition that had to be passed through and not held onto.

[m] See above, pages 54 and 55.

Although the book was published only after the war (Jung always dated his prefaces when he had finished the book, so it was completed by the spring of 1920), all the research and most of the writing was done during the war. It is interesting that his one long volume that is concerned mainly with *conscious* psychology was conceived at the time of his "confrontation with the unconscious." But, again, the one belongs to the other, for, as Jung used to emphasize later, it is impossible to face the strange world of the unconscious unless the foundations of consciousness are well and truly laid. We have already seen how important Jung's normal life was to him in these years (his family, profession, military service) and one can also understand how helpful it must have been to work on the history and consolidation of consciousness at one and the same time as he was experiencing the depths of his own psyche and the collective unconscious. In later years he always said that people should be well and truly rooted in the conscious world *before* they try to explore the unconscious, that such an anchor is indispensable, and we see how well anchored he was himself. Although in a way it was a matter of two separate fields of study, yet they had already met in the book *Psychological Types* itself, in what he said of inferior functions, for instance, and the necessary transformation of consciousness.

With the discovery of the mandala as the symbol of the Self, the totality of the psyche, Jung reached the conclusion of his "confrontation with the unconscious." This discovery, and most of the preparation of *Psychological Types*, brings us to the end of World War I. Before we proceed, we must consider the changes that had taken place in Jung himself in what was roughly the first decade of his fifty-two years in Küsnacht, for undoubtedly, of all the decades of his life, it was the most important, the time in which, to quote his own words, "everything essential was decided."

It is difficult, if not impossible, to overestimate the change that took place in Jung during this decade for, little as people realize it now, it is above all the journey into the deep unconscious that makes the difference between the mana personality (the outstanding human being) and ordinary people. Mankind has not always been so unaware of this point as modern man has unfortunately become. Even today in unspoiled primitive tribes, who continue to live as their and our own ancient forefathers did, we find that the most revered man of the tribe, more respected even than the chief, is the shaman or medicine man who has made the journey into the depths of the unconscious in some form or other. It is only through this dreaded venture that the shaman is qualified to undertake the function of spiritual guide to his tribe. The medicine man undertakes this journey, as it were, to ascertain the will and reach the guidance of his gods and in order thus to help both the individual and the tribe to greater health and prosperity. It is unfortunately also possible to undertake this journey for purely egotistical reasons, in order to gain power over other people and to exploit the tribe for purely personal gain. This latter class of "medicine man" is composed of the so-called black magicians, who are hated and feared more than anyone else in the tribe. But even so, such a man stands out from other people because he knows and has experienced far more, but he uses his knowledge destructively and for his own egotistical purposes and always in the long run comes to a bad end.

It was partly—if not mainly—for this reason that Jung used to say that a sensitive sense of morality was *essential* in anyone who wished to go through the process of individuation. He used to point out that this was the quality that far too many pupils of Lao-tzu lacked. Therefore, even before the master's death, many of his pupils deserted the essentials in his teaching and caused it to degenerate into mere magic. Unfortunately, the same fate, in a modern form, overtook too many of Jung's own patients and pupils, a fact that greatly saddened his last years. He used sometimes to say sorrowfully: "He (or she) has given up Jungian psychology and is practicing prestige psychology instead." On occasion he said it of a whole group.

Another way of describing the "confrontation with the unconscious" is to view it as an enormous gain in self-knowledge. The realization of the importance of self-knowledge did not, of course, begin with Jung. The words "know thyself" were written on the walls of the Delphic oracle temple in early days and since then have been revived from time to time by wise and farseeing men all over the world. Perhaps one of the clearest descriptions of the value of self-knowledge is to be found in the writings of Richard de St. Victor (a Scotsman), one of the most famous and learned monks of the Victorine order in the twelfth century, who, in his book *Beniamin Minor,* wrote:

> The first and fundamental task of the mind, which strives to climb the summit of knowledge, must be to know itself. It is the summit of knowledge to know that one knows oneself completely. The complete knowledge of the reasonable mind is a great and high mountain. It is higher than the peaks of all worldly knowledge, it looks down from above on all the wisdom of the world, and on all the knowledge in the world.

Richard de St. Victor continued by pointing out the weakness of philosophy in this respect and said:

> What has Aristotle found of this kind, what has Plato found, what of such things has the great multitude of the philosophers found? Verily and without doubt, if they had been able to climb this mountain of their penetrating mind, their effort would have sufficed to find themselves;

had they known themselves perfectly, they would have never inclined
to the hill of things created, they would never have lifted their head
against the creator. Here the searchers failed in the search. Here, I say
did they fail, and therefore it was impossible for them to climb the
mountain. "Man lifts himself on high in his innermost and God is
uplifted." (Ps. 63). Learn to meditate, O man, learn to meditate on
thyself, and thou wilt ascend in thine innermost. The more thou
improvest daily in self knowledge, the more thou wilt climb above
thyself. He, who reaches perfect self knowledge, has already reached
the top of the mountain.[23]

Anyone who knew Jung well will have realized that it was just this
knowing himself that made him what he was. There are no empty theories
in his psychology; everything is founded on rock-bottom experience and is
genuine through and through. It is thus—in my experience at least—the one
thing in life that never proves disappointing.

Naturally, the mountain of self-knowledge that Richard de St. Victor
praised so highly is not mere ego knowledge, not just personal psychology,
as Richard makes very clear when he quoted the Sixty-third Psalm: "Man
lifts himself on high in his innermost and God is uplifted." Richard is saying
the same thing here, in medieval Christian language, that Jung said seven
hundred years later in different words: As to this self knowledge, this real
penetrating knowledge of our own being, do not make the mistake of
thinking that it means seeing through the ego. To understand the ego is
child's play, but to see through the self is something totally different. The
real difficulty lies in recognizing the unknown. No one need remain
ignorant of the fact that he is striving for power, that he wants to become
very rich, that he would be a tyrant if he had the chance, that he is pleasure
seeking, envious of other people and so on. Everyone *can* know such
things about him- or herself, because they are mere ego knowledge. But
self knowledge is something completely different; it is learning to know of
the things that are unknown.

It was in recognizing the unknown in himself that Jung most excelled and
as a result laid the foundation for his whole psychology during the decade
we are considering. I think Richard de St. Victor would have said that he
reached the "top of the mountain" as few, if any, had done before him. Nor
would Richard have accused him of inclining "to the hill of things created"
or of lifting "his head against the creator," as he does not scruple to accuse
the philosophers of doing, even such famous men as Aristotle and Plato.
This is all the more remarkable when we remember that Jung grew up in the
last quarter of the nineteenth century when the whole spirit of the age was
turning more and more toward materialism. In spite of their great
achievements in the field of personal psychology, both Freud and Adler
succumbed to this trend and were unable to see beyond the material and

personal. So it must have been particularly difficult for Jung to swim right against the current of his time and never "incline to the hills of things created." And, as the reader knows, the spirit of the time was also dead against the value of the individual, and turned more and more to sinking the individual in the mass. Even in those countries where some rights are still left to the individual, all introspection or self-examination is dismissed as morbid, yet Jung never wavered but remained faithful all his life to "climbing the mountain of self-knowledge" and thus, as Richard said, not only saw all the wisdom and knowledge of the world spread out before him but saw far beyond to the eternal man in us or, in his own language, to the No. 2 personality, the Self.

But climbing the mountain of self-knowledge and, above all, getting a clear, objective view of the Self entails having it out with the opposites. It is easy enough to accept these intellectually and to talk of the really scalding hot pair of opposites—good and evil—as if they were dark and light, hot and cold, or any other natural pair of opposites. But Jung was a parson's son and I remind the reader of his experience when he was only eleven of God and Basel Cathedral,[n] which shows as nothing else can the agonizing problem that the opposites of good and evil represented all his life. Some seventy years later in *Memories*, in the chapter "Late Thoughts," Jung wrote on the same subject:

> Light is followed by shadow, the other side of the Creator. This development reached its peak in the twentieth century. The Christian world is now truly confronted by the principle of evil, by naked injustice, tyranny, lies, slavery, and coercion of conscience. This manifestation of naked evil has assumed apparently permanent form in the Russian nation; but its first violent eruption came in Germany. That outpouring of evil revealed to what extent Christianity has been undermined in the twentieth century. In the face of that, evil can no longer be minimized by the euphemism of the *privatio boni*. Evil has become a determinant reality. It can no longer be dismissed from the world by a circumlocution. We must learn how to handle it, since it is there to stay. How we can live with it without terrible consequences cannot for the present be conceived.[24]

When one thinks of the state of the world and of evil as a collective problem, it can still in no way be conceived how we can live with it and survive. But, as Jung emphasized again and again, it is only in the individual that any important problem can be solved and, in his own individual psychology, Jung certainly searched for, especially during his "confrontation with the unconscious," and found a way to live with the

---

[n] See above, page 45 ff.

dark side of himself and with that of the Creator. He once told me that the experience of God and Basel Cathedral had been the guiding line of his whole life. He realized then, once and for all, that God at times demands evil of us and that then we must obey whatever it costs us. To do evil—or good, either, for that matter—lightly, without making the utmost efforts to ascertain the *kairos* (the opportune and decisive moment), is indeed purely destructive; but to do evil consciously and when it is asked by the Self, as Jung thought that blasphemous thought to the end, is purely creative.

Probably enough has been said to show the reader why this first decade in his house by the lake changed Jung through and through. The work on the unconscious was completed and never had to be repeated. From then on Jung knew he had to live with the opposites and could never again indulge himself in living merely as a "good man." But, naturally, he still had to learn how to live with evil for many decades, for although we all thought at the end of the First World War that evil had reached and even perhaps passed its summit, how wrong we were and what an awakening was still in store for us.

As we saw in the chapters on Basel University and Burghölzli, Jung had fulfilled the task set him by his dream at the end of his school days.° He had faced outer life in his No. 1 personality and kept his little lamp burning. And in this chapter and the preceding one we have witnessed his turning around once more and facing his No. 2 personality. From then on he once again had to live both personalities but differently from before. As a child he had mainly done so unconsciously and, when he at times became aware of it, he experienced it as a terrible conflict. But now he was fully conscious of the problem, and after finding the mandala as the symbol of the Self, he was able to do so harmoniously and no longer felt torn in half by it. Saint Paul had obviously found something of the same phenomenon when he said: "I live; yet not I, but Christ liveth in me" (Galatians 2:20). Indeed, to oversimplify, we may say that after these years Jung still lived his No. 1 personality and accepted all the responsibilities involved, but his real life was lived, not by himself, but by his greater No. 2 personality. Or, as he once expressed it, "One could say that every evening I go to the bottom of the river where the meaningful life is lived, but in the morning I get up and put on the persona of Dr. Jung and try to live that also as fully as possible." He learned more and more, as the years went on, that this is essentially *not* two but one.

° See above, page 56.

# 8

# The Frontiers Open
# 1919–1925

It was a good thing for Jung that the frontiers of Switzerland were relatively closed during the war. He had the largest capacity for work I have ever seen in anyone, but even he could hardly have managed to cope with a large practice during the time of the "confrontation with the unconscious." The only other work he ever did that could even compare with the latter was finding his way through the unknown jungle of alchemistic texts, and at that time had to cut down his practice to two or three days a week. His other writing was all done during holidays. He always took longer holidays than most analysts and I can testify that these were an advantage to his analysands, rather than the reverse. It is good for everyone to test from time to time how far he can be independent, and long holidays prevent either analyst or analysand from going stale. But the longest holidays are too short when it comes to exploring the hitherto completely known.

Although just before the war came to an end Jung had completed the "confrontation with the unconscious," he still felt that something more was needed. He had kept a record in writing of all he had experienced and had painted a great many pictures of the contents of the unconscious which he had seen, but he still had the feeling that things recorded only on paper did not yet have a real enough form. He felt: "I had to achieve a kind of representation in stone of my innermost thoughts and of the knowledge I had acquired. Or, to put it another way, I had to make a confession of faith in stone. That was the beginning of the 'Tower,' the house which I built for myself at Bollingen."[1]

This feeling, though strong and persistent, was still rather vague when the war came to an end, and it took a few more years before he could realize it in concrete reality. Besides, the frontiers were hardly open before numbers of foreigners descended on Jung. They came from many countries, but it was at this time that the Anglo-Saxons began to predominate, as they were fated to do throughout the years between the two world wars, so that Jung gave most of his seminars in Zürich also in English. Of course, the frontiers were never again crossed with the complete freedom which had prevailed before the war. We now not only had to accustom ourselves to passports, but for some time after the frontiers reopened there were considerable formalities at all consulates, to obtain a visa for this or that country. These activities settled down remarkably quickly, however, or else people became so accustomed to them they were no longer bothered by them.

One of the first English doctors to come to Jung in Zürich was Godwin Baynes[a] (always called Peter), who soon realized the value of Jungian psychology and, in spite of a rather checkered career, devoted his whole life to it, until his death during World War II. He was a tall man, even a few inches taller than Jung, a university "rowing blue," and outstanding in sport and games. He came to Jung originally because his first marriage had run on the rocks while he was in service abroad. One of the first tasks he undertook was the translation of *Psychological Types* into English, so that it was able to appear in 1923, soon after the first German publication, in 1920. Since Peter Baynes did not, at that time, know German very well, his translation of this volume has the advantage of being the only translation of any of Jung's books into any language that Jung himself went through word for word.

Peter Baynes was an extravert and an exceedingly friendly person; he very soon made himself at home in Zürich. Emma Jung and Toni Wolff were particularly fond of him, and before long he began his first term as Jung's assistant. In many ways he was the best assistant Jung ever had, for he was singularly free of a certain jealousy and a sense of inferiority that working with an outstanding man like Jung unfortunately seems to breed in other men, even those considerably younger. Baynes was a medical doctor but free of the usual medical prejudices and limitations. He never for a moment wanted to go "beyond Jung," a phrase one hears too often nowadays, though almost always from young men who are still far from beginning to understand where Jung stood or who he was. This period as assistant was the first of several during all of which Peter Baynes was able to be of great aid to Jung in his overburdened practice.

Peter Baynes once told me that beyond doubt his true vocation was to be Jung's assistant, but his extraverted, open nature constantly involved him in other plans. As a result, he was always torn between England and

[a] He is best known as the author of *The Mythology of the Soul* and *Germany Possessed,* and also as a translator of Jung's books.

Switzerland, and even spent some time in America. His spells as Jung's assistant were therefore never of very long duration, so in the autumn of 1922, he went back to England. He had meanwhile met and fallen in love with Hilda Davidson (niece of the then Archbishop of Canterbury) and had married her some time before returning to England.

Two years earlier, in the summer of 1920, Jung had held his first seminar in England. As far as Esther Harding[b] remembered the seminar was arranged by Constance Long,[c] probably assisted by Peter Baynes. It was held at Sennen Cove in Cornwall and its subject was a book called *Peter Blobb's Dreams*, but as far as I know no written record of the seminar exists. The attendance was small, only about twelve people, which must have been extremely pleasant for Jung. He always loved small groups and much regretted the fact that his seminars inevitably increased in size as time went on. Apparently everyone stayed in one boarding house at Sennen Cove and Jung gave analytical hours as well as his seminar. Such seminars and free social contact with Jung continued, with variations, until long after the Second World War, and were almost as helpful to the development of his patients as was analysis itself.

This first seminar in Cornwall brought another doctor to Zürich who was destined to devote her life to Jungian psychology and to play a leading role in its development in the United States. Eleanor Bertine[d] was one of the first women doctors at Bellevue Hospital in New York. Later, while in general practice, she discovered Jung through his books. In 1920 she went to London to work with Constance Long, and thus came to attend the seminar at Sennen Cove. Directly afterward she went to Zürich for about a year to study with Jung and, when he was on holiday, at his suggestion, she and Peter Baynes analyzed each other's dreams. It was while she was in Zürich for the second time, in 1922, that she met the English doctor Esther Harding, and these two, together with Dr. Bertine's old friend Kristine Mann, later founded the first Jungian group in New York. This was uphill work, for publicly the Freudians were much the first in the analytic field. Eleanor Bertine told me once that she always warned all the young people who came for analysis and wanted to become professional psychologists that they must hope for no *outer* support in their careers, for she was not in a position to give it. This had an enormous advantage, for none of the early

---

[b] I owe most of my knowledge of the Anglo-Saxon side of these years, just after the First World War, to the kindness of Dr. Harding, well known as the author of *The Way of All Women, Psychic Energy, Woman's Mysteries, Journey into Self, The I and the Not-I,* and *The Parental Image.*

[c] Dr. Long translated Jung's *Collected Papers on Analytical Psychology* (London: Bailliére, Tindall and Cox, 1916).

[d] Author of *Human Relationships* (New York: Longmans, Green & Co., 1958) and *Jung's Contribution to Our Time* (New York: C. G. Jung Foundation and G. P. Putnam's Sons, 1967).

patients of these doctors stayed with them for reasons of career or ambition, and they were therefore able to found a group that relied entirely on the *inner* way and on self-knowledge.

Even today, when Jungian psychology has become so much better known and therefore, unfortunately, far more attractive to purely ambitious people, one feels the beneficial effects of this early training in New York. In the summer of 1968, the late Franz Riklin Jr., Marie-Louise von Franz, and I were invited from Zürich to give lectures at the celebrations for Esther Harding's eightieth birthday on Bailey Island in Maine. I have never taken part in a congress where the atmosphere was more relaxed and related and where there was such freedom from personal ambition and intrigues. I realized then—even more than before—how much the American group owed to the genuinely Jungian approach of Eleanor Bertine and Esther Harding. And I should like to record that shortly before his death, Jung mentioned with the greatest appreciation how well both of them had done.

Even before the first (1920) English seminar in Cornwall, Jung was able to go where he "had longed to be: in a non-European country where no European language was spoken and no Christian conceptions prevailed, where a different race lived and a different historical tradition and philosophy had set its stamp upon the face of the crowd." He continued: "I had often wished to be able for once to see the European from outside, his image reflected back at him by an altogether foreign milieu." He described this journey to North Africa in *Memories*,[2] so I will draw attention to only a few points from this unforgettable experience of which I often heard Jung speak. Actually he spoke much more often of his longer and still more interesting stay in East Africa in 1925 but, having spent six months myself in Tunisia, I was especially interested in his impressions of that country, for it had also made an unforgettable impression on me and left me with a great many unanswered questions.

The African trip was the first of the journeys Jung took for the chief purpose of gaining a *point de repère* outside his own civilization and in order to understand totally different cultures. It was the only trip on which the language barrier was almost complete. Only in the hotels and big towns could some few Arabs speak French, and Jung knew no Arabic at all. He once told me it was the only language he entirely failed to learn and he attributed this curious circumstance to the fact that his father knew the language well. At all events, it gave him a different approach from that of his later journeys on which he could talk to people and ask questions.

The Arab cafés off the beaten track are particularly fascinating in Tunisia—you seem to be literally in another world—and Jung spent many hours in such cafés, listening to conversations of which he did not understand a word, but acutely observant of gestures and the emotions they were evidently expressing. He soon learned that what Europeans regard as "Oriental calm and apathy" is really only a mask. What interested him most was the subtle change in their features when North Africans were speaking to a European, and thus he "learned to see to some extent with different eyes and to know the white man outside his own environment."

Jung went to North Africa in the spring of 1920 with Hermann Sigg, a Swiss friend, who had to go on a business trip. They landed in Algiers, then traveled by train along the coast for thirty hours to Tunis. He gave a vivid account of this journey and of his first impressions of Africa in a letter to his wife (part of which is published in Appendix III³ to *Memories*). He told her that he was still completely bewildered and that though he knew Africa was speaking to him, he had as yet no idea of what it was saying. After Tunis the two men went South to Sousse, where Jung left Sigg to transact his business while he went on alone into the desert, to Tozeur, from where he rode with his dragoman on swift mules to the oasis of Nefta.

The desert and its oases are a world apart from the African cities, but it was the people who interested Jung most. He said that he "felt cast back many centuries to an infinitely more naïve world of adolescents who were preparing, with the aid of a slender knowledge of the Koran, to emerge from their original state of twilight consciousness, in which they had existed from time immemorial, and to become aware of their own existence, in self-defence against the forces threatening them from the North."

One vast cultural difference between the Moslem and Christian world dawned on Jung only some twenty years later when he visited the Taj Mahal in India. The incredible height of the Himalayas and the Taj Mahal were two of the most vivid impressions he brought back from India. The beautiful Taj Mahal—built in A.D. 1632 by the Emperor Shah Jahan as the mausoleum of his favorite wife and in which he also was later buried—struck Jung as the most perfect temple of love ever erected. As he sat, letting it speak to him, he realized that the Moslem religion is founded on the Eros principle, that is, the feminine principle of relationship, whereas Christianity, indeed, all the other great religions, are founded on the Logos principle, that is, the masculine principle of discrimination. In his last long book, the *Mysterium Coniunctionis*, Jung presented his most pictorial description of these two principles. He wrote:

Logos and Eros are intellectually formulated intuitive equivalents of the archetypal images of Sol and Luna. In my view the two luminaries are so descriptive and so superlatively graphic in their implications that I would prefer them to the more pedestrian terms Logos and Eros, although the latter do pin down certain psychological peculiarities more aptly than the rather indefinite "Sol and Luna."[4]

Shortly before this passage, Jung had made clear that in the bright light of the sun everything can be seen and discriminated, and that the sun therefore represents a much lighter consciousness, whereas the mild light of the moon merges things together rather than separates them:

It does not show up objects in all their pitiless discreteness and separateness, like the harsh, glaring light of day, but blends in a deceptive shimmer the near and the far, magically transforming little things into big things, high into low, softening all colour into a bluish haze, and blending the nocturnal landscape into an unsuspected unity.[5]

Jung described Logos and Eros as gods in the Swanage seminar of 1925.[6] He pointed out that if we had lived in the time of Sophocles we would have realized "the great god Eros, god of relatedness" and also "Logos, the god of form." He explained that the principle of Logos does not produce logical or intellectual thinking, for Logos is an experience, a revelation. Saint Paul and the Gnostics still thought according to the laws of Logos (one thinks of the former's revelation on the way to persecute the Christians at Damascus, for example). So we may assume from Jung's experience in the Taj Mahal (as the most perfect temple of love which has ever been built) that an experience of the god Eros led to the foundation of the Moslem religion, whereas the god Logos was the determining force in the case of all the other great religions. We can even prove this in the case of the Christian religion, for the beginning of Saint John's gospel equates Christ himself with the Logos.

The foregoing provides some idea of the difference between these two principles and indicates how his realization of this difference in the Taj Mahal answered questions that had remained unanswered with Jung through all the previous years. He did indeed have a dream on the last night in Tunis which "summed up the whole experience" in Africa and which helped him to digest his overabundant impressions and ideas. He gave this dream and its interpretation in considerable detail in *Memories*,[7] but since it not only was the climax of his journey but contained almost unbelievably much of the future in which these two principles and the dark and light opposites found their place, I will remind the reader of its main line.

In his dream, Jung was in an Arab city, walled and with four gates, therefore a mandala. In the center was a citadel, a casbah, in itself typically North African, but surrounded by a moat, like a European medieval castle. The gate beyond the wooden bridge was open, and, eager to see more, Jung began to cross the bridge, but the young Arab prince to whom the citadel belonged met him halfway and tried to knock him down. They wrestled wildly, crashed into the railing, and fell together into the moat. The prince then tried to force Jung's head under the water in order to drown him, but the latter succeeded in getting the prince's head under instead, not to kill him, for he felt great admiration for him, but to save his own life and to subdue the prince. Jung evidently succeeded in this for they were then sitting together in a large octagonal room in the center of the citadel and he was forcing the unwilling prince "with paternal kindness and patience" to read a magnificent book in the "Uigurian script of West Turkestan." This nevertheless was Jung's book and had been written by him. To read this book was absolutely essential and, just as the dream ended, the prince yielded.

Royal and aristocratic figures in dreams always refer to the Self; therefore, as Jung pointed out, although on account of his dusky complexion the prince was clearly a shadow, he could be no personal shadow, but rather represented a so-far-unknown shadow of the Self. If we look back, we remember that the No. 2 personality, that representative of the Self in Jung's childhood, always turned out to be positive, and we can say the same of the "confrontation with the unconscious," where this figure appeared first as Elijah, turning later into the helpful Philemon. But as a symbol of the totality, this figure must be negative as well as positive, and now its other side appeared and even tried to extinguish life. In *Memories* Jung reminded the reader of Jacob's struggle with the angel of the Lord, Jehovah's own dark side which does not know men and so tries to kill them.

At the time, Jung realized that this dream was a result of the terrific impact of North Africa; five years later, on his next visit to Africa, he further comprehended that he had been in danger of being *submerged,* for the dream was the first hint of "going black under the skin," a danger which, as he pointed out, is too little acknowledged by Europeans in Africa. Jung also pointed out that when he went to Africa to find a psychic observation post outside Europe, he had been unconsciously motivated by a wish: "to find that part of my personality which had become invisible under the pressure of being European." Until then, since this part of him was in opposition to his conscious personality, he had tried to suppress it, but now it had burst forth to become fully visible for the first time, for these apparently "alien and wholly different Arab surroundings" had awakened an archetypal memory. This was one of the dreams which Jung at the time could content himself only with "noting the phenomenon and hoping that the future, or further investigation, will reveal the significance of this clash with the shadow of the Self."

The revelation of all that it meant was indeed far in the future, for it was only when he was studying alchemy, nearly twenty years later, that its full significance must have dawned on him. Marie-Louise von Franz drew my attention to an extraordinarily close parallel which Jung quoted much later in his paper "Arbor Philosophica," [8] from the *Arabic Book of Ostanes*.[e] In this text there is a description of the alchemistic lapis (the Self) which represents it as a tree which grows on the tops of the mountains, as a young man born in Egypt, and as a prince from Andalusia, who torments the adepts who are searching for the lapis, and even kills their leaders.[9] On the next page, Jung quoted another text which says literally: "Unless thy stone be thine enemy, thou will not attain to thy desire." [10] We see clearly from these two alchemistic parallels that had Jung not met this dark side of the Self, his "confrontation with the unconscious" would not have been adequate or complete. This dream, then, the outcome of his first visit to Africa, can be called the first epilogue to that confrontation. When I pointed out that his work on the unconscious never had to be repeated, I meant that by far the major part of his confrontation had been successfully carried through and brought to a close, but there were still constant additions to it, epilogues that really continued all his life, for no human being can ever exhaust the infinite extent of the collective unconscious.

It is interesting that although the anima appeared *first* in her negative aspect (as is usual with most figures that represent some aspect of the unconscious) until now the Self had always appeared in a beneficent form to Jung. This is a Just-So Story which cannot be explained, but it almost seems as if the unconscious itself wanted to be made conscious. Therefore, as Jung was the pioneer in this field, apparently his No. 2 personality encouraged his investigations and reserved the revelation of its dark and destructive side until Jung was fully and finally convinced of the reality and efficacy of the unconscious. He had already experienced the dark side of God in his childhood, both in his early phallus dream[f] and when he was forced to think the blasphemous thought to the end at the age of eleven,[g] so the idea was not by any means entirely new to him.

Jung ended his account of this first visit to Africa with the words:

I did not at the time have any glimmering of the nature of this archetypal experience, and knew still less about the historical parallels. Yet though I did not then grasp the full meaning of the dream, it lingered in my memory, along with the liveliest wish to go to Africa

---

[e] Ostanes is one of the most ancient alchemistic authors we know. This special text is transmitted to us by Arabic tradition and we find it in Berthelot, *La chimie au moyen âge* (Paris, 1893), but Ostanes also appears in his *Collection des anciens alchimistes Grecs* (Paris, 1887–88).

[f] See above, page 23 ff.

[g] See above, page 45.

again at the next opportunity. That wish was not to be fulfilled for another five years.

When Jung returned to Zürich in the spring of 1920, he was obliged, by all the patients and pupils who flocked to him and by the invitations for lectures and seminars abroad that poured in on him, to live a much more extraverted life than he had been used to during the war. Jung always gave himself wholeheartedly to whatever he was doing, but by temperament and nature he had a great longing for introversion. He met this need by his rather long holidays. But Jung was always ready, even during his holidays, to see anyone who was in genuine need. Later he frequently came down to Küsnacht from time to time during the holidays for at least one whole day's work.

During the years we are considering in this chapter (1919–25), it was the need for a really introverted refuge which struck Jung more and more. There was an island off Schmerikon, at the end of the upper Lake of Zürich, on which he had spent a number of camping holidays and he was much taken with the idea of buying this island and building on it a stone representation of his "innermost thoughts and knowledge." At the time, the island indeed had enormous advantages. It was a really introverted refuge where no one could get to him except by boat or by an exceptionally long swim. Yet it was only about twenty miles from Küsnacht, so that he could always be reached for real emergencies. He was disappointed when his efforts to buy this island failed. Many years afterward, he used to point to it and say that it reminded him of how fortunate it was that one so often is prevented from getting one's heart's desire. It would obviously have been impracticable for an old man, whereas his Tower at Bollingen remained his greatest pleasure to the end of his life.

It was not easy, however, to find the right site. He remained true to the upper Lake of Zürich, which even now has remained real country with few houses on its shores.[h] It proved so difficult to find the right piece of land that he even thought of buying some land above Bollingen which had a magnificent view of the lake and mountains, quite near the spot where Marie-Louise von Franz, at his advice, built her tower over thirty years later. But he never really meant to build anywhere but on the shore of the lake for, as he said in *Memories*, "It was settled from the start that I would build near the water."

[h] Most unfortunately Bollingen village has now been declared a *"Bauzone"* (building area). This will not come into force until drainage is installed—since one cannot now get a permit to build without it—but it is only, I fear, a question of time. Company's water has already been brought all over the Bollingen area. I do not mean that it is likely to become suburban, but that a great many vacation houses will probably be built there, though I hope the shores of the lake will remain exempt.

At last, in 1922, this ideal site became available. He was able to buy a large piece of land—large by Swiss standards, for there is a great scarcity of land in Switzerland—with a long frontage on the lake. It was secluded and yet accessible, for it was only just over a mile from Bollingen station, from which there were infrequent but direct trains to Küsnacht. Indeed, the railroad line which formed the boundary of Jung's property on the land side turned out to be a curious protection to his privacy. It was not near enough to the Tower to be a noisy disturbance, but it formed[i] a dangerous crossing, particularly later, in the days of the automobile. There was a primitive approach, two heavy poles forming the two gates, and it was necessarily near a bend in the line so that one was aware of the approach of a train only at the last minute. It always struck us as singularly suitable that Jung's Tower should be guarded by a dangerous approach.

Jung did not take to a car until seven years after he bought this land. One of its great advantages was that, whenever he had time, he could reach one of his houses from the other by sailboat. This was his favorite way of transportation and he always felt it to be particularly suitable, because he was thus between the water (chief symbol for the unconscious) and the air (with a view of the outer, conscious world). He still much favored a bicycle as a means of getting about, though in the early days he usually used the railroad and walked from Bollingen station. Jung was always patient with the train journey, although it was slow and dawdley in those days, since he had extraordinary powers of concentration.

Jung described the building of the Tower and the additions that were made to it in *Memories*.[11] He began the first building in 1923 and did a great deal of the actual construction of the original Tower with his own hands. One wonders how he had time, for it was a particularly busy year. Peter Baynes had gone back to England in the autumn of 1922, leaving him without a male assistant. Toni Wolff was proving herself to be an able woman assistant, but one analyst can never quite replace another, particularly since some patients need a woman analyst and others must work with a man. Moreover, Toni was not a doctor, and—as she told me—Jung at first was anything but delighted at the idea of her becoming an analyst and discouraged it for some time. By the beginning of 1929 however, when I came to Zürich, Jung had accepted her completely as an assistant, and sent a lot of people to her, though he was always careful—as indeed he was with all his assistants—to send her only those people who were suited to her. In fact, if he felt at all doubtful, he would ask them to come back and tell him if it did not go well. Within these limits, however, she did excellent work and was of great assistance to him in his overburdened practice, as well as to the analysands themselves.

---

[i] Several years after Jung's death it became possible to reach the Tower by a circuitous route with a bridge over the railroad.

I once asked him why he had at first been so much against Toni's becoming an analyst. He replied that since he believed her to have an unusual literary ability, he had been keen for her to devote herself to creative work. He was afraid if she became an analyst she would do little writing. That turned out to be the case: she did write some excellent papers and lectures but they were few.[12] I was reminded of what Jung had said when she was writing the longest of these papers for the *Festschrift* for his sixtieth birthday, on July 26, 1935. Her other papers usually started as lectures for the Psychological Club, sometimes slightly enlarged and revised later. But when she wrote her long *Festschrift* paper, for the only time in her life she drastically reduced or even cancelled her analytical hours as far as she could. On the other hand, she wrote with enthusiasm and seemed to feel great satisfaction in the work during the one or two years she devoted to it. I asked her near the end of her life whether she ever regretted not having written more. She replied she would rather have spent her lifetime helping other people than as an author; I cannot say that she altogether convinced me. It was a pity she could not combine the two forms of work. She would indeed have been most unusually qualified to write a full-length book, and I cannot help regretting that she never did.

In July, 1923, Jung again went to England to give another seminar, this time at Polzeath in Cornwall. The occasion was organized by Peter Baynes and Esther Harding, and twenty-nine people attended, including Emma Jung and Toni Wolff. Mrs. Jung told me later that, though she had enjoyed it very much, she had been puzzled then and for some years afterward by the English. They struck her as much more extraverted and scattered in their affections than the Swiss. She had yet to experience America and to learn what a really extraverted life is like. She did not visit the United States until 1936, and then she came back positively breathless.

Although the Polzeath seminar had been given nearly six years before I came to Zürich, all of Jung's pupils who had attended it were still constantly talking about it, most especially Esther Harding, on whom it had made a deep impression. Since several of the things he spoke of then, which he had noticed in the dreams of individuals, have become worldwide threats today, I often find myself thinking of what Esther Harding and others told me about that 1923 seminar.

Jung already saw then that, with the decline of the influence of the Church, man's impersonal ideas, which he later called "archetypal images," were floating in the air, so to speak, for our present *Weltanschauung*[j] is completely deficient in receptacles for it. This energy thus

---

[j] *Weltanschauung:* this descriptive German word has no adequate English equivalent. It is usually translated as "philosophy of life," but it means much more than that; it contains the whole subjective attitude to life and to the unconscious.

falls into the unconscious from whence it returns in archaic and very unacceptable forms. A good example—then ten years in the future, after the Polzeath seminar—is the way the old wanderer, Wotan, came to life in Germany when the Nazis came into power. Such archaic contents had already given Jung much trouble, for they would suddenly erupt and disturb a smooth and harmonious relationship in the so-called transference.

Although Jung agreed with Freud as to the importance of the transference, he took a very different view of its content. Freud took *all* the projections of the patient to be personal, whereas Jung thought that only the upper layer had a personal origin. Therefore he did not think that remaining bound by the transference, after all the personal projections had been worked out, was necessarily infantile, but was more usually caused by impersonal contents which no longer find their place in our religion. How this works out in practical analysis is shown most clearly in a case which Jung gave in his essay "The Relations between the Ego and the Unconscious," in which the factor that caused such a prolonged transference turned out to be the image of the patient's lost god.[13] Of course, in such cases it is fatal to break off the analysis prematurely.

Jung gave four chief causes for the repressions which had already sent the impersonal elements into the unconscious. These points made a deep impression upon me, because I had suffered from all of them in my early connection with the Church. The first of these tendencies was the way the Church increasingly excluded nature. But it must be emphasized that Jung always pointed out the difference between Christ's original teachings and what the Church has made of them. Christ himself evidently had an excellent relation to nature. I will quote only one logion as evidence of this: "Wheresoever there are (two, they are not without) God: and where there is one alone I say I am with him. *Lift up the stone and there thou shalt find me: cleave the wood and I am there."* [14]

Outer developments since 1923 reinforce Jung's conclusion. Art has almost entirely abandoned nature, in favor of all kinds of abstractions. Builders no longer seem to take any notice of the landscape in which their buildings are set. The most beautiful old medieval cities are surrounded by great boxlike apartment houses, each more hideous than the last. The waters of our rivers and lakes are increasingly polluted for the sake of great industries. The younger generation of farmers seems to have lost all feeling for nature and flocks to the cities. If we go on as we have been doing for the last fifty years, there will soon be no nature left in the overpopulated countries. On the other hand, nature is coming back into the consciousness of quite a number of people. Natural science arose in the nineteenth century, and for the first time the real miracles of nature were investigated as a science. There is also a general tendency to make expeditions into nature, to seek it again, as it were, and national trusts have arisen to protect particularly beautiful countrysides from building, and so on. But unfortunately, in spite of anti-litter campaigns, there is a growing and deplorable tendency on the part of the public to ruin such places with orange peels, empty bottles, cigarette butts and the like, for nature has been neglected too long and this neglect is too deeply written in the blood of "Christian" man.

The second point Jung made was that the Church increasingly excluded animals. But again, here it was the Church and not Christ himself, for from the apocryphal (Oxyrhynchus) sayings we learn that the disciples asked him: "Who are they that draw us to the kingdom that is in heaven? Jesus answered: The fowls of the heaven, whatsoever is under the earth, the fishes of the sea, and these are they that draw you and the kingdom is within you."[15] Appreciation of the animal kingdom could hardly go further; evidently Christ himself thought that grace could be found most directly through the birds and fishes.

This attitude of the Church has, more than anything else, alienated man from his own as well as from the larger impersonal instincts and has since produced a deplorable state of affairs all over the world. As naturalists like Gerald Durrell, Bernard Grzimek, and Konrad Lorenz always emphasize, many species of animals are in danger of being entirely exterminated. Everywhere, man is their greatest danger, killing them recklessly for his own profit and regarding them as of no account except for profit. As far as the Christian world is concerned—and it is the people brought up in Christian countries who are the worst sinners in this respect—this could never have happened had the Church not excluded nature and animals. But again there is also a countermovement, and animals are also appreciated today as never before. Laws are made for their protection, most countries have a society for the prevention of cruelty to animals, and never were more animals kept as valued pets. But this is only of recent years, and unfortunately it seems to have made little difference to the exploitation or even to the extermination of animals where "Christian" man thinks there is a profit to be made.

The third exclusion is perhaps the worst from the psychological point of view, because it has prevented man from recognizing his own shadow. It consists in the exclusion of the inferior man. The latter was condemned as sinful and had to be completely repressed. He was very largely equated with sexuality, which was permitted only for the purpose of propagation. The fact that the church bells were even rung in South America to remind man of his duty to produce more souls for the Church's flock has always remained in my mind. Jung always used to say that sexuality had two aspects: reproduction, which is carnal sexuality, but it can also be used to worship, so to speak, the god Eros, that is, relationship. It was the latter aspect that the Church condemned as sinful.

The outer results of this repression have become so obvious that it is hardly necessary to enumerate them: overpopulation—which Jung regarded as a greater danger to mankind in the long run than even the atom bomb—is an ominous threat all over the world. Youth indulges far too much (as an enantiodromia from the too little of the Church) in carnal sexuality and hardly knows any longer that real relationship between the sexes exists or that it has anything to do with sexuality. The so-called inferior, or rather—as he is now called—the underdeveloped, man is a burning problem everywhere, though perhaps principally in Africa. The black and white problem is one of the worst that the United States has had to face, and very soon England will have exactly the same problem. These phenomena would never have developed so negatively had the Church not excluded the inferior man, so that the problem of *our own shadow*, which alone would qualify us to deal with what we call the inferior or underdeveloped man outside, has never been dealt with. But again one must not forget the opposite movement; slavery was abolished only in the nineteenth century and only quite recently have we begun to study the customs of primitive man with the idea that we might learn something from them; before that ethnology was the study of a curio. Moreover, outwardly at any rate, we have begun to do something about the so-called inferior man *among* us. (Deplorably though, only the very few do anything about him *in* themselves.) We have now begun a sort of science of human weakness and have changed our attitude to it radically.

The fourth repression was of creative fantasy. If fantasy is given full freedom it will probably lead the individual to find a divine spark in himself, his own No. 2 personality, to use that much later formulation. Such individual production of symbols would have undermined the authority of the Church, which is what it wanted to avoid at all costs. But this led to our lamentable lack of an impersonal attitude and to the suppression of many creative people through the centuries.

The Church indeed has apparently little influence nowadays, yet—as suggested before—these long repressions are written, as it were, in man's blood and continue to function in quite other areas. Industry, for instance, has taken over the repression of creative fantasy, in the soul-killing repetitive work it demands from the great majority of its employees. Many of these workers have small creative forces within themselves, and while they worked independently, or in small businesses, they had ample scope to employ them while using some initiative and choice in their work. In the old building or carpentry trades, for instance, there was scope for creative fantasy, but in the modern factory there is none, only a deadly repetition of just the same work day after day. It is this monotony and mechanical treadmill that is largely to blame for the industrial troubles all over the world. Naturally, the workers *long* for more change and fantasy in their lives and hope vainly to be able to buy it with higher wages.

A few attempts have been made by certain farsighted employers to introduce more change into the work and this has met with most encouraging success. But centuries of the repression of creative fantasy by the Church are very difficult to repair. Perhaps it is in this fourth category that the most damage of all has been done.

I hope that enough of the content of this seminar has been recalled to show how early Jung became aware of these dangers that are threatening our very existence today. Shortly before his death he wrote much more about them, for he was always very mindful of what a danger man had become to himself.

We must now return to the Tower which, for Jung himself, was by far the most important acquisition of this year. The form in which he had to represent his innermost thoughts in stone was not planned ahead, but grew gradually, as he recalled in *Memories*, "following the conrete needs of the moment." It was only later, after several additions to the original 1923 Tower, stretching from 1927 to 1956, that he could see "how all the parts fitted together and that a meaningful form had resulted: a symbol of psychic wholeness."[16] But the first Tower was in its roundness already a perfect, simple mandala, which was for Jung an expression of the Self, the ultimate that he could attain.

Over the door of the original round Tower he chiseled the following words into the stone: "Sanctuary of Philemon, penitence of Faust."[7][k] Later, when, in making additions to the house, this inscription had to be walled in, he repeated it above the inner door to his "retiring room," which he built in 1934.[18]

The Tower was built primarily as a place where Jung could be "reborn in stone," and where he could be entirely himself, "a place of spiritual contemplation." There were also "concrete needs of the moment" from the very beginning. He could never forget the part that Toni Wolff had played in his "confrontation with the unconscious," when her sympathy and courage had contributed so much to the successful outcome of those difficult years, thus enabling him to make his "confession in stone" of the deepest insights which he had then gained. And the Tower also profited Toni, for she loved being there. Not that she appreciated it at first. Jung was very amusing about her initial reactions, for such a primitive way of life—doing everything for themselves, "all the simple acts that make man simple," as Jung purposely intended—was completely outside Toni

[k] "Philemon" means "the loving one." This was the name of Jung's spiritual guide to the unconscious and symbol of the Self during his "confrontation with the unconscious" (*MDR*, pp. 182 ff). "Faust's penitence" refers to the murder of Philemon and Baucis (toward the end of *Faust*, Part II) when Faust's ambition to increase his land led to the death of this innocent old pair of loving servants of the gods. All of the inscriptions at the Tower are in Latin or Greek.

Wolff's previous experience. They cut their own wood, drew their own water, at first filtering lake water, for it was only in 1931 that Jung got a water diviner and discovered his own excellent spring, which still, however, needed to be pumped by hand; and of course they did all their own cooking, cleaning, and dusting. "Toni's hair literally stood on end whenever we got a new pot," he said, and still laughed when he told me about it, around 1934. But Toni soon learned to love the simple life and to reckon the time she might be in Bollingen as by far the happiest part of the year.

I never heard Jung complain of noise, not even after a bathing beach had been opened next to his garden at Küsnacht, but one can well understand his growing need for a secluded place entirely his own. Although at times he shared it with his family or his friends (for instance, Hermann Sigg, at whose instigation he had undertaken his first journey to North Africa, often sailed up with him for a day or two at the Tower), Bollingen was primarily a place where he could be quite alone and where even his nearest and dearest could not "drop in" on him while he was working, and he loved it more than anything else from the beginning to the end. Only about two years before his death, I was sitting with him one day as he was chopping wood beside the lake. We were speaking of the Buddhist belief in reincarnation. I remarked that I hoped that, if that were how things were, this would be the last time I had to reincarnate! Jung began to agree with me warmly, as he always had before in such discussions, but he suddenly stopped and looked all around him in silence. Then he said: "No, I am wrong. If I might have Bollingen, I would be willing to come again."

Jung emphasized in *Memories* that Bollingen was primarily the home of his No. 2 personality, that timeless or eternal figure in man which yet needs the No. 1 personality to experience three-dimensional reality and the here and now in this moment of time. He said:

> At Bollingen I am in the midst of my true life, I am most deeply myself. Here I am, as it were, the "age-old son of the mother." That is how alchemy puts it, very wisely, for the "old man," the "ancient," whom I had already experienced as a child, is personality No. 2, who has always been and always will be. He exists outside time and is the son of the maternal unconscious. In my fantasies he took the form of Philemon, and he comes to life again at Bollingen.[19]

I do not know whether it has anything to do with the fact that Jung's land and much of the surrounding country is the so-called area of St. Meinrad and is old church land, but Bollingen certainly has a special quality. You feel far more in yourself there than elsewhere and after any illness it has a singularly healing quality. I first realized this fully from something Jung once said. Even before Marie-Louise von Franz bought her land there, we were a good deal at Bollingen. At first I used to stay with my old friends, Hans and Linda Fierz, and after their deaths, Linda most kindly bequeathed to M.-L. von Franz and myself a *Gastrecht*[1] in their house, which was close to Jung's. While I was staying in Bollingen, if I used the privilege sparingly and tactfully, I was allowed to look in at the Tower from time to time. But once, when I was down at Küsnacht for my whole vacation, I asked Jung if I might occasionally drop in from Küsnacht, providing I was prepared to go at once should the moment not be propitious, as was always the arrangement when I was in Bollingen. I at once met with an unqualified refusal. He explained later that when I was staying for some time in Bollingen, I did not upset him, but if I came up from Küsnacht, I would bring quite a different atmosphere and that would inevitably be a disturbance.

I had from the first visit felt a most special quality in the Tower, in its view over the lake, above all in Jung himself, but it was only when I was meditating on Jung's refusal that I got my first dim idea of what this quality was. Jung was, as it were, completely in his No. 2 personality at Bollingen, and that, or something in the place itself, stopped one worrying about the thousand and one trifles with which the No. 1 personality is always concerned. To a certain extent, I suppose, one also got into one's own No. 2 personality there and was therefore no disturbance to Jung. But this was not so when one came up from Küsnacht; one was automatically an upsetting influence then, so one just had to learn to keep away.

This, of course, does not mean that Jung never invited people from the world of No. 1 to visit him in Bollingen. He did often, but then he knew they were coming and was prepared for them. It was the unexpected "dropper in" from an alien atmosphere who had to be discouraged, or Jung found his time being wasted with having to find his way back into the world of No. 2. One also felt the presence of his No. 2 personality in Küsnacht or wherever one met Jung in the outside world. But he wore the No. 1 personality, the persona of Prof. Dr. C. G. Jung, over it. At Bollingen that was not the case, except when he was prepared to meet people from the outside world. His very clothes were those of No. 2, in the sense that they had nothing to do with the prevailing fashion but were old comfortable clothes, eminently suitable for the simple life he led at Bollingen, chopping wood, cooking, and so on.

As the No. 2 personality was so entirely constellated at Bollingen, it is natural that the most important part of his creative work was also done there. When he first got there from the outside world, he always spent some

---

[1] I know no English equivalent, but when her sons were not using the house we might have it to live in, the time to be arranged by mutual agreement.

days acclimatizing himself to the place, doing all those jobs that have to be done in the simple life there or even just staring at the lake. Then, when he was thoroughly in tune with the world of No. 2, his best ideas came to him, and he wrote as No. 2 wished, although of course No. 1 did the actual writing, translating ideas too strange into language that could be understood. He also wrote a great deal at Küsnacht, especially later, when he had more time, but the most creative part was always done at Bollingen.

From the beginning, Jung was alone a great deal at Bollingen. He wrote in *Memories* of some curious visions or psychic events that came to him in his solitude[20] and he also gave many of the reasons that made his Tower a suitable residence for No. 2. It was built—mostly at four-year intervals— from 1923 to 1956, the beginning dating from two months after his mother's death, the last part being built some months after his wife's death in 1955. Therefore, as he pointed out, the Tower was a place that "was connected with the dead."

Jung's mother died unexpectedly in January, 1923, while he was staying in the Tessin. He described in *Memories* the terrifying dream he had the night before and his surprising journey back to Zürich when two opposite emotions so strangely made place for each other. These two emotions about death are indeed an archetypal motif; I mention only the example of Saint Augustine's interpretation of Christ's death as a *hieros gamos* (sacred marriage) with the mother, therefore as a cause for mourning *and* rejoicing. He said:

> Like a bridegroom Christ went forth from his chamber, he went out with a presage of his nuptials into the field of the world. He came to the marriage-bed of the cross, and there, in mounting it, he consummated his marriage. And when he perceived the sighs of the creature, he lovingly gave himself up to the torment in place of his bride, and he joined himself to the woman (matrona) for ever.[21]

Jung had indeed had a dream where his father questioned him about marital psychology about two months before, which he thought afterward might have warned him, but at the time it never occurred to him that it could refer to his mother's death.[22]

Jung's mother had moved, with her daughter, to Küsnacht some years before, in order to be near her son and her grandchildren, whom she adored. Emma Jung once told me that the children often stopped in to see their grandmother on their way home from school, and that this had solved a problem which might otherwise have been difficult. Neither Emma Jung nor her husband attended church, yet they were quite sure that children should be brought up with a religious background. Emma Jung told me that, while the children were still very young, old Mrs. Jung was an ideal solution, for she still believed, or at any rate thought she believed, the Christian creed implicitly and was delighted to teach it to her grandchildren. Jung knew from his own childhood that his mother "was somehow rooted in invisible ground" which had to do with nature,[m] so that he was not afraid of the children being taught a too conventional, rootless religion. Altogether, from all I have heard, especially from her great-nephew,[n] Franz Riklin Jr., it must have been a great loss when she died; she was seventy-five years old.

The year 1923 was a very eventful one for Jung, crowded with impressions. As far as I know, 1924 was a comparatively quiet year, but 1925 again must have been one of the most eventful and crowded years of his life. He was in America at the beginning of the year, and in January undertook his productive journey to the Pueblo Indians with three American men.

[m] See above, page 128.
[n] Actually, Franz Riklin's mother and Jung were first cousins, but he always called them Uncle and Aunt.

# 9

# Journeys
# 1925–1926

The journey to the Pueblo Indians of New Mexico began at latest in the very first days of 1925. Fowler McCormick could not remember the exact day they gathered in Chicago, but his impression was that it was between Christmas of 1924 and New Year. At all events, two of the three Americans who made this journey with Jung met him in Chicago. The first of these was Fowler McCormick himself, the son of the Mr. and Mrs. Harold McCormick who were so active and helpful in founding the Zürich Psychological Club in 1916.[a] Fowler was a good deal in Switzerland as a boy during his mother's long stay there, although he actually went to school in America and not, like his sister, in Switzerland. He knew Jung well and, as he was growing up, also had some analytical hours with him. He was a young man in his twenties when he went with Jung to New Mexico; he thoroughly realized what an interesting chance this was and immediately accepted Jung's invitation, although it was not easy to fit in with his other engagements.

The second member of the party was George Porter who had often been to Zürich and whom Jung valued highly. When he died some years later, Jung was much distressed and said that if he had only known about George Porter's difficulties he would have gone to America at once to do all he could to help him. The third member of the party, whom they met in Santa Fe, was Xaime de Angulo, whom Jung knew much less well, if at all. It was probably Cary de Angulo, who played such a positive role in Zürich, who suggested that de Angulo accompany them, because he was especially well acquainted with the country and the Indians themselves. Cary and Xaime de Angulo were divorced by 1924, but they remained good friends. At all

[a] See above page 130 ff.

events, Fowler McCormick said that de Angulo was a pleasant fellow and an addition to the party. He was a Spanish aristocrat, but I believe he had become an American citizen by the time he married Cary.

Jung, McCormick, and Porter traveled by train from Chicago to Santa Fe and after meeting de Angulo went first to the Pueblo Indians. It was of these that Jung almost always spoke, for they seem to have made by far the strongest impression upon him. But the trip was more extended than one would gather from the "Extract of an Unpublished MS." which is all that appears in *Memories*.[1] Fowler McCormick said that they also paid a short visit to some more primitive Indians, who lived in caves and small houses in the Canyon de los Frijoles, also in New Mexico. Unfortunately I have not been able to trace any record of this part of the journey.

After this they all went to see the famous Grand Canyon and rode down into the Canyon on mules. Jung had learned to ride during military service, and though I never heard of him doing so as a recreation, he had not the slightest difficulty when his journeys required transportation on horses, mules, or camels. The scenery, both from the edge of the Canyon and inside the huge abyss, made a strong impression upon him. The party separated after the Grand Canyon, Jung going on to New Orleans with Fowler McCormick, since he also wanted some contact with American Negroes, a great number of whom were working at that time in the forests near New Orleans.

The main reason that took Jung to New Mexico was that he still felt a great need to see the white man from outside, for, as he pointed out, we always need a place to stand *outside* in order to be able to criticize ourselves at all. The journey to North Africa had not satisfied him, particularly since he had not been able to talk to the Arabs. Though he studied their reactions whenever he saw them speaking to a white man, he could not get them to tell him anything about their own impressions. He also, of course, wanted to know as much as he could about the Indians themselves, especially their religion, but this proved much more difficult than to get them to tell him their opinion of the Americans.

Jung made great friends with a chief of the Taos Pueblos and found himself able to talk to him as he had only rarely talked to a European. With Europeans, he said one is constantly running onto the sandbank of things long known but never understood, but with this Indian "the vessel floated on deep, alien seas." This chief, whose name was Ochwiay Biano, which means Mountain Lake, was highly critical of the white man. Jung was astonished to hear that the Indians believe the Americans to be mad because they think in their heads! Jung asked him where the Indians think; he replied, in their hearts.

This made a great impression on Jung; I often heard him say that we make some of our worst mistakes with other races because we assume that, like ourselves, they do their thinking in their heads. Not only do the Indians think in their hearts but many more primitive, races think still lower down, in their bellies, for instance. This really lays different races wide open to misunderstanding each other.

After many talks with Mountain Lake and humbly accepting most of his criticism of the white man, Jung realized that he would never reach the mysteries of the Pueblos' religion by direct questions. He could win Mountain Lake's confidence only slowly and by degrees. He judged his progress in this respect mainly by signs of emotion, which Mountain Lake could not avoid: his eyes filling with tears, for instance, when they were getting close to the religious mysteries, which the Indians still guard as carefully as the mysteries were guarded at Eleusis. One day, when sitting together in the sun on the roof of a pueblo, they were speaking of the Americans—a subject about which Mountain Lake had no wish to be reticent. He spoke with particular bitterness of their attitude to the Indian religion. After a long silence, he said: "The Americans want to stamp out our religion. Why can they not let us alone? What we do, we do not only for ourselves but for the Americans also. Yes, we do it for the whole world. Everyone benefits by it." ² Jung realized by his growing emotional excitement that they were approaching something of great importance concerning the Pueblo religion, probably the mysteries themselves. This would be very delicate ground, so he only asked why the whole world benefited. Mountain Lake told him then that the Pueblo Indians were a people who lived on the roof of the world, nearest therefore to God and the sky, and they were thus quite specially "the sons of Father Sun and with our religion we daily help our father to go across the sky. We do this not only for ourselves but for the whole world. If we were to cease practicing our religion, in ten years the sun would no longer rise. Then it would be night forever."

This was the most impressive moment of all Jung's time with the Indians. He wrote even then that this made him realize "on what the dignity, the tranquil composure of the individual Indian, was founded. It springs from his being a son of the sun; his life is cosmologically meaningful, for he helps the father and preserver of all life in his daily rise and descent." Jung pointed out that, though most white men would smile at this naïveté and feel enlightened and superior, this reaction really comes from a secret, unadmitted envy that the Indian still has so much more meaning in his life, and in order to avoid seeing our own poverty in this respect. Looked at rationally—thinking in the head—it seems perhaps absurd to believe that man can have any influence on the sun, yet if we remember that the sun for them is God, and that the Christian religion also "is permeated by the idea that special acts or a special kind of action can influence God—for example, through certain rites or by prayer, or by a morality pleasing to the

Divinity," we can see the matter differently. It is not primarily the idea that man can influence God (for the Indians, the sun) that is strange to us, but the idea that man can *help* God. Our prayers are all directed to asking favors of God; the Indian has far more dignity, for he *thinks with his heart* and wishes to give as well as receive. His heart tells him that not only does all life need the warmth and light of the sun, but he is also sure that the sun needs man and the Indian ceremonies to assist him in his daily journey. Essentially, it is the same idea as Jung's favorite Chinese rainmaker story, for that old Chinese was also sure that if man only had the right attitude, if he was in Tao, as the "rainmaker" would call it, could the weather be favorable to the crops and to the welfare of mankind.[b]

If we take the trouble to try to think in the heart, instead of rationalizing in our heads, we can see at once how near the truth that Indian chief was when he said that the American, who stands for the white man in general, is mad always to think in his head, to rationalize everything, and to live by the intellect and reason alone. The Indians, who think in their hearts, speak a mythological language, but how much nearer they are to the archetypal world of the unconscious, and how far more meaning and dignity they have in their lives. In the chapter "On Life After Death" in *Memories*, which he wrote more than thirty years after his visit to New Mexico, Jung said: "The decisive question for man is: 'Is he related to something infinite or not?' That is the telling question of his life."[3] The Indian certainly has this relationship and has all the dignity and repose of soul which it brings. But it is an individual question for the white man in our days, and one that too many white people never even ask themselves.

Mountain Lake's scathing criticism of the white man caused Jung to "fall into a long meditation," for not only did the Indian maintain that Americans are mad because they say they think in their heads, but he pointed out how cruel all white men look. He said: "Their lips are thin, their noses sharp, their faces furrowed and distorted by folds. Their eyes have a staring expression; they are always seeking something. What are they seeking? The whites always want something; they are always uneasy and restless. We do not know what they want. We do not understand them."[4] Jung had found what he had been searching for so long: a completely outside standpoint from which to view the white man. He considered our whole history in the light of what he had learned, for this Indian "struck our vulnerable spot, unveiled a truth to which we are blind." In his long meditation on what Mountain Lake had said, Jung involuntarily saw "the Roman legions smashing into the cities of Gaul, and the keenly incised features of Julius Caesar, Scipio Africanus and Pompey." He saw "the Roman eagle on the North Sea and on the banks of

[b] See above, page 128 ff.

the White Nile . . . and the pillaging and murdering bands of the Crusading armies . . . and the hollowness of that old romanticism about the Crusades.'' And then, of a more recent time, he saw all the harm done by our well-meaning missionaries, trying to bring Christianity (the religion of love) into ''these remote pueblos dreaming peacefully in the Sun, their Father,'' and the harm done to the peaceful peoples of the Pacific islands by the importation of ''fire water, syphilis and scarlet fever.''

Jung said this meditation was enough. He saw another face behind all our well-meaning missions and what we call ''spreading civilization.'' It was ''the face of a bird of prey seeking with cruel intentness for distant quarry—a face worthy of a race of pirates and highway men.'' He realized then that ''all the eagles and other predatory creatures that adorn our coats of arms'' are ''apt psychological representations of our true nature.''

Recent events, all over the world, have proved, even more clearly than in Jung's lifetime, how right Mountain Lake's judgment was, and nothing could be more foolish and short-sighted than for us to project it all onto the other side of the Iron Curtain. It was only Jung's painful investigation of his own shadow that made him so ready to accept the unfavorable light which Mountain Lake threw on the white man in general, for anyone who is still full of illusions about his own well-intentioned side being the only side would have rejected it all out of hand. But it made a permanent impression on Jung, and he frequently recalled it in later years, as the Second World War and subsequent history showed ever more clearly the justice of the accusations. At last Jung had found what he had wanted when he undertook his first journey to North Africa; seeing Europe from outside was then no longer the *primary* motive during the rest of the American trip or on any of his later ones.

One more experience with the Pueblo Indians must be mentioned because Fowler McCormick told me that Jung spoke of it often at the time. In fact, McCormick thought that the old man mentioned in it made a still greater impression on Jung than had Mountain Lake himself, although he saw him only once very briefly. This incident is described in detail in *Memories*.[5] Jung was by the river looking up at the mountains which rose nearly another six thousand feet above the high plateau on which he stood. Suddenly an old Indian materialized noiselessly beside him and asked him in ''a deep voice vibrant with emotion . . . 'Do you not think that all life comes from the mountain?' '' Jung heard the special emotion in the word ''mountain'' and remembered being told that the Indians celebrated their secret rites on the mountain. With that ready and deep understanding with which Jung could meet every sincere human being, he replied: ''Everyone can see that you speak the truth.'' It was one of those very short encounters when someone seemed to touch Jung's life only for a moment in order, as it were, to deliver a message.

Jung was also interested in the Indians for another reason. When he first went to the Middle West, some years before his journey to the Indians, he stood one day with an American friend, watching a stream of hundreds of workers as they poured out of a factory. He remarked to his friend that he had never imagined the percentage of Indian blood in Americans to be so high. His friend laughed and replied that he was willing to bet that there was not one drop of Indian blood in all these hundreds. This was before Jung had analyzed enough Americans to be aware of the curious "Indianizing" of the American people, which probably is the result of their having settled on soil which had been lived on before only by Indians.

Jung often warned his pupils when they began to analyze that they must be much more careful in talking to the American about his shadow than to the European. The reason for this, he said, was that the European had been settled on his own soil for many centuries, but there was a big gap for Americans because they had all comparatively recently left their roots in Europe and sailed across the Atlantic. He used to say: "The European has a door in the corner of the room of his consciousness with a reasonable flight of stairs which leads down to his shadow. He may refuse ever to open the door, but it is quite safe for him to do so. But when the American opens a similar door in his psychology, there is a dangerous open gap, dropping hundreds of feet, and in those cases where he can negotiate the drop, he will then be faced with an Indian or Negro shadow, whereas the European finds a shadow of his own race."

There is a great deal about the role played by the Indian and Negro in the psychology of the American in a lecture Jung gave in Darmstadt in 1927 (two years after this journey) called "Seele und Erde."[6,c] When he and Fowler McCormick went on to New Orleans after the Grand Canyon because Jung wanted a chance to contact the Negroes there, it was mainly in order to understand their contribution to the psychology of his American patients. His visit to the Indians had already been enlightening regarding the Indian look which the very soil seems to have imparted to the "Yankee type of emigrant." He was already convinced that the mixture of Indian blood was almost, if not quite, negligible, and he was also intensely interested in the Negro contribution to American psychology, an instance in which there was no mixture of blood at all.[d] It was not any physical resemblance in this case, but the extraordinarily strong influence which the Negro exercised upon white American behavior. In the 1927 lecture he spoke of their amazing Negroid laugh, also of the curious walk with loose limbs and swinging hips which one so often sees in Americans. Both these characteristics he found in the Negro foresters near New Orleans in their

[c] The translation of the German word *Seele* (soul or psyche) as "Mind" is an apt example of how right Mountain Lake was to say we think in our heads.

[d] The lecture in 1927 was given, of course, many decades before the recent racial problems in America.

original, pure form. Jung also pointed out that both purely American music and dancing have found their chief inspiration in the Negroes. Many of their most emotional religious revivals come straight from the same source, to say nothing of their naïveté, both in its charming and less acceptable forms. Jung also compared American newspapers to the endless chattering in the Negro village! The ever-open American door; the fact—strange to European eyes—that many American gardens, even in the most luxurious estates, are not walled in or even fenced but are wide open to the street; the lack of intimate privacy and the boundless sociability and social life were all, Jung felt at all events in 1927, reminiscent of the primitive life in open huts and the *participation mystique*, even identity, that one finds in the daily life of the Negroes. One can well understand why Jung felt that his visit to the Indians would not be complete without including one to the Negroes.

On the way back from New Mexico, Jung spoke in New York at the house of Kristine Mann, who with Eleanor Bertine and Esther Harding founded the Analytical Psychology Club of New York in 1936. Since this lecture could be given in a private house, the group must have been small, something Jung appreciated. He used to say that the larger the group the stupider it became, until, at about one hundred, it was just a large *Wasserkopf* (literally, "head filled with water")! He was always anxious for the Psychological Club, and later the C. G. Jung Institute, in Zürich to remain small. Unfortunately, both have grown enormously since his death.

When Jung returned to Küsnacht in the very early spring of 1925, he started the first long seminar to be given in Zürich in the English language. This lasted from March 23 to July 6, and since it consisted of sixteen lectures, it must have been given almost every week. Moreover, a great many people were with him for analysis. We owe a multigraphed report of this seminar to the members of the class, especially to Cary de Angulo (later Cary Baynes). By this time Cary de Angulo (who first came to Zürich in 1921) was settled in a house on the other side of the lake with her sister, Henri Zinno, and her little daughter, Ximena de Angulo. Except for short intervals, Cary and her family remained in Zürich until shortly before the Second World War. Their house was always a center for the Psychological Group, particularly for Anglo-Saxons, and their warm Southern hospitality was a godsend to many people. Both Cary and Henri were unusually intelligent women; the conversation at their house was always well worth while and taught many newcomers a great deal of Jungian psychology.

Almost immediately after the end of the English seminar in Zürich, Jung went to England to give another seminar at Swanage in Dorset. There were about one hundred people in this third seminar in England, which was far more than Jung liked in such a group. Nevertheless, he gave twelve lectures, from July 25 to August 7, on the subject "Dream Analysis." Jung liked the place itself very much, enjoying the sea, as he always did. The

seminar, although of "great historical value" to Jungian analysts, is I think
of less interest to the general public, for "Dream Analysis" was also the
subject of many later seminars. It is a subject, moreover, which is often
treated in Jung's books.[7]

While Jung was in England he made up his mind to take his journey to
tropical East Africa, and the rest of the summer and early autumn of 1925
was occupied with his preparations for that journey and arrangements to
leave his large practice for several months, a longer time than he had as yet
been away from Switzerland. Nevertheless, he found some time for
introversion and inward preparation for his journey in his beloved Tower at
Bollingen, although necessarily much less than was usual during the
summer holidays.

During the summer of 1925, when Jung was in England for the big
seminar at Swanage, he visited the Wembley Exhibition in London and was
so "much impressed by the excellent survey of the tribes under British
rule" that, as mentioned above, he "resolved to take a trip to tropical
Africa in the near future."[8]

This was a much more complicated journey, involving a great deal more
preparation, than any he had as yet undertaken. His journey to North
Africa, made at the suggestion of his friend, Hermann Sigg, largely
followed the route of the latter's already arranged business trip, with
extensions decided on the spur of the moment. The three American friends
with whom he went to the Indians in New Mexico either knew the ropes or
were easily able to get the required information. But a trip to a remote tribe
in tropical Africa, arranged with two Americans and one Englishman none
of whom were acquainted with the area, required a great deal of planning
and carefully chosen equipment. It seems quite remarkable that he was
able to carry out his plan so quickly, for there were permits to be obtained
from the British government and endless camping equipment and food to
purchase, mainly from the Army and Navy Stores in London. The
preparations did not go altogether smoothly, and Jung began to want a
direct message from the unconscious, to assure him that his plans were in
accordance with its present constellation.

He decided to consult the *I Ching*, an ancient Chinese oracle method by
which the unconscious can express itself. Jung had been interested in the
method, even before he met Richard Wilhelm. He wrote in Appendix IV of
*Memories*[9] that he had made an "all-out attack" on the book one summer,
for he was determined to know "whether the *I Ching*'s answers were
meaningful or not." He was fascinated by the "amazing coincidences" he
encountered even then and, when Wilhelm's translation appeared in 1923,
he found to his "gratification that Wilhelm took much the same view of the
meaningful connections" that he had.

Jung first met Wilhelm at Count Keyserling's, during a meeting of the

"School of Wisdom" at Darmstadt. I think this must have been in 1922, for in 1923, Wilhelm had already been invited to speak on the *I Ching* at the Psychological Club in Zürich. Jung then had the opportunity to discuss the *I Ching* with him at length, for Wilhelm knew the entire literature on the subject and was able to fill in many gaps for Jung. They became great friends; Wilhelm often came to Zürich and stayed with the Jungs.

So by 1925, on the eve of his African journey, Jung was already well acquainted with the *I Ching* and had no doubt of its meaningful answers. When he consulted it about his proposed journey, he threw hexagram No. 53 with a nine in the third place.[e] This line included the words "the man goes forth and does not return," which made him face the fact that, though the whole hexagram "development" (Gradual Progress) evidently meant that the unconscious was in favor of the expedition, it was likely that he would have to pay for the journey with his life. He said that the impression was particularly strong throughout the voyage to Mombasa. In East Africa, although it remained at the back of his mind as a possibility, it no longer occupied the foreground.

He accounted for its being so particularly strong during the voyage by the fact that several of his fellow passengers, who were going to Africa to live, died within their first months in the country. This included the young man who sat opposite him at table in the dining saloon. The *I Ching* had obliged him to face the fact that a similar fate might be lying in wait for him, but, he said, he thought it was kept in the foreground of his mind during the voyage by the presence of death in the air, and one could not tell whom it might strike. Otherwise, Jung enjoyed being on the sea. He used the voyage to teach himself the Swahili language, so that he might speak directly with the natives and he succeeded to a remarkable extent, but he said it had been more difficult to learn than any language he had previously attempted. He accounted for this by the fact that while one is young, one's mind is comparatively empty, but every year it fills up more, so that it is much more difficult for the ramifications of a new language to find space for themselves.

Peter Baynes, the English friend who accompanied Jung to Africa, had a still more difficult start to his journey. When he was packing to go, his second wife died quite suddenly under tragic circumstances. To make it at all, Peter had to go overland to Marseilles and join the Woerman liner, on which Jung and his young American friend, George Beckwith, had already embarked. His wife's death made the African journey difficult for him, although it also meant a great deal to him, especially in retrospect. Peter once told me—with the endearing self-criticism of which he was capable—that he had been a terrible wet blanket on the trip, because his anima got

---

[e] Nines and sixes unlike sevens and eights, emphasize the lines they occur in and make them the most important part of the oracle.

completely out of hand and he fell from one bad mood into another. Although his moods were sometimes annoying to Jung, the latter was nevertheless able to understand and to remain objective to the situation; the much younger George Beckwith could not tolerate them at any price however, and became more and more irritated.

George Beckwith also had a tragic destiny. Jung was fond of him and said once it was because of the high courage in the manner in which he met his fate. He was killed in an automobile accident a few years later; Jung said that his dreams had shown so clearly that he had not been given a trustworthy ship for the journey of life, and that Jung had been obliged to tell him in the course of his analysis that it was likely to sink early. George Beckwith replied that he had always suspected something of the kind, faced it completely, and lived his short life to the full. Except for his difficulty with Peter Baynes's anima he enjoyed himself enormously on the African expedition.

The fourth member of the party was to have been the American, Fowler McCormick. At the last moment, however, when his equipment was on the way to Africa, he was unavoidably prevented from going. Jung found himself in a difficult position, for George Beckwith declared that their trio was too difficult a proposition for him, and that unless a fourth member was introduced he could not go through with the program.

A letter from the governor of Uganda[10] asking the expedition to take charge of Ruth Bailey was therefore really a godsend to Jung. George Beckwith immediately declared himself completely satisfied if she should come to make their fourth. They knew her already from their stopover in Nairobi and knew that she was the sort of girl who could take difficulties in her stride. She had four brothers to whom she was devoted and with whose exploits she had always tried to keep up. Jung used to say later her brothers were a great blessing to him, for if she made any trouble at all, they would say: "Ruth, snap out of it," and unlike most women she really did "snap out of it."

Ruth Bailey found herself in a difficult position when she got to East Africa. Her youngest sister was engaged to an Englishman who had a good post in East Africa. The young pair were eager to get married as soon as possible, but he was unable to return to England to fetch his bride. Mrs. Bailey would consent to her daughter's being married in East Africa only on condition that her elder sister, Ruth, go out with her. They had come out on the same ship as Jung's party, but, as was true of almost everyone on board, they did not get to know them on the voyage. They were naturally in the bright, young, game-playing, dancing set who called Jung and his two friends "the three Obadiahs."[f] Jung for the most part read, studied Swahili, or walked silently about the deck. But in Nairobi Ruth found

[f] From a music hall song much in vogue at the time.

herself in a tense situation, for she felt *de trop* with the young couple, who were nevertheless determined to look after her and tried to keep her constantly with them.

At a dance on Armistice night (November 11) at the hotel in Nairobi things reached a climax when Ruth found that her brother-in-law intended to dance half the dances with her! She saw Dr. Jung sitting alone writing at a table. In desperation she walked up to him and asked if she might sit beside him as long as it did not disturb him, and thus free the young couple. From then on, until they left Nairobi, Ruth saw a certain amount of Jung and his friends, who all liked her and appreciated her keen sense of humor and thoroughly sporting attitude. Before leaving, Jung told her she should find a way to live *her own life* and not that of the young couple during the months she was still to be in Africa. I do not think any of the party really expected to meet Ruth again.

It would have been hardly possible to find a girl anywhere more suited to the expedition than Ruth Bailey, so the governor of Uganda's request fell on well-prepared soil. Ruth was over twenty years younger than Jung, strong and healthy, and more or less the age of and with the same tastes as George Beckwith. She herself always says that she provided the "comic relief" for the party. Nevertheless, Jung was taking no risks. They were already on Mount Elgon, right at the back of Beyond, when the governor's letter arrived. Jung wrote to Ruth saying they would take her under their protection, as requested, provided she could join them in their camp. He invited her to come to stay with them on the mountain. A native would be sent to show her the last part of the way, a climb that could be done only on foot, but he left her to find her way to the *rendezvous,* Kimilili, as best she could. One need only read Jung's account of their own journey to Mount Elgon, after the railroad came to an end, to realize how remote their camp was and the enormous difficulties it would present to a girl of her age. Ruth was not yet thirty when she undertook the journey to Mount Elgon.

This was typical of Jung. He usually made people show their mettle before he invested in them. Ruth, therefore, found herself faced with the most difficult task of her life. Her very conventional and most conscientious brother-in-law was all against the plan and put every obstacle he could in the way, and the difficulties of finding transportation to such out-of-the-way places would have daunted most girls. But since everyone recognized her at sight as a good companion, she always got people to help her, to give her lifts in her almost impossible journey. She finally arrived at Kimilili, where the boy sent by Dr. Jung was awaiting her. However, to the young Englishman who gave her her last lift, Kimilili did not recommend itself as the right place to leave an English girl. Fortunately, at that moment, she caught sight of a native who had a water carrier on his back marked "C. G. Jung," so she was able to prove to her escort that she really had been met as arranged!

The man did not speak a word of English. Carrying her things, he led the way silently along a lion path through the bush in the stifling heat for two hours. Ruth could not help wondering what would happen if they met the lion, but, intrepid girl that she was, she followed him without protest. When at last they reached the camp, she naturally felt a considerable sense of achievement and announced proudly to Jung: "I have arrived!" "So I see," he returned calmly as if she had dropped in from the neighboring house. Once she had won her spurs, however, and proved her mettle, she found herself most genuinely taken under the group's protection. She was always ready for any exploit, and did her full share of work in the camp. It cannot have been long before Jung definitely decided to take her with them on their arduous journey to Egypt. In fact, George Beckwith declared he would not go unless she made one of the party.

I have just given the outer reasons that led to this decision, but Jung himself gave the deeper reason that set this rather surprising chain of events in motion. He pointed out that owing to Fowler's being prevented from joining the party "an unconscious or fated constellation: the archetype of the triad" had been called into being, and that that archetype is always calling for a fourth to complete it, "as we see again and again in history." [11][g] Jung mentioned the episode in order "to suggest the subtle modes by which an archetype influences our actions." In terms of the diagram on page 17, this was a case of an archetypal image from below coming up and influencing outer events.

Jung gave a wonderful account of this entire African journey in *Memories*. By summarizing what I believe to be the chief gains of this journey, I hope to show what it was that the fruitful years 1919–26 added to what Jung already had achieved after his "confrontation with the unconscious." The African journey was probably also one of the happiest times in his life, particularly the stay on Mount Elgon. He said:

My companions and I had the good fortune to taste the world of Africa, with its incredible beauty and its equally incredible suffering, before the end came. Our camp life proved to be one of the loveliest interludes in my life. I enjoyed the "divine peace" of a still primeval country. Never had I seen so clearly "man and the other animals" (Herodotus). Thousands of miles lay between me and Europe, mother of all demons. The demons could not reach me here—there were no telegrams, no telephone calls, no letters, no visitors. My liberated psychic forces poured blissfully back to the primeval expanses.[12]

Before the journey started—with his *I Ching* hexagram, 53, 9 in the third place—Jung had faced the fact that his life might end on this African trip.

[g] Pythagoras, in the sixth century B.C. pointed out that four was the number of totality.

This was not an easy accomplishment at that time: Jung was only fifty—at the height of his strength—and he knew that a great many people were dependent on him. This was not in a financial sense, for if he had died his family would have suffered no material hardship, but in a spiritual sense. He was at the height of his practice and he knew well that many of his patients and pupils were not yet ready to stand alone. This deeply bothered him in making his decision to go, but he told me he felt strangely unconcerned in Africa itself. He once described the effect the heat had on him: an extraordinary detachment which nothing could touch. Lying in his deck chair one hot afternoon, he actually tried to break this detachment by thinking of all his worst European worries, such as the patients who gave him most cause for anxiety, but it all seemed remote and unimportant. When he got back to Europe it was different, but the time in Africa itself was a period of complete detachment.[h]

As far as I know, this was the first time Jung had to put into concrete reality a conviction which grew on him from the time he had passed from the first to the second half of life. He felt that in the second half of life one can live completely only if one has fully faced the fact that one is no longer going *out* into life but ultimately facing inward, with the goal of inevitable death. He often said, after he had been ill, in the last decade of his life: "I thought it was the end and I think that is why I have so unexpectedly been granted a new lease of life." Perhaps it was because he had fully faced the possibility that he might have to pay for his journey to Africa with his life that such abundant and meaningful life was granted him in Africa. At all events, from all I ever heard him say about his time in Africa—and he often spoke of it—it was indeed "one of the loveliest interludes" of his whole life and also perhaps the most productive.

Even at the risk of repeating material that is in his own account, I should like to give my own impression of the enlightenment that came to Jung in Africa, in the sequence it seems to me to have taken. Perhaps the moment when he woke up on the railroad journey from Mombasa to Nairobi and saw the "slim, brownish-black figure . . . motionless, leaning on a long spear, looking down at the train"[13] was the first enlightenment. Jung was enchanted. He knew it was something he had never seen, entirely outside his experience in this life, and yet at the same time he had the "most intense *sentiment du déjà vu*," accompanied by the feeling that he "had always known this world which was separated from me only by distance in time. It was as if I were this moment returning to the land of my youth, and as if I knew that dark-skinned man who had been waiting for me for five thousand years."

---

[h] The medieval German mystical theologian, Meister Eckhart, found detachment the "best and highest virtue."

This happened to him after he had been in Africa (at Mombasa) only two days and seems to me the exposition of his whole stay there. Both his No. 1 and No. 2 personalities were constellated and active at one and the same time. No. 1 felt the dark-skinned man as alien, for he had never in his fifty years of life seen or experienced anything like him; but the timeless No. 2 reached right down through the layers of the unconscious to the primeval ancestors and naturally felt as if he already knew the man who was separated from him only by time. Such a complete constellation of Self and ego seems to me the necessary prologue to the tremendous impression that Africa was to be to Jung. Indeed, he reported that the "feeling tone of this curious experience accompanied me throughout my whole journey through savage[i] Africa."

Both personalities were indeed absolutely necessary for his next overwhelming experience, which was no less than the discovery of our own myth. Early in his "confrontation with the unconscious," he had realized painfully that he no longer lived by the Christian myth, that it had lost its meaning for him. The longing to find his own myth began then, but it had been particularly intense since early that year (1925) when the Indian Mountain Lake, told him that the *raison d'être* of his Pueblo was to help their father the sun to cross the sky each day. Jung said: "I had envied him for the fullness of meaning in that belief and had been looking about without hope for a myth of our own.[14] Now, suddenly and completely unexpectedly, he found it, alone on the Athi Plains near Nairobi, among the gigantic herds of grazing animals, gradually moving forward like slow rivers. I often heard Jung describe this moment, and I also heard a great many people say that they are unable to follow him here. Indeed, without some experience of the Self and the ego, it is hard, if not impossible, to grasp.

Before speaking of this experience of Jung's on the Athi Plains, I would like to refer to a later passage in *Memories*, in which he mentioned that the eternal Self needs the limited ego in order *to experience itself in outer reality*. It can thus, in earthly form, "pass through the experiences of the three-dimensional world, and by greater awareness take a further step toward realization."[15] In other words, No. 2 personality needs No. 1 as much as vice versa.

Perhaps the first time Jung fully realized this truth was as he stood there, that day on the Athi Plains, out of sight and hearing of his friends, in "the stillness of the eternal beginning," of "the world as it has always been." Of course those animals have existed there on the plains for untold ages, but it suddenly dawned on Jung that this was only potential existence until someone gave them "objective existence" by creatively knowing they

---

[i] The German is *"durch das wilde Afrika."* I cannot quite agree with translating *"wilde"* as "savage" here, though as a whole the translation of *Memories* is excellent.

were there. This, he wrote, is what the alchemists meant when they said: "What nature leaves imperfect, the [alchemistic] art perfects." Thus "the cosmic meaning of consciousness became overwhelmingly clear" to him, and he knew that man could continue creation, in fact he was even "indispensable for the completion of creation." If man does not accept this task, the world is bound to go on "in the profoundest night of non-being down to its unknown end." But if people can only realize this vital myth of man, that he is "indispensable for the completion of creation," then our troubled age may yet rediscover as much, or even more, meaning in life than it has lost.

The next incident to make a deep impression on Jung was at the provisional terminus of the Uganda railroad, where the party was waiting for two automobiles, in which they were to complete the next stage of their journey, to be loaded with their equipment. Jung was sitting, smoking his pipe on a "chop box," when he was joined by an elderly Englishman who sat down beside him, also smoking a pipe. He asked if Jung had just arrived and wanted to know where he was going. Then he asked if he might give Jung a piece of advice, since he had been there forty years. "You know, Mister, this here country is not man's country, it's God's country. So if anything should happen, just sit down and don't worry." Then he got up without another word and disappeared into the horde of Africans swarming around them.

Never has a piece of advice made a stronger impression on its recipient. Jung was profoundly grateful to that unknown Englishman, and whenever things went wrong in Africa, he remembered to "sit down and not worry," always with the best results. So impressed was Jung with this advice and with how it helped him in Africa, that he passed it on to all his pupils who were fated to go through the "confrontation with the unconscious," for what applies in the jungle or bush also applies to the unconscious.

Although it may seem strange to those not familiar with Jungian psychology, it is a fact that the same conditions prevail in very primitive countries and in the collective unconscious. If we think again for a moment of the diagram on page 17, there is nothing surprising in this. Africa, when Jung was there in 1925–26, was a very primitive country, "the dark continent" as it was always called in those days; therefore you were in the lowest layers of the collective unconscious when you were in Africa, among the primeval ancestors, even the animal ancestors in general. Of course, in Africa you are in a way meeting those layers *outside,* and in the "confrontation with the unconscious" you are meeting with the *inside,* but both aspects are, as that wise old Englishman told Jung, God's country and not man's country. Or in psychological language, it is the country of Self, not of the ego. We have already seen how this works practically when the Self, or Jung's No. 2 personality, had the "most intense *sentiment du déjà vu*" when he saw the dark-skinned man leaning on his spear and looking down on the train, as if he had been waiting for him for five thousand years. The ego, the No. 1 personality, on the contrary, could register only a completely new experience, one which even seemed alien. But we can also see here just how important the ego is to the Self, for it was the former that became *conscious* of the impression, that gave it three-dimensional existence, *definite* existence, whereas five thousand years are as yesterday to the Self, whose knowledge may indeed even be absolute, without ever registering in the here and now, in this moment, and thus giving it definite or objective existence.

When Jung set forth from what was then the terminus of the Uganda railroad, he left civilization, as he had always known it, behind him, and had only the trails that stretched all over Africa before him. As he thought over the old Englishman's advice, he realized it was the quintessence of his forty years' "experience; not man but God was in command here—in other words—not will and intention, but inscrutable design." It was really much the same experience as he had had himself in his "confrontation with the unconscious": accepting the inscrutable design that reveals itself and never trying to push through his own way. In fact: "Sit down and don't worry" until the "inscrutable design" reveals itself, instead of trying to control the uncontrollable.

When at last they got to Mount Elgon, that "loveliest interlude," freed from the usual plagues of civilization, such as telegrams, telephones, letters, and visitors, which he characterized as demons bred by Europe, he was able to let his "liberated psychic forces pour blissfully back to the primeval expanses," and there was able for a time to enjoy the "world as it has always been," the "stillness of the eternal beginning." But his consciousness was always alert to learn all he could about that beginning. For that purpose, he arranged a palaver every morning with the natives, who stood around the camp all day long watching their "doings with never-fading interest." It was very difficult, however, to extract any information about their dreams or religion or what was really vital to them. Although the Elgonyi were then still unspoiled, later, gold was discovered close to their territory and then the Mau-Mau movement arose "among those innocent and friendly natives." Even then, however, at the happy moment Jung and his friends were among them, there were signs that they were losing the connection with their deep religious roots that are so essential to the well-being of a tribe. For instance, after much rather fruitless inquiry about their dreams, Jung discovered that they were no longer guided by the dreams of their medicine men, as is usually the case with unspoiled tribes and had been formerly with the Elgonyi. This was because the medicine men themselves labored under the delusion that their dreams were no longer necessary, on account of the presence of the district commissioner and the fact that the English knew everything.

In the palavers, which always took place with the sun high in the sky,

Jung was at first tremendously impressed by their optimism: animals, even the large beasts of prey such as the lion, were "good and beautiful," and diseases had no power to arouse fear for, while they could lie in the sun, they found everything good. But he soon discovered that at sunset this optimism suddenly disappeared and they became the helpless victims of fear. The god that ruled the dark was as sinister and dangerous as the god that ruled the day was good and benevolent. This fear was mainly fear of ghosts. Indeed, one day when they were passing through a wood on Mount Elgon in the middle of the day, Jung suddenly perceived that this fear of ghosts was not confined to the night, but was also connected with certain places. I once heard Jung describe this incident more or less as follows: The usually willing natives complained that they were tired and the corporal made every kind of excuse. By using the simple and effective method of walking behind them, Jung forced them into the wood. But they showed such signs of anguish that at last he said to the corporal: "You are usually so efficient, what is the matter with you?" He would not say anything, but when Jung whispered in his ear the taboo word "Ghosts?" the corporal, greatly relieved, replied: "Yes, ten thousand." Jung then saw how fear works on these people and how real it is to them. It seems to be exceedingly uncanny to walk in a bamboo forest on the trail of a rhinoceros; you are never sure you will not meet it, and you have to stoop as you walk because the rhinoceros is shorter than man. These are the only paths and they are unpleasant enough, even for a European, but the green twilight, with its impression of being under water, where all is still and damp and dead, overcomes the native completely. He is much closer to the collective unconscious than we are; we have a comparatively thick layer of consciousness on the top, which is only occasionally broken through, but the native spends nearly all his time in the unconscious.

Very soon Jung discovered what perhaps impressed him most during all of his stay on Mount Elgon. At dawn, when the sun first comes up over the horizon, the natives emerged from their huts, spat into their hands, then turned the palms upward toward the sun. They could not explain this action to Jung; it was just what they had always done. But then, as he pointed out, how many Europeans can explain the candles on the Christmas tree or why we hide colored Easter eggs? But he did find out that only at the moment of rising is the sun *mungu*, God. At the same time he discovered that the new moon, as the first delicate golden crescent, is also God. But at other times, the Elgonyi never worship either sun or moon, or regard either as God. Spittle is soul substance to the primitives, so in effect they were saying: "I offer to God my living soul," a "wordless acted-out prayer which might equally well be rendered: Lord, into thy hands I commend my spirit!"[16]

That it was just the moment of the coming of the first light which they worshipped made a tremendous impression on Jung, and all the while he was in the camp, he formed the habit of taking his camp stool out in order to watch every morning the extremely impressive spectacle of sunrise in those latitudes. Even the usually noisy baboons, who inhabited a high cliff near their camp sat almost motionless, as if they also were waiting for the sunrise. It was the archetypal image in nature, foreshadowing Jung's discovery of man's myth: it is the birth of consciousness—the light of the sun has always symbolized consciousness—that is the meaning of life, what the ego can do for the Self. In nature it is repeated endlessly, dawn after dawn and it is left to man to continue this act of creation, to capture the moment in time, to hold it and find its meaning. The fact that the Elgonyi acted out this ceremony, dedicating their souls to it every morning, as the *unconscious* acting out of the myth of man, must have made a tremendous impression on Jung. This was particularly so because he was fresh from the experience of discovering that becoming *conscious* of such things is the task of modern man and the myth that can restore the lost meaning of his life.

As they later worked their way slowly from the sources of the Nile to Egypt, Jung was increasingly struck by the enormous Hamitic contribution to the ancient and differentiated culture of Egypt. We have just seen how impressed he had been by the cloudless optimism of the Elgonyi during the day, which gave way, without inner contradiction, to terror and pessimism during the night. This shows us vividly how close the opposites are in primitive people, entirely without the wide and painful gap which civilization has opened up between them. Jung learned that the Elgonyi believe implicitly that a wholly benevolent god, whom they call *adhista* and greet as the rising sun, rules the day, yet at sunset gives way naturally to *ayik*, the principle of darkness, the breeder of fear. When Jung got to Egypt he found with surprise that these two gods flow down with the Nile and appear again as the two acolytes of Osiris: Horus, the principle of light (*adhista* renamed), and Seth, the principle of darkness (*ayik* renamed). Of all he learned while he was with the Elgonyi, this seems to have impressed him the most, and he spoke of it frequently in seminars and conversations.

As he floated down the Nile he was struck by the great role played by the sun myth in the Egyptian religion and by how purely African this myth is. He had seen its beginning when the Elgonyi spat into their hands and offered their spittle (soul substance) to the rising sun. In Egypt it could be called the central myth of the Egyptians' religion. The sun god Ra moves over the sky, with a new symbol for every hour, then sinks as a crocodile in the west and takes his sun boat through all the dangers of the underworld, to rise again as a scarab in the east the next morning. Jung often pointed out that the Christian sun (light of consciousness) motif came from Egypt, not vice versa, as is often maintained. This theme has been most interestingly worked out by Dr. Helmuth Jacobsohn in his lecture at the 1968 Eranos conference.[17]

Since it was definitely settled that Ruth Bailey should return with the three men through Egypt, she was obliged to leave Mount Elgon before they did in order to go back to her sister and brother-in-law, where she had left her luggage, to settle all her affairs. She would now have to leave the young couple at once, instead of staying for six months as had originally been planned. She found her brother-in-law as averse to her accepting the protection of the "three Obadiahs" to Egypt as he had been to her visit to the mountain. But her sister took a different view, telling her she would be a fool to miss such a chance. Ruth left them before Christmas, which she spent in Nairobi, sent her big luggage back by boat, then applied herself to the problem of getting to Jinja on Lake Victoria, the place where she was to meet the three men. As usual she landed on her feet, actually arriving at Jinja some days before Jung's party. Here she was met by a man she had known on the ship who, when he heard her plan, first hailed her as a fourth Obadiah! Then, he persuaded her to help him in the meantime to run the hotel, understaffed through illness, which she did with her usual efficiency.

In the meantime Jung's blissful stay on Mount Elgon had come to an end, as all such interludes in life too quickly do. With heavy hearts the group struck camp and trekked along the southern slope of Mount Elgon into the territory of the Bugishu, the tribe which had given its name to the whole expedition when it started from London. They stayed for some days in the resthouse of Bunambale, with its magnificent view of the broad Nile valley. Then they made their way to Jinja on Lake Victoria, where, to their great surprise, they found themselves being officially shown their rooms by Ruth Bailey. She detached herself rapidly from her duties at the hotel, and they all four then traveled by the narrow-gauge railroad to Lake Kioga. There they found a paddle-wheel steamer to take them on the next stage of their journey, which they began at the New Year, 1926.

Wherever it was possible, they traveled by any means they could get, but there was one long stretch where there was no transportation at all.[j] About the middle of their exhausting walk they had the adventure which Jung describes vividly in *Memories*.[18] I often heard Peter Baynes, Ruth Bailey, and Jung himself talk about that night of the native dance, which might have had a very different end had Jung not been able to control the wild excitement that seized the dancers. Later he heard that this tribe was

[j] Ruth Bailey wrote me the following account of this stretch: "We had intended to walk from Nimule to Rejâf, about 100 miles! But we only walked for two days (about 40 miles), in exhausting heat, and with very little water. We walked from 5:30 A.M. to 9:30 A.M. After then it was impossible and we sheltered at so-called rest stations (a roof on four uprights). We were feeling rather desperate on the third day, when we met a battered old truck which had been sent to collect a German naturalist. But C. G. commandeered the truck and we piled into it and drove to Rejâf where the truck was sent back for the German scientist! We waited at Rejâf for a week for the flat-bottomed boat which navigates through the Sud." Since the twenties, Anglo-Saxons who knew Jung well called him "C. G." I think the custom originated with Peter Baynes, but I am not sure. Later it spread to other nationalities.

reckoned a dangerous one, that they had actually speared two Europeans at a similar dance a fortnight before.

On the night, however, that Jung and his party were present, Jung as yet knew nothing of all this, but he was not exactly reassured by the sight of this tribe, which consisted of the blackest and wildest natives they had yet encountered. However, he accepted their offer of a dance gladly, hoping it would "bring their better nature to the fore." But it was formidable, to say the least, when, after dark had fallen and the tired party were "longing for sleep," they began to hear the drums. Then some "sixty men appeared, martially equipped with flashing lances, clubs, and swords." All the women and children of the tribe followed them and settled around a huge fire, kindled in spite of the heat, which was well up in the nineties. Then the dancing and singing began, the natives forming a protective ring around the women and children, then advancing toward the four Europeans, dancing more and more wildly around them and toward the four whites seated at a short distance in deck chairs. Jung said:

> It was a wild and stirring scene, bathed in the glow of the fire and magical moonlight. My English friend [Peter Baynes] and I sprang to our feet and mingled with the dancers. I swung my rhinoceros whip, the only weapon I had, and danced with them. By their beaming faces I could see they approved of our taking part. Their zeal redoubled; the whole company stamped, sang, shouted, sweating profusely. Gradually the rhythm of the dance and the drumming accelerated.
>
> In dances such as these, accompanied by such music, the natives easily fall into a virtual state of possession. That was the case now. As eleven o'clock approached, their excitement began to get out of bounds, and suddenly the whole affair took on a highly curious aspect. The dancers were being transformed into a wild horde, and I became worried about how it would end. I signed to the chief that it was time to stop, and that he and his people ought to go to sleep. But he kept wanting "just another one."[19]

I have more than once seen Jung in somewhat similar though much milder situations in Europe, when the excitement at masked carnival balls, for example, threatened to get out of bounds. I always had the impression on such occasions that the Self—Jung's No. 2 personality—took over and restored order calmly and entirely without effort,[k] so I was very interested when Ruth Bailey told us one evening that on that occasion in Africa Jung

[k] One sees something similar in the large group sculpture in the Museum at Olympia (Greece), where the sculptor has succeeded most admirably in depicting Apollo stopping the rape of women by the drunken Lapiths, as if saying: "Now it is enough."

seemed to grow in stature before their eyes until he apparently towered over the natives. Evidently a deep level of the unconscious had been reached, a level common to European and African, for although Jung knew no word of this tribe's language, the people seem to have understood him at once, as he cracked his whip and swore at them genially in Swiss German! They capered off, scattering into the night, leaving Jung and his friends to sink exhausted into bed. They could still hear "jovial howls and drumming in the distance," but the tension was dissolved, the danger banished.

This was really a moment—similar to the moment when Jung saw the native who seemed to have "been waiting for me for five thousand years"—when we can easily see how both Jung's personalities were constellated at one and the same time. The No. 1 personality had never experienced such a scene and was even rather frightened, but No. 2 was completely at home and could deal with the situation with effortless ease.

Very soon after this memorable evening, the group's trek came to an end at Rejâf in the Sudan. From then on they could follow the Nile, under more or less civilized conditions. All the time Jung had been in Africa, his dreams, disappointingly enough, had been of home and personal problems; now, as the really strenuous part of the journey came to an end and they were safely on the Nile, he had his first dream of a dark-skinned man. This man was not, however, anyone he had seen in Africa, but dated from a stay in America twelve years before. He was a Negro barber who, ominously enough, was preparing in the dream to crimp Jung's hair—in other words, to give him Negro hair! He realized immediately that he had been long enough in the blissful peace of the beginning and that he was in danger of "going black," a danger that threatens Europeans who settle in Africa. It was clearly time to draw some conclusions from the numerous notes he had taken of all that happened while he had been in Africa.

After long consideration, he came to the painful conclusion that his real motive in undertaking the journey was not primarily a scientific investigation into primitive psychology but rather to seek an answer to the embarrassing question: "What is going to happen to Jung the psychologist in the wilds of Africa?"[20] He even had to own—very painfully—that he was largely impelled to his venture by the atmosphere in Europe, which was becoming too highly charged for him.

It may be difficult for younger readers to realize how highly charged and uncertain the years between the two world wars were. On Armistice Day, 1918, for instance, when we all felt we should be rejoicing that at last the 1914 war was over, I for one was happy about it only on the surface; below I had an even more ominous premonition of disaster than at any time during the war. That this was not a purely personal feeling was soon borne in on me by the fact that many other people had shared my apprehension. The Spanish flu, which actually killed more people than the war itself, may have accounted for some of it, as it broke out all over the world just as the first war ended. Even when that epidemic was over, however, the tension remained. Of course we all tried to get back to a normal life, but the feeling of uncertainty and doom—mainly a terrific tension—continued just under the surface. One could, of course, say with complete truth that things are even more ominous now, but now the dangers are more visible and, though probably even worse, they are at least not hidden from any thoughtful person, as they largely were between the two wars, particularly in the twenties. As we can see, Jung had to go to East Africa to see Europe from an entirely different world, to realize that the atmosphere in Europe had become "too highly charged" for him.[21]

In his journeys to North Africa and to the Indians in New Mexico, Jung's avowed purpose was to see how the white race looked from a totally different standpoint, but his conscious purpose in undertaking his journey to tropical Africa had been more as a scientific investigation of primitive peoples. Then when he came to draw conclusions from his notes of the trip, as they floated down the Nile toward Egypt, after the dream that showed the danger of "going black," he found to his astonishment that his unconscious took no interest whatever in this project. It was, however, vitally interested in what the journey was doing to Jung's own psychology and had encouraged it because it forced Jung to go deeper than ever before, "until it touched every sore spot in his own psychology."

Jung took two months going through the Sudan and Egypt, feeling that he understood its marvelous old culture far better for having entered it from Africa instead of by the usual route from Europe. After all, *Egypt is Africa,* and it has really been influenced almost entirely by what has flowed into it down the Nile, and comparatively not at all by anything it may have gained from early contact with Greece and the rest of Europe. The Nile is the life stream of Egypt; all its cultivation depends on the waters of this river and this has been so since its earliest beginnings.

Only at Khartoum, as far as I know, was Jung obliged to function as the famous psychologist. Gordon College there managed to get him to give some lectures. But this had its advantages for at least one of his party, for Ruth Bailey had her only attack of malaria and was thankful to have it when they were staying at a hotel for a week, where she need be no impediment to the expedition. It was naturally important to her to "carry her weight" on the trip, and in this aim she succeeded admirably.

They proceeded slowly down the Nile to Cairo, with long stays at Aswân and Luxor. Jung was not only deeply impressed by the monuments of the ancient culture of Egypt, but was also greatly struck, as he had been in North Africa, by the Islamic religion. Eight years later I heard him describe the vivid impression that one mosque in Old Cairo made on him. Seven years before he was in Cairo, at the end of the "confrontation with the unconscious,'' Jung had discovered the mandala, which was for him the ultimate culmination of all he had discovered.[1] But during all those years he had neither written nor spoken publicly of the mandala, for he was not yet sure if it was a subjective discovery or whether it was an objective symbol belonging to all mankind. It was still three years before he would break his silence. In the meantime, one can imagine how he welcomed this experience in Cairo. By 1933, when he publicly spoke of it, he was already speaking and writing freely on mandalas.

He described this mosque in considerable detail, saying it was a perfect square with very beautiful broad pillared corridors on each side. The House of Ablution, where the ritual washings take place, was in the center. A spring of water welled forth there and formed the bath of rejuvenation, of spiritual rebirth. Jung described the dusty, crowded streets outside, and said that this vast hall seemed like entering the Court of Heaven, as if it were heaven itself. He had the impression of perfected concentration and of being accepted in the immense void of heaven, and this religion, where God is really a call, at last became comprehensible to him. (We must remember that it was six years since he had first come in contact with it in Tunisia.) He spoke of hearing the call—"Allah"—echoing through this vast hall, and of feeling that the call itself penetrated to heaven.

Such impressions and those of the far more ancient culture were so enthralling to Jung that he was utterly astonished when the two young members of the party, Beckwith and Ruth Bailey, thought perhaps they had had enough of pyramids in Gaza and suggested that they might bathe that afternoon in the Mena House Hotel swimming pool, instead of going to see the pyramids of Seqquara. Such a choice was really incomprehensible to Jung, so profoundly was he enjoying everything he saw in Egypt. Seeing how shocked he was, the young people decided after all for the farther pyramids.

It was also in Cairo that the only serious case of illness they had on the whole trip overtook them. George Beckwith came down with a very serious attack of tropical malaria, which may even have been blackwater fever. Jung spoke in *Memories* of how thankful they were during this illness to have the nursing experience of Ruth, who had been a V.A.D. in France for most of the First World War. They were very much afraid that it would be impossible for Beckwith to catch their ship at Port Said, but he just made it. He showed his usual courage, during the time that it seemed doubtful he would recover, and murmured, with what they were afraid might be his dying breath: "It was a good trip!" Actually the sea air seemed to aid his return to good health.

The realizations which Jung made in Africa still took him some years to

---

[1] See above, page 126 ff.

digest and work out. As we have seen, there were epilogues to the "confrontation with the unconscious" when more illumination as to what he had faced then became more evident to Jung, but they no longer formed clearly marked changes or advances in his attitude and personality.

# 10

# Back to Europe
# 1926 –1933

When Jung returned to Küsnacht in the early spring of 1926, he felt challenged to find a new attitude to Europe. This must be seen against his painful realization in Africa that his decision to travel had been largely motivated by the fact that "the atmosphere had become too highly charged" for him in Europe. Although many people had realized at the time of the armistice—and during the conference of Versailles—that nothing had really been settled by the war, yet by the twenties a reaction had set in, and most people were blithely trying to reestablish the peaceful and comparatively carefree life they had led before the war. This was a vain endeavor, for a great deal more was forever gone than most of us were then willing to admit.

The unconscious is never fooled by such endeavors, and something in us—perhaps it was our No. 2 personalities—led us to an ominous feeling that disaster was lying in wait for us in the not too distant future. A terrible tension always builds up when there is too much contrast between our conscious outer lives and the real state of the world, which is always known as it really is in the unconscious. From the pain of his realization in Africa, it is clear that even the psychologist Jung had not up until then been quite free from the general reaction of the twenties. He was probably temporarily a bit blinded by the lure of open frontiers, by the realization of his wish to travel—leading to two extended journeys in one year—and by the extraordinary peace of his glimpse into "the stillness of the eternal beginning" that Africa had given him. But the most perfect interludes end all too soon. While his party was making its way down the Nile into Egypt, Jung had begun to look at his trip more objectively and to come to the painful conclusion that, since he had not sufficiently recognized the tension in Europe, there was in his travels something of a flight from it, concealed behind his genuine wish to study the primitive peoples of tropical Africa.

Jung had already learned that collective tension, if not realized, can have disastrous effects. In the world as it was before 1914, Western man had also repressed an intolerable tension by his conscious conviction that war was impossible in our civilized and enlightened days. Jung's visions of Europe bathed in blood were an attempt on the part of the unconscious to open his eyes to the collective tension and to show him the catastrophe lying in wait for the world. As we saw, he did not understand then the clear language the unconscious was speaking—as we can see easily enough *after* the event—but took the visions as referring to the subjective state of his own individual unconscious. He would never make the *same* mistake again, but this time, as far as I know, the unconscious sent him no revealing dreams or visions, and he had to learn again the hard way: through his extraordinary gift for self-criticism.

It was not pleasant to realize that the Wembley Exhibition had had much less to do with his decision to go to Africa than an *unconscious* wish to escape from the atmosphere in Europe. But Jung had also learned modern man's living myth in Africa, and now he knew beyond doubt that our consciousness, even of the most painful truths, is "indispensable for the completion of creation." He thus realized more than ever before the vital importance of *becoming conscious*. He knew that when he returned to Europe he must face this tension which he had been unconsciously trying to ignore, and that the would-be carefree optimism of the twenties must be sacrificed completely as groundless illusion. From then on Jung allowed himself no illusions about the state of Europe and the probable further disasters which would most likely overtake his generation before its life-span was over.

This was a difficult way to follow in the twenties. Once again Jung found himself forced to swim against the tide of his time, as he had done as a student when he refused the materialistic standpoint that was sweeping the "educated" world. The strong current of public opinion in the twenties felt that there had been suffering enough in World War I and "peace in our time" was believed to have been *earned* and to be a just reward for "the war to end war" that had cost so much. But Jung was quite aware of the tension that was piling up, and he frequently warned his pupils to avoid any illusions. It was still another seven or eight years before he knew where the danger was likely to break, but in 1926 he already knew the full futility of hoping that World War I had done anything toward "ending war."

When he got back to Switzerland he was confronted as usual by a tremendous demand on his time and energy: patients and pupils who had been waiting impatiently during his absence and the usual demand for lectures and seminars abroad. But although he met these outer demands unstintingly, he realized more and more that it is the inner life that counts, and that his efficiency in outer tasks depended entirely on how unflinchingly he faced the demands that the unconscious made to become conscious. So the following year, 1927, he made Bollingen still more habitable and undertook his first addition to his "confession in stone," an annex to the original round Tower that he had built in 1923.

Before he could do this, however, he had to suffer a great loss when his friend Hermann Sigg died suddenly on January 9, 1927. As noted earlier Sigg often sailed up to the Tower from Küsnacht with Jung. Because he was connected so closely with the first years at the Tower, Jung undertook his first long Latin inscription on the stone wall of the kitchen as a memorial to him. The 1927 annex had a great practical advantage for it contained a study where Jung could work undisturbed indoors. This was not yet the "retiring room" of which he spoke in *Memories*; that was not built until four years later, in 1931. But at all events, during the day this study was entirely his own, although it was as yet by no means ideal, for the bedroom that was always used as a spare room opened out of it. Moreover, there were two entrances in those days, one to the original Tower and one to the new annex, so that in bad weather one had to go out in the rain to get from one to the other. (The building was at this stage when I first stayed at the Tower in December, 1929.) The annex was a most useful addition, for there was also an excellent and very cool storeroom below the study which was used as a larder as well, thus relieving the original round kitchen of a great deal for which it must have been difficult to find a place.

Jung always thoroughly enjoyed building onto his Tower and was never disturbed by the noise. He was there as much as possible himself at such times to prevent the builders from making mistakes. From the beginning, being at Bollingen was not only his greatest pleasure, the place where he was most within himself, but it was also there that he could best face such things as the tension in Europe. Nevertheless, he very soon found that he could enjoy it only at the right times and that he must never go there when his work needed his presence in Küsnacht. He ordinarily went during his holidays and for an occasional weekend—usually by himself—in the term.

The years after his experience in tropical Africa were busy ones. In 1926 and 1927 he went to America for lectures and seminars, and although he did not give any more English seminars in Zürich until the autumn of 1928, his practice became larger and more demanding each year. Although circumstances forced him to lead such an active *outer* live in the world, these years while he was readapting to the tension in Europe were mainly years of *inner* enlightenment; they could even be called the first fully conscious epilogue to his earlier "confrontation with the unconscious," for the dream in Tunis was understood only much later.

His interest in the mandala had never wavered throughout all these nearly ten years, but his knowledge of it was greatly increased by a dream he had in 1927. This dream led to the painting of two particularly significant mandalas, the last he felt the need to execute. This was because the dream

"depicted the climax of the whole process of development of consciousness" and it satisfied him completely. He even felt the dream to be "an act
of grace."[a]

The dream is recorded in detail in *Memories*[1] but its main outline is worth
repeating because it formed such a vital climax. He dreamed that he was in
Liverpool with about half a dozen other Swiss men in the most disagreeable
conditions: dirty, sooty streets on a dark winter's night in the rain. It
reminded him of a section of Basel, where one walks up from the market to
a raised plateau by the so-called Alley of the Dead. When they reached the
plateau, however, they found everything arranged in mandala form. The
quarters of the city were placed radially around the center, and each of the
individual quarters was also arranged radially around its own central point,
thus forming a small replica of the whole. In the center of the greater
mandala, in contrast to the rain, fog, and smoke of the periphery, there was
a round pool and in the middle a small island in blazing sunlight with a
beautiful flowering magnolia in the center. While Jung was carried away by
the extraordinary beauty of this island, he noted with surprise that his
companions did not see it all. They only grumbled at the horrible weather
and expressed surprise that "another Swiss" had settled in Liverpool and
lived in this vicinity. Jung thought he knew "very well why he had settled
here." Each of the quarters of the city had its own central point,
illuminated by a larger streetlamp, and forming a small replica of the
glowing island in the center of all.

Although he did not mention it in *Memories*, he told me once that the
great discovery of this dream, which he illustrated by a painting,[2] was that
the "other Swiss" lived in the "vicinity of one of these secondary centers"
and not near the center of the whole mandala. This was his first vivid image
of the nature of the Self, which is collective in the main central island (open
and accessible to all who are able to see it) and individual in the small
unique replica, where, like the "other Swiss," each of us must live. He thus
first learned that our place is *not* in the center of the mandala, but at the
side, in a small individual replica of our own. He thus began to distinguish
his own personal myth from the myth of modern man as he had realized it
on the Athi Plains in East Africa, nearly two years before. We all have the
task of completing creation, of becoming conscious of *all we can* and thus
to give it "objective existence." The fact, however, that none of his
companions in the dream, about half a dozen Swiss men, could see the
island, or apparently become conscious of its existence, taught him that his
own individual myth had to do with becoming conscious of the center of all,
as well as of everything concerning his own individual replica and the
relation between the two. The former constitutes a kind of image of the

[a] The reader will remember Jung's first experience of "the miracle of grace," when he was
only eleven years old, after he found the courage to think his blasphemous thought to the
end. (See above, page 46.)

destiny of mankind in general, the latter of each individual. The constituents are all in the central image, but the selection and combination of these constituents are different, even unique, in each individual replica.

The dream also gave him new hope in coming to terms with the too highly charged atmosphere in Europe. When he first got back from Africa, in the period before the dream, he suffered from a tendency to depression and a feeling of hopelessness. He even reported that the dream of dark, rainy Liverpool

> represented my situation at the time. I can still see the grayish-yellow raincoats, glistening with the wetness of the rain. Everything was extremely unpleasant, black and opaque—just as I felt then. But I had had a vision of unearthly beauty, and this was why I was able to live at all. Liverpool is the "pool of life." The "liver," according to an old view, is the seat of life—that which "makes to live." [3]

From that dream on, however hopeless things seemed in daily life, in his patients, or in the world situation, Jung was never tempted to despair. He knew there was a light at the center of every individual life, even a sunlit island—where the opposites are harmoniously united (as they are in light and shade wherever the outer sun shines)—at the center of the life of every individual and of the world, however lost it appears to be in misunderstanding, unconsciousness, and strife. How many people can open their eyes wide enough to become aware of this? It almost seems as if the future of the whole world depends on the answer to this question.

This illumination—for it was no less—finally showed him, even more clearly, all that he had learned in the "confrontation with the unconscious," nearly ten years before. It also made his task in analysis much plainer. He knew then that everyone who came to him came for more consciousness, in some form or other—for that is the general myth of mankind in our day—but that the level of consciousness and the things each patient needed to become conscious of were different. The majority—like Jung's Swiss companions in the dream—have as yet no inkling of the existence of the central island. Their task—and often it is all that is asked of them—is to become conscious of things which others seem to have known long ago. Jung once explained this by saying that some people do not yet know that a mountain exists; they may even have to spend their whole lifetime learning this, as it seems to us, obvious fact.

The first of the two mandalas that Jung painted represented the arrangement as it was in the dream itself. To anticipate for a moment: in 1946, during Winston Churchill's visit to Switzerland, Jung was invited to a dinner party given for Churchill by the city of Zürich and was seated next to the guest of honor. He was greatly struck by the fact that the tables were arranged in exactly the same radial formation as on the plateau in his

Liverpool dream twenty years earlier, and that the table at which Churchill and he were sitting was just where the "other Swiss" had settled in his dream!

In 1928, a year after his dream, Jung felt moved to paint another mandala, this time with a golden castle at the center. He was struck as he painted it by its Chinese character, and asked himself why. He had hardly finished it when, out of the blue, Richard Wilhelm sent him the manuscript of an old Taoist-alchemical treatise, *The Secret of the Golden Flower,* and asked him to write a psychological commentary on it. Jung devoured the manuscript at once, for it gave him "undreamed of confirmation" of his own ideas, even describing it as "the first event which broke through my isolation." It impressed him so much that he later wrote beneath this mandala:[4] "In 1928, when I was painting this picture, showing the golden, well-fortified castle, Richard Wilhelm in Frankfurt sent me the thousand-year-old Chinese text on the yellow castle, the germ of the immortal body." Such synchronicity always made a deep impression on Jung, though it was still many years before he called the phenomenon by this name.

There is an even clearer description of what this meant to Jung in the Foreword to the Second German Edition to *The Secret of the Golden Flower,* which was published in 1938. He wrote:

My deceased friend, Richard Wilhelm, co-author of this book, sent me the text of *The Secret of the Golden Flower* at a time that was crucial for my own work. This was in 1928. I had been investigating the processes of the collective unconscious since the year 1913, and had obtained results that seemed to me questionable in more than one respect. They not only lay far beyond everything known to "academic" psychology, but they also over-stepped the bounds of any medical, purely personal, psychology. They confronted me with an extensive phenomenology to which hitherto known categories and methods could no longer be applied. My results, based on fifteen years of effort, seemed inconclusive, because no possibility of comparison offered itself. I knew of no realm of human experience with which I might have backed up my findings with some degree of assurance. The only analogics—and thcse, I must say, were far removed in time—I found scattered among the reports of the heresiologists. This connection did not in any way ease my task; on the contrary, it made it difficult, because the Gnostic systems consist only in small part of immediate psychic experiences, the greater part being speculative and systematizing recensions. Since we possess only very few complete texts, and since most of what is known comes from the reports of Christian opponents, we have, to say the least, an inadequate knowledge of the history as well as the content of this strange and confused literature, which is so difficult to evaluate. Moreover, considering the fact that a period of not less than seventeen to eighteen hundred years separates us from that age, support from that quarter seemed to me extraordinarily risky. Again, the connections were for the most part of a subsidiary nature and left gaps at just the most important points, so that I found it impossible to make use of the Gnostic material.

The text that Wilhelm sent me helped me out of this difficulty. It contained exactly those items I had long sought for in vain among the Gnostics. Thus the text afforded me a welcome opportunity to publish, at least in provisional form, some of the essential results of my investigations.[5]

Already in 1919, as we have seen, Jung knew that in discovering "the mandala as an expression of the Self" he had attained what was for him the ultimate reality, but he had as yet no empirical proof that it had collective and not just subjective validity. Therefore, it was only after he came upon this proof in the old Chinese text that he published his discovery of ten years before. Most people find it difficult to realize that psychology is no invention, but an *empirical science*. It becomes easier when they can see the same symbol in totally different empirical material.

Jung said later in the same Foreword that, at the time we are considering, he had not yet realized that *The Secret of the Golden Flower* is not only a Taoist text of Chinese Yoga but also an alchemical tract. His discovery of the paramount importance of alchemy was still some years in the future; he said it was this text "that first put me in the direction of the right track. For we have in medieval alchemy the long sought connecting link between Gnosis and the processes of the collective unconscious, observable to us today in modern man."

It was indeed no meaningless chance that this synchronicity took place while he was still facing the intolerable tension in Europe, which he had first realized in Africa. The opposites are seen far more clearly in the East, whose gods are always positive *and* negative, and the mandala is the expression *par excellence* of the Oriental's effort to deal with this tension. But the East always tries to escape from the tension of the opposites into Nirvana, into non-being. This solution, however, denies the value of the No. 1 personality, or, in other words, the value of human life in three-dimensional reality. We should make a great mistake if we adopted the Eastern solution; it was a mistake which Jung never made. Unreality was always "the quintessence of horror" to him, and however fascinated he was by his fantasies at the height of his "confrontation with the unconscious," he still always knew that everything he was experiencing was ultimately directed at the real life he was living in the world. He was always determined to meet "its obligations and fulfill its meanings."[6]

Where the West can learn a great deal from the East is in its full acceptance of the equality of the opposites. The Christian religion has perhaps torn the opposites farther apart than any other great religion, thus making them fully visible. But it has also made less effort to reconcile them; it always strives to overcome the negative and to help the positive to conquer it. The former is represented in the Christian religion by the devil, Satan, who must at all costs be vanquished by the Saviour, Christ. It is unfortunately an illusion to believe that one opposite can ever permanently overcome the other. Such a repression is bound to lead sooner or later to an intolerable tension which, if not realized, will result in an enantiodromia, when the repressed opposite will inevitably gain the upper hand. Today, we are witnessing on all sides the flourishing of the dark and evil opposite as never before; but in the twenties this was not nearly so visible, and it was still the attempted repression of the dark opposite that was producing the unbearable tension that had secretly contributed to Jung's journey to Africa. Jung saw this clearly as he began to find the right attitude to the highly charged atmosphere in Europe. He saw more and more clearly the danger to which the West was exposing itself by *again* repressing one opposite and that everything depended on reestablishing an equilibrium between the opposites. He had known this intellectually for many years, as anyone can see by reading his definition of the symbol in *Psychological Types*. But now he had to see this in concrete reality and to meet it as an everyday problem. He had already done this in his own psychology to a great extent, but he now had to learn the effect that the same opposites *in the collective* world can have on one if *not realized*. It was indeed not by chance that *The Secret of the Golden Flower* should fall into his hands at just that time, and that he should learn that a thousand years ago the Chinese had already known the enormous difference between *knowing* and *not knowing*, being conscious or unconscious. "Indolence of which a man knows and indolence that he does not know are a thousand miles apart,"[7] declared that text.

This was an objective confirmation, widely separated in both space and time from all his outer experience in his No. 1 personality, of a fact he had known in his own psychology since he was a schoolboy, when "neurosis" developed after he had been knocked down from behind in the Cathedral Square in Basel. He was genuinely ill just as long as he forgot that he had thought as he lay on the ground: "Now you won't have to go to school any more." But as soon as he faced this painful truth, he recovered and never suffered a relapse. A great deal of his most successful therapy was based on this experience, as we saw, for example, in the case of the woman at Burghölzli who also recovered without relapse when she was faced with the fact that for a moment she had known she wished to murder her child. Jung's realization, on the Athi Plains, of the living myth of mankind, that it is only human consciousness that can continue the work of the Creator by giving an objective existence to the world through becoming *conscious* of it, is also closely related to this therapy.[8] Now *The Secret of the Golden Flower* told Jung that the wisdom of China had already known this fact, a thousand years before; so it is indeed no wonder that he felt his isolation had at last been broken into and that his lonely experience had been confirmed by other human beings.[9]

Nothing prevents people from realizing the vital importance of consciousness more than not wanting to face the so-called shadow, that is, the part of our personality that we fear because we do not know it, and which is liable to play us such tricks as forgetting we *meant* to escape school, for example, or that we *really* wanted to blot out all trace of a marriage, in order to become free for the man we had just learned was after all obtainable. It is admittedly painful to learn such facts about ourselves, but it is the way *par excellence* that leads to a worthwhile and meaningful life, in which we can learn to live in our replica of the central mandala and to find out the *purpose* of our individual life, *why* we exist at all. It was undoubtedly because Jung was always willing to face the most painful facts about himself that he was free to learn, not only his own individual myth, but even the myth of modern man.

Almost directly after Jung had read and digested *The Secret of the Golden Flower*, he must have begun to write his psychological commentary to it, for it was published in 1929. This forced him—more than anything he had encountered before—to an *"Auseinandersetzung"* with the East. The most profound realizations of mankind come from the deepest levels of all, from the layers of "primeval ancestors," as illustrated in the diagram on page 17, or even from the two lower layers, "animal ancestors in general," or life itself, "the central fire." But the fourth "large group" layer already produces realizations of which the ancient experience of man differs in East and West, for instance; we cannot adopt these, as is far too widely practiced, without doing violence to the structure of our own inheritance.

Yet in a profound text like *The Secret of the Golden Flower* there is a great deal from the lowest layers that is exactly the same in East and West. Jung therefore found amazing confirmation and parallels to his own "confrontation with the unconscious" and to the material that was being brought him by some of his patients. This commentary contains one of the clearest descriptions of the method of active imagination which he ever wrote,[10] as well as a remarkable exposition of what we can learn from the East and the great dangers of any imitation. Writing this commentary took all the time available to him from his demanding outer life during the end of 1928 and the beginning of 1929.

I first came to Zürich in January, 1929. While I was waiting in my hotel room for my appointment with Jung, but before I knew anything of his interest in the mandala or anything beyond what he had already published about his psychology, and nothing of him as a man, I was surprised to see, with my inner eyes, four priests in a wood who then formed a square. I was a painter in those days, so I immediately made a sketch of what I had seen and dated it, but I said nothing to Jung about it in my first interview.

In the autumn of 1928 Jung had resumed his English seminars in Zürich for the first time since 1925. These seminars were held once a week at the Psychological Club, during the terms, and continued regularly until February, 1939. I was fortunate to arrive after only six lectures had been held, and to have subsequently heard them all, almost without exception. Until the end of the summer of 1930 the subject of these seminars was a series of dreams by a man. From the autumn of 1930, until the end of the winter term in 1934, Jung dealt with a woman's long series of visions (active imagination). From the summer term, 1934, until he ceased to give this seminar, in February, 1939, the lectures were on Nietzsche's *Zarathustra*.

My impression of Jung at the time of my first interview on January 14, 1929, are still vivid. He was in his fifty-fourth year and, except for his gray, almost white, hair, he still looked a young and exceptionally vigorous man. It is difficult to describe him in words, since his expression altered constantly. He could look very serious, and then something would amuse him, and the sun broke through, so to speak. Altogether, the expressions that went over Jung's face were very like certain days in nature when the landscape seems to alter all the time. He was a tall man, about six feet, two inches, and broad, but with little spare flesh. His eyes were dark brown and he always wore gold-rimmed spectacles. He had a habit, however, of looking at people over the rims of the glasses and then one saw that his eyes were not really very large; they were rather on the small side, but extraordinarily expressive. He could convey more with an almost imperceptible wink than anyone else I ever saw. Altogether, his eyes, usually in analysis looking at one directly over his glasses, conveyed almost as much as what he said.

His forehead was high, though not unpleasantly so, as it sloped slightly backward, and his nose and chin were very decided. He wore a small mustache but was otherwise clean-shaven and his mouth was nearly as expressive as his eyes. When he came to fetch me from the waiting room, he held his pipe in his hand and was accompanied by his large gray Schnauzer dog who was evidently used to drawing his own conclusions about the people who came to see his master.[b]

Although I was certain I had never seen Jung before, or even seen a photograph of him, I yet had the strongest *sentiment du déjà vu* that I had ever experienced. At the same time, I was certain that this was the most whole person I had ever seen. In my painting, I had always been drawn by

[b] This dog, Joggi by name, was Jung's faithful friend for many years and died, at the unusually old age of nineteen, asleep in his basket (his mandala!) one night during World War II.

this quality which one finds untouched in animals and in most children, but which so far I had seen in adults only among primitive people untouched by civilization and often in old European peasants who had lived all their lives on the soil. I had long since given up any hope of finding it in educated people, for up to the moment of seeing Jung I had always found that, in these highly specialized days, they lacked that indefinable look of the complete, natural human being. Jung, on the other hand, might have been a Swiss peasant rooted for centuries on his soil; at the same time, he obviously had by far the best mind I had ever encountered. Considerably shattered by these strong impressions, I bent down to pat the dog, until I was recalled by Jung asking dryly, "Did you come from Paris [where I was living at that time ] to see the dog or me?"

One is so used in these days to experiencing the opposites separated from each other that it is surprising to find a human being in whom they exist simultaneously. I felt at one and the same time that Jung could be more direct, even ruthless, than anyone else I had known—and indeed *he was* when necessary, even in the first hour—and yet he also obviously had the warmest possible heart and a rare love of humanity. You experienced these two qualities, each made curiously relative by the presence of its also fully accepted opposite, *simultaneously* and could take the one because of the other. Above all, his geniality and lively sense of humor made him completely acceptable, however ruthless he chose to be.

I had read all his books before coming to Zürich. I therefore thought I understood and greatly appreciated something of his thought, but my first interview was enough to convince me that his psychology was embodied in the living man and that he himself was far more convincing than all his books put together. Even now, writing so many years after his death, I often observe that my students are far more convinced by seeing him on the B.B.C. "Face to Face" television interview than by anything they learn in other ways. I am glad to record that up until now this film has been shown to the students every year by the C. G. Jung Institute in Zürich.

Although Jung could well have claimed, with his already far too full practice and the effort of writing his commentary to *The Golden Flower*, that his time was fully occupied, he nevertheless resumed his English seminars on January 23, 1929. These seminars were a vivid experience, and were heard by the great majority of Jung's older pupils who are now doing their best to uphold his psychology—each in his own way—all over the world. Jung never allowed his audience at these seminars to get very large, and I was most fortunate in being allowed to attend them from the beginning (a privilege I owe to Toni Wolff, with whom I worked during my first time in Zürich) because I had read all of Jung's published books. Incidentally, he was surprised to hear that I came to see him entirely on account of his books. At that time it seems that seldom or never happened.

In these 1929 seminars there were about thirty people in the audience, mainly American and Swiss, with a sprinkling of English and other nationalities. In spite of all Jung's efforts, the number increased in later years but never, right to its end in 1939, did it exceed about fifty. Therefore, he was able to speak much more freely than in his lectures or books and to try out his new ideas. As he says in his commentary to *The Secret of the Golden Flower*, he kept his discoveries about the mandala to himself for ten years and it was only after he received this old Chinese confirmation that he wrote and spoke of it in lectures. Curiously enough, the second dream I heard him analyze, in January, 1929, was of a steam roller in a wood, which was not, as the dreamer expected, making a road which led from one place to another but was making an intricate pattern in two rhythms which, looked at, as the dreamer did, from above, turned out to be a square. Inside it, at the center, was a spiral footpath leading to the center of all. The dreamer had done a drawing of this at Jung's request, which was shown to us and is reproduced in the seminar notes that were made at the time and subsequently multigraphed for the use of the class. This led to Jung's telling us a great deal about mandalas, not only in the Chinese parallel he was working on, but many others from all over the world which his investigations had discovered.

The fact that this symbol must be basic in human nature was empirically proved to me when I looked at the sketch I had made, *just before* seeing Jung for the first time, of the four priests in a wood who formed a mandala. Both Jung's patient's mandala and my own were in a wood, frequent symbol of the unconscious. This seminar was full of material from the East in which Jung's main interest was centered at the time, for, though the series of dreams was dreamed *before The Secret of the Golden Flower* reached Jung, it was full of symbols which synchronistically were also old Chinese symbols. I was therefore fortunate enough in my first weeks in Zürich to begin with this basic symbol of the mandala, which exactly fitted into the passion for wholeness which my painting had already roused in me.

I was also exceedingly fortunate in coming to Zürich in January, 1929, for it was still early in the several years during which Jung undertook no long journeys. As far as I can remember, he did not even go to America between 1927 and 1936. It was a time when he stayed relatively put, so to speak, and let all his pupils come to him, instead of visiting them in their various locations. With the exception of some lectures in neighboring countries, Jung remained in Switzerland during those years, devoting himself to his practice and to the group of pupils and patients that had formed around him. Not only did the English seminar thrive and attract many doctors and others from abroad but also the Psychological Club flourished as never before.

Founded in 1916, the Psychological Club had gone through some difficult times, of which I know only by hearsay. At one point Jung even left it, although the continuity was insured by the continued presence of Emma

Jung and Toni Wolff and by many of his most loyal pupils. It was not long, however, before Jung yielded to their entreaties and returned. He had already realized, long before this contretemps, that lectures and scientific discussions were not enough to keep a group together. So he not only encouraged many social occasions, but laid considerable emphasis on the social contact and the refreshments which were always served during a pause, between the lectures and subsequent discussions. By this time the Psychological Club was fortunate enough to have secured Fräulein Anni Ammann as its resident housekeeper. (She remained well over forty years, and was extraordinarily and unusually warmhearted and almost universally beloved. She retired in the spring of 1970, to the lasting regret of the members.) She fed not only the members of the club on her excellent sandwiches and tea, but also, at Jung's request, the members of the English seminar. These mornings—it was always on Wednesday morning, the middle of the working week—consisted of two-hour lectures, too long for both lecturer and audience. Jung found, after he had instituted this social tea pause, that the atmosphere improved enormously. The seminar lectures were completely informal. Jung spoke freely without notes except those on the material he was discussing. He asked questions, and we were all free, even encouraged, to ask him questions ourselves.

Not only were there social pauses between lecture and discussion in the Psychological Club but there were always dinners at Christmas and certain evenings were reserved for members, at which the "club problem" was frankly discussed. Jung, moreover, invented a special game for such occasions, called the Alleluia game. In it all the members sat around the room with one member in the center. A knotted cloth (usually a napkin) was thrown from one to the other. It was *de rigueur* to throw it as far across the space in the middle as possible, not just to pass it to your nearest neighbors. The member in the center had to catch it on its way; when he succeeded in doing so, he might sit down, and his place was taken by the member who had thrown the cloth. The game often waxed fast and furious and always efficiently banished stiffness and formality. It had an amazingly relating effect bringing the group together in an almost magical way.

Unfortunately, I was not yet in Zürich when this game was initiated though I played it several times in my first years as a member, so I do not know quite how it started. It is, of course, connected with the early ceremonial "ball-dance" of the Church, in which the officiating priests danced "in time with the rhythmical sounds of the chanted sequence" and the ball was handed or thrown to the dancers in turn or together. Such a ceremony was danced in the Cathedral of Auxerre, and probably in many other churches and cathedrals, as late as the sixteenth century. Then an outcry was raised against its secular character, and it was forbidden, to the great regret of some of the priests.[11] There were also many earlier *"jeu de puume" (pilota* or *pelota)* games rather like tennis played in the churches.

I do not know how far Jung was acquainted with these medieval parallels when he introduced this game to the club, but he must have known something about them because of the name he gave—"The Alleluia Game"—for the "Burial of the Alleluia" and "The Whipping of the Alleluia" were also ceremonial rites of which "we can find traces in the medieval churches."[12] According to G.R.S. Mead, the Alleluia was "personified as a feminine potency, and not only personified but made to suffer death, burial and resurrection." Mead quoted Abbé Lebeuf (early eighteenth century) as reporting that in the cathedral of one of the dioceses near Paris this ceremony took the form of whipping. One of the choirboys whipped a top (which was inscribed with the name "Alleluia" in golden letters) "down the pavement of the Church and out of doors." Lebeuf was much intrigued by what he called *cette bizarre comédie*, but apparently failed to discover whether (as he assumed probable) there was also a "Whipping-back of Alleluia" on Easter Day to celebrate her resurrection.

I do not know how much Jung took over medieval customs in the game. We know that he regretted that all such rituals were banished from the Church so early, for, as he pointed out in *Psychology and Alchemy*, all traces of such games and of "divine intoxication" which had played such a role in earlier religions, especially the Dionysian, vanished entirely from the sacred precincts and became secular. He even ended this interesting paragraph with the words: "Our solution, however, has served to throw the gates of hell wide open."[13] Certainly the psychological reason was that the napkin, which was knotted into a ball, symbolized the Self, and the game was intended to unite the members *in the Self*, or via their No. 2 personalities, to use that phraseology, and to prevent their fellowship with each other from falling apart in mere personal and transitory interests. Probably something of the same kind was at the bottom of the *jeu de paume* and "ball-dances" in the Church. Dancing is even attributed to Christ Himself,[14] but, as the original tradition fell a victim to rationalism, the symbolism of the ball (the round, complete object) was forgotten.

In the before-mentioned paragraph (182) of *Psychology and Alchemy* Jung also regretted that all traces of the carnival were banished from the Sacred Precincts. He had been brought up, of course, in Basel, where the carnival (although not in the Church) has a long historical tradition behind it which not only gives it far more atmosphere and life, but definitely prevents it from getting out of acceptable bounds, as it easily does in towns or countries where this tradition is lacking. If one compares the spirit of carnival in Basel and in Zürich (which is a much more commercial and newer city, with far less tradition behind it), one can see at once why Jung regretted that all of that side of life had been banished from the Church, for it was thus cut off from its oldest roots and tradition and from all religious form. By the latter I mean, to use psychological language, it was taken out of the precincts of the Self (or the No. 2 personality) and given over entirely to the egotistical aims that prevail in the outer world (or to the No. 1 personality). Therefore, at Jung's instigation, the Psychological Club gave its first large Carnival Ball in February, 1930, at the Hotel Sonnenberg in Zürich.

This evening (although it was somewhat difficult for people like myself who had been brought up in countries that did not celebrate carnival) was perhaps the most memorable evening in the whole history of the club. Jung himself, at a much later club evening (where photographs of past events, including this ball, had been shown), said that it was so for him. He recalled that he went home from it with more hope for the club and his own psychology than he had ever experienced before or since, and added that he himself had enjoyed every moment of it from its start, when he was received by a beneficent angel[c] at the door, until he went home about six o'clock the next morning.

Although he tried hard to keep out of the limelight by changing his costume and mask three or four times during the evening, he was nevertheless the center and inspiration of the party, however little he wanted this role. This was, I think, because the opposites were so much united in him, and he was by this time so whole, that more one-sided people were inevitably drawn to him to get at least a glimpse back into their own lost wholeness.[15] It was, of course, a projection, but it was a fruitful projection, for that missing quality in themselves was often seen in him for the first time in adult life. (If it remained forever a projection, it naturally became regressive, but, in a successful outcome, it was gradually seen to be a projection, the projector thus becoming aware of his or her No. 2 personality for the first time.) At all events, on an evening such as this first Carnival Ball in 1930, everyone—patients, pupils, and, by far the majority, complete outsiders—turned toward him as their center. Not that they all congregated around Jung, giving their whole attention to him; the ball had its own life and the pairs were also quite naturally absorbed in each other. A good deal of wine was drunk and from time to time this threatened to go beyond the bounds of good taste. But the unconscious seemed to warn Jung each time this threatened and he was there at once with exactly the right joke to bring the people back to the divine and saving quality of humor. It was the same sure instinct in Jung that had saved his party the night of the native dance in Africa.[d]

The Psychological Club was entering its very best years at the end of the

---

[c] This was our dear Fräulein Ammann, the club housekeeper, in an angel's costume and mask.
[d] See above, page 178.

twenties, for Toni Wolff took over the presidency for nearly twenty years in 1928. Before then the presidency had changed hands frequently. This also had its advantages, for it made the members more active and perhaps more responsible for the welfare of the club. But in such outstandingly capable hands as Toni Wolff's, the advantages of a more permanent presidency soon made themselves felt. She worked herself right into the job, had the club's welfare constantly at heart, and gave herself endless trouble to get interesting outside lecturers from other fields and to inspire the members of the club to take up some research where she would be sure of reaping a good lecture in the end. At first the other members of the club's governing committee were all men, but in 1934 one of their number (there were five members of the committee including the president, all automatically coming up for reelection every year) suggested that, since such a large number of the members were women, a ratio of four males to one female on the committee was unsuitable. He accompanied this suggestion with his own resignation,[e] and from then on the sexes were more or less evenly divided on the committee. As long as there was a high level in the lectures at the club (they took place every alternate Saturday evening), Jung attended them regularly, taking a most lively part in the subsequent discussions. He also frequently lectured there himself during Toni's presidency and the club gradually became the place in which he gave his first lecture in any new field of research. In those days the audience was a real sounding board and the lecturer felt the most sympathetic support that I, at all events, have ever experienced.

I was not admitted to the lectures at the Psychological Club with the same speed and ease as to the English seminars, because, although I had had a German governess for five years as a child, my German had become rusty in the intervening years. It took me some time to convince either Jung or Toni Wolff that, though I spoke it so badly, I did really understand the language. So, to my lasting sorrow, I was not admitted to the last lecture of Richard Wilhelm in February, 1929. It was Jung's German seminar at Küsnacht in 1931 that finally convinced him that I understood the language quite well enough. Then I soon found that the language difficulty was only a pretext. There were really quite different reasons behind Toni's reluctance to admit me to the club, although she was, I am sure, well disposed to me, particularly at that time. I finally succeeded in becoming a member in the the spring of 1933.

I mention this in order to show what an efficient guardian of the threshold Toni was! Of course she knew Jung's wishes as to keeping the club small,

---

[e] This was Fritz Allemann, a most valuable member of the club until his death in 1968. He was a distinguished businessman who had lived for a long time in Egypt. The finances of the club owe a great deal to his advice, which continued even after he left the committee. "Let us ask Mr. Allemann" was our constant cry during the seven years I was on the committee and he always came to our rescue.

and everyone had to pass a tremendous fire of resistance before there was any chance of becoming a statutory guest, much less a member. While Linda Fierz was on the committee, the Fierz sons nicknamed Toni "the club tiger," and I must admit this was an exceedingly apt description. Though it naturally did not always add to her popularity, this was really one of her most valuable adjuncts as president, for it not only kept the club small but also raised the standard of admitted candidates. I can testify that it took a great deal of conviction, persistence, and courage to stand up to Toni in her role as club tiger!

When I first got to Zürich, Jung—surprisingly enough—had neither a car nor a secretary, and at first he came to the seminars by bicycle or train. But by the time of the Easter holidays in 1929, the former situation began to change. Jung was at last persuaded to buy a car. He was a grandfather before he learned how to drive, but he already knew the roads well from bicycling, and he soon began to see that his freedom and radius would be considerably improved by driving a car. He could, for example, get to Bollingen much more quickly and waste less time on travel to Zürich from Küsnacht. So it was not very long before he had bought *two* cars: a two-seater Chrysler for his own use and a large Dodge limousine for the family.

Before long Emma Jung and Toni Wolff felt they must follow his example and learn to drive a car too, but it was much more difficult for them. Although they were younger than he,[f] they had had no previous experience of the roads. There were, however, plenty of people to drive Emma, unless she actually wanted to drive herself. Their faithful gardener, Müller,[g] for example, was taught to drive and to look after the cars.

Toni had the greatest difficulty of all, for she had no aptitude whatever for driving a car. With driving lessons before breakfast every morning, it took her nearly a year to pass her test and get her driving license, but she persisted until she succeeded. She was always a very erratic driver, but she was in such good contact with the unconscious that she was somehow mercifully preserved from serious accidents[h] and drove with considerable pleasure until her death in 1953. She bought herself a very large Chrysler at the end of 1929, the most unsuitable car for a beginner that can be imagined. Her next Chrysler was only slightly smaller, but when she got her B.M.W., about 1938, she calmly and rather reproachfully informed us that *at last* she had a suitable car. (As if all her friends had not been imploring her from the beginning to get a smaller car!)

---

[f] Emma Jung, born in 1882, was seven years younger than her husband; Toni, born in 1888, was thirteen years younger.

[g] Müller—who adored Jung and loved the whole family—was a typical old family servant and was with Jung until his death in 1961. I still see him about, driving his own little car in Küsnacht.

[h] Neither Jung nor Mrs. Jung ever had an accident, beyond an occasional scratched fender. Such scratches were very frequent with Toni.

In December, 1929, and August, 1930, I was fortunate enough to stay for two days in Bollingen. It is most unlikely that I should have been asked there so early in my analysis had Toni not been to stay with my family for a month in England in July and August of 1929. My father was still Dean of Chichester—though on the brink of retiring—and staying in a cathedral close and in our small Sussex country house were new and therefore interesting experiences to Toni. As her mother, Frau Wolff, was as yet too traditionally Swiss to welcome a stranger so soon to her house, Toni paid back the hospitality by asking Jung to invite me to Bollingen.

I was frankly terrified when I first arrived at the Tower. It was very cold weather and Jung was cooking in his original round kitchen in a long Oriental robe which he often wore in cold weather. He looked like a picture I had once seen of an old alchemist at work among his retorts. He looked more whole than ever, but different from the way I had seen him in the seminars and in the two analytical hours which were all I had had with him up until then. I seemed to be back in the Middle Ages, with the lamp and firelight making a small illuminated circle in what struck me that evening as a huge circular circumference of darkness.[i] Toni, who was also staying there, just gave me some tea and told me to take a chair by the fire and watch Jung cook, then busied herself with fetching the things he asked for and her own jobs. Jung was entirely engrossed in some absorbing cooking and in watching the fire. (He was a most unusually good cook and used in those days to cook the most complicated dishes. I remember one sauce with no fewer than sixteen ingredients!) Although I learned only later how many of his ideas came to him while working on such things, I felt instinctively that I had better say nothing. I did not yet know him well enough to feel it as a companionable silence (which I learned later to enjoy more than anything), so after two or three hours I took an opportunity, when he did not seem quite so engrossed, to murmur: "I am scared stiff." Although only a faint amused smile indicated that he had even heard my remark, the ice was broken and I began to feel at home. After a bit he gave me an aperitif (at the Tower he always called that a "sun-downer"), then I even got a small job or two to do, and finally we were ready to sit down at the round table. The marvelous food and wine rapidly banished my fear, though I was fortunate enough still to say nothing, except for a few appreciative gruntlike murmurs while we were eating. That was indeed fortunate because, as I learned later, Jung *hated* to talk while he was eating a really good meal. (He used to quote his mother, who said that chattering was disrespectful to good food.) The only remark I remember him making during that first meal was: "Oh, well, you already know how to enjoy your food, that is *one* thing [emphasis on the one!] I shall not have to teach you!"

[i] The Tower kitchen is not really large at all, as I saw next morning.

After supper the silence was over, and the ensuing ease lasted for the rest of the visit. For a long time I felt more at ease with Jung in Bollingen than anywhere else, except in analysis. I remember that after washing up we played some card game which Jung won easily, with Toni a good second, while I was unplaced! (Neither then nor at any subsequent time, though Jung fairly often played card games—though never bridge—did I ever see or hear of him playing for even the smallest stakes.) He quite enjoyed teasing me as a dunce, however, but by that time I did not care at all.

Next morning we went for about a three-hour walk in the large woods on the hill behind his house. Those woods are most confusing, as the valleys take unexpected directions, and that first morning he kept asking me to point in the direction of the lake, apparently delighted that I always got it wrong. Only much later did I realize that Toni, who had no sense of direction at all, had told him that, as I had such a (to her) marvelous power of finding my way, I must after all be a sensation type, and he wanted to prove the obvious fact to her that I was not. Jung once told me that these mistaken diagnoses of type, although Toni was totally unconscious of them, were sometimes extraordinarily fruitful in an analysis, for by being sure her analysand's inferior function was superior and conscious, she developed it in a remarkable way.

My summer visit to the Tower, about eight months later, was totally different. I felt perfectly at home from the beginning, the weather was as hot as the first visit had been cold, and we bathed in the lake instead of walking. On such an enchanted summer evening one was powerfully attracted in two directions: the lake lapping within a few yards of the door, with that healing quality that is peculiar to Bollingen; and Jung himself engrossed in cooking in the round kitchen, with whom one might sit in an already companionable silence and also be healed by his wholeness. Later I went there often, but those two first contrasting visits have remained particularly vivid in my mind, although they are now well over forty years ago.

The building was in the stage of the original round Tower and the first more or less square annex. There was as yet no built-in area to eat out-of-doors. On hot days or evenings a table was placed at the edge of the lake, the trees providing complete seclusion on the land side, but if it rained meals were still taken in the kitchen. The walls were very thick, so the kitchen was seldom unpleasantly hot, even after considerable cooking. Jung was already occupied with plans for his second addition, which came into being in the summer of 1931. This addition joined the original round Tower with the 1927 annex and added a new long room with an open fireplace, where Jung later did a great deal of his cooking, even in the summer.

The 1931 addition provided a flat roof outside his study and the towerlike annex—provided by the original 1927 addition—was extended and the retiring room,[16] of which Jung spoke so warmly in *Memories*, came into being. Jung had already put at least two paintings on the walls of the bedrooms above the kitchen; now he undertook to paint all the eight walls of his retiring room, a tremendous job which took him several years to finish. As he said himself, these paintings "expressed all those things which have carried me out of time into seclusion, out of the present into timelessness. This second tower became for me a place of spiritual concentration." Jung would often spend most of the day painting or meditating in his retiring room, and he only seldom asked people into it. *Very* occasionally, when he was uncertain about some technical point, I would be asked in to give my opinion, because of my earlier training as an artist, but it was so much his own place that it was best just to answer his question as well and quickly as possible, then rapidly disappear.

In February of 1931, there was a repetition of the Carnival Ball at the Sonnenberg. That evening also had a satisfactory life of its own. The Anglo-Saxon pupils had prepared an amusing play: finding the remnants of Jung's discoveries in two thousand years. It was, however, the last big ball given by the Psychological Club at the Sonnenberg, for things always lose impact in repetition, and Jung seldom or never encouraged repetition of *anything*. There were masked dinner dances every carnival time at the Bahnhof restaurant, for a few more years, but they were organized by the committee of the club, and Jung attended them at their request; he was never again so entirely and wholly involved in them as he was in the first.

Having served my apprenticeship during two years with three of Jung's assistants, I started analysis with him in January, 1931. I am glad it was that way around, for it would have been very frustrating to work with *anyone* else after once experiencing what it was to work confronted with Jung's wholeness.[j] He let nothing through, and one was constantly challenged in one's most inferior and unconscious areas. I never again worked with anyone else, but my analysis with Jung stretched over many years. At first he usually saw me twice a week, then only once, then only for occasional hours when I could *prove* it was necessary. I was thus able to pass naturally from transference to an objective relationship.

---

[j] I must, however, testify that the other three were all excellent analysts in their own way. Both Toni Wolff and Peter Baynes had had a lot of experience before I worked with them, and I feel especially grateful to the former's genius for accepting with a unique calm the most extraordinary fantasies and ideas from the unconscious. Emma Jung was only just beginning to analyze when I worked with her in the summer of 1930. She took me only because I dreamed that she added a new dimension to my life, and Jung told her that she could not refuse such a challenge from the unconscious. I worked with her during one summer term, but she gave me an unusual amount in that time, partly because her superior sensation function stimulated my own very inferior sensation. Moreover, the analysis laid the foundation for my later important relationship to her.

Until after his illness in 1944, Jung never analyzed in his library. There was a small, separate room, off the library, which made an ideal consulting room. The analysand sat in a comfortable armchair and Jung sat at his desk, but with the chair well pushed back, so that he faced his *vis-à-vis* directly. I remember Peter Baynes telling me that, when he asked for advice in some difficulty, Jung inquired where he sat while analyzing and then exclaimed: "For heaven's sake, man, come out from behind your desk!" Peter added: "I should never have thought of it, but when I did the difficulty vanished."

In the summer in good weather Jung liked to analyze in the "garden room," [17, k] which was a small square room at the corner of his garden, directly on the lake. It was mainly on account of this room that the Jungs were horrified when the land on the Erlenbach side of their garden was developed as a public bathing area. They did their best to buy the land, but found later that it disturbed them far less than they had expected. The bathing season was mainly during the long vacation when Jung was at Bollingen anyhow, and although he had to give up working in the garden room in the afternoons, he was not disturbed when working at the other side of the garden, also directly on the lake.

When working indoors, Jung liked to pace up and down, especially when he was analyzing dreams. He told me his long hours of analysis prevented him from taking enough exercise. His pacing never disturbed me in the least, I even rather liked it; but he evidently knew very well whether it disturbed the analysand or not. In later years, I learned with surprise that some people, who had analyzed with him for years, had never seen him walk up and down at all! Altogether, analysis with Jung was very informal and differed with each individual. After 1944, when he was doing much less analysis, he usually saw people in his library. Then each sat in a comfortable armchair, with a beautiful view of the garden and lake, at a convenient distance from each other, as Jung was slightly deaf during his last years.

In 1930 and 1931 Jung held a German seminar in the Hotel Sonne, Küsnacht, in early October at the beginning of the winter semester. The first was on active imagination, the visions of an American woman, with special emphasis on the pictures she had painted of all the most important images. The second, in 1931, was devoted to several similar cases, also with pictures, but a different course was taken in each case. A great many Germans came from all over Germany, also other nationalities, and Jung's Zürich pupils could also attend, insofar as they knew German. Unfortunately I was delayed in England in October, 1930, and missed the seminar that year. Thus I had my first experience of those concentrated seminars,

---

[k] Marie-Louise von Franz has an excellent account of how Jung analyzed in this room, taking every natural event, such as insects flying in, the lake lapping more audibly than usual, and so on, as belonging synchronistically to what was being said in the analysis.

with a lecture from Jung every day for a week and a dinner and dance at the end, in October, 1931.[1]

In the early summer of 1931, Jung had had a successful lecture, with an extremely large audience, in Berlin, but came back from it unusually tired. He said that in spite of the success, or rather because of it, he had found it *very* trying and was determined to reduce lectures in large halls to a minimum. As mentioned before, he always had a great difficulty in putting up with large audiences. As far as his short, concentrated seminars were concerned, he had to accept, although unwillingly, that more and more people attended them. But from then on he gave lectures in large halls only when it was absolutely necessary. Success never blinded Jung in the least; the important thing to him was that a few people really understood. Later he used to tell those of his pupils who went abroad to lecture: "Remember that it really does not matter if you have a success or a failure. What matters is whether somebody really gets it or not." When we got back, he said, on more than one occasion: "I hear you *suffered* a success."

We have lost sight of Peter Baynes since the return from Africa in March, 1926. He had a bad time getting back into himself, but was much helped by a growing friendship with Cary de Angulo. They married in 1927 and spent the first years of their marriage in Carmel, California, and in England. As far as I know, he did not work as Jung's assistant again until September, 1929, when he and Cary returned to Zürich, intending to settle there permanently. Jung was very glad to have him again as assistant, and everyone found the Bayneses a great addition to the Zürich group.

Although Jung did not have time to write a long book between *Psychological Types* in 1920 and *Psychology and Alchemy* in 1944, he produced a great many lectures and short essays. Perhaps the most important were two separate essays, several times revised and reprinted, which were translated by Peter and Cary Baynes and which appeared in English in 1928 as *Two Essays*.[m] These essays, in the original Baynes translation, were called "The Unconscious in the Normal and Pathological Mind" and "The Relation of the Ego to the Unconscious." The first was translated from the already published German text, but the second first appeared in its 1928 form in English. (Jung sometimes made alterations in, or most often additions to, his earlier works when they were translated into English.) The latter essay is one of the clearest expositions of his psychology that Jung ever wrote.

[1] We owe it to Olga von König-Fachsenfeld that both seminars were preserved in multigraphed form for the use of those who were there. These notes have recently been reprinted, but are still only circulated privately. It is to be hoped that such reports will be produced later for a wider circulation.

[m] Now Vol. 7 of *Collected Works*. The second of these essays was originally given as a lecture in Paris during the First World War, in 1916, but it was much enlarged and changed later.

A further collection of Jung's lectures and essays appeared in German in 1931 under the title *Seelenprobleme der Gegenwart* (roughly, *Psychological Problems of the Present Day*), and a similar volume in 1934 under the title *Wirklichkeit der Seele* (*Reality of the Psyche*). By 1928 the two Bayneses had already translated and published several such lectures and essays, under the title *Contributions to Analytical Psychology*, so that more than one of these must have appeared in the English translation before the German original. (Later Jung often wrote in English, but not at the time we are considering.)

The Baynes translations were a godsend to the English-speaking public. On all the social occasions in Zürich in the early thirties, the two were almost equally valuable. Peter, as a most sociable extravert, was always an extremely lively element; Cary, in her quieter, introverted way, was an unfailing support to any introvert who was feeling out of the party. Jung highly valued all this in the couple as a married pair, and he was fond of them both, but he nevertheless had some misgivings from the beginning regarding the permanence of their marriage. One cause of these misgivings was that they were both unusually good swimmers and had got engaged far out at sea. He was afraid this might be symbolic of their having been too far in the unconscious to be conscious of what they were doing. The other cause was that, although Cary was an attractive and unusually intelligent woman, she was not, Jung feared, Peter's anima type at all; he might meet such a woman later and have difficulties in sticking to his present marriage.

This latter misgiving proved only too well founded. About 1931 Peter did actually meet such a girl, twenty years younger than himself, but really the image of what Jung had already described as Peter's anima type. Peter not only was very fond of Cary, but also felt that it was his true vocation to be Jung's assistant in Zürich. Jung said firmly that if he left Cary, he must also leave Zürich for good. Since Cary and her sister, Henri Zinno, were settled in Zürich, it would be an impossible situation. Once again, as in Africa—though quite differently—Peter had a very bad time, changing his mind again and again. Eventually he decided on divorce and married the English girl.

I do not want to say a word against this marriage, for I believe Peter to have been happy in it. The pair settled in England, which was, of course, a great gain to the London group. But the loss of his best male assistant was a serious privation for Jung, and it was also a great loss to the whole Zürich group. It was the second bad experience that Jung had with a foreign doctor as his chief assistant. Some years before this, a German doctor, W. M. Kraneveldt, was to have been his assistant. He came to Zürich and put in his application to the Police of Foreigners for a permit to stay for this work. Jung warned him in the strongest terms against analyzing *anyone* until he had the permit. Unfortunately, Kraneveldt did not listen to Jung's advice; he therefore failed to get his permit and even had to leave Switzerland.

After these two experiences, Jung had only Swiss assistants[n] or foreigners who had already got their green permit to settle.

As mentioned before, when I first came to Zürich in January, 1929, Jung had neither a car nor a secretary. His wife and his third daughter, Marianne, later Mrs. Walter Niehus, stepped into the gap when Jung was no longer able to cope with his correspondence or his accounts, because of his enormous load of analyses and lectures.[o] But it was not congenial work for either of them; particularly, the patients' bills were inclined to be inaccurate. I do not think that in that year or two I ever got a correct bill, and the mistakes were always in my favor! Jung knew, had known for some years, that he should get a secretary, but it was difficult—almost impossible—to find the right one. Then in the spring of 1932 the god-sent answer to the problem unexpectedly appeared.

It began in a way that was a great grief to Jung. His old friend Dr. Hans Schmid, of Basel, died unexpectedly in an accident. Jung told us at the time that his death had taken a strange form. A short time before, a tree that he regarded as his life-tree had died, and this so much preyed on Dr. Schmid's mind that he had had a series of accidents, the last of which was fatal. He left a widow, a son, and two daughters, of whom the elder, Marie-Jeanne, was a trained secretary and extremely good at languages. She had just spent a year or two in England and spoke English fluently, with hardly a trace of a foreign accent. Her mother had come from French Switzerland and had always spoken French with her children. Since they were brought up in Basel and with a German-Swiss father, their German and Swiss German were also faultless.

Now, the great difficulty in finding the right secretary for Jung was that it was necessary for such a secretary to know some psychology, but the possible candidates with this qualification all had transferences[p] of some form or other to him. He felt that this would lead to complications that would give more trouble than their work would be worth to him. But Marie-Jeanne knew him from quite a different side: as an old friend of her father's who had visited them from time to time since her earliest childhood, he was just a familiar figure who generated no excitement at all. Moreover, since her father was one of the original Zürich group, she knew enough about psychology not to be at sea in the work.

Marie-Jeanne Schmid was Jung's secretary for twenty years, and in the end turned out to be virtually irreplaceable. By which I do not mean she made no mistakes—she was human enough to make quite a lot and never to

[n] It was at this time that Dr. C. A. Meier came from Burghölzli to work as assistant to Jung. He was later president of the C. G. Jung Institute in Zürich soon after it was founded in 1948.

[o] Jung's sister, Gertrud, was also very helpful, mostly, I believe, in typing his manuscripts. She died in 1935.

[p] I hope it is already clear that this necessarily involves projection of elements of the Self which would be disturbing in a practical and objective job such as secretarial work.

imagine herself to be "the perfect secretary." She fitted like a glove into the Jung household and was really an enormous help to him during all those years. She was the age of the younger daughters and had played with the Jung children all her life. Therefore, although she had her own flat in the neighborhood, she was always in Jung's house on the Seestrasse at lunch, was capable of helping Mrs. Jung as well as her husband, and of making no trouble in the family. After all those years of coping with the clerical side of the work as best he could, for Jung a trained secretary, who took charge of his correspondence and manuscripts, introduced an unknown method and order into them, and could always put her hand on anything he asked for, was a totally unexpected joy. It was also pleasant to him that she had her own private life, which was considerably more exciting to her than he was.

Marie-Jeanne was only about twenty when she came to Jung. She was like a cheerful, roly-poly schoolgirl at that time, but unusually intelligent and efficient. Both she and her sister were "very well covered" and she ruefully used to tell a story of a farmer who envied her father his daughters as if they were particularly fat little pigs. She cooked well and was never above setting to and preparing a good meal. Not that this was often necessary; the Jungs had two maids at that time, for there was little or no difficulty in getting good household help in Switzerland until after the Second World War. Nearly everybody liked Marie-Jeanne and she was really a godsend to Jung. Long after she married and left him, he had a dream about her which made him say: "I shall always be related to Marie-Jeanne. She belonged in my life."

It was in the autumn of 1932 that the Indologue, J. W. Hauer, at that time professor for his subject in Tübingen, came to Zürich to give us a seminar on Kundalini Yoga.[q] This was a thrillingly interesting parallel to the process of individuation, but, as always happens when a perfected Indian philosophy is placed before a European audience, we all got terribly out of ourselves and confused. We were used to the unconscious taking us into this process very gradually, every dream revealing a little more of the process, but the East has been working at such meditation techniques for many centuries and has therefore collected far more symbols than we were able to digest. Moreover, the East is too far above everyday reality for us, aiming at Nirvana instead of at our present, three-dimensional life. Jung was confronted with a very disoriented group who had greatly appreciated but had been unable to digest Hauer's brilliant exposition of Kundalini Yoga. When this was over, therefore, Jung devoted the first three lectures of his English seminar to a psychological commentary on Hauer's lectures which got us all back—the richer for the experiences—into ourselves.[r]

---

[q] This seminar was given in both English and German.
[r] This Hauer seminar, like all the English seminars, was recorded with Jung's supplementary lectures and multigraphed for the use of those who had attended. In the autumn of 1930, Mary Foote (a well-known American portrait painter) had taken over the work of editing

In 1932 the city of Zürich awarded Jung its literature prize. This pleased him far more than much more famous honors, such as the honorary doctorates which were increasingly bestowed on him from abroad, because it was the first recognition from his own country. He gave the lecture on the occasion in the Rathaus, an old building by the so-called vegetable bridge (there are open stalls on and around it which sell flowers and vegetables). The audience was large. It was a most impressive occasion.

At the end of the winter semester, 1933, about the middle of February, Jung was extremely tired and felt the need of a complete change and rest. Although his health and strength were good, he was liable to catch influenza, at least once in a winter, and that is always an exhausting disease. Moreover, as I mentioned before, he was unusually "stay at home" during those years, so when Hans Fierz suggested a cruise on the Mediterranean, he accepted at once, as he had in 1920 when Hermann Sigg had suggested North Africa. Professor Fierz had taken a sudden fancy to this trip. He engaged berths for his wife and himself, then discovered that she did not at all like the idea of being so long on the sea. Finding himself with an extra berth, he had offered it to Jung, although he did not know him at all well at that time. Jung was considerably surprised, but then thought the unconscious had really inspired Hans Fierz to offer him just what he required. It also shortened the semester by about a fortnight, which he felt was just what his exhausted state required.

This was the only voyage of the kind that I ever knew Jung to take, for the short nibbles such voyages offer at interesting places, so far unknown to him, such as Athens, were not really his "cup of tea." But he loved the sea, it was a complete rest, with no traveling arrangements to make, and it was really the right thing at the right time. He came back rested and well, having enjoyed himself greatly.

There was a rather surprising epilogue to this journey. Some months before, Jung had been obliged to buy some more land at Bollingen. The new land had a long lake front but was a much narrower piece of land than his own, and therefore nearer to both railroad and road. It bordered Jung's driveway to the road and it would have been disagreeable to him to have it sold as building sites,[s] but, as he complained, the peasant wanted more for it than he felt he could really afford. So, on the Acropolis of all places, he

all the English seminars. At first they were arranged from the notes of several of the class, but very soon Mary Foote was able to persuade Jung to allow a stenogram. She found an excellent stenographer, a Mrs. Koeppel, an English girl married to a Swiss who went on faithfully and steadily reporting every seminar that Jung gave in English. As the written word is necessarily different from the spoken word, Mary Foote gave her whole time to her editing work until the end of the English seminars in 1939. By that time, all the earlier volumes were sold out, and she then gave her time right into her old age to eliminating mistakes and generally improving on her work for a new edition. We owe her a great deal for the preservation of so much material. She died in 1968 at an age well over ninety.

[s] This was before it became difficult or impossible to get a permit to build by the lake.

decided to sell this land to Hans Fierz. Since the latter had been looking for a site to build a vacation house, and such a lovely site by the lake was really a blessing to him, he was willing and glad to give Jung a good price for it. On the other hand, Jung was rather afraid of having people he knew and who amused him so close, for Bollingen, as a place of spiritual concentration, must remain a completely secluded retreat. This difficulty was got over by the arrangement of a flag which Jung always from then on put up when he wished to be entirely undisturbed. Even when it was not up, he made it very clear that he must not be disturbed too often and only at certain times of the day, but when the flag was up, it was never to be passed on any account.

# 11

## Storm Clouds over Europe
## 1933–1937

In 1926 Jung had already become painfully aware of the tension in the atmosphere in Europe. In fact, it is clear, from what I have heard of the Polzeath seminar in 1923, that he had been uneasy about Western man's lack of an impersonal attitude ever since the First World War showed up the inability of the Church to fill this need in the great majority of Europeans. Some dreams of his German patients, as early as 1918, had indeed drawn his attention to the situation in Germany, but he did not know with any certainty where trouble would first break out. Yet from the beginning of my time in Switzerland, he frequently mentioned that he was especially uneasy about Germany, because Christianity had been forced by the sword upon the Germans and therefore their Christian veneer was thinner, their pagan roots much nearer the surface, than elsewhere.

In the early thirties this uneasiness was greatly increased by the dreams of his German patients, some of which were very ominous indeed. For some years before Hitler and his party seized power, Jung had kept an anxious eye on Germany, wondering what form a pagan revival was likely to take.

Some time before the fatal change of German government took place, Jung had accepted an invitation from the C. G. Jung Gesellschaft (the Psychological Club of Berlin) to give a seminar in July, 1933, at the Harnackhaus in Dahlem, near Berlin. Rather unusually, he made no objection to about half a dozen of his pupils going with him to Berlin, for the C. G. Jung Gesellschaft had invited the members of the Psychological Club, Zürich, to attend. So it happened that I drove by myself from Küsnacht to Berlin, thus witnessing the whole of Germany on its feet, a phenomenon which the reawakening of Wotan from his sleep in the unconscious had brought about. I asked Jung before I set out whether he thought I could risk the drive, in view of the state of Germany then, and after careful consideration he replied: "Yes, risk it! Mind you, I don't know what will happen, but it will be an interesting experience."

That was exactly what it was. There were hardly any cars on the road, but the route was literally crowded with hikers, and one could go hardly fifty yards without being asked for a lift. Every time I went to a garage for gasoline I was warned in the strongest terms against giving anyone a lift. Most of the hikers were harmless enough, the garage attendants admitted, but there had been many hold-ups, even stolen cars, so they insisted on my promising to take up *no one* before they would fill my tank! So I drove through that crowd of hikers, feeling a brute, but only twice, when I was asked at garages and so had time to judge the hikers, did I take anyone with me. Both were perfectly harmless and threw an interesting light on the general exodus: "I just think it could not be as bad somewhere else and perhaps I shall be able to find work at Nuremberg,"—or Leipzig, Berlin, or wherever they were going.

Jung himself, with Emma, Toni, and a few others, went by train, and we all met at the Harnackhaus in Dahlem. The meeting of the club opened on the first evening with a lecture by Heinrich Zimmer, the Indologue. Then followed Jung's seminar of six lectures, which took the rest of the week. This was, I believe, only Jung's second meeting with Zimmer, a man who was destined to become a great friend not only of Jung but of us all. We not only met him nearly every year at Eranos (Ascona),[a] but he lectured frequently at the Zürich Psychological Club. He was a charming person, lively, interested in everything, particularly his own subject, but with curiously childlike hands which made Jung anxious about him from the beginning, with only too much reason as it turned out.

That first lecture in Berlin was really a masterpiece. Zimmer held the audience spellbound, a feat, since he was little known at that time and the large audience, which had collected from all over Germany and abroad, had come primarily to hear Jung and were disappointed that he was not lecturing that first Sunday evening. But Zimmer had not only an excellent knowledge and grasp of his subject but also a very creative mind and an extremely lively delivery; in short, he was one of the best lecturers I have ever heard. Curiously enough, although he had an unrivaled knowledge of Sanskrit and of the old Indian texts, he had never been to India, a gap that was to have been filled in the autumn of 1939 when he planned to go there, probably with Peter Baynes, but was—alas, for always—prevented by the outbreak of war.

Although Jung's lectures in themselves were absorbing, I felt more and more uncomfortable as the week went on. I could make little or no contact with anyone at the seminar and even had difficulty in speaking to the people from Zürich whom I knew so well. One morning—it was about the middle of the week—Jung stopped me on the stairs and said: "Take care, you are getting dangerously out of yourself." I knew he was right but had no idea why, until he added: "These people are all in a panic, they are scared stiff and have no idea where all this is leading. I am afraid nothing can save them and that they are heading for inevitable disaster, but at least we will earn the merit of trying to help them as long as we can." That was enough to save my situation, for I realized at once that, since I had not seen their panic, I had become infected, via the unconscious. The next day, seeing that I was once more in myself, Jung had a long talk about the whole thing with an English friend and me.

I had seen from his few words on the stairs that he was taking a dim view of the new government and the prospects for Germany, but now—as he told us—he had still more reason to do so. He had been persuaded by a German doctor[b] that one of the high officials of the new government[c] felt very uncertain of the course of events and was most anxious to consult him, so, though unwillingly, Jung had consented to go to see him. But the moment he got into the room he realized he had been misled, that the official had also been told that Jung wanted to see *him*![d] Jung was angry at such a foolish, time-wasting deception, and left as soon as possible, but with added apprehension concerning the future of Germany in such hands. He never spoke to any of the other leading Nazis, but he felt hopeless from the beginning about the colleagues of such a windbag as he had seen.

He spoke again at greater length of the panic that was gripping the German people and of his fear that nothing could stop a disaster. At least, the only thing that could possibly stop it, he said, would be for enough individuals to become *conscious* of the possessed state they were all in. Therefore, he said, for as long as we could we should give them the benefit of the doubt and help as many as we could to become more conscious. He did this himself mainly via the individual (he had many German patients at that time), but his article in the *Neue Schweizer Rundschau* on "Wotan"[1] was one of his rare efforts to wake up a wider public to the real state of affairs. Jung had been afraid for some years that the thin Christian veneer in Germany was likely to crack. Already, in the Polzeath seminar of 1923, he had deplored the lack of an impersonal attitude, which was thereby present only in the unconscious, from which it was likely to return in archaic and unacceptable forms.

As soon as he read in the newspapers that the Germans were restlessly on the move, wandering from place to place, he was reminded of the

---

[b] I think it was Dr. Otto Curtius, the brother of a former chancellor of Germany, but my memory may be at fault.

[c] As far as I remember, this was Goebbels.

[d] I must say for Dr. Curtius (or whoever it was) that he was not the only one of Jung's admirers who was firmly convinced that he could make *anyone* see reason if only he would talk to them. Jung told me during the war that he had received a number of letters from people imploring him to stop the war by explaining their errors to the dictators.

wanderer Wotan and realized that this was the "archaic symbol" that was certainly going to produce an unacceptable situation in Germany, unless enough individual Germans could become *conscious* of the danger in time. It may be remembered that much later, some years after the Second World War, when Jung was asked if he thought there would be an atomic war, he replied that he thought it depended on "how many people could stand the tension of the opposites in themselves." ᵉ He could also have expressed it in other words (as he did that day in Berlin): it depended on how many people could become *conscious* of the situation in time. He had already learned painfully in Africa how necessary it was for the individual to realize the outer collective tension fully, and he had known before—at least since his "confrontation with the unconscious" or even much earlier—that one *must* first learn to stand that tension in oneself. But that day in Berlin was the first time I realized how much fate itself depended on the individual and why Jung was trying with all his might to wake up the *individual* Germans with whom he came in contact.

After I had written the above from my recollection, I came on a description by Jung of the difficulties he encountered in dealing with the Germans in these early days of the Nazi regime. I quote the most relevant part in full:

When Hitler seized power it became quite evident to me that a mass psychosis was boiling up in Germany. But I could not help telling myself that this was after all Germany, a civilized European nation with a sense of morality and discipline. Hence the ultimate outcome of this unmistakable mass movement still seemed to me uncertain, just as the figure of the Führer at first struck me as being merely ambivalent. It is true that in July 1933, when I gave a series of lectures in Berlin, I received an extremely unfavourable impression both of the behaviour of the Party and of the person of Goebbels. But I did not wish to assume from the start that these symptoms were decisive, for I knew other people of unquestionable idealism who sought to prove to me that these things were unavoidable abuses such as are customary in any great revolution. It was indeed not at all easy for a foreigner to form a clear judgment at that time. Like many of my contemporaries I had my doubts.

As a psychiatrist, accustomed to dealing with patients who are in danger of being overwhelmed by unconscious contents, I knew that it is of the utmost importance, from the therapeutic point of view, to strengthen as far as possible their conscious position and powers of understanding, so that something is there to intercept and integrate the contents that are breaking through into consciousness. These contents

ᵉ See above, page 129 ff.

are not necessarily destructive in themselves, but are ambivalent, and it depends entirely on the constitution of the intercepting consciousness whether they will turn out to be a curse or a blessing.

National Socialism was one of those psychological mass phenomena, one of those outbreaks of the collective unconscious, about which I had been speaking for nearly twenty years. The driving forces of a psychological mass movement are essentially archetypal. Every archetype contains the lowest and the highest, evil and good, and is therefore capable of producing diametrically opposite results. Hence it is impossible to make out at the start whether it will prove to be positive or negative. My medical attitude towards such things counselled me to wait, for it is an attitude that allows no hasty judgments, does not always know from the start what is better, and is willing to give things "a fair trial." Far from wishing to give the beleaguered consciousness its death-blow, it tries to strengthen its powers of resistance through insight, so that the evil that is hidden in every archetype shall not seize hold of the individual and drag him to destruction. The therapist's aim is to bring the positive, valuable, and living quality of the archetype—which will sooner or later be integrated into consciousness in any case—into reality, and at the same time to obstruct as far as possible its damaging and pernicious tendencies. It is part of the doctor's professional equipment to be able to summon up a certain amount of optimism even in the most unlikely circumstances, with a view to saving everything that it is still possible to save. He cannot afford to let himself be too much impressed by the real or apparent hopelessness of a situation, even if this means exposing himself to danger. Moreover, it should not be forgotten that Germany up till the National Socialist era, was one of the most differentiated and highly civilized countries on earth, besides being, for us Swiss, a spiritual background to which we were bound by ties of blood, language, and friendship. I wanted to do everything within my feeble powers to prevent this cultural bond from being broken, for culture is our only weapon against the fearful danger of mass-mindedness.

If an archetype is not brought into reality consciously, there is no guarantee whatever that it will be realized in its favourable form; on the contrary, there is all the more danger of a destructive regression. It seems as if the psyche were endowed with consciousness for the very purpose of preventing such destructive possibilities from happening.[2]

To anyone who, like myself, was with Jung in Berlin in July, 1933, and who saw and heard him frequently during the next twenty-eight years, the libel that Jung was a Nazi is so absurd and so entirely without foundation that it goes against the grain to take it seriously enough to contradict it.

Moreover, for the most part it is believed only by the people who *want* to believe it, and it is always useless to waste energy on them. I learned this in 1914 and I have never forgotten the lesson. When the Germans were sweeping through Belgium and the north of France and neither the French nor the British expeditionary force seemed in the least able to stop them, somehow a rumor started, and swept through England, that Russian reinforcements were being landed in Scotland, and one was even told quite seriously that it *must be true,* because they had been seen stamping the snow off their boots. Undeniable facts, such as the Scotch temperature in August, were absolutely useless, because the people who told the story wanted to believe that huge Russian armies were going to be thrown in to stop the German advance.

The rumor that Jung had any sympathy with the Nazi program is just as absurd. If the one shows incredible ignorance of meteorological facts, the other shows equal ignorance of the elements of Jung's psychology, which lays its whole emphasis on the *individual.* Jung says, for example, of the "isms" (and from the start he always said Nazism and Bolshevism, as it was called then, were two names for the same thing):

> The political and social isms of our day preach every conceivable ideal, but, under this mask, they pursue the goal of lowering the level of our culture by restricting or altogether inhibiting the possibilities of individual development. They do this partly by creating a chaos controlled by terrorism, a primitive state of affairs that affords only the barest necessities of life and surpasses in horror the worst times of the so-called "Dark" Ages. It remains to be seen whether this experience of degradation and slavery will once more raise a cry for greater spiritual freedom.[3]

And in another place:

> The great events of world history, are, at bottom, profoundly unimportant. In the last analysis, the essential thing is the life of the individual. This alone makes history, here alone do the great transformations first take place, and the whole future, the whole history of the world, ultimately spring as a gigantic summation from these hidden sources in individuals. In our most private and most subjective lives we are not only the passive witnesses of our age, and its sufferers, but also its makers. We make our own epoch.[4]

These two short quotations should suffice to show how completely incompatible Jung's psychology is with *any* political movement, and how impossible it is that Jung was ever in sympathy, even for a moment, with anything concerning the Nazi regime.

To return to Berlin in 1933: Jung's seminar was taken down at the time in an unusually good stenogram and multigraphed for the use of the class in almost verbatim form. I have reread my notes with the greatest interest, to remind myself how Jung had dealt with the Germans in their panic at the time. Although he did all he could to open the eyes of the individual to the myth of Wotan that was possessing Germany, he did not speak of it or refer to the political situation *at all,* when addressing his large German audience in Berlin. But he did do his utmost to open their eyes to the reality of the psyche and the inner life. He also spoke a good deal of the danger of being unconscious and of getting caught in *participation mystique* and mass emotion, but he always spoke in general terms and left the individuals in the audience to apply it to their own present situation. He certainly managed to calm his audience. I have never felt a general atmosphere change so quickly, nor have I ever heard such enthusiastic and persistent applause as at the end of the final lecture.

Jung was constantly being asked in Berlin about the extraordinary self-confidence of German youth. This made him feel that he needed to know more of Swiss youth and of how it was developing. By 1933 his own children were rapidly marrying and leaving home, and his grandchildren were still quite small. Therefore, when he got home from Berlin and was settled at Bollingen, he asked a nephew of Toni Wolff, Pablo Naeff, who had been brought up in the Argentine but was then in his last year at the Zürich Freie Gymnasium and on the threshold of the university, to bring a few members of his class to spend a day at Bollingen. Jung gave them both lunch and supper and told them a lot about his psychology, watching their reactions with the greatest interest. Pablo Naeff had asked six other boys and just one girl (Marie-Louise von Franz, who at eighteen years old was thus first introduced to Jung and his psychology) to form the party which visited him at his Tower that day.

It was in August of this same year (1933) that Jung lectured for the first time at the Eranos Tagung in Ascona. These annual meetings were organized by Olga Fröbe-Kaptyn and had been in existence for some years. Judging from the paintings on the walls when we first went there, these early meetings must have been rather Theosophical in character. Jung had no sympathy whatever with Theosophy—for he always felt it speculated in the air, with no empirical foundation—so I do not know how Frau Fröbe originally persuaded him to lecture at Ascona. At all events, his presence so completely changed the character of the meetings that later Frau Fröbe herself used to speak of the Tagung as having begun in 1933. She had built a large lecture hall (which could hold about two hundred people) in the beautiful garden of her villa at Moscia, a hamlet between Ascona and Porto Ronco. It was a perfect setting for such summer gatherings, situated directly on Lake Maggiore, with a delightful bathing place beneath, which

Frau Fröbe generously allowed those who attended the Tagung to use.

The general subject of this first Tagung was "Yoga and Meditation in East and West." Frau Fröbe had persuaded not only Jung to lecture but also Heinrich Zimmer; Erwin Rousselle, who was director of the China Institute in the University of Frankfurt (where he had succeeded Richard Wilhelm in 1930); Ernesto Buonaiuti[f] of Rome; G. R. Heyer, a well-known psychiatrist from Munich[g] and a few others.

Jung lectured extemporaneously that year on the "Empirical Basis of the Individuation Process." It is due to the merit of Toni Wolff that the lecture was preserved in the 1933 *Eranos Jahrbuch*, since she was able to contribute a written version. Jung subsequently produced a "thoroughly revised and enlarged version" and published it in *Gestaltungen des Unbewussten* (Zürich, 1950). This version is translated as *A Study in the Process of Individuation* in the *Collected Works*.[5]

From 1933 until 1939, Jung stayed for the duration of the Tagung at the Monte Verità Hotel, up on the hill at Ascona, with a magnificent view of the lake and mountains. It belonged to Baron von der Heydt, who had a large collection of both Eastern and Western art, which at that time hung mainly in his private villa and in all the rooms of the hotel.[h] The Baron, a strange being,[i] had nothing to do with the management of the hotel, but lived in his own villa and only occasionally put in an appearance. It was a large hotel and in many ways unique, with enormous sitting rooms which more nearly resembled comfortably seated picture galleries, and large balconies and grounds, all with the wonderful view of Lake Maggiore. Many of the other lecturers, as well as Jung, were quartered there by Frau Fröbe.[j] Emma Jung, Toni Wolff, and quite a large number of our group also stayed there; in fact, anyone could who applied early enough for a room. I was lucky enough always to obtain one, from 1933 until 1939 (at the end of which year the hotel shut down for the duration of the war), and used to look forward every year to our ten days in such idyllic surroundings.

There were a great many interesting discussions, of which Jung was always the center, both on the terrace at Eranos after the lectures and at the hotel after meals. These were on a variety of subjects, as well as on the

[f] Professor Buonaiuti, a well-known scholar on all early Christian subjects, who had been excommunicated for heretical views in 1926 and deprived of his professorship for refusing to take the oath to Mussolini in 1931, lectured for many years at Eranos, and those who understood Italian greatly appreciated his lectures; he was also much liked by everyone.

[g] For Dr. G. R. Heyer, see below, page 289.

[h] Most of it is now at the Rietberg Museum in Zürich.

[i] In 1933 he was already separated from his wife, Baroness Vera von der Heydt, who married him while still a very young girl. (He was a very rich banker.) Later she became interested in Jungian psychology, and worked first at the Davidson Clinic in Edinburgh, then as an analyst in London.

[j] I believe Baron von der Heydt to have been very generous to Eranos, and to have charged little or nothing for having the lecturers at his hotel.

current lecture, with the lecturer himself often present. At such times the discussion was mainly between Jung and the lecturer, with a large appreciative audience. There were also what Frau Fröbe used to call "round table discussions," with just her own guests, after meals in her garden. Jung took part in these regularly only after the Hotel Verità closed, that is, during the war and for several years after. The Jungs never went to another hotel but were housed by Frau Fröbe in a lovely apartment she had built over the lecture hall. They had their meals in her villa or more often at the large round garden table which was her dining table whenever the weather was fine. While the Jungs still stayed at the Verità and we had our cars, there were often expeditions to fascinating small Tessin villages where there was usually a hotel with exceptionally good food. The cooking at the Monte Verità itself in those days was often a trial to Jung; being such a *cordon bleu* himself, he hated to see good food (it was all of the best quality) indifferently cooked.

It was also in 1933 that Jung began to lecture again at the Eidgenössische Technische Hochschule in Zürich, for the first time since 1913; this time the lectures continued, almost without interruption, until 1941. They were always on Friday in the late afternoon, and were welcome to all his students; with the English seminar on Wednesday mornings they gave us two lectures from Jung each week. He began these lectures on October 20, 1933, to an enormous audience, for the curiosity of the general public was aroused to see a fellow citizen who had become world famous by that time. To Jung's great disgust, therefore, he had to give his lectures in the Auditorium Maximum, which holds 435 people and was always practically full. As mentioned before, Jung hated large groups except occasionally for single lectures, and he found his mammoth audience every week exceedingly tiring.

I do not know whether he did it on purpose to reduce his audience (although it had that effect, in that he was able to give all his later courses in a smaller hall, still one of the largest, but not the unwieldy Maximum), but his first course of lectures was rather difficult. (He said afterward they were *too* difficult, that the majority of the audience had understood little or nothing.) The first four were a brief survey of the history of psychology, in which he traced its forerunners in the writings of many philosophers, beginning with Descartes (1596–1650) and going through to William James (1842–1910). After this, he demonstrated the empirical background of the psyche; then a description of Justinus Kerner's famous *Clairvoyante of Prevorst*, with the many attendant diagrams showing the psychological background, took seven further lectures. The remaining five lectures were devoted to Flournoy's[k] case of Hélène Smith, who became a famous medium, and a diagram concerning consciousness which, after being applied to the Seherin, the subject of Kerner's work, and Hélène Smith, he extended to

[k] Flournoy of Geneva, see above, page 98.

Freud, to Rockefeller, to the so-called Normal Man; to the Swiss saint Niklaus von der Flüe; to Goethe; and finally to Nietzsche. These lectures were in German. Una Thomas, Elizabeth Welsh (original translator of most of *Essays on Contemporary Events*), and I pooled our notes and translated them into English, for the benefit of Jung's students who did not know German. This was later developed into a multigraphed edition, circulated privately among the various Anglo-Saxon groups.[1]

In 1934 Jung also began a seminar on children's dreams, this time for a much smaller audience, consisting mainly of the students of the E. T. H. and the university. These seminars were all recorded in a German stenogram by Riwkah Schärf-Kluger and are being printed—also in a private edition—in German. They really opened up a new field, for many of the children's dreams on which Jung commented contained a prognosis of the whole future course of the child's life. Dreams where this could be proved were mainly provided by older pupils and friends of Jung, many of whom vividly remembered their earliest dreams.

By 1933 Jung had already found himself on the horns of a dilemma regarding the International General Medical Society for Psychotherapy (and its publication, *Zentralblatt*), of which he was an honorary president. The members of this international society came from many nations, but the Germans had always dominated it and held the principal executive positions. Together with the *"Gleichschaltung"* (unification) forced on every German society by the Nazi government, this situation had become impossible, and the president, Ernst Kretschmer, resigned "on account of the general upheaval." I do not think that Jung had ever consented to be president of anything in the almost twenty years since his resignation from the presidency of Freud's International Association in April, 1914. As we saw then, such posts and the correspondence they involved were anything but congenial to Jung. Nevertheless, the whole world of psychiatry was being threatened in Germany, and Jung saw that the only hope for the existence of the society lay in total reorganization. Clearly, that could not be carried out by a German president; so some "leading members of the society" pressed Jung—he expressed it as "fervently"—to take the chair. He wrote in a newspaper article:

Thus a moral conflict arose for me as it would for any decent man in this situation. Should I, as a prudent neutral, withdraw into security

---

[1] There is some idea of publishing these lectures. They are not complete, as Jung wished to be free to repeat himself, but they cover the most interesting semesters in six volumes. Since they were public lectures, they could be published but we had only a German stenogram (by Rikwkah Schärf-Kluger) for the later volumes. The earlier ones, therefore, represent only a synopsis of the lectures.

this side of the frontier and wash my hands in innocence, or should I—as I was well aware—risk my skin and expose myself to the inevitable misunderstandings which no one escapes who, from higher necessity, has to make a pact with the existing political powers in Germany? Should I sacrifice the interests of science, loyalty to colleagues, the friendship which attaches me to some German physicians, and the living link with the humanities afforded by a common language—sacrifice all this to egotistic comfort and my different political sentiments? I have seen too much of the distress of the German middle class, learned too much about the boundless misery that often marks the life of a German doctor today, know too much about the general spiritual wretchedness to be able to evade my plain human duty under the shabby cloak of political subterfuge. Consequently no other course remained for me but to answer for my friends with the weight of my name and independent position.

As conditions then were, a single stroke of the pen in high places would have sufficed to sweep all psychotherapy under the table. That had to be prevented at all costs for the sake of suffering humanity, doctors, and—last but not least—science and civlization.[6]

At that time—in fact, during most of the thirty-two years I saw Jung—I used to write down afterward all I could remember of my analytical hours, seminars, and especially interesting conversations. I take the following from what he told me when he returned from the next congress of the society, which took place in Bad Nauheim, on May 10–13, 1934. (My notes are dated May 14, 1934, so the congress must have been fresh in his mind.) This was the congress at which Jung presented his scheme for the total reorganization of the society.

Jung struck me as unusually exhausted but on the whole satisfied with the outcome of the meeting. In fact, he said, by far the hardest work had been in the preparation of his proposals; the various points were accepted surprisingly easily at the time. In order to give the society a still more international basis, a system of independent national groups had been decided on, and the society had been freed from German domination by a rule that no national group could muster more than 40 percent of the votes. On the other hand, every national group was entirely free to make its own regulations; but—and this was the most important point—every individual member was also free to become a member of his own national group *or*, if he preferred it, to join the International Society independently as an "individual member." This was the regulation that Jung had been the most anxious about, and he said he had got it through only by mentioning neutral countries, such as Switzerland and Holland, and describing how disagreeable it would be if there were individual doctors who disapproved of their own national regulations and were thus debarred from taking part in the broader views of the whole International Society.

Now, of course, every intelligent doctor present knew that Jung was putting this through for the sake of the German Jewish doctors, who could thus either form a group of their own or simply join the International Society as individual members. He was also inevitably leaving the German group free to make any National Socialist regulation they wished or were forced to adopt, but only, of course, for their own group. Jung said that after the point was passed without opposition from the German group, in fact without the German situation being mentioned at all, there was a lot of speculation among the other nationalities as to why the Germans had not opposed it. The more optimistic thought they were glad to be able to turn a blind eye without loss of face, while others thought they had no idea what they had consented to.

Both before and after this congress, the *Zentralblatt*, the periodical published by the International General Medical Society for Psychotherapy, presented the worst problems. The president, who was automatically its chief editor, had always been a German, and its managing editor and staff were all German; moreover, it was published in Germany. Because of the tyranny of the Nazi government, no one knew what might be ordered next. The society itself was saved by the system of national groups and individual members, but Jung hoped also to forestall Nazi interference in the *Zentralblatt* by giving orders to the managing editor to print *a special issue, "for exclusive circulation in Germany,"* of a political manifesto by the president of the German group (Prof. M. H. Göring, a psychiatrist who was a cousin of the infamous Göring) and told him *on no account* to print it in the general *Zentralblatt*. But to Jung's "surprise and disappointment" the managing editor disobeyed him (he was probably more afraid of the German authorities) and the manifesto appeared in the general *Zentralblatt*. Jung said: "The incident is naturally so incriminating as to put my editorship seriously in question."[7] He was, I know, at this point much tempted to throw over the whole uncongenial job, but he decided to stick to his friends for, as he said, "What is help or friendship that costs nothing?"

There were, unfortunately, many elements in psychiatric circles (both inside and outside the International Society) that were attempting, as Jung summed it up two years later, "to render objective discussion impossible from the start by sowing political suspicion on the one hand and sectarian discord on the other."[8] He then mentioned two of these: "The Freudian spirit of sectarianism put the greatest obstacles in the way of an Austrian group[m] and a political campaign was started in the press by the

[m] It must be remembered this was some years before Germany annexed Austria.

corresponding elements in Switzerland." This latter campaign was begun on February 27, 1934, by just such an element, a Swiss doctor and psychiatrist, G. Bally, who wrote a letter to the *Neue Zürcher Zeitung* which began:

> The political situation in Germany obliged every learned society to undertake a reorganization which is referred to there by the word *Gleichschaltung* [unification]. The essential point consists in the expulsion of all members who are not pure German nationals and of all Jews. The General Medical Society for Psychotherapy has also been unified in this way.

As this, of course, applied *only* to the German group and *not* to the International Society, Dr. Bally quickly switched from the society to its *Zentralblatt*, which had been made into a genuinely suspicious document by the managing editor's disastrous blunder. It is possible that at the time Dr. Bally wrote his letter, he did not know the real circumstances, but if this was the case, why did he not admit it later? Anyway, he wrote literally: "Dr. C. G. Jung (Küsnacht, Zürich) admits to being the editor of this *gleichgeschaltete* [unified] periodical. A Swiss, therefore, is the editor of the official organ of a society which—according to Dr. M. H. Göring, a leading member—expects all its members before they write or speak—to have carefully and scientifically studied Adolf Hitler's fundamental book *Mein Kampf* and accepted it as their foundation."[9] Or, as we would say, "accepted it as their Bible."

Jung wrote a reply[10] to the same paper a fortnight later. He began: "I wish to discuss no surmises with Dr. Bally but prefer to report the facts," and then went on to do so objectively, particularly stressing that his presidency (with its accompanying editorship) was "*not* of the *German* but of the *International* Society as is stated in the issue from which Dr. Bally quotes." This mistake (or misrepresentation) of Dr. Bally's has been particularly long-lived. I saw it stated, in an otherwise friendly—if somewhat uninformed—article about Jung in an American periodical some ten years ago, that one could not deny that Jung was swept away into sympathy for the Nazi movement at its start because one could not otherwise explain his having accepted, and kept after the attacks on the Jews had begun, the presidency of the *German* Medical Psychiatric Society.[11] The author went on to mention a "hardly less reprehensible Freudian parallel" when, according to Ernest Jones, "the Freudian group, with the Master's consent, allowed their Jewish members to resign in order to preserve analysis in Nazi Germany." It is quite evident that this author is not one of those who *wanted* to believe such a libel and that he genuinely believed it was the *German* society. There are many like him, and I

therefore go into more detail than this distasteful subject warrants.
To quote a little more of Jung's "Rejoinder to Dr. Bally":[12]

Since the German section of the International Society *has* to be *gleichgeschaltet*, and since, moreover, the *Zentralblatt* is published in Germany, there naturally arose so many difficulties that more than once we doubted the possibility of a reorganization. One of these concerned the oath of allegiance and the "purity of political sentiment" required of the German Society. We in Switzerland can hardly understand such a thing, but we are immediately in the picture if we transport ourselves back three or four centuries to a time when the Church had totalitarian presumptions. Barbed wire had not been invented then, so there were probably no concentration camps, instead the Church used large quantities of faggots.

The second point of which Dr. Bally accused Jung, and which has also led to a particularly long-lived libel, was anti-Semitism. Here he based his accusations on what Jung had written in his "Editorial" to the same number of the *Zentralblatt*.[13] Jung said:

. . . It will therefore be the primary task of the *Zentralblatt* to give impartial appreciation to all objective contributions, and to promote an over-all view which will do greater justice to the basic facts of the human psyche than has been the case up till now. The differences which actually do exist between Germanic and Jewish psychology and which have long been known to every intelligent person are no longer to be glossed over, and this can only be beneficial to science. In psychology more than in any other science there is a "personal equation" disregard of which falsifies the practical and theoretical findings. At the same time I should like to state expressly that this implies no depreciation of Semitic psychology, any more than it is a depreciation of the Chinese to speak of the peculiar psychology of the Oriental.

Dr. Bally quoted this passage in part, then not only denied that any such differences exist, but accused Jung of opportunism in bringing up the subject at that particular moment in time when it would exactly suit the Nazi book. The editor of the *Neue Zürcher Zeitung* in introducing Jung's "Rejoinder to Dr. Bally" even went so far as to assert that Jung began to acknowledge racial psychology only at this particular moment.[14]
To dispose of the last accusation first, I must state that from the beginning of my time in Zürich Jung always laid great emphasis on the necessity of realizing the differences in racial and national psychology. I remember, for example, telling him once of something Toni Wolff had done in 1929 in England. He found it very amusing and added: "However could

she do such a thing in England? Has she no idea of the difference between English and Swiss psychology?'' He often mentioned the great importance of realizing these differences in his seminars and writings. For example, in 1918, Jung wrote:

> Christianity split the Germanic barbarian into an upper and a lower half, and enabled him, by repressing the dark side, to domesticate the brighter half and fit it for civilization. But the lower, darker half still awaits redemption and a second spell of domestication. Until then, it will remain associated with the vestiges of the prehistoric age, with the collective unconscious, which is subject to a peculiar and ever-increasing activation. As the Christian view of the world loses its authority, the more menacingly will the "blond beast" be heard prowling about in its underground prison, ready at any moment to burst out with devastating consequences. When this happens in the individual it brings about a psychological revolution, but it can also take a social form.
>
> In my opinion this problem does not exist for the Jews. The Jew already had the culture of the ancient world and on top of that has taken over the culture of the nations amongst whom he dwells. He has two cultures, paradoxical as that may sound. He is domesticated to a higher degree than we are, but he is badly at a loss for that quality in man which roots him to the earth and draws new strength from below. This chthonic quality is found in dangerous concentration in the Germanic peoples. Naturally the Aryan European has not noticed any signs of this for a very long time, but perhaps he is beginning to notice it in the present war;[n] and again, perhaps not. The Jew has too little of this quality—where has he his own earth underfoot? The mystery of earth is no joke and no paradox. One only needs to see how, in America, the skull and pelvis measurements of all the European races begin to indianize themselves in the second generation of immigrants. That is the mystery of the American earth.[15]

And in 1928 he wrote, in *The Relations Between the Ego and the Unconscious:* "A collective attitude naturally presupposes this same collective psyche in others. But that means a ruthless disregard not only of individual differences but also of differences of a more general kind within the collective psyche itself, as for example differences of race." In a footnote to this sentence he added:

> Thus it is a quite unpardonable mistake to accept the conclusions of a Jewish psychology as generally valid. Nobody would dream of

[n] The First World War.

taking Chinese or Indian psychology as binding upon ourselves. The cheap accusation of anti-Semitism that has been levelled at me on the ground of this criticism is about as intelligent as accusing me of an anti-Chinese prejudice. No doubt, on an earlier and deeper level of psychic development, where it is still impossible to distinguish between an Aryan, Semitic, Hamitic or Mongolian mentality, all human races have a common collective psyche. But with the beginning of racial differentiation essential differences are developed in the collective psyche as well. For this reason we cannot transplant the spirit of a foreign race *in globo* into our own mentality without sensible injury to the latter, a fact which does not, however, deter sundry natures of feeble instinct from affecting Indian philosophy and the like.[16]

These quotations should suffice to prove beyond doubt that since 1918, if not before, Jung had been emphasizing the importance of realizing the great differences that exist not only between the Jewish and Aryan races but between *all* races and *all* nations. We have tried to keep this fundamental characteristic of Jung's psychology in mind from the beginning, through frequent references to the diagram on page 17. We must now consider a little of what he said on this subject in March, 1934, in his "Rejoinder to Dr. Bally":

Admittedly I was incautious, so incautious as to do the very thing most open to misunderstanding at the present moment: I have tabled the Jewish question. This I did deliberately. My esteemed critic appears to have forgotten that the first rule of psychotherapy is to talk in the greatest detail about all the things that are the most ticklish and dangerous, and the most misunderstood. The Jewish problem is a regular complex, a festering wound, and no responsible doctor could bring himself to apply methods of medical hush-hush in this matter. . . .[17] If I were in the position—as Dr. Bally supposes me to be—of not being able to point to a single difference between the two psychologies, it would amount to exactly the same thing as not being able to make plausible the difference between the peculiarities of the English and the Americans, or the French and the Germans. I have not invented these differences; you can read about them in innumerable books and newspapers; as jokes they are on everybody's tongue, and anyone who fails to see that there are one or two psychological differences between Frenchmen and Germans must have come from the back of beyond and know nothing about our European madhouse. Are we really to believe that a tribe which has wandered through history for several thousand years as "God's chosen people" was not put up to° such an idea by some quite special psychological peculiarity? If no differences exist, how do we recognize Jews at all?[18] . . . All levelling produces hatred and venom in the suppressed and misjudged; it prevents any broad human understanding. All branches of mankind unite in one stem—yes, but what is a stem without separate branches? Why this ridiculous touchiness when anybody dares to say anything about the psychological difference between Jews and Christians? Every child knows that differences exist.[19] . . . I express no value-judgments, nor do I intend any veiled ones. I have been engaged for many years on the problem of imponderable differences which everybody knows and nobody can really define. They are among the most difficult problems of psychology and probably for that reason are a taboo area which none may enter on pain of death. To many people it is an insult if one credits them with a special psychological idiosyncrasy, and in dealing with parties and nations one must be even more careful. That is why any investigation of these imponderables is so extraordinarily difficult, because , as well as doing his work, the investigator has to perform a grotesque egg-balancing dance around highly charged sensibilities. It is high time the practising psychologist understood more about these psychic imponderabilia, because from them arise a good half of the things that go wrong in the world. Anyone who could define the nature of these imponderable differences would truly have gazed deep into the mystery of the human soul. For my part, I do not belong to those savants who concern themselves exclusively with what is known already—an extremely useful activity, no doubt—but prefer to sniff around territories where nothing is yet known.

Consequently I am amused to find myself cast in the role of the nitwit who is unable to spot a single difference between Jews and Christians. It is, in spite of Bally, an undoubted fact that the difference exists, just as water existed before the chemist discovered $H_2O$; but it cannot be grasped as yet, because all the views that have been put forward so far are unsatisfactory.[20]

Jung ended his answer to Dr. Bally:

It is, I frankly admit, a highly unfortunate and disconcerting coincidence that my scientific programme should, without any assistance of mine and against my express wish, have been lined up with a

---

° "Put up to" appears to be a very unfortunate translation. The German is: *"zu einem Gedanken ermächtigt wäre."* *"Ermächtigt"* means *authorized,* which seems to me to give the meaning far better.

political manifesto. But an event of this kind, although regrettable in itself, often has the consequence of ventilating problems which would otherwise be sedulously avoided.[21]

Although Jung said that it is necessary "to perform a grotesque egg-balancing dance around highly charged sensibilities," he was always a bit too optimistic about hoping that reason would prevail. He undoubtedly still told himself at the time that Germany was "a civilized European nation with a sense of morality and discipline," and he still hoped that the Germans might come to their senses regarding the Jews, if they could only be made to see and understand the racial differences that lead to all such misunderstandings. It was much too optimistic, for he had already realized the Nazis were projecting their shadow on the Jews and therefore were not in a position to see the real Jew at all. How anyone could see this as anti-Semitism is beyond my understanding. When I remember how exhausted Jung was when he came back from the reorganization of the International General Medical Society for Psychotherapy and how pleased he was that, as he optimistically hoped then, the Jewish doctors had one society at least where they were fully accepted and free, and how many Jews were always highly valued members of our Zürich group, I am forced to the conclusion that here also it is mainly, if not entirely, a matter of people *wanting* to believe a rumor. Jung also took endless trouble later to help Jewish emigrants from Germany to settle in other countries. Many leading Jews—such as Dr. Gerhard Adler of London—have themselves publicly denied that there was any truth in the rumor, apparently entirely without effect, so it seems useless to say more.

Dr. Bally's letter created little stir at the time, and that little quieted down completely after Jung explained the facts of the matter in his "Rejoinder to Dr. Bally." But the poison evidently went on smoldering underground, only rarely sending a spark to the surface during the next eleven years. After the war when feeling ran so high and the worst thing that could be said of anyone was to accuse him of being a Nazi, the temptation proved too overpowering to those who wanted to discredit Jung. They revived all of Dr. Bally's mistakes and ignored Jung's reply and the real facts of the matter. When these attacks are not anonymous, they, sad to say, can usually be traced to other psychologists, such as the Freudians, who seem to be suffering from what the Germans call *"Futterneid."*[p]

Jung was usually completely detached from the whole storm. His No. 1 personality was indeed from time to time most understandably and

___

[p] This apt German expression can only lamely be translated into English as "envy" or "jealousy."

humanly indignant that such lies could be so peristently circulated about him; but his No. 2 personality was completely untouched.

In May, 1934, Jung began his English seminar on Nietzsche's *Zarathustra*. At the end of the previous term, in March, 1934, the class had been asked to give its opinion as to whether Jung should continue with the series of visions, which had been the theme of the seminars since the autumn of 1930, or whether he should change to *Zarathustra*. The class voted for the latter. Jung, who was of course principally concerned, took the vacation to consider whether he would venture on this long and difficult book. At the beginning of the summer semester, however, he announced that he had decided to accept the vote of the class, but warned us that the responsibility was on our own heads. *Zarathustra* would certainly not be easier than the visions, for it was a "hell of a confusion" and extraordinarily difficult. Jung said that he had broken his head over certain problems and that it would be very hard to elucidate the book from a psychological angle.

Jung had often reminded us that, although we were fortunately still able to live our ordinary lives, we should never forget the storm clouds hanging over Europe. He had also mentioned that he thought Nietzsche's idea of the Superman was the direct forerunner of the German idea that they were the *Herrenmenschen* (the Master- or Supermen), so it is possible that the vote of the class was swayed by the hope that we would get more understanding of and insight into the strange events that were taking place so near us, just over the German border. But, as in Berlin, Jung seldom or never mentioned the outer situation directly. Nevertheless, since a good many Germans attended the English seminars in those years, it is probable that he hoped that the study of this prototype would help to produce the consciousness he thought was the only hope of averting the catastrophe he had felt looming so ominously in Berlin the year before. At all events, Jung faithfully continued to "elucidate the work from a psychological point of view" until the end of the English seminar in February, 1939.

We reached the episode of the fate of the rope-dancer in the summer term of 1934. As he was dying, Zarathustra said to him: "Thy soul will be dead even sooner than thy body." This, Jung said, was the "prophetic word," for—as is well known—Nietzsche's soul was dead before his body. As Jung noted then: "His soul died in 1889, when his general paralysis began, but he lived on for eleven years more. His body lived, but his soul was dead. So the fate of that rope-dancer symbolizes Nietzsche himself." Right through this long seminar Jung made it abundantly clear that Nietzsche had become insane because of his identification with the Superman. And right through these years the German was being urged by his Führer to regard himself as the Superman, destined to rule mankind. Nietzsche's rope-dancer symbolized only too certainly the fate not only of Nietzsche, but of the whole of Nazi Germany, a fate of which Jung already had a foreboding when he talked to us that day in Berlin.

The general subject for the lectures at Eranos that year was *"Ostwestliche Symbolik und Seelenführung"* (Symbolism and Psychogogic Methods in East and West), and Jung lectured on "The Archetypes of the Collective Unconscious." From the beginning, although he allowed his lectures to be printed in the *Eranos Jahrbuch* as he had delivered them, Jung reserved the right to go on working on his papers later, to extend them and, in their new form, to reprint them as he wished. Therefore, many of his most important papers, even of his books, appeared in earlier, briefer form as Eranos lectures. Very often, still earlier versions had been given at the Zürich Psychological Club. This lecture on "The Archetypes of the Collective Unconscious" was given first at Eranos, then extended to two lectures on the same subject at the club in November of the same year (1934). The final form of this lecture appeared in *Von den Wurzeln des Bewusstseins (Concerning the Roots of Consciousness)* in 1954. It gave its name to the whole first part of the ninth volume of the English *Collected Works*.[22]

The 1934 Tagung was considerably longer than the year before, and several new lecturers were added to the original seven, who all lectured again. I will refer to only two of the new Eranos lecturers in 1934: J. W. Hauer (whose Zürich seminar on Kundalini Yoga has already been mentioned)[q] and the well-known Martin Buber. Each of the lecturers took the general theme for the year from the point of view of his own field of study.

I think 1934 was the first year that several motorists in the Zürich group drove over the Gotthard in their own cars, keeping in touch with each other at various *rendezvous* along the way. Until World War II deprived us of gasoline, this became a sort of yearly event. Jung usually preferred to start in the afternoon, to drive only as far as Hospental and to spend the night there, driving on the next morning, but sometimes we drove straight through. In 1933 Toni Wolff had found her large Chrysler terribly unwieldly in the narrow Tessin Lanes, so in 1934 she suggested we should take only one car (hers as a rule, but sometimes it was mine) and drive in turns. As I had driven a great deal longer than Toni or either of the Jungs, I found myself their chauffeur in the dark or on the most difficult roads, and thus began to drive Jung about, an activity that was to increase (particularly after he gave up driving himself) right up to one month before his death, and to which I owe a great many of our most interesting conversations. In this way I was able to see him without wasting any of his precious working time.

q See above, page 206.

Jung had been puzzling for years about the meaning of a dream (circa 1926) in which he had found himself shut into a courtyard, after driving across the Lombard Plain in the horse-drawn wagon of a peasant, who exclaimed, as the gates clanged to behind them, "Now we are caught in the seventeenth century."[23] Jung had not come to any satisfactory interpretation of this dream, however, during the subsequent years. His interest in alchemy, to which he realized only much later that the dream referred, began quite independently. In 1928, although he was fascinated by *The Secret of the Golden Flower*, he did not realize that it was an alchemistic text. It must have stirred some chord in him, however, for he then asked a Munich bookseller to notify him whenever he found an alchemical book. In this way he bought the 1553 edition of the *Artis Auriferae*—which contains the "Rosarium Philosophorum" that he was later to quote so often[24]—but, except for looking at the pictures, he did not attempt to read it for over two years, dismissing it at first as "nonsense."

The earliest date I can give for certain as the beginning of his serious study of alchemy is the spring of 1934. Marie-Louise von Franz had a strikingly alchemistic dream around Christmas, 1933, and by the spring she had plucked up her courage to ask Jung for an appointment in order to understand it. He told her that he had definitely made up his mind to study alchemy and that she could have the analysis she longed for but could not afford if she would pay him by looking up some of the Greek and Latin texts which he needed to understand the confused web of alchemy. He told her that his Latin, and particularly his Greek, were rusty from lack of use, and that to look through all the necessary Greek and Latin texts would take too much of his time. He told her the volumes he needed to know and instructed her to go right through them and pick out the bits that were "symbolically interesting." She was terrified, for at that time she knew nothing of symbols. But she turned out to have what amounted to a genius for picking out the right bits, thus saving him untold time and trouble. She had just entered the university and was studying classics, but she had already been distinguished at the gymnasium for her Latin and Greek. Jung told her that when she was at Bollingen the summer before, he had already had a curious irrational feeling that she had something to do with alchemy.

As Marie-Louise brought in her reports of the required volumes, he soon realized what his dream of the seventeenth century had referred to (for by far the majority of the most interesting medieval treatises were written in the seventeenth century), and also that his study of alchemy was a fateful thing which it was impossible for him to avoid. At first it all seemed a strange impenetrable labyrinth, but gradually he began to see light and to see that "analytical psychology coincided in a most curious way with alchemy."[25] In alchemy, where the concern for the wholeness of man, so to speak, had been preserved as the Church became more and more one-sided, he had at last found the missing link between his own "confrontation with the unconscious" and the Gnostics.

I will leave the full description of Jung and alchemy to Dr. von Franz, for she was his collaborator in alchemy from 1934 until his last alchemical book, the *Mysterium Coniunctionis,* of which she wrote the third volume.[26] Jung said in his Foreword: "For Parts I and II I am responsible, while my co-worker, Dr. Marie-Louise von Franz, is responsible for Part III. We have brought out the book jointly, because each author has participated in the work of the other."[27] Jung originally planned to publish all three volumes under both names. To his considerable disappointment—because it would have been a continuation of an old alchemical tradition of the adept and his *soror mystica* working together—there was such a jealous uproar that he sent for his co-worker and asked her permission to give up the plan, since he felt his health would hardly stand the foolish turmoil. During his old age everyone who was really fond of him put his health above every other consideration, so Marie-Louise consented at once, though also naturally with considerable disappointment.

This is an anticipation indeed, for the foregoing happened just before Jung's eightieth birthday, for which the first volume appeared, but I mention it here to show why I leave this theme almost entirely to Marie-Louise and to show how highly qualified she is to deal with it.[28] It is true that Jung did talk to me quite a bit about it while he was doing his research on alchemy, but in a different connection, for I know little Latin and no Greek, so could be of no use whatever in this respect. It was of the "curious coincidence" between alchemy and analytical psychology that Jung spoke when he talked to me at the time. (I should mention here that Jung frequently spoke with his pupils about his current researches, and to each probably of a different aspect.) The fact gradually became increasingly clear to him that what he called "the process of individuation"—first recognized as a natural process of the human psyche in himself and his patients during his "confrontation with the unconscious"—was *the* central underlying archetypal pattern. Therefore it was always uncovered in every honest and sustained attempt to establish a relationship to "something infinite." In *Memories* he said that this is "the telling question" of every human life since the infinite is the only "thing which really matters" and prevents us from "fixing our interest upon futilities."[29]

Of course, it took many years of study before he recognized this underlying fact in alchemy. At first he felt well and truly lost in the puzzling language of the texts, although he soon realized how wrong he had been to dismiss them as "nonsense." In spite of himself, they "persistently intrigued" him, and he knew he must go into it all more thoroughly. Then it dawned on him that the alchemists were talking in symbols—his old acquaintances—and at that moment the doors clanged to behind him, as in his dream, and every spare moment was used in studying alchemy. One wonders how he could possibly have found the time in these particularly full years—it was not until the autumn of 1936 that he drastically reduced his practice and discontinued the English seminar for the whole winter. He was, however, so fascinated that I do not think he could have continued his analytical work and his lecturing had he not pursued this overwhelming interest in alchemy. It overworked him, but it also imbued him with new life and energy.

Quite at sea at first as to what these queer old texts were really driving at, he made an enormous card index of recurring phrases, with cross-references, the sort of work that would have employed most people for at least a year working at it full-time; he made it in the sparse, spare time left after eight or nine hours' analytical work each day. Of course, he also worked on it in the holidays, but it got more and more difficult to transport all the necessary books to Bollingen.

During these years I went to Bollingen regularly, at least once every holiday, in order to do a pencil drawing of Jung (facing page 202). I had never thought of making such a drawing, but during a dinner at the Sonnenberg, early in 1932, Jung quite unexpectedly leaned across the table and asked me *when* I intended to do a portrait of him. (I must mention that at that time Jung was anxious for me to continue my profession as an artist, although he changed his mind later.) Thus challenged, I took the first opportunity to discuss possibilities with him, for I was afraid of taking more time than he could afford. On the other hand, I was willing to dispense with regular sittings and to work while he read or wrote. The drawing was done only at Bollingen and he was always occupied with his own work while I drew. He was naturally in an introverted mood and I thus drew a side of him that few people knew. When it was finished (for his sixtieth birthday, in July, 1935) he said that although he liked it— "because it had something that none of the other portraits have"—it would never be popular, and I must be prepared for a great deal of negative criticism. He explained that people were used to his being there *for them*, and I had drawn him in a totally withdrawn mood. He said they would feel almost rejected by him when they looked at it and it would thus be only natural for them to dislike it. I sometimes found it difficult to proceed with it and at such times Jung took over and drew for a short time on it himself!

In 1935 Jung attained the age of sixty. Although there was a constant stream of congratulatory telegrams, presents, and letters, it was still possible for him to celebrate the day at Bollingen with his family. From his seventieth birthday on—every five years—this became impossible, and he was forced to be in Küsnacht and to attend large celebrations. The Swiss are very keen on such anniversaries and make much more of them than do the Anglo-Saxons.

Toni Wolff—assisted by Linda Fierz and Emil Medtner—brought out a *Festschrift* in quite a large volume for this sixtieth birthday. Since Jung had little or no curiosity about mundane matters, he had no idea that anything of the kind was in preparation and was genuinely astonished when a copy, beautifully bound in leather, was laid on his pillow the evening before his birthday. Toni Wolff's long contribution, with which the book opened, was in my opinion the best thing in it.[r] Naturally, it was a great pleasure to Jung that she had made such an effort to do the creative work he was always so anxious for her to do, but which she was unfortunately usually too willing to neglect. Although indeed she did so only in order to save him work in analysis, I think it was a mistake and that she might have remained with us much longer[s] if she had developed her creative potential more. At all events, in later years, Jung would allow no pupil to remain in his vicinity unless he devoted most of his energy to creative work in some form or other.

The subject at the Eranos Tagung that year was much the same as in 1934: "Psychogogic Methods in East and West." Jung's paper was on "Dream Symbols of the Process of Individuation," the first version of what later became the second part of his book *Psychology and Alchemy*, under the title of "Individual Dream Symbolism in Relation to Alchemy." There were not so many lecturers as in 1934, which had proved to be almost too many. There was a single appearance that year by Robert Eisler (author of *Orpheus, the Fisher*), who was a most entertaining person and who told us several stories that really amused Jung.

This year of his sixtieth birthday also contained a great pleasure at Bollingen for Jung. It was four years since his last addition to the Tower, and as he wrote in *Memories*:

> the desire arose in me for a piece of fenced-in land. I needed a larger space that would stand open to the sky and to nature. And so . . . I added a courtyard and a loggia by the lake, which formed a fourth element that was separated from the unitary threeness of the house. Thus a quaternity had arisen, four different parts of the building, and, moreover, in the course of twelve years.

Perhaps this was the greatest improvement of all to the seclusion of the house. Before it was built, though complete in itself, the house opened straight onto open ground on the shore of the lake. Although the number of boats that passed was almost negligible, yet it had been impossible to sit anywhere out of doors that was not open to the lake. After this addition,

[r] Albert Oeri's "A Few Recollections of Jung's Youth" was by far the most amusing.
[s] Toni Wolff died in her sixty-fifth year, in March, 1953.

C. G. JUNG

*A pencil drawing by Barbara Hannah*

there was not only a walled courtyard with two doors, which were kept locked, but also a raised loggia[t] with an open fireplace where Jung in future did most of his cooking on summer nights. The loggia could be open, with a lovely view of lake and mountains, though a low wall and its height from the ground screened it from the view of passing boats, or when there was wind or he felt specially introverted, there was a great sailcloth curtain that gave it all the protection of a tent.

Jung enjoyed this courtyard and loggia immensely from the first and also used the latter sometimes when he felt like working out of doors, but he never regretted those twelve years without it. He even told Marie-Louise von Franz, when she was building her Tower, in which he took a lively interest, on no account to build an outside loggia until she had lived for some years in her house. "It takes that time," he said, "to see what you really want and to know how to build exactly the right thing." His own certainly justified the delay, for it was exactly right. The courtyard also provided much more privacy from visitors, who were now obliged to knock at the courtyard door. There was a small, almost invisible window, so the visitor could be inspected before the door was opened. Unless he was there alone Jung never went to this outer door himself.

One cannot speak of Bollingen without mentioning the Kuhn family, who lived in a house on the road, not quite half a mile from the Tower. The eldest boy, Hans, played quite a role in the life at Bollingen, since he frequently helped Jung with the heavy work, such as felling and cutting up trees. He was absolutely devoted to Jung and even now cannot speak of the days at the Tower without his eyes filling with tears. About 1932 Jung got him the position of chauffeur and general factotum to Mrs. Alice Crowley, one of his American pupils who settled in Zürich, and as Jung got older, Mrs. Crowley was increasingly generous in lending him Hans. He was a simple-minded, faithful soul, and he often played a positive role in Jung's dreams.

Jung always got on well with peasants and, as he was getting older, he occasionally had Hans to stay with him, in order to help with the heavier work, when he wanted to be alone at the Tower. Hans was absolutely no disturbance to Jung, and Toni Wolff also fitted in with him well. Emma Jung sometimes complained that he was lazy, except when directly helping his idol, and much later Ruth Bailey also had something to complain of in that respect. But on the whole he was the right person in the right place and a real addition to the Bollingen life.

In the autumn of 1935, Jung went to London to give five lectures at the Tavistock Clinic to an audience of about two hundred, mostly doctors. These lectures, although *extempore* have been published in book form as

---

[t] Jung built a roof over this loggia later, in 1951.

*Analytical Psychology, Its Theory and Practice.* [30] Dr. E. A. Bennet began his excellent Foreword with the following words:

In 1935 the late Professor C. G. Jung, then in his sixtieth year, gave a course of five lectures in London to about two hundred doctors, at the Tavistock Clinic.[u] A report of the lectures and the succeeding discussions was recorded in a typescript volume edited by Mary Barker and Margaret Game, and this is now published in book form.

Jung's work was well known to his audience but few had heard him speak. His lectures attracted a representative group of psychiatrists and psychotherapists of every "school" as well as many from the mental hospitals and a sprinkling of general practitioners. His custom was to lecture for an hour and follow on with a discussion for a second hour. Right from the start his unusual material, his informal manner, and a surprising fluency in colloquial English, established an easy and stimulating atmosphere, and the discussions ran far beyond the appointed time. In addition to his fascination as a speaker Jung selected his words with care and he had the knack of saying precisely what he meant in comprehensible form, free from doctrinaire jargon.

Both Toni Wolff and I attended these lectures and worked afterward on the typescript, which was multigraphed at the time. Mere words can give more than a dim idea of the living content of the lectures and discussions and their effect on the audience, particularly on doctors from more or less opposing schools, who, as the week went on, seemed to drop all doctrinaire theories from fascinated interest in the empirical facts. Doctrinaire theories have a nasty way of reestablishing themselves later, but for the time they became irrelevant in face of the new facts which Jung brought, and above all in the face of his own wholeness, convincing integrity, and inimitable humor. Laughter helps more than anything to bring a group together.

I had just bought a new car which had to be driven five hundred miles in order to have its first service before leaving England, so Jung used it freely while he was in London. Thus for the first time I witnessed how much at home he was everywhere in England and how well he fitted in. He once told me that when he first went there, he had one of his strongest feelings of *déjà vu*. He felt we had not enough evidence to have a definite opinion concerning reincarnation, but he said then, "If I have lived before, I am sure I was at one time an Englishman."

The next year, 1936, was also exceedingly full. It must be remembered that all these years when he was studying alchemy so intensively he was

---

[u] Founded in 1920 as the Tavistock Square Clinic, its name was changed in 1931 to the Institute of Medical Psychology, and a few years later this became the Tavistock Clinic.

keeping up, almost without a break, his English seminar at the Psychological Club, his lectures and seminar on children's dreams at the E.T.H., and never giving less than four to nine hours[v] analysis a day. He also never failed to appear at Eranos during those years, and I marvel how he did it when I remember how at peace with himself—almost at leisure—he seemed all the time. I think all of his pupils who have gone on with their process of individuation since his death and got old enough to realize the full value of time must now regret more than anything else how they often worried him unnecessarily with futilities, for time, I am quite sure, was more valuable to him than anything else, especially in those years. I remember Toni Wolff once arranging an auction at the Psychological Club to raise momcy for some important project. All club members gave things of value to be auctioned, and Jung was persuaded to give an hour of his time. He then bid for it himself and did not give up until it was well over a hundred francs! Though Jung had a good attitude to money, he never threw it about, so his bidding convinced the members of the club of what a high value he set on his own time.

The summer of 1936 was further burdened with preparations for lectures he was to give on a visit to America in the autumn of that year, and at Eranos in August he spoke on alchemy for the first time to a wider audience. He had, it is true, given an earlier formation in three lectures at the Zürich Psychological Club in the late autumn of 1935, but it was still difficult for him to speak on the subject, since neither he nor Marie-Louise von Franz had yet had the time to go through anything like all the texts they had collected, and he still complained that he often felt lost in the impenetrable labyrinth of the alchemical texts.

The general subject of the Eranos Tagung that year was "Formations of the Idea of Redemption in East and West." Jung gave what the Eranos Index describes as four lectures on "The Idea of Redemption in Alchemy"; but, if my memory does not fail me, he gave these in double hours on two mornings of the Tagung to a specially enthralled audience, for it was the first time that most of the people had realized that alchemy was infinitely more than a foolish medieval attempt to make gold. The final version of these lectures forms Part III of Jung's book *Psychology and Alchemy*,[31] first published in 1944. This was altogether a very interesting Tagung at Eranos. I remember particularly vividly how interested we all were in the lecture of a French professor, H. C. Puech, on the "Concept of Redemption in Manicheism."[32] I think this was the only time that Professor Puech lectured at Eranos.

---

[v] He kept up a steady eight hours a day, although of course this had to be reduced on his seminar and lecture days, and was sometimes increased when he could not get through his absolutely necessary work.

During his summer holiday in 1936, Jung found a dead snake, with a dead fish sticking out of its mouth, a most curious parallel to his thoughts at the time. He was so much struck by this synchronistic event, that he carved the incident on the wall of the courtyard in Bollingen.

Jung's idea was that the serpent represented the pagan spirit, which is emerging so strongly in our times, and that it is trying to eat the Christian spirit, represented by the fish. The new reconciling symbol, for which the alchemists were searching, will be born from these two opposites.

Toward the end of August, Jung went to the United States again, this time accompanied by his wife. Emma Jung had not had much (or any) desire to travel while her children were young, for she was an exceptionally devoted mother and always very anxious concerning her children's welfare. But as they got older, Jung increasingly encouraged her to develop a life of her own, for he knew better than anyone else how valuable undivided interest is to small children, and yet how this very devotion becomes destructive as soon as the children are old enough to form their own lives. Therefore, much encouraged by her husband, Emma Jung learned both Latin and Greek, when her children were all in school, and she was thus very valuable to him in the scientific side of his work. Now he encouraged her to enlarge her horizon still more and to go with him to America. I remember that she was rather in two minds about it herself, but eventually decided to go.

Jung always went to America, in fact, wherever he went overseas, by ship. Air travel was of course much less usual in those days than now, and although Jung once—I think it was in 1935—flew back from England, he never liked the idea of flying, for he felt one got there too quickly, thus leaving pieces of one's psyche behind! He even advised his pupils much later, in the fifties, when flying had become cheaper and much easier, on no account to go to America by air, for they would find they had left bits of themselves behind and would be unable to be fully present during their lectures and seminars. So the Jungs embarked on a large North German Lloyd steamer and thoroughly enjoyed the voyage.

When they landed in America they went first to Harvard University in Cambridge, Massachusetts. Harvard was celebrating its Tercentenary Conference of Arts and Sciences, and had invited Jung to lecture. He did so under the title "Factors Determining Human Behavior."[33] This lecture seems to have been especially appreciated, but Jung was rather taken aback when he found his hostess dissolved in tears after the lecture, sobbing: "It was so beautiful!" "Now what moved her?" Jung asked when he got home, "For I am sure she did not understand a word of it." Such things often happened, and for a long time they invariably surprised him. He wrote and spoke from his wholeness, so that all four functions (thinking, feeling, sensation, and intuition) naturally entered in, but at the time we are considering he had not yet fully realized this. When feeling types, for instance, were deeply *moved* by what he had just intended to be *understood,* he was always astonished.

Both the Jungs enjoyed themselves at Harvard and wanted to stay longer than originally intended. But in the meantime over a hundred people had gathered on Bailey Island in Maine for a seminar. Esther Harding told me shortly before her death—still very ruefully—that it had fallen to her lot to telephone Jung at Harvard and explain the situation to him. Jung gave himself so completely to congenial circumstances that time sometimes became somewhat relative to him, so, with his usual optimism, he had been sure that only a few people would travel so far to hear him and that those few were sure to be spending their vacation up in Maine and would therefore, like himself, be in no hurry. But when he heard there were so many who had come only for the seminar, and with engagements directly afterward, he was horrified and changed his plans immediately.

This seminar had been arranged by the three leading Jungian doctors in New York: Eleanor Bertine, Esther Harding, and Kristine Mann. They had a house together on Bailey Island, analyzed there for at least a month every summer, and always spent the long vacation in that wonderful spot. The island is divided from the mainland not only by the sea but also by another island, and there are amazingly engineered bridges over both short stretches of water. Jung was immensely impressed by the Maine coast and felt it to be still virgin country on which man had made little or no impression, living more in its past than in the present. At that time the island had far fewer houses than it has today, and I remember Jung saying it had made a strange and unique impression on him. He said to me: "Go there if ever you have a chance," advice which I was able to follow only thirty years later, seven years after his death.

The Jungs stayed with the three doctors in their large house right above the sea, and he gave some analytical hours as well as his seminar. When he could, he gladly and with the greatest enjoyment went sailing and exploring the coast. Meanwhile Emma Jung, though she had enjoyed herself enormously and found it all a different world, was getting increasingly breathless at the pace of American life and the amount of extraversion expected of her. In fact, one had the impression that she was still panting when Dr. E. A. Bennet, his wife, and I met them at Waterloo station with our two cars, for Jung also had some lectures in London on his way home from the States.

Dr. and Mrs. Bennet had found them some really delightful rooms in a small hotel just off Regents Park, quiet and quite close to the Bennets' own house, where Jung saw people for analytical hours and was looked after by Dr. Bennet's efficient secretary. When they got out of the cars and looked at this tiny hotel—not much larger than a moderate-sized country house—Jung remarked to his wife: "Could there in the whole world be a greater contrast?" They had stayed at one of the largest hotels in New York

(I think it was the Waldorf Astoria) and the contrast must indeed have been extreme. But they soon loved their quiet little hotel, with no traffic noise at all and every home comfort introduced by the Bennets, and Emma Jung found it an indescribable rest after her enjoyable but nonstop weeks in the States.

When they returned to Küsnacht, Jung arranged at last to take some extra time off from work, for the summer had left him no time for his beloved alchemy. He gave no English seminar nor lectures at the E.T.H. during the following winter. He also cut down his analytical hours to a minimum and at last had some time to find his way through the impenetrable jungle of alchemistic texts. Though it was especially hard work—even comparing it to his "confrontation with the unconscious"—he thoroughly enjoyed the winter that year and found it highly rewarding.

When the Easter holidays were over, however, he took up all his work again, and the summer schedule that year was again particularly heavy. The change of work had done him good, though, and he tackled it with renewed zest. The summer holidays were also eaten into, for he had promised to give the three Terry Lectures at Yale University, and all his time before the usual Eranos Tagung was occupied in the preparation of those lectures directly in English. An English-speaking publisher told Jung that he greatly preferred the papers which he wrote himself in English to any translation, for they were infinitely more alive, but naturally it took him rather longer than writing in German. His lecture for Eranos was rather time-consuming, since he spoke on the visions of Zosimos, which are in Greek.

Jung was due to go to India toward the end of 1937, and this made his visit to America that year very much more hurried than the year before. After the Terry Lectures[34] at Yale, he gave a seminar in New York which was a continuation of the Bailey Island seminar of the previous year. This proved to be his last visit to America, although, since he was only just over sixty, no one thought of such a thing at the time.

The unconscious always seems to know such things in advance, however, and the speech, which he gave at the farewell dinner on the evening the seminar closed, was singularly impressive, as if he knew he was speaking last words to many of his audience. Several people spoke to me of this speech, including Esther Harding. They were unusually unanimous as to its main line of thought and the points which had made an indelible impression on them.

Since he had already spoken twice that day, Jung was not willing to speak again, but then he said he would try to see if anything came to him to say, so that clearly most of the speech came to him directly from the unconscious itself. Since he had just given his Terry Lectures on "Psychology and Religion," that subject was naturally uppermost in his mind and so he continued with this theme in his speech.

As I have often heard him remark on other occasions, he spoke that night of what difficult days we live in, for the archetypal images of the collective unconscious are no longer content to flow into the prevailing religion. They have come loose from their moorings, so to speak, and are troubling modern man with the restless state of the energy which has been contained in the Christian religion for the last two thousand years. Some of this energy has gone into science, it is true, but that is too narrow and rational to satisfy anything like all of the floating archetypal images. This is the reason for our many isms today, and it confronts the modern free individual with the task of coming to terms with them in his own life.

Jung spoke for some time about Christ as a human being and showed what a difficult problem he was faced with. As an illegitimate child, he naturally had a life-long battle with the power devil. This is clear in the temptation in the wilderness, but he had the most unusual sense of integrity to refuse all of Satan's offers. Yet he did not quite escape them; his kingdom was not of this world, but it remained a kingdom all the same. And the strange incident of his triumphal entry into Jerusalem seems to stem from the same root. But all such convictions deserted him on the cross, when he uttered the tragic words: "My God, my God, why hast Thou forsaken me?" That was Christ's moment of utter failure, when he saw that the life he had led according to his best convictions and with such integrity had been largely based on illusion. On the cross he was deserted by his mission, but he had lived his life with such devotion that, in spite of this, he won through to a resurrected body.

Then Jung said to his audience—and this is what struck so many of them as last words—that we could only follow Christ's example and live our lives as fully as possible, even if it is based on a mistake. We should go and make our mistakes, for there is no full life without error; no one has ever found the whole truth; but if we will only live with the same integrity and devotion as Christ, he hoped we would all, like Christ, win through to a resurrected body.

# 12

# Indian Intermezzo
## 1937–1938

The journey to India in 1937–38 had a very different background from any of Jung's previous journeys. The first two, to North Africa and to the American Indians, were undertaken in an effort to see Europe from the *outside*. The journey to East Africa and Egypt had the ostensible purpose of studying primitive psychology and approaching Egypt from Africa, down the Nile, instead of, as is usual, across the Mediterranean. I am sure the revelation which Jung's unconscious gave on the Nile impressed him deeply: that the unconscious itself had had a very different reason for encouraging him to take that journey, namely, to bring up the rather embarrassing question, "What is going to happen to Jung the psychologist in the wilds of Africa?" [1] It was probably the further unconscious reason which he then discovered, that escape from the rising tension in Europe had also played a considerable role in his decision, which made him refuse a tempting suggestion that he go to China about 1934.

He had been enormously impressed by Chinese wisdom, even before meeting Richard Wilhelm, when he first experimented one summer with the *I Ching*.[a] He gave up a burning wish to learn Chinese only when his studies in alchemy convinced him that he could never find the time to learn that most difficult of all languages. He also longed to go to China to form his own conclusions about Chinese culture there, so I do not think there was anything he would have liked better than to accept a proposal that he go on a long journey through China[b] which would have taken at least six months. When he told me he had decided against it, he added sadly: "I realized my

[a] See above, page 165.

[b] As far as I recall, the proposal originated with Erwin Rousselle, who was then director of the China Institute in Frankfurt.

right place at present was *here*!'' Unfortunately, during his lifetime I did
not see the connection between this decision and his realization on the
Nile, and was not able to ask him whether such a connection existed, but I
am convinced that it was the feeling he should not escape a second time
from the mounting tension in Europe that made him deny himself this
longed-for journey.

By 1937 he had somehow found time to read a great deal "about Indian
philosophy and religious history," and he "was deeply convinced of the
value of Oriental wisdom."[2] Therefore the invitation of the British
Government of India "to take part in the celebrations connected with the
twenty-fifth anniversary of the University of Calcutta," which were being
held in January, 1938, came as a welcome opportunity to see something of
the Orient after all. The guests landed in Bombay in December, 1937, and
were taken to see quite a lot of India on the way to Calcutta. Jung did not
want to be bound by a fixed itinerary, so he suggested that Fowler
McCormick also go with them, and that he and Fowler make some
expeditions on their own, especially to South India and Ceylon, after the
celebrations in Calcutta were over. The whole journey, however, took less
than three months, so he was away for a much shorter time than he would
necessarily have been had he gone to China.

It was not easy, however, to add this journey to a year which already
included the Terry Lectures at Yale and a seminar in New York. He cut
down his time in America to a minimum; even so, there were only a few
weeks between his return from America and his departure for India. Since
he was leaving his patients and pupils for so long, he saw them all as often as
possible, although that winter he necessarily omitted the English seminar
and all his lectures at the E.T.H. Unfortunately, he did not allow sufficient
time for his personal preparation for the journey (such as inoculations), and
Toni Wolff was always convinced that his illness in Calcutta was a result of
this omission.

I do not know if Jung cast an *I Ching* for this journey, as he had before
going to Africa, but I certainly got the impression, when I saw him for the
last time before he departed, that he was reckoning with the possibility that
he might not return. At least it seemed to me, from one or two things he
said, that he was preparing his pupils for that eventuality. A dangerous
illness did indeed stand before him, the first of many he was to go through
before his death. Jung was sixty-two at this time and already considerably
detached from life, although at the same time he still gave himself to it
completely.

He told me that day what a different attitude he had toward this coming
journey. Before Africa, for example, he had been caught up in the prospect
of the coming journey and would have been bitterly disappointed if it had
been put off. "I look forward immensely to experiencing India and Indian

culture for myself," he said, "yet should it suddenly be cancelled I should not really be disappointed. Instead of traveling to Marseilles next Friday, I could quite easily settle down to doing something else that day." He fully realized, as he made clear in *Memories*, that this time he must remain in himself, "like a homunculus in the retort," as he expressed it. "India affected me like a dream, for I was and remained in search of myself, of the truth peculiar to myself." We can see clearly how far Jung's inner development had progressed in the twelve years since his return from Africa.

That he was not so set on the journey was also partly due to his being so engrossed at the time in his intensive study of alchemy. He even called the journey to Indian an intermezzo in that study, and he took with him a large volume, the first of the *Theatrum Chemicum*, and read it from beginning to end before he returned. This volume contains the principle writings of Gerard Dorn, which Jung then read for the first time. Readers familiar with the *Mysterium Coniunctionis* will remember that Jung quoted Dorn at considerable length in the last chapter, "The Conjunction," because Dorn had seen deeper and knew more of alchemy's subjective side than any of the other alchemists.

Jung described the effect of this reading during the journey to India:

Thus it was that this material belonging to the fundamental strata of European thought was constantly counterpointed by my impressions of a foreign mentality and culture. Both had emerged from original psychic experiences of the unconscious, and therefore had produced the same, similar, or at least comparable insights. [3]

Returning to the diagram on page 17: both his reading of Gerard Dorn and much of what he was seeing in India evidently came from the deepest levels of the unconscious, from "the primeval ancestors" layer or even lower. We have already seen the same phenomenon at work when we were considering the writing of Jung's commentary to *The Secret of the Golden Flower*.[c] But, as he stated: "India gave me my first experience of an alien, highly differentiated culture." This "alien" element came in from the higher levels, beginning with the large group layer and going on through the nation, clan, etc. In the culture which Jung was absorbing, which came from these higher layers, the insights were by no means entirely the same, similar, or even comparable to his own psychic experiences, and it was these aspects of Indian culture that—during the rush of sight-seeing on the part of the whole group—proved completely indigestible to Jung. He told us when he got home: "I could not digest India, and that is why I had to be

[c] See above, pages 187 and 188.

so ill in Calcutta." Dysentery is a disease connected with digestion, and in his case it became so severe that there was no escape from ten days in the hospital during the celebrations in Calcutta. Jung always hated not being able to meet obligations he had undertaken. Therefore, he was, on the one hand, very embarrassed not to be able to attend all the celebrations for which he had been invited to India. On the other hand, however, it was *force majeure* and in no way his own fault. So the advantages on this occasion outweighed the disadvantages and, as he recalled in *Memories,* this enforced rest in the hospital was a "blessed island in the wild sea of new impressions, and I found a place to stand on from which I could contemplate the ten thousand things and their bewildering turmoil." [4] In fact, such an opportunity for introversion was a godsend in the extra-verted rush of his journey to India.

This journey necessarily followed the program arranged for the delegates to the Indian Science Congress at Calcutta. In view of their itinerary between landing at Bombay and arriving in Calcutta it must have been a very full schedule. Not only did they see one place of enthralling interest after the other but the program included "a good many dinners and receptions," at which Jung learned a great deal about the social life and the individual psychology of many educated Indian men and women.

When he got back to Zürich, the women in his environment were obliged to reconsider their orientation toward being a woman. He had been enormously struck in India by the skillful behavior of the Indian woman and by the fact that she really lived by her Eros principle, and thereby giving the men in her environment the opportunity to live their principle, supported on the feeling side by every woman they met, instead of—as is all too general in Europe—being douched with cold water from breakfast time on. Soon after his return to Europe, he wrote about this, in *The Dreamlike World of India:*

I had a chance at these [dinners and receptions] to talk to educated Indian women. This was a novelty. Their costume stamps them as women. It is the most becoming, the most stylish and, at the same time, the most meaningful dress ever devised by women. I hope fervently that the sexual disease of the West, which tries to transform woman into a sort of awkward boy, will not creep into India in the wake of that fad "scientific education." It would be a loss to the whole world if the Indian woman should cease to wear her native costume. India (and perhaps China, which I do not know) is practically the only civilized country where one can see on living models how women can and should dress. . . . It is a sad truth, but the European woman, and particularly her hopelessly wrong dress, put up no show at all when compared with the dignity and elegance of the Indian woman and her costume. Even fat women have a chance in India; with us they can only starve themselves to death.[5]

He did not, however, think so well of the Hindu man's clothing; the Indian male, he wrote, is "too fond of ease and coolness." But he also felt that Indians knew a great deal more about how to behave in a large family than Westerners do. He said later in the same article:

> You have to adapt yourself to the family and know how to talk and how to behave, when twenty-five to thirty members of a family are crowded together in a small house, with a grandmother on top. That teaches you to speak modestly, carefully, politely. It explains that small twittering voice and that flowerlike behaviour. The crowding together in families has the contrary effect with us. It makes people nervous, irritable, rough, and even violent. But India takes the family seriously. There is no amateurishness or sentimentality about it. It is understood to be the indispensable form of life, inescapable, necessary, and self-evident. It needs a religion to break this law and to make "homelessness" the first step to saintliness. It certainly seems as if Indians would be unusually pleasant and easy to live with, particularly the women; and, if the style were the whole man, Indian life would be almost ideal. But softness of manners and sweetness of voice are also a part of secrecy and diplomacy. I guess Indians are just human, and so no generalization is quite true.[6]

Jung went in for generalizations as little as anybody I ever knew. I realized painfully at the time, however, that it is unfortunately a fact that Western woman is going through a stage in which it is very difficult for her to live by her own principle, Eros. As he made very clear in *Woman in Europe*,[7] this is primarily because circumstances have forced her to live her masculine side. He added: "Masculinity means knowing what one wants and doing what is necessary to achieve it. Once this lesson has been learned it is so obvious that it can never again be forgotten without tremendous psychic loss."[8]

Jung in no way advised the European woman to try to put the clock back and return to earlier models. When she still wears her national *Tracht* (costume), European woman dresses very meaningfully, if never quite so successfully as her Indian sister. But now that she has opened the door to greater consciousness, she can never shut it again "without tremendous psychic loss." To realize how far one's essential femininity has been lost is a very helpful though painful lesson, and those of us in Zürich gained a lot when Jung pointed this out to us on his return from India. All these impressions were naturally very tiring for him and, although still very vigorous and enterprising, Jung was considerably exhausted when he reached Calcutta.

Jung often spoke of his experiences in India, but I never heard an exact itinerary of the route they took from Bombay, where they landed, to Calcutta, where the prearranged part of the journey culminated and ended. A glance at the map shows one that they traveled right across India; they certainly visited Delhi, the hill of Sanchi, Agra, Allahabad, Benares, Darjeeling, and undoubtedly many other places as well. The universities of Allahabad and Benares, as well as the university in Calcutta, bestowed doctorates upon Jung.

I have mentioned the deep impression—one could even say enlightenment—that he received at the Taj Mahal.[d] He was certainly equally moved by the stupas on the hill of Sanchi. Later he often spoke of this experience, which eventually revealed "a new side of Buddhism to him."[9] There is a vivid description of it in *Memories*[10] but another one, in *The Dreamlike World of India,* is less well known and at least equally vivid:

> Not very far from Agra and Delhi is the hill of Sanchi with its famous stupa. We were there on a brisk morning. The intense light and the extraordinary clarity of the air brought out every detail. There on the top of a rocky hill, with a distant view over the plains of India, you behold a huge globe of masonry, half buried in the earth. According to the Maha-Parinibbana-Sutta, Buddha himself indicated the way in which his remains were to be buried. He took two rice bowls and covered the one with the other. The visible stupa is just the bowl on top. One has to imagine the lower one, buried in the earth. The roundness, a symbol of perfection since olden days, seems a suitable as well as an expressive monument for a Tathagata. It is of immense simplicity, austerity and lucidity, perfectly in keeping with the simplicity, austerity and lucidity of Buddha's teaching.
>
> There is something unspeakably solemn about this place in its exalted loneliness, as if it were still witnessing the moment in the history of India when the greatest genius of her race formulated her supreme truth. This place, together with its architecture, its silence, and its peace beyond all turmoils of the heart, its very forgetfulness of human emotions, is truly and essentially Indian; it is as much the "secret" of India as the Taj Mahal is the secret of Islam. And just as the perfume of Islamic culture still lingers in the air, so Buddha, though forgotten on the surface, is still the secret breath of life in modern Hinduism. He is suffered at least to be an avatar of Vishnu.[11]

[d] See above, page 143.

This passage also provides considerable enlightenment concerning the difference between the two vivid impressions at the Taj Mahal and on the hill of Sanchi. It was the "secret of Islam" that was revealed to him in the former, the secret of India on the latter. The first fell on well-prepared soil. It was eighteen years since he had first come face to face with Islam, on his journey to North Africa in 1920, and he had been pondering it ever since. Therefore, its central secret, that is based on Eros, not on Logos, as the other great world religions are, could be brought up into consciousness at once, answering many questions that had been consciously puzzling him through all the intervening years. These questions had been renewed in 1925, when he again very often came face to face with Islam on his journey to East Africa and down the Nile. But this was his first direct contact with India; therefore, the levels above the primeval ancestors were still strange, even alien to him. One fact indeed rose from the very deepest levels of all:

> [He ] grasped the life of Buddha as the reality of the Self which had broken through and laid claim to a personal life. [Jung had already realized much the same in regard to Christ. ] For Buddha, the Self stands above all gods, a *unus mundus* which represents the essence of human existence and of the world as a whole. The Self embodies both the aspect of intrinsic being and the aspect of its being known, without which no world exists. Buddha saw and grasped the cosmogonic dignity of human consciousness; for that reason he saw clearly that if a man succeeded in extinguishing this light, the world would sink into nothingness.[12]

Jung had already experienced this fundamental realization from the deepest layers of the unconscious, for himself and quite independently, on the Athi Plains in Africa, twelve years before he stood on the hill of Sanchi.

Although this fundamental realization probably came to him then and there, there was still so much entirely new to him on the Asian and Indian levels of the unconscious that one cannot doubt that it was also this experience on the hill of Sanchi that contributed to the "wild sea of new impressions" which landed him in hospital at Calcutta. In fact, he related in *Memories* that at Sanchi he "was overcome by a strong emotion of the kind that frequently develops in me when I encounter a thing, person or idea of whose significance I am still unconscious."[13] There was still a great deal about Buddha and Buddhism that needed years before it would rise to consciousness, exactly as we have seen was the case with "the central secret of Islam."

In *What India Can Teach Us*[14] Jung spoke of the strange fact that:

> Buddha has disappeared from Indian life and religion more than we

could evei imagine Christ disappearing in the aftermath of some future catastrophe to Christianity. . . . India is not ungrateful to her master minds. Universities like Calcutta and Benares have important philosophy departments. Yet the main emphasis is laid on classical Hindu philosophy and its vast Sanscrit literature. The Pali Canon is not precisely within their scope. *Buddha does not represent a proper philosophy. He challenges man*! This is not exactly what philosophy wants. It, like any other science, needs a good deal of intellectual free play, undisturbed by moral and human entanglements. But also, small and fragmentary people must be able to "do something about it," without getting fatally involved in big issues far beyond their powers of endurance and accomplishment. This is on the right road after all, though it is a *longissima via*. The divine impatience of a genius may disturb or even upset the small man. But after a few generations he will reassert himself by sheer force of numbers, *and this too seems to be right*.[15]

Jung said earlier in the same article:

The remote goal of the transformation process, however, is very much what Buddha intended. But to get there is possible neither in one generation nor in ten. It obviously takes much longer, thousands of years at all events, since the intended transformation cannot be realized without an enormous development of consciousness. It can only be "believed" which is what Buddha's, as well as Christ's followers obviously did, assuming—as "believers" always do—that belief is the whole thing. Belief is a great thing, to be sure, but it is a substitute for a conscious reality which the Christian wisely relegates to a life in the hereafter. This "hereafter" is really the intended future of mankind, anticipated by religious intuition.[16]

These passages—especially the words "and this too seems to be right"—show very clearly Jung's amazing tolerance and acceptance of every man as he was. He took *every* human life seriously, at whatever level of consciousness it had to be lived. He was convinced that mankind's greatest need is more consciousness, and he did everything he could to achieve this end himself and to help other people to do so. Sometimes, his own "divine impatience of a genius" did disturb or even upset the small people in his environment, yet fundamentally he never rejected them for a smallness they could not help; although he deplored the general unconsciousness, he never condemned those who were unable to escape from it, for he knew that this also "seems to be right."

His principal concern in India, however, as he reported in *Memories,* was "the psychological nature of evil." The burning problem of evil— which had concerned Jung since his childhood—had now, with the rise of the Nazis, forced its way into the front row of European problems. As he wrote, many years later, in "Late Thoughts": "Evil has become a determinant reality. It can no longer be dismissed from the world by a circumlocution. We must learn how to handle it, since it is here to stay. How we can live with it without terrible consequences cannot for the present be conceived."[17] Although Jung struggled all his life with this problem, we can see from the above words that he by no means regarded it as solved, even at the end of his life. And he soon discovered in India that, though we can learn a great deal from the Indians' very different conception of evil, yet they have not solved the problem either, at all events not from our point of view.

Even before Jung went to India he had been very much impressed by the way the Indian has integrated this problem of evil into his spiritual life. His recognition of this achievement cast a new light for him on the whole subject, and he now realized how well the Oriental can integrate so-called evil without losing face, a thing we cannot do at all in the West. But he soon saw the disadvantages of the Eastern point of view; good and evil have no outline and are never seen as quite real. He remarked that we are thus left with "the paradoxical statement that Indian spirituality lacks both evil and good, or is so burdened by contradictions that it needs *nirdvandva*, the liberation from the opposites and from the ten thousand things."[18]

The problem of morality takes first place with the Westerner but this is by no means the Indian point of view. The Indian regards good and evil as "merely varying degrees of the same thing." The Christian strives for good and succumbs to evil, the Indian declares the world to be only an illusion and strives to be liberated from it. The Indian practices meditation and Yoga to achieve this end, whereas Jung realized, right through his "confrontation with the unconscious," that the most important stage in meditation is above all to realize what has come to us from within in our own *actual life*.[19] Real life was always the most important thing of all to Jung, for he recognized it as the unique opportunity for the eternal Self to "enter three-dimensional existence."[20]

When Jung got home from his Indian journey he told me that, in some ways, it had been the most bewildering experience of his life; but that as a result of it he had eventually found a standpoint, through realizing that the most important quality to cultivate is what the French call *sagesse*. He then quoted—for the first time that I remember—the essence of Greek wisdom in the sentence he afterward quoted in *Psychology and Alchemy:*[21] "Exaggerate nothing, all good lies in the right measure." It seems to me that the motto he used at the beginning of *The Psychology of the*

*Transference,*[22] and which he sometimes also quoted, is nearly related: "A warring peace, a sweet wound, an agreeable evil." (John Gower: *Confessio amantis.*)

Although the Indian sees the outline of the opposites far less clearly than we do, he undoubtedly lays far more emphasis on their union and for that reason has taken sexuality into his religion in a way completely unknown in the West. The Indian realizes fully that sexuality is not just a personal matter between man and woman, but is also the meaningful symbol for the reconciliation of all the opposites that remain torn apart so disastrously in the West. Jung said in *What India Can Teach Us:*

> If you want to learn the greatest lesson India can teach you, wrap yourself in the cloak of your moral superiority, go to the Black Pagoda of Konarak, sit down in the shadow of the mighty ruin that is still covered with the most amazing collection of obscenities, read Murray's cunning old *Handbook for India*, which tells you how to be properly shocked by this lamentable state of affairs, and how you should go into the temples in the evening, because in the lamplight they look if possible "more (and how beautifully!) wicked"; and then analyse carefully and with the utmost honesty all your reactions, feelings, and thoughts. It will take you quite a while, but in the end, if you have done good work, you will have learned something about yourself, and about the white man in general, which you have probably never heard from any one else. I think, if you can afford it, a trip to India is on the whole most edifying and, from a psychological point of view, most advisable, although it may give you considerable head-aches.[23]

Jung very often referred to the "Black Pagoda of Konarak," to the obscene sculptures, and to the amazing remarks made to him by the pandit who was with him.[24] These obscenities were there "as a means to achieve spiritualization." Jung objected that, judging from the open-mouthed delight shown by the young peasants, it was more likely they were having their heads filled with sexual fantasies. That, the pandit replied, was just the point; they must be reminded to fulfill their karma or these "unconscious fellows" might forget it. (One is reminded of the church bells being rung in South America to remind man of the need for propagation, as Jung mentioned in the 1923 Polzeath seminar.) He was even more amazed when the pandit confided in him, as they left the temple and were walking down a lingam lane, that, as Jung had been so understanding, he would tell him a great secret: "These stones are man's private parts."

Jung used to say when he spoke of this experience: "I was dumbfounded; with us every child knows that fact, and in India it is the great secret." I never heard him say more than just to tell the story to illustrate the essential difference between the way sexuality is regarded in East and West, and to advise us to ponder it. It seems to me, however, that the main difference is that, in the West, we regard sexuality almost purely biologically, as a means of propagating the species and to further personal relationships between man and woman, whereas, in the East, it is (or was) regarded as belonging to the gods, a matter for them alone. It is, therefore, the great secret that man has also a physical right to participate in the mystery. The Indian obviously lives sexuality much as we do, but perhaps even more unconsciously and purely instinctively. Jung always said that the more primitive a people were, the less important sexuality was to them; it is no problem to them because it is not repressed as with us. Food, Jung used to say, is far more problematic to the primitive because it represents much more uncertainty. When I speak of the Indian as "primitive," I do not, of course, mean the educated Indian, who knows his own wonderful ancient culture, but the teeming multitude in the streets and the peasants to whom the pandit was referring when he spoke of the purpose of the temple obscenities at Konarak.

It was the specific way the Indian regarded sexuality that amazed Jung, not the fact that it was attributed to the gods, for he had seen "its spiritual aspect and its numinous meaning" over twenty years before; it was indeed, as we have seen, the main cause of his break with Freud. One could say that Jung's wholeness led him to see *both* aspects of sexuality, long before he met it in India or in his reading about Eastern religion and philosophy. Freud, on the contrary, saw sexuality only as it is usually regarded in the West: as a purely biological and personal matter, although he was profoundly affected unconsciously by its other religious and spiritual aspect, so that it was his real, but unrecognized, religion.

All these bewildering new impressions were too manifold and diverse for even Jung's digestion, and in Calcutta he finally had an opportunity to catch up with them, while he was in the hospital. He said that he returned to the hotel "in tolerably good health," but Fowler McCormick recalled that he still looked very ill and that his condition gave Fowler cause for anxiety, both then and during their whole journey together through Southern Indian to Ceylon. Jung refused, however, to let his health interfere with his profound interest in, and even enjoyment of, the end of his stay in India, or with his time in Ceylon.

In the meantime, while still in his Calcutta hotel, his unconscious sent him a dream which ignored his present environment, as did the dreams he had when he was in East Africa, and imperiously "wiped away all the intense impressions of India and swept me back into the too long neglected concerns of the Occident, which had formerly been expressed in the quest for the Holy Grail as well as in the search for the philosopher's stone." He recorded this dream in full detail in *Memories*.[25] It concerned the search for the Grail, which urgently had to be in its castle that very evening for a special celebration. Jung realized that it was the task of the group he was with in the dream to bring the Grail to the castle. Six of them set out on an exhausting walk toward an uninhabited house where the Grail was hidden. They found that it was on an island divided from where they were by an arm of the sea and Jung's exhausted companions camped where they were and fell asleep. Jung had just concluded that he must swim this last stage *alone* when he woke up.

Jung reported that this dream took him out of the world of India and reminded him that India was not his task, but only an admittedly significant part which would carry him closer to his goal. He said that the dream was asking him: "What are you doing in India? Rather seek for yourself and your fellows the healing vessel, the *servator mundi*, which you urgently need. For your state is perilous: you are all in imminent danger of destroying all that centuries have built up."[26]

We are reminded of Jung's realization in Africa that the unconscious was interested only in what "was going to happen to Jung the psychologist in the wilds of Africa" not primarily interested in Africa itself. But there is an enormous difference and progress between the two experiences. This time there was no reproach: Jung was not escaping from something he did not realize sufficiently in Europe, but it was now time to turn the searchlight of his mind onto the European problem and how it could best be served by the healing vessel of the Grail. We shall see, from what happened in Europe only a few weeks after Jung got home, how urgent the problem was and why it was so vital for the Grail to be in the Grail Castle that very evening, to speak in the symbolism of Jung's dream.

Ceylon, the last stage of Jung's journey, no longer seemed to be India but more nearly related to the South Sea Islands with their touch of paradise. Two things happened to him in Ceylon which made an especially strong impression on him and of which he often spoke later. Two peasants collided and got stuck with their carts in a narrow street. Jung waited for the furious mutual accusations that would certainly follow such a mishap in Europe but, to his amazement, "They bowed to each other and said: 'Passing disturbance, no soul!' That is to say, the disturbance takes place only outwardly in the realm of Maya, and not in the realm of true reality, where it neither happened nor left a mark. One might think this almost unbelievable in such simple people. One stands amazed."[27] Jung then went on to give other examples.

Many years before Jung was in Ceylon, I had been enormously struck by a similar incident. On my second visit to Bollingen in 1930, Jung hit the doorpost with the fender of his car while backing out of the garage. I expected him to be very much annoyed and upset (as most people are by such things), but not at all. It did not seem to touch him in any way. Evidently it was just "a passing disturbance, no soul," and left no mark at all in the world of reality!

It was easy to overlook this quality of Jung's, but as a matter of fact he never allowed himself to be upset by such superficial "passing disturbances." The reason many people overlooked this was that he could sometimes be very irritable and annoyed with *apparently* trivial mistakes. But if one looked back carefully and objectively at the incident, instead of feeling ill-used one could always see that much more was involved than appeared at first sight. In my own case I usually learned that something unconscious in me—animus or shadow, in Jungian language—had thrown a monkey wrench in the works without my knowledge, or in other words, these things had a double floor of which at first I had seen only the superficial aspect. If what happened touched "the realm of true reality," it also touched Jung, but not otherwise.

Later one saw the same thing in Jung's reaction to the annoyingly persistent rumor that he was a Nazi. It never touched him in "the realm of true reality." Though the persistence of this unfounded rumor sometimes seemed to be longer than a "passing disturbance," in the eyes of his No. 1 personality, he remained essentially unmoved.

Since the busy international port of Colombo in Ceylon had little to interest Jung, he soon left it and went inland. In Kandy, the old royal city, there was a small temple (containing the relic of the Holy Tooth of Buddha) which held a special charm for him. He often spoke of an evening ceremony in that temple which deeply impressed him. It was preceded by a "one-hour drum concert" which he described in detail in *Memories*[28] This music, which does not speak the white man's language of the head, appeals to an even deeper layer than the American Indian's language of the heart. It speaks the most "ancient language of the belly and solar plexus," right from the deepest layers of the human soul: the layer of the primeval ancestors and the layers below. Prepared by this music, Jung was moved to see young men and girls pouring enormous quantities of jasmine flowers into mounds in front of the altars and singing a *mantram* under their breath. Naturally, Jung thought they were praying to Buddha, but the monk who was with him explained: "No, Buddha is no more. He is in nirvana, we cannot pray to him. They are singing: 'This life is transitory as the beauty of these flowers. May my God [in sense of *deva* = guardian angel] share with me the merit of this offering.' " Jung felt this to be an illumination of his life-long preoccupation: "The thorny problem of the relationship between eternal man, the Self, and earthly man in time and space."[29] It was certainly one of the most important impressions that India left on him.

By the time he set out on his homeward voyage he had such a plethora of impressions that he stayed on the ship at Bombay, once more entirely engrossed in medieval alchemy. He ended the chapter on this journey in *Memories* with these words: "But India did not pass me by without a trace; it left tracks which lead from one infinity into another infinity."

# 13

## Darkening Clouds
## 1938–1939

When Jung returned to Switzerland from India in February, 1938, he was still far from well. He consulted a Swiss specialist for tropical diseases, and was obliged to give up his intention to start work at once. He had to rest for two or three weeks. This was helpful, just as his time in the hospital at Calcutta had been. It enabled him to go on sorting out his impressions much better than if he had begun to see people outside his immediate family circle at once. He always complained that, whenever he came back from an interesting journey, everybody wanted to hear about it *at once,* long before he felt ready to talk.

Jung had not, however, been back long before his peace was shattered by the Nazis' marching into Austria. This destroyed his last hope that a second world war could be avoided and was a terrible blow to him. It was now very clear why the unconscious had drawn his attention to the "imminent danger" threatening Europe and the perilous state that all of Europe was in.

Franz Riklin Jr.—at that time nearing thirty and just starting his medical career—was chosen by some exceedingly rich Swiss Jews to go into Austria *at once,* with a very large sum of money, to do all that he could to persuade leading Jews to leave the country before the Nazis had time to start persecuting them. Franz said he was largely chosen for this work because of his exceedingly Teutonic appearance: no one would suspect him of any connection with the Jews. He also was a very resourceful young man who would obviously be adept at throwing dust in the eyes of the Nazis and at persuading the Jews to take advantage of the opportunity. In general he was *exceedingly* successful in carrying out his mission, but in one place, where he perhaps most wanted to succeed, he failed entirely.

Before he left Zürich, his father, Franz Riklin Sr., had pressed him to try above all to persuade Freud to leave Austria and to take advantage of the most unusual facilities which he could offer. His father had known Freud very well in the old days. Both he and Alfons Maeder had left the Freudian group at the same time as Jung, but none of that counted anymore in comparison with Dr. Riklin's very human wish to see his old friend in safety.

Franz Jr. went to see Freud as soon as he got to Vienna and explained the situation to him. He was bitterly disappointed when Freud answered: "I refuse to be beholden to my enemies." Franz had been a very young child when Freud visited his parents, but he remembered him well. He did his best to persuade Freud that neither his father nor Jung felt any enmity toward him; on the contrary, he said, they really only wanted to know that he was safe. He also pointed out that there was no need for Freud to stay in Switzerland, for once there he could travel wherever he liked. It was all to no avail. Freud merely repeated that he would accept no favors from his enemies. The Freuds were very friendly to Franz himself; he was much too young to have been involved in the quarrel. They even asked him to dinner before he left Vienna, but nothing he could say was able to shake Freud's iron determination.

This was a great disappointment to young Franz, for he knew how much it would disappoint his father, who was counting on him to bring Freud back with him. He knew that Jung, of whom he had always been particularly fond, would also be very sorry. The latter, however, had known Freud better than the Riklins. He was sad but not surprised. When reproached, as he sometimes was, for not doing more to help Freud leave Austria, Jung always replied: "He would not take help from me under any circumstances." It is rather ironic that when Freud did go to England much later, he had to owe his satisfactory house in London to a Jungian: Dr. E. A. Bennet.

Jung saw all his patients and pupils at least once before he went to his beloved Tower at Bollingen for the Easter holidays. I was staying next door with the Fierzes, during those holidays, so I witnessed the next stage in Jung's cure: the doctor he had consulted insisted on his taking a long walk every day. Fond though he was of the Bollingen woods, he felt he needed more variety, if he was to keep up the hours of walking prescribed. So, for the only time I remember, he took his car to the mountains each day and got quite enthusiastic about thinking out new and exciting walks.

There was one friend of his who found Jung's illness not at all to his taste: his Schnauzer, Joggi, found himself banished from Bollingen for the first time in his life. Joggi was becoming an old dog by this time, and when at Bollingen he always disturbed them in the night, at least once and usually more often, because he insisted on going out and, just as they had gone to sleep again, barking to come in. Jung, who of course felt that his first task was to recover his health completely, hardened his heart and left Joggi at

Küsnacht. He had a large garden at his disposal there and his every need was cared for, but he did not have his master, which was, of course, the chief thing in his life. This led him into a very clever piece of E.S.P., the recollection of which still amazes me. One afternoon when I was going down to Küsnacht Jung asked me to stop at his house and get some things he wanted from his secretary, Marie-Jeanne Schmid. While we were collecting the things, I must have left the door of my car open, for when I came out onto the drive, there was Joggi sitting in the passenger's seat. Now he was not a dog that cared for motoring and he had never been in my car before. But there he was and there he intended to stay, and we had to get the gardener, Müller, before he could be induced to get out and then only with great difficulty. How did he know that that car was going back to Bollingen and that this was his chance to rejoin his beloved master? Jung had used his own car in Bollingen, so mine cannot have still smelled of him, since he had not been in it since before going to India.

The rest and the long walks, plus whatever treatment he had to undergo, did their work, and after the Easter holidays Jung took up the full burdens of his work again: not only his private practice, but also his lectures and seminar at the E.T.H., and the English seminar at the Psychological Club were all resumed. Jung remained practically in full harness for the next six years—until his illness in 1944—but I think he never *quite* recovered his perfect health after his illness in India. He did as much work, but one felt it was sometimes a considerable effort, which it seldom had been before.

Just before the 1938 Eranos meeting—which was on the theme of the "Great Mother"—Jung went to Oxford for the 10th International Medical Congress for Psychotherapy, which was held in England that year.[1] (It had been held in Copenhagen the year before.[2]) While in Oxford he received an honorary doctorate from the university there. A great many universities bestowed degrees on him, but the only time I remember Jung being at all excited by such an honor was at Oxford. This was not because of his own recognition, but because the whole traditional ceremony, the many treasures belonging to the colleges, the buildings themselves, and the medieval atmosphere which still hung over Oxford at that time delighted and fascinated him. He was full of it on the way to Ascona. I was delighted that England had once more found favor in his sight, for the only time he ever really sharply criticized the English was after his return from India, when he spoke more than once of how unnatural and stiff the Englishman was in India and how little he had adapted to his environment. It was not the government he criticized but the lack of adaptation and naturalness in the individual Englishman. Particularly, the English voice in India got on his nerves. He says of this in *The Dreamlike World of India*:

> You cannot help noticing how a great number of perfectly nice and decent Englishmen elaborately imitate a he-man voice. God knows

why. It sounds as if they were trying to impress the world with their throaty rumbling tones, or as if they were addressing a political meeting, which has to be convinced of the profound honesty and sincerity of the speaker. . . . What a superhuman burden it is to be the overlords of a continent like India![3]

After returning from Oxford, Jung at once attended the Eranos Tagung and contributed his lecture, "Psychological Aspects of the Mother Archetype." Although the subject interested him and he subsequently revised and enlarged his lecture and published it in *Von den Wurzeln des Bewusstseins* in 1954,[4] it was yet a considerable sacrifice to give his time to writing it when he was longing to get back to his study of alchemy. Eranos was, however, the last disturbance in his time at Bollingen during the summer holidays of 1938.

In the autumn of that year, in his course at the E.T.H., Jung began to lecture on Indian texts. He had begun speaking of dreams in the summer semester, and in the late autumn he began lecturing on active imagination and on Indian Yoga as a parallel to our Western efforts. This was welcome to his audience, for India was still fresh in his mind, and we heard a good deal of his journey and of what had impressed him most in India. It was also in that winter that he wrote the two articles on India, to which I have already referred more than once, and both were published in New York in the magazine *Asia* early in 1939.[5] He wrote these articles in English, and by then I had the privilege of correcting all he wrote for publication in that language. He did a good many articles, introductions, and lectures in English during the following years, always in a most amazingly expressive English, far more vivid often than pedantically correct English could ever be. I always found it difficult to alter it any more than was absolutely necessary, and probably I altered too little, but I must own to regretting that it has been so thoroughly corrected in the *Collected Works*.

In the meantime, however, Europe had received yet another blow to any hope of peace that may have survived the annexation of Austria: the Nazis marched into Czechoslovakia. A woman in Switzerland had dreamed in March, 1938, that a semi-divine woman had rebuked Hitler for taking Austria, had warned him that he would be punished even more if he took Czechoslovakia, and if he touched Poland that would be the end. Jung was, therefore, not quite unprepared for Czechoslovakia being the next on the list, but it is usually, if not always, impossible to say at the time whether such dreams really foreshadow future events or whether they have only a subjective meaning. At all events, Jung was never for a moment deceived by Chamberlain's declaration after Munich: "Peace in our time." He did not condemn Chamberlain and his colleagues for not interfering with Hitler's moves *to the east* for the following reason: by this time he was quite sure that war was inevitable, but he hoped it would break out first between Germany and Russia and thus weaken the former before the unavoidable final clash with the Western nations. He had indeed regarded war as inevitable ever since he saw how each nation was piling up armaments: "They don't spend all that money on arms to keep them unused," he used to say very sadly. One cannot avoid being afraid that the same is true of the political situation today, although in the meantime Jung has given us a faint gleam of hope: if enough people can stand the clash of the opposites *in themselves*, modern man might still just avoid the worst catastrophe of all. At the time (1939) we are discussing, however, I had never heard him say anything so clear.

Jung had given his English seminar as usual in the summer and autumn of 1938, but when 1939 dawned he began to feel he must cut down his activities somewhere, since three lectures in the week and an over-full practice left him no time at all for himself, his writing, or his beloved alchemical books. By February, 1939, he decided to stop giving the English seminar. He had been interpreting Nietzsche's *Zarathustra* for nearly five years, and he felt that that was enough. So on February 15, after having given five lectures since Christmas, he announced to the class that he was not going on with the English seminar until he felt more at leisure. I do not think that at the time he intended to take more than a long holiday from it, probably the rest of that term and the summer of 1939. However in the autumn, when he found that there were many fewer Anglo-Saxons in Switzerland on account of the war, he realized that the English seminar, of all his lectures, was the one to discontinue. So February 15, 1939, saw the end of the regular English seminar.

I do not know whether or not the discontinuance of the English seminar had anything to do with the fact that Jung was particularly interested in the material he was using at that time in his lectures at the E. T. H. He had been lecturing on Indian texts through the winter, and since the end of December, 1938 he had been interpreting an especially interesting Tantric text: *Shri-Chakra-Sambhara Tantra*.[6] He came to the end of this text very soon after he gave up the English seminar and then began a comparison of the sequence of its symbols with those of alchemy. This must have helped him a lot with all the impressions he had absorbed in India, from reading Dorn's chief works in the *Theatrum Chemicum*, and the similar or contrasting images he had found in India. The similarities in the symbol sequences were most striking and he was evidently very much interested in them. At the beginning of the summer semester he went even further, giving us a "psychological parallel" to the two previous sequences, by which we could see clearly how both "had emerged from original psychic experiences of the unconscious."[7]

The English Royal Society of Medicine invited Jung to give a lecture on April 4. He went to London, accompanied by his wife, at the very end of

March. Since it was a cold spring that year, I did not take my own car across France—as on previous occasions when Jung went to London—but borrowed a car from my sister who was in Canada at the time.

The lecture at the Royal Society of Medicine[8] was enthusiastically received, in fact so enthusiastically that I could not resist asking him, when he told me about it as I drove him the next morning, whether his anima by any chance was dancing on his forehead again. (This referred to a previous occasion, in 1931 or 1932, when he had lectured in Germany and had come home *very* dissatisfied with the wild success he had had. He said to me, at that time: "I positively felt my anima dancing on my forehead and fascinating the audience on her own!") He was considerably annoyed by my remark and got out of the car, when we arrived at his destination, without his usual word of thanks for the transport. But when I fetched him at lunchtime, he remarked: "Of course, it was like that last night." This was a most endearing characteristic of Jung's. One really might take him completely at his word when he wrote:

> The touchstone of every analysis that has not stopped short at partial success, or come to a standstill with no success at all, is always this person to person relationship, a psychological situation where the patient confronts the doctor on equal terms, and with the same ruthless criticism that he must inevitably learn from the doctor in the course of his treatment.[9]

Whenever it was justified, Jung always accepted this "ruthless criticism," if not immediately, then shortly afterward, when he had had time to think it over. For instance, in the foregoing typical example: after all the rejection he had received from the medical profession, he was at first a bit too pleased with being completely accepted and wildly applauded in the stronghold of English traditional medicine to be able to see the connection with the much earlier German example. Soon afterward, however, he saw the resemblance for himself, and accepted it with his own special brand of humility.

As was usual when Jung went to England, he also gave lectures and discussions to the Psychological Club and to the Guild of Pastoral Psychology. He did not stay very long in London, however, for Emma Jung was especially anxious to spend some time in the West Country, visiting Glastonbury and other places connected with the Grail. She had been much interested in the whole history of the Grail for a long time and worked at it very intensively from several years before the war until her death in 1955. Unfortunately, or perhaps fortunately, she was so often asked to give lectures on it that the enormous material she collected on the subject was never condensed into book form, nor had she yet been able to work out the thorny problem of Merlin. Marie-Louise von Franz, therefore, was confronted with a trunkful of rather scattered material when Jung asked her, after his wife's death, to finish the task.[10] He was exceedingly pleased with the result, which was published in German during his lifetime.[11]

In early April, 1939, I drove the Jungs down to West Byfleet, where they continued the journey to the West Country with Peter and Anne Baynes. An incident on the drive may amuse the reader. My sister's car (which I was using on this trip) was a great deal broader than my own and I stupidly touched a coster's cart with my fender as a result of misjudging the breadth of the car. It was entirely my fault and no harm was done to either vehicle, but to prevent an argument, Jung let down his window and said to the coster, with an air of gentle reproof: "Why did you push your cart into the lady's way?" The coster was evidently greatly taken by the way he was addressed and apologized profusely and with great good humor. A European version of the incident Jung had witnessed in Ceylon: "Passing disturbance, no soul!"[a]

Things looked very bad indeed regarding the possible outbreak of war when the Jungs got back from the West Country, and as Jung was longing for Bollingen, they returned to Switzerland the next day. I dined with them the evening before their departure. Jung was inclined to be very pessimistic after he had listened to the evening news on the radio. We even wondered whether I should not cut short my stay in England and get back to Switzerland in a few days. But the next morning, as I drove them to the station, he said he was *sure* he had been too pessimistic the previous evening, it would hold a bit longer, and I should certainly carry out my original plans for a round of visits in Sussex and the West Country. To my lasting regret I acted on his first apprehension and did not change to his amendment. I was not to see England again until 1947, when several of the relations and friends I had been going to visit had died. It was usually safer to follow Jung's considered opinion than remarks he sometimes let fall at the moment. As he once said in a seminar: "In the course of a long day, I drop a good many unripe cherries, and it is very annoying when people pick these up and treasure them!"

I saw vividly that April what he meant when he said it was necessary for him to acclimatize himself to Bollingen before beginning his creative work. This time, when he got back to Bollingen, he had to write an introduction to W. Y. Evans-Wentz's *The Great Liberation,* and he told me while we were in London that it was going to be difficult to get it finished in the short time left of the holidays. "Nevertheless," he added, "I can't do it straight from here or I shall not be able to get into its atmosphere, so I must stare at the lake for some days!" When he gave me the manuscript to correct, the first two or three pages were written in the style he had used for his lecture to the Royal Society of Medicine and only later did he get into a style that was

[a] See above, page 251.

suitable to the book. When I pointed this out to him, he took it back, rewrote the pages in question, and returned them a few days later with the remark: "I saw at once what you meant; evidently I did not stare at the lake long enough!"

The tension in Europe was almost unbearable that summer and culminated in an unusually dramatic Eranos Tagung in August. Even the weather seemed affected; I never remember so many violent thunderstorms and downpours of rain as during July and August that year. Jung felt an extraordinary pressure on the drive over the Gotthard, and insisted on all the cars in his party getting on as fast as they could. He was at once proved right, for we were hardly up the north side of the pass when there was an extensive landslide which blocked the road behind us for two or three days. Several friends who drove separately to Ascona found themselves obliged to put their cars on the train, a much slower and more complicated business then than it is today.

The theme for the Eranos Tagung that year was "The Symbolism of Rebirth in the Religions of all Times and Places." Jung had not written a lecture that year, but was nevertheless persuaded to give two extemporary talks, "on the spur of the moment" as he expressed it,[12] "The Various Aspects of Rebirth." A stenogram of the lectures was taken at the time, and he was further persuaded to put it into written form for the *Eranos Jahrbuch.*"[13] He used this stenogram but said:

> Certain portions had to be omitted, chiefly because the requirements of a printed text are different from those of the spoken word. However, so far as possible, I have carried out my original intention. . . . I have also endeavoured to reproduce my analysis of the eighteenth Sura of the Koran as an example of a rebirth mystery.[14]

Jung further revised and expanded these lectures when they were printed in *Gestaltungen des Unbewussten.*[15] This is the version which appears in the *Collected Works.*

That August—separated by—a few weeks from the outbreak of the Second World War—we were reminded in the lecture hall itself of the ominous state of nature. Lake Maggiore had overflowed its banks, and the bathing facilities between the lake and the lecture hall were all under water. The water was within a few feet of the terrace of the lecture hall, with a lot of the garden below it submerged. In the thirty-eight years I have known it I have never experienced the lake in a comparable state.

For the first time there was considerable tension between the Germans and the other Westerners at the Eranos Tagung. I do not think that any of the Germans present were Nazi sympathizers, but they were nevertheless in a peculiarly possessed state. We had already experienced this terrifying state of possession in Berlin in 1933.[b] This time it was different. The Germans had all been exposed to Nazi propaganda for over six years, which even when they did their best to be objective, had caused a peculiar *abaissement du niveau mental*. As mentioned before, Jung always said that the Germans are characterized by a specially low threshold between conscious and unconscious, and this was never more evident than in Ascona in August, 1939.

One morning after the lecture I was driving the Jungs back from Eranos to the Monte Verità, when a German woman, whom we all knew and liked and who was a special friend of Emma Jung, asked for and was given a lift up the hill. Jung asked me to stop at Pancaldi's in the main street of Ascona, so that he could buy a newspaper. As he was getting out, the German woman remarked with poignant regret: "I am afraid England and France are *determined* to have war." I leaped out of the car, opened her door, and informed her that if that was how she felt she could find some other way of getting home to the hotel. This amused Jung, and he laughed and laughed, whereas Emma Jung looked aghast. Such clashes were not at all to her taste and I can still see the horror depicted on her face. When Jung recovered from his amusement he said to our German friend: "That is quite right, you know. What you said was a pure projection. If anyone wants war it is most certainly Germany." The poor German woman was completely bewildered. Propaganda had told her so often that the Allies, especially England, were determined on war that although she had studied psychology and knew all about projection, she could hardly take it in. However, she murmured a sort of apology and—chiefly on account of Emma Jung's distress—I relented and drove her up the hill to the hotel. She remained bewildered, however, and constantly discussed the matter with all three of us for the rest of the Tagung.

Now I must emphasize that this woman thoroughly disliked the Nazi regime even then, and later, when her only son was killed in the war, she fully realized that the blame rested with the Nazi warmongers; but at this time (1939) she was really too possessed to be able to take an objective standpoint and could only realize how thoroughly bewildered she was. When I read in the papers, much later, and saw photographs of the bewilderment of the German sailors after the *Bismarck* was sunk, I was reminded of this incident. They had heard so often that their ship was unsinkable that they simply could not believe their eyes when it went down.

A very high Swiss official in the Red Cross told Jung an incident that makes clearer the conditions which prevailed that year at Ascona. He had an interview with Hitler just after Danzig, on matters connected with the Red Cross. He found Hitler unusually quiet and apparently peaceful, and

[b] See above, page 210 ff.

therefore thought it was a good opportunity to broach a point on which he knew there was a difference of opinion. But he had no sooner dared to differ, than Hitler flew into an ungovernable rage, began tearing down the window curtains and destroying them, in fact went completely berserk. The Red Cross man was removed unobtrusively from the room before Hitler could attack him directly, and to his amazement they hurried some dancing girls into the room as if the "Führer" was some old Roman emperor.

Jung told me this amazing incident some weeks after the outbreak of war, and he added that it was not only Hitler who was possessed but the whole German nation: "It is no use saying you are not at war with the German people, you are; they are all possessed like Hitler and absolutely unapproachable." Indeed, Jung, who had made such untold efforts to make the Germans conscious of what was happening in their country, more or less gave up at this point because he saw the case was hopeless; it could only proceed toward inevitable disaster.

This approaching disaster was sadly evident during that last Eranos Tagung before the war, but except when some incident forced it on his notice Jung seldom spoke of the coming war. He evidently believed in carrying on with our normal lives as long as possible. Life, therefore, at the Monte Verità hotel went on much as usual. There were expeditions to remote Tessin villages and long discussions after meals. But there were several people present whom we were never to see again, even such close friends as Peter Baynes and Heinrich Zimmer, and although we did not know this, such events cast their shadows before. Heinrich Zimmer was already in considerable trouble. He was married to the daughter of Hugo von Hoffmannsthal, the Austrian poet, who was of Jewish descent. Although Zimmer was of pure Aryan descent, he had forestalled trouble by very regretfully resigning his professorship at Heidelberg and emigrating to Oxford. But he was German through and through and, although very hospitably received and with near relations of his wife already in England, he was unable to accustom himself to Oxford. The very next year he emigrated to the United States, where he worked first at the Johns Hopkins University in Baltimore, then at Columbia University. In 1939 Zimmer was busily cheering himself up at Ascona with the prospect of at last visiting India in the autumn, but I do not think he really believed that war would be delayed long enough for him to go.

Jung expressed the whole atmosphere of this Tagung when he said that there was "a feeling of the Last Judgment in the air." He used to say later that 1939 was by no means the only time when he felt a Last Judgment air at Ascona: "One always somehow has the feeling there that one must say all the important things, for it will be the last time one can do so." But it seems as if August, 1939, set a stamp on the Tagung which it was never quite able to shake off in the subsequent years I attended it, until about 1954.

Since we always saw Dr. Jolande Jacobi at Ascona and since it was about this time that she moved to Zürich, this may be a convenient place to speak briefly of her earlier acquaintance with Jung. I first heard of her in 1931 when Jung gave a lecture at the Kulturbund in Vienna.[c] Dr. Jacobi had really created the Kulturbund, much as Frau Fröbe had created Eranos, and Jung came back from Vienna very much impressed by her unusual efficiency and energy. He lectured there again in 1932[16] and she also visited Zürich. The acquaintance was always kept up by meetings at the Eranos Tagung each year, when she used to stay at the Monte Verità hotel and was a most dynamic element, especially at the evening parties, for she had great social gifts. When the Germans marched into Austria, Dr. Jacobi moved back to Budapest, her hometown, for she was Hungarian by birth. Her husband had been living in Budapest part of the time she was in Vienna, and she rejoined him there.

When the Germans moved into Czechoslovakia, however, she thought it would not be long before they also took Hungary, so she decided to move to Switzerland. Jung did everything he could to help her, as he always helped Jews who were threatened by the Nazis. Nevertheless, he was very doubtful as to whether Zürich was the right place for such a dynamic extravert. Although he always appreciated her energy and efficiency, they were very difficult for each other. Her goal, for which she strove passionately and constantly, was to put Jung on the map on a grand scale, whereas he felt he was already much too much on the map.

Although no introvert could quite agree with her goal, the way she shouldered her difficulties when she first came to Zürich must command respect. After being a rich and famous hostess in Vienna, she began again from the bottom in Zürich, with very little money and temperamentally anything but in sympathy with the introverted Swiss. In a surprisingly short time, however, she made good. She held her own during the war, although that was not a time when her extraverted talents could unfold as they did later.

When the Eranos Tagung was over in 1939, we all went our several ways. The Jungs usually went off by themselves in their own car at the end of the Tagung, for a short expedition before returning home, but I forget where, or even if, they went that year. Many of our group went home via Geneva, since the Prado had sent most of its Velázquez paintings for safekeeping to Switzerland during the Spanish Civil War. That war was now over, but the Spanish permitted the Swiss to exhibit the pictures in Geneva before they were returned.

We were all home again and Jung was at Bollingen when the news of the unholy alliance of Germany with Russia burst upon a horrified Europe.

[c] In the German first volume of Jung's letters, there are some to Dr. Jacobi dated much earlier. She is best known as the author of many popular books on Jungian psychology.

Jung was further disturbed by a most indigestible dream which he had immediately afterward. He dreamed that Hitler was "the devil's Christ," the Anti-Christ, but that nevertheless, as such, he was the *instrument of God*. He told me it took him a long time and much effort before he was able to accept this idea. Although Jung had been occupied with the idea of the dark side of God since his childhood, it was still many years before he finally faced the problem in *Answer to Job*, and the idea that a dangerous madman like Hitler could be the instrument of God was still far from his consciousness when he had this dream.

Jung was in Küsnacht for a day or two when war actually broke out. Marie-Jeanne Schmid was having the only long holiday (about three months) that she had in the twenty years she was Jung's secretary. Therefore Riwkah Schärf (later Mrs. Yehezkel Kluger) was helping him with his necessary correspondence from time to time. She told me he was in the garden when she arrived that afternoon. Looking stricken to the heart, he said: "A second world war in one lifetime, how can that be endured?" Later, he sometimes used to say, when things looked very black in the fifties: "I do not think I could survive a third world war." The prospect of such a war, with the general suffering it would produce, made it almost unbearable for him to contemplate, though he knew that reality cannot be ignored.

# 14

## The Second World War
## 1939–1945

In the autumn of 1939, Jung spent the time between Eranos and his return to work in the middle of October at Bollingen. He did indeed go down to Küsnacht for a day or even for a few days whenever it was necessary, but Bollingen was always by far the best place for him to come to terms with things like the mounting tension in Europe (which he had first realized in 1926) and such catastrophes as the outbreak of another world war. This was, I think, because the Tower was especially the place of the Self, with its totally different standpoint toward things that happen in space and time.[1]

A dream which a woman had some years ago, during one of those periods when a third world war looked almost inevitable, may make this clearer. In the dream she was as near panic about the war as she felt in reality, then she was infinitely reassured by a goddesslike figure coming toward her, saying: "But even if war does break out, it will not be worse to me than a bad dream." The East tries to identify with this point of view, declares the world to be mere illusion, and seeks liberation from the warring opposites in Nirvana. But Jung thought that in the West we should make every effort to become *conscious* of the eternal standpoint, then do our best to reconcile it with three-dimensional reality in our *actual life*, in the here and now. Therefore, if we are obliged to live through another world war, that is a painful *fact* with which we must reckon and certainly no illusion.

Jung made this idea of two standpoints particularly clear in his commentary on *The Secret of the Golden Flower*. He wrote of the fact that, in favorable cases, some people seem to outgrow a problem that would destroy others. They gain a new level of consciousness, as it were, from which they can see even the worst problem in a totally different light. He explained:

What, on a lower level, had led to the wildest conflicts and to panicky outbursts of emotion, from the higher level of the personality now looked like a storm in the valley seen from the mountain top. This does not mean that the storm is robbed of its reality but instead of being in it, one is above it. But since in a psychic sense, we are both valley and mountain, it might seem a vain illusion to deem oneself beyond what is human. One certainly does feel the affect and is shaken and tormented by it, yet at the same time one is aware of a higher consciousness looking on which prevents one from becoming identical with the affect and can say: "I *know* that I suffer." What our text says of indolence, "Indolence of which a man is conscious, and indolence of which he is unconscious are a thousand miles apart"[2] holds true in the highest degree of affect.[3]

By this time Jung was always able to reach both these standpoints (mountain and valley, Self and ego) wherever he was, but Bollingen was the place that lay directly beside the mountain, so to speak, where its outlook was most accessible to him. Jung had a very unusual and profound love of humanity, and always took every human life seriously, so that general catastrophes, like a world war, were very hard indeed for him to accept. It was, however, a fortunate circumstance for him that war broke out in the long summer holidays when he was always at Bollingen. It was evident when he came back to Küsnacht in October that, although the war was still an agony to him in the valley, he could also see it objectively and calmly from above, from the mountain. Both these points of view were present simultaneously, although the one that fitted the situation was often more evident. One could also express it quite differently and say that in Bollingen he became fully conscious of all the suffering involved and accepted it sufficiently to be able to say: "I *know* that the world including myself is going through an incomprehensible amount of suffering."

The point of view obtained from the mountain was particularly visible at the E. T. H. lectures, which he resumed on November 3, 1939. He had finished his Eastern texts in June and had devoted the last four lectures of the summer semester to "The Exercitia Spiritualia of St. Ignatius of Loyola," as a Western example of his general theme of active imagination. When he resumed these lectures, he pursued the same course as he had in Berlin six years before: he hardly referred to the outer situation but tried to open the eyes of his large audience to the *reality* of the psyche, to the inner life and its different point of view. The material itself, however, led him to make a most telling point, which really struck home to many in his audience. I remember vividly thinking at the time: "At last one sees a meaning in the war."

Jung was speaking of an introduction to the Ignatian "Exercitia

Spiritualia" by an old Spanish Jesuit, Izquierdus, who lived in the early seventeenth century. When defining the difference between mortal and venial sin, Izquierdus had said: "There is really only one mortal sin, which consists in placing the goal in the creature instead of in God," and "For the man who stands in mortal sin there is no God, no Heaven and no salvation." Jung commented that, according to this, practically the whole of Western humanity was in mortal sin.

Translated into the language Jung used in his commentary on *The Secret of the Golden Flower*, practically "the whole of Western humanity" finds its only goal in the valley, because it no longer knows that the mountain exists. Yet it is only from the mountain that the goal Izquierdus calls God can be seen. Therefore—from his point of view—Western humanity is practically all in mortal sin. We really come back again to Jung's realization of the myth of modern man fifteen years before on the East African Athi Plains: man's consciousness is "indispensable for the completion of creation" if it is not to go down to its unknown end "in the profoundest night of non-being."[4]

There was an unpleasant uncertainty in the air after Germany conquered Poland, and the so-called *drôle de guerre* had begun in the West. Military circles in Switzerland were much disquieted by the concentration of German troops on the northern border. At that time it was thought only too likely that Germany, instead of attacking the so-called impregnable Maginot Line, would violate Swiss neutrality and attack France by that route. There was never anything like panic, for Switzerland knew itself to be well armed and was determined to defend itself to the last man.

Even when the Maginot Line was forced and the German armies were pouring into Belgium, Holland, and France, the pressure on Switzerland did not relax. On the contrary, still more German troops were concentrated on the Swiss border and it was afterward revealed that had France not crumpled so quickly, Germany would have tried to attack her through the comparatively level northwest of Switzerland. The troops from the more primitive "Inner Schweiz" even swore that the Germans were prevented from crossing the Swiss border only by the Swiss saint, Niklaus von der Flüe! Officers of these regiments told us afterward that many of their men were convinced they had seen him, preventing the Germans from touching Swiss soil.

Be this as it may, it was an unpleasant fact that the Swiss main line of defense was in the mountains, behind Zürich. I spent an evening with Emma Jung about this time and she told me how worried she was about her many grandchildren. Emma was afraid Jung would refuse to leave his practice, but the whole family had taken a small pension near Saanen, in the Bernese Oberland and she hoped, if they were informed that the situation was desperate, he would at least consent to see them all into safety. All the younger men in the family—her son and sons-in-law—were on active service in the army. She was worried about whether or not they had enough room in their car to transport all the children,[a] so we arranged to take my car too. Our gasoline allowance was shrinking each month but I had enough saved up for any such emergency.

Nevertheless, I was considerably taken by surprise (for of course I did not know then that Jung had received an urgent warning from Bern) when Marie-Jeanne Schmid rang up early one morning to say the Jungs would be grateful if I would transport two of their grandchildren as soon as possible to Saanen in the Bernese Oberland. Since that left me with one free seat, I also took Elizabeth Welsh, who had arrived from England shortly before and was also living at the Hotel Sonne in Küsnacht. We got to Jung's house as soon as we could, though not before their car had started, but the children whom I was to transport were still there.

Of course I knew our destination but I did not know whether Jung would go by the Brünig Pass or by Bern. I decided on the former route, since I felt big towns were better avoided under the circumstances. I was, however, very glad indeed to be passed by the Jungs' car—with Jung driving—in the Sihltal, some ten miles out of Zürich. (They had also been taken by surprise and had had to go to the bank in Zürich to get money.) Although there were a great many controls on the road, we just missed them all, and met for lunch on the other side of Lucerne at Alpnachstad, just by the funicular which goes up Mount Pilatus.

Here we learned what had caused the Jungs to take their grandchildren and daughter-in-law so suddenly to the mountains. He had been telephoned from a very high place in Bern, late the night before, and asked to leave Zürich immediately. The Swiss authorities had learned that Jung's name was on the Nazi blacklist and they did not want the Germans to have an opportunity to capture him. This information—added to Emma's previous anxiety—left him with no choice: he had to drive the family car to Saanen, although one could see it went terribly against the grain to leave his practice at such a moment. That morning, moreover, he had been called by a friend in the High Command of the army who said that Switzerland was almost sure to be attacked that very day. We made a rendezvous at Spiez, on the Lake of Thun, where the Jungs were to meet one of their younger daughters who was taking her own children direct. I was probably to take the children I had in my car to their other grandparents on the Lake of Thun.

When we met the daughter, however, she told us it had been decided that it would be safer to take all the children to Saanen. So we delivered them to the charming little pension the whole family had rented, situated with a

---

[a] The Jungs eventually had nineteen grandchildren, but not all of them had been born by 1940.

beautiful view up above Saanen. We then went on ourselves to a hotel near Gstaad, three or four miles away. When France collapsed so quickly, the Germans refrained after all from attacking, for they knew the Swiss army could account for at least half a million of their men. This was by no means the only time during the war that the Germans massed their troops against Switzerland, but they always thought better of it at the last moment. They used to call Switzerland "that prickly little hedgehog."

It was only a very few days before Jung went back by train to his practice in Küsnacht, and from then on, until early July, he divided his time between there and his family in Saanen. He was usually in Küsnacht for the middle of the week and in Saanen for a long weekend. By this time, moreover, two or three more of Jung's pupils had joined us at the hotel near Gstaad, and Jung used to walk over nearly every weekend to give those pupils who were still in analysis with him an hour, then stay to lunch, walking back in the early afternoon. I was fortunate enough to have sufficient gasoline to take Jung back to Küsnacht on two of his visits. (Quite a few filling stations in the empty tourist centers conveniently "forgot" to ask cars with numbers from another canton for coupons!) These were strange, memorable drives, through a fully armed countryside, on roads that were almost empty except for military traffic. In the meantime, the fall of France had relieved the pressure on the Swiss border, and Jung spent all the rest of the war in Küsnacht or Bollingen.

There was no regular Eranos Tagung that summer, but at Frau Fröbe's urgent request Jung went down to Ascona to take part in a sort of token Tagung. It consisted of two lectures, one by Jung and one by Prof. Andreas Speiser,[b] to a very small audience. Jung, who wished to keep this token Tagung small, discouraged his own pupils from going. The 1940 Eranos Tagung was therefore the only one I missed in twenty years. Both Jung and Professor Speiser spoke on the Trinity from the viewpoint of very different fields. Jung spoke extemporaneously—as he had the year before—but a stenogram was taken and he eventually revised and expanded this lecture into "A Psychological Approach to the Dogma of the Trinity." It appeared in German in *Symbolik des Geistes* in 1948, from which version the English is taken.[5]

The rest of the summer vacation was spent as usual in Bollingen, with days in Küsnacht when necessary. By this time life had returned more or less to normal in Switzerland and Jung resumed his work in the autumn, both analysis and lectures at the E.T.H. There were, of course, many fewer foreigners in Switzerland, by this time, only those of us who had settled there and occasional short-time visitors who somehow managed to get over

---

[b] At that time, he was professor of mathematics at Zürich University, but in 1944 he moved to Basel University.

the frontiers. There was strong anti-German feeling all over Switzerland—it would not be exaggerating to call it hatred—and this time the Swiss were practically unanimous, not divided, as in World War I. The few of us who were here had the great advantage of being a very small group, a thing always much appreciated by Jung.

By the autumn of 1940 private cars no longer received a gasoline allowance. By the spring of 1941 they were no longer allowed on the roads at all, even if their owners still had some gasoline saved up. Doctors who had to visit their patients were naturally given a ration, but consultants like Jung, who worked in their own houses, got none. I remember a French-woman, who had somehow succeeded in getting a permit to visit Jung from Paris, being unable to believe that he had no fuel for his car. "But of course there is petrol for someone like you," she said to him. He assured her that the Swiss made no such exceptions and that he had no more petrol than anyone else. Whether he could have got any for his work at the E.T.H., I do not know, but I am quite sure he never asked. He just patiently walked nearly a mile to the station, went into Zürich by train, then took a trolley up to the university. It must have been very tiring, but I never heard him complain.

Jung also submitted patiently to every regulation made for wartime conditions. For instance, he plowed up the required percentage of his ground at Bollingen for the planting of potatoes. I remember one day, when we were all working on those potatoes, he found a dead mouse and, thinking it would interest my Cairn terrier, threw it to her. For some reason, however, she took this as a personal insult and came to me complaining bitterly. He was amused at her offended dignity and quite amazed, when she saw him again three weeks later, that she cut him dead on the platform of Küsnacht station. Since she generally greeted him with the greatest enthusiasm wherever she met him, he asked: "Whatever is the matter with the dog? She simply turns her back on me." I said I expected it was still the mouse. "Oh, dear," he replied, "I quite forgot my bush manners when I did that!"

The great Swiss doctor and alchemist, Paracelsus, died in 1541. In spite of the war, the four hundredth anniversary was much celebrated in Switzerland and Jung was asked to lecture both at Basel, on September 7, and at the big celebration in Einsiedeln, on October 5. The first lecture was called "Paracelsus, the Physician." [6] The second—which went much deeper—was called "Paracelsus as a Spiritual Phenomenon." [7] Both lectures were published in German together in 1942 as *Paracelsica* but, whereas the first was published almost as it was given, Jung took a lot of trouble in the autumn of 1941 to work out and enlarge the second, for, as he explained in the Preface to *Paracelsica*, it was not possible in a lecture to give any idea of the enigmatic figure of Paracelsus himself, who is hidden behind his numerous medical, scientific, and theological writings. In fact, Jung said that it is very difficult to solve the riddle of Paracelsus and that the reader should consider his essay as a mere attempt to see something of the secret philosophy of Paracelsus and not think that he laid claim to having said anything conclusive on this difficult subject. Be this as it may, he certainly held his large audience in Einsiedeln spellbound, that October evening, in the large lecture hall that lies behind the cathedral and monastery buildings adjacent to the fields containing the young stock of the horse breeding center for which Einsiedeln is famous throughout Switzerland.

Altogether, those few days which we spent in hotels in Einsiedeln were a most welcome oasis in a particularly dark time of the war, when Germany was practically the ruler of Europe. Although very different, it reminded us of earlier years at Ascona, when we had all stayed at the Monte Verità Hotel. Einsiedeln is indelibly connected with Paracelsus, for he was born in a cottage, still standing, only two or three miles away. Something of his atmosphere still remains. Moreover, it is a place of pilgrimage. The Black Madonna of Einsiedeln is said to have brought about many cures and rescues. The monastery, with its large boys' school and its horse breeding establishment, also has a special charm of its own. Jung once spent a few days' holiday in Einsiedeln later during the war and came back unusually pleased with its abbot and the other monks, and with the whole restful atmosphere of the place.

Although the Einsiedeln Paracelsus celebration stands out in my memory as an unusually meaningful time, the two Eranos meetings of 1941 and 1942, though much changed from before the war, were also worthwhile gatherings. No one came who was not living in Switzerland, but in 1941 Jung gave one of his best Eranos lectures on the "Transformation Symbolism in the Mass,"[8] and in 1942 another alchemical lecture, "The Spirit Mercurius."[9] The Hungarian professor Karl Kerényi, who later took refuge in Switzerland and who was destined to become a veritable pillar of Eranos, lecturing every year until quite recently, first came in 1941.[c] Max Pulver, the Swiss graphologist, also became a regular lecturer in 1941, and some other Swiss professors replaced the foreign professors who could no longer attend the meeting.

Of course, life was very different without our cars and we missed the Jungs in our daily life, for from then on they stayed in the flat over the lecture hall. But there was a very nice hotel, the Collinetta, in Moscia, quite close to Eranos, where Toni Wolff and many of our old Verità group lived happily in 1941 and 1942. Then, unfortunately, it ceased to be a hotel. After that there was no general hotel and everybody had to lodge in Ascona, or

[c] Professor Kerényi died in 1973.

very near it, with a transportation problem to Eranos in the hot August days.

It was in 1942 that Jung was asked by some leading Swiss and a German psychiatrist to help in an attempt they planned to make to reestablish peace. Jung threw himself into this project at first with considerable enthusiasm. It was kept completely secret at the time, of course, and I knew about it only because Jung thought I would be a suitable person to take their message to England. "No one would ever suspect you," he said. Moreover, since the person they wanted to approach in England was Archbishop Temple (whom Jung knew, respected, and liked), I should—from my past—have had no difficulty in getting an interview with him.

The German doctor was far from being a Nazi, but through his profession he had direct access to Nazi headquarters. He reported that Hitler was becoming doubtful if he could really win the war and might be willing, the doctor thought, to make a peace treaty acceptable to the Allies. Jung was enormously attracted by the possibility of saving many lives and much suffering, and spoke to me of the project as something very close to his heart. He asked me to hold myself ready but not as yet to ask the British Consulate for my papers. It would, of course, have been easy and would have looked quite natural for me to ask to be repatriated to my own country. On the other hand, it was most unlikely that I could get back to Switzerland until after the end of the war. It was, therefore, with a heavy heart—for I already felt Switzerland to be my home, containing all my dearest friends—that I accepted; it was something which I realized at once could on no account be refused.

Jung told me of the project in June. Toward the end of July he asked me up to Bollingen for the day, since he evidently wanted to discuss the matter. He was waiting by the garage when I arrived, for he had not said a word about it even to his wife or Toni Wolff; it was at that time so hush-hush that even now I can hardly make myself write about it. He told me the latest developments. He was very hopeful that it would go through but he was not certain it would, and he told me to continue to delay asking for my papers. I had dreamed of the project for the first time the night before and, when he heard this, he at once asked for the dream.

I dreamed that it was his son, still a very young man in the dream, who was running the project, and a voice informed me that nothing could come of it. But, it added, it should never be held against him, for it was motivated by the very purest love of humanity. Jung swore quite fluently and said: "Oh, damn it! Am I being too naïve?" He then added that somewhere he had always feared it was a pipe dream, but that we would still wait to see what happened, before making a decision of any sort.

Some weeks later, at a concert one evening during the Eranos Tagung, he came to sit by me and murmured under cover of the music: "Yours was an Abraham's sacrifice, we have had to give up the whole idea!" He added: "The Nazis are too evil, no peace can be made with them, the whole thing will have to be completely destroyed, whatever it costs." The next day, during the journey back to Küsnacht, he told me what had happened. When it was mentioned to Hitler, he had flown into one of his berserker rages, and the German psychiatrist had saved his life only by escaping to Switzerland, where he had to remain for the rest of the war. Jung told me that since the unconscious had begun criticizing the project, he had lost his enthusiasm and his earlier trust in it, but was glad, under the circumstances, that it had settled itself without his being forced to withdraw his support. This was typical of Jung's attitude to the unconscious: he always sacrificed his ego will to the superior wisdom of the unconscious; in this case it was a great sacrifice, for he had been set on the hope of saving untold suffering and lives; but he never obeyed it blindly or hastily, only after a careful consideration of all the pros and cons. Once this question was settled, I never heard him mention it again.

The war revealed the most ardent patriotism in Toni Wolff. I always knew Switzerland mattered tremendously to her, but she was over fifty when the war broke out and I admit I was surprised that she put her time and her car voluntarily and unstintingly in the service of the Frauen-hilfsdienst (roughly, Women's Helpers Service). She was already threatened by arthritis and the rough life was anything but good for her, but she spared herself nothing. She was in the motorized section and of course had to sleep in dormitories, often under cold and uncomfortable conditions.

Jakob Bosshard, a mutual friend of Toni's and mine, who had been a young colleague of Toni's father in Japan, told me that he knew her commanding officer and he had told him that Toni was the most valuable asset her unit possessed: not because she was a good driver, in fact she was seldom allowed to drive a car, but because she had such a marvelous influence on her much younger companions. She could inspire them to work as no one else could and never countenanced any relaxation until the last job was done. She never spared herself, in spite of her much greater age and increasing arthritis, and her example worked miracles in her environment.

She continued too long, however, after the doctors had begged her to let them demobilize her, and paid for it by constant pain during the last years of her life. It also gradually cut her off from the greatest pleasure of her life: her stays with Jung at Bollingen. His Tower was too near the lake for her; when there her hands went back on her and refused the service she asked of them. I never once heard her complain, though I doubt if she was ever out of pain, but, unless one asked, she never mentioned it, and forced herself to do everything as long as she possibly could.

The year 1943 was the first time, since he began in 1933, that Jung did not lecture at Eranos, although he and Emma Jung attended the meeting as usual. Jung's creative libido was already flowing into his greatest book, the *Mysterium Coniunctionis*, and he felt he could not divert it in order to write a lecture for the Eranos Tagung that year, whose theme was "Old Sun Cults and the Symbolism of Light in Gnosis and Early Christianity." This was, of course, a great loss for the Tagung and a grief to Frau Fröbe-Kapteyn, though she was somewhat consoled by Jung's consenting to attend. He also took a leading part in the discussions, held on the terrace after the lectures, or at Frau Fröbe's own round table.

The lectures were enriched that year by the French professor Louis Massignon who somehow managed to attend. He had lectured before the war at Eranos, from 1937 to 1939, and we had all appreciated his lectures on Islam and his experience of Islamic countries. I no longer remember how he managed these appearances in the midst of the war, but I know we were pleased to see him. Another addition to the lectures in 1943 was Prof. Hugo Rahner from Innsbruck. He belonged to a Jesuit community which had taken refuge from the Nazis in Switzerland. He continued to lecture at Eranos all the while his order was in Switzerland. He was a specialist on the writings of the Fathers of the Church, a well-known author and an unusually good lecturer, as well as a charming personality.

Jung had much more time for his alchemical studies and writing during the war than he had ever had before. He still had a very large practice, but with most of his foreign patients and pupils segregated by the war in their own countries, he no longer had to work such long hours. He had already given up his lecturing and the children's dreams seminar at the E.T.H. in 1941, and for the first time since the "confrontation with the unconscious" he had some time for himself, freed from the pressure that had been incessant since 1919. He still went every other Saturday evening to the lecture at the Psychological Club. He repeated his Eranos lectures there, for naturally only a very small percentage of the club had heard them in Ascona. He also had small discussion groups from time to time, and no one sincerely asked him for help without response. But at last he had time to write books on alchemy, as he had been wanting to do for so long.

The first result was *Psychology and Alchemy*,[10] completed, to judge by the date of the preface, by January, 1943. The first Swiss edition, however, was not published until 1944. Although Parts II and III had originally been his Eranos lectures of 1935 and 1936, they were so much revised, enlarged, and rewritten that they seemed almost new to his readers, and the long and particularly illuminating introduction and the end of the book were entirely new.

*Psychology and Alchemy* had hardly been completed before Jung started on his *opus magnum*, the *Mysterium Coniunctionis*. The first chapters of that book were all written before Jung's illness in 1944. Although the suffering of the war was always hard for Jung to bear, World War II was nevertheless an exceedingly creative time for him.

The year 1943 brought the loss of two very dear friends: Heinrich Zimmer and Peter Baynes. In 1940, Professor Zimmer had left Oxford—where he never felt able to take root, although he made a good connection with the Analytical Psychology Club in London and made friends with Peter Baynes—and with his family had gone to New York. We knew at the time only that he was teaching at Columbia University and was apparently all set for a successful new career in America, when he died quite suddenly on March 18, 1943, of pneumonia. We heard, however, after the war from a mutual friend that once again, as in Oxford, he had been unable to take root and never felt at home in New York. The language was a great difficulty, he never really mastered English, and this friend—who was American by birth but completely bilingual—said that he always insisted on talking German, even in public, which was naturally anything but politic. Jung reminded us that he had always been apprehensive, on account of the extraordinarily childlike quality of Zimmer's hands, about his ability to grasp a difficult reality. It was a tragedy that he had to leave his beloved Heidelberg, and one feels that if only he had been able to remain, he need perhaps not have died at the early age of fifty-two.

Peter Baynes, who had been Jung's assistant more than once and a member of the Zürich club for twenty-three years, was an even closer friend, so it was a great shock to hear that he had also died, in England on September 6, 1943. He was eight or nine years older than Zimmer and had been suffering from a duodenal ulcer for some years. But, as we heard later, he had died quite unexpectedly of a tumor on the brain, which no one, not even Jung, had for a moment suspected. He was an irreparable loss to Jungian psychology in England and his death was a great grief to everyone who knew him well, for he was, and always had been, a most lovable person. Jung was much distressed by both these deaths.

Perhaps the greatest milestone in Jung's attainment of wholeness—with the solitary exception of his "confrontation with the unconscious"—was provided by his illness in 1944. I do not wish to assert that Jung attained complete wholeness; it would go against his whole *Weltanschauung* for me to make any such claim. He always said the Self, and therefore wholeness, reached *far beyond* our comprehension, and that we should regard everything we learned as a temporary stage *on the way* to comprehension. Therefore I would claim only that Jung attained the maximum amount of wholeness that was attainable *to him*.

Early in 1944—on February 11 to be exact—Jung was out for his daily walk. Since his return from India in 1938, he had continued to walk as much as possible, and when the war gave him more leisure he walked several miles every day. He was a mile or two from his home when he slipped rather badly on the snow. This was very unusual, for right into old age Jung was unusually surefooted in snow. He did not fall but felt that he had hurt his leg seriously. He limped to the nearest house—fortunately it was quite close—and telephoned for a taxi to take him home. His own physician, Dr. Jakob Stahel Sr., who was the very pattern of the old family doctor, was away, but his son, then a very young doctor, came at once and diagnosed quite correctly that Jung had broken his fibula. He insisted on Jung's going immediately to a large private hospital called Hirslanden on the outskirts of Zürich, and put him under a very able young surgeon. Like many surgeons, particularly at the beginning of their work, this one probably thought more of what was right for the broken leg than for an active old man of nearly seventy, so he insisted on the limb being kept quite still. At first Jung read his alchemistic books quite happily, but soon his active body rebelled against inactivity, and about ten days after entering the hospital he had a very bad thrombosis of the heart and two others which went to his lungs. It was totally unexpected. Emma Jung was in town and was contacted with great difficulty. She stayed in the hospital with him—she was able to obtain a room in another wing but quite close—until he could go home. Jung was at death's door and remained so for several weeks. His life was saved by a heart specialist—Jung spoke of him as Dr. H. in *Memories* [11] [d]—who was perhaps the most famous heart specialist of his time, at all events in Switzerland.

As Jung related in *Memories*, [12] he became very worried about his doctor because he had seen him in a vision "in his primal form, as a *basileus* of Kos." [e] After his illness, particularly after Dr. H. died, Jung was still distressed by the idea that this death might be connected with his own almost miraculous recovery. He pointed out that Zeus himself was said to have killed Aesculapius by a thunderbolt because he had brought back patients from death. Later, in the Aesculapian sanctuaries, doctors might save any lives they could among their patients but were forbidden to bring anyone back from the dead. Should they break this law, they had to pay for it with their own lives. Jung was somewhat consoled, however, when he heard that a friend of Dr. H.—another well-known Zürich specialist—had been distressed about him several months *before* Jung's illness began. He said that he had implored Dr. H. to watch his step and to permit a thorough medical examination, because, as his doctor friend stated, he looked and seemed really unwell. Like most doctors, Dr. H., however, did not follow the advice he would certainly have given to any of his patients, and was evidently not in good health, even prior to Jung's illness.

This vision took place when Jung was very near death. As he related in

[d] Dr. Theodor Haemmerli-Schindler.
[e] See above, page 57.

*Memories*,[13] he felt he was leaving the earth, which he could see below him as if from a thousand miles in the air , and felt "the whole phantasmagoria of earthly existence" fall away or being stripped from him, until he was left with just what he was. In other words, he was left with the degree of wholeness he had attained during his earthly life. At first there was a sense of annihilation, as everything familiar was stripped from him, then this became of no consequence, for he had everything he was and "that was everything."

Jung was on the point of entering a temple hollowed out of a "gigantic dark block" of "tawny granite," which he was longing to do because he knew all his questions would be answered there, for he would meet all the people to whom he really belonged and these were those who knew the answers to his burning questions. Just before he entered, Dr. H. floated up in his primal form from the earth and said that he had been delegated to bring Jung a message: there was a protest against his leaving the earth, he had no right to do so and must return. Jung was profoundly disappointed, and at that point the vision ceased. This was the only time I know of in his whole life that Jung lost all desire to live; for several weeks he longed only to get back into the reality he had experienced in his visions and took a long time to regain his old conviction of the importance of this life, or rather that he had not already lived everything that belonged to his life on earth. He did eventually regain this conviction and lived another seventeen years, during which he wrote his most important books and attained still further wholeness.

There were many strange synchronistic events in the environment during the time that Jung lay between life and death. I will mention only two of these. One of his pupils had the worst attack of flu of her life and was also very near death. Then she had a sudden vision of Jung approaching her urgently, saying: "I have decided to go back to the earth; get back into your own body as quickly as you can." Another pupil, who also had a very bad attack of that year's virulent flu was suddenly horrified to find that her watch and the clock beside her bed had stopped at exactly the same moment. She was terrified that this might mean that Jung had died at that moment and went through great agony before she could get news of him.[f]

---

[f] It was certainly not by chance that it was just these two pupils of Jung who had these synchronistic experiences, for one of them had dreamed about three weeks before Jung broke his leg, that she was on a ship that was just at the point of sailing from a port on the west coast of Greece. The ship was crowded, but the only passenger she recognized was the other pupil (although they were not close friends). She said to her: "I thought Jung was coming on the ship, but I don't see him anywhere." Her fellow pupil replied: "Oh, yes, he is on the bridge," at which moment the ship sailed. After some time, for unknown reasons, it turned around and went back to the port from whence it had sailed. When Jung heard the dream, during his convalescence, he said that evidently those two pupils, or at all events the one who had the dream, would have died also, had he not been recalled to earth, for the boat in that dream must have been Charon's boat which set out to take them all over the Styx but had turned back for then unknown reasons.

As regards the "protest from the earth," there was great suffering among Jung's friends and pupils because no bulletins concerning his condition were issued, and it was next to impossible to get any reliable news. This gave rise to wild and alarming rumors. This custom is typically Swiss; illness is regarded as something that concerns *only* the family,[g] so no bulletins are given out—even on famous people—as they are in other countries. When the worst was over, I had occasion to talk over this past situation with another of Jung's pupils who, not being Swiss herself could not understand it. She felt somewhat bitter toward Emma Jung for not having realized the situation. I suggested that perhaps it was right psychologically, for perhaps everybody around Jung had to suffer the maximum in order to recall him to the earth. At that moment there was a loud report in an old tallboy in my room. (Immediately we were both reminded of the time this happened in Freud's bookcase.[14]) My friend said: "Why then it must be true." Immediately there was a second report, then no more.[h] Although Mrs. Jung was sorry when she learned how much suffering her silence had caused, and Jung himself gave orders that, in any future illness of his, regular and completely truthful bulletins were to be issued, I have always wondered whether that Swiss custom was not a blessing in disguise.

Jung had already written the early chapters of the *Mysterium Coniunctionis,* and before we consider the most important visions of his illness, those of the *hieros gamos* (the sacred marriage), I must anticipate for a moment, in order to report something he said after his illness to Marie-Louise von Franz, who worked with him on the *Mysterium Coniunctionis* both before and after his illness. He said of his previous work on the book: "All I have written is correct. I need not change a word, but I only realize its full reality now." He even told me once that his illness had been necessary, or he could never have *known* the full reality of the *mysterium coniunctionis*. In fact, it was presumably only because of his long and arduous work on the subject before that these visions, which he described as "the most tremendous things" that he "ever experienced," were revealed to him.[15]

Jung had suffered since early childhood from the opposites at war. One

---

[g] Some years before, at the beginning of the war, Jung had suffered from this ingrained Swiss habit. He had known Toni Wolff's mother was ill, but not that there was any immediate danger. Therefore, Toni was to go to Bollingen on a certain day. Instead, he received a telegram saying she had been prevented. He actually learned of the death of her mother from the newspaper. When he remonstrated later, Toni replied: "But naturally I could not let the post office at Bollingen know about that death until it was announced." Jung told me she was so convinced of this "fact" that he could only apologize for having been so dense as not to think of it! From the amazed way he told me, I saw that Jung himself had become more international than Swiss on this point—Swiss to the core though he was, he did not suffer from Swiss prejudices.

[h] I have known the tallboy all my life and still have it, but this is the only time I ever heard it make any noise.

need only remember this suffering when forced to think the blasphemous thought about God and his beautiful Basel Cathedral.[16] In fact, it started even earlier, at Laufen before he was four,[17] when he began to distrust the Lord Jesus, from realizing the dark, destructive side of this radiantly positive figure. We have also seen how he suffered from the two world wars, when the opposites clashed against each other on a worldwide scale. Perhaps it needs this amount of suffering from the separated and warring opposites to appreciate their union, as Jung appreciated the unique visions of the *mysterium coniunctionis* or *hieros gamos,* which he had every night for about three weeks while he was dangerously ill and while the days were still unmitigated hell. He told me later that, after those three weeks were over, this blissful state returned only once for about twelve hours when he had a pulse of 180.

He reported these visions fully in *Memories*. They all concerned the *hieros gamos*, the mystical marriage, the *coniunctio*. First he felt himself to be in the garden of pomegranates, where the wedding of Tifereth with Malchuth was taking place.[i] Or it was Rabbi Simon ben Jochai, whose disciples and friends celebrated his death as a marriage in the Beyond.[j] Later it was the Marriage of the Lamb in a festively decorated Jerusalem. And, as the last image, it was All-father Zeus and Hera, who at the end of a wide valley, which formed a classical amphitheater, were consummating the mystic marriage, as it is described in the *Iliad*. During all these visions[18] he reported that he felt in an utterly transformed state. He wrote:

> It was as if I were in an ecstasy. I felt as though I were floating in space, as though I were safe in the womb of the universe—in a tremendous void, but filled with the highest possible feeling of happiness. "This is eternal bliss," I thought. This cannot be described; it is too wonderful.[19]

When he was released from the hospital, he was still feeling, as it were, homesick for this "eternal bliss" and often said we would experience freedom from the tension and clash between the opposites only after death, as if it were "a consummation devoutly to be wished."[20] But many years later, after his "belief in the world had returned"[21] and he was doing his "best to form a conception of life after death"[22] and to describe this

---

[i] In Cabalistic doctrine, Malchuth and Tifereth represent the female and male principle within the Godhead.

[j] This idea of the *Todeshochzeit* (the death marriage) reminds one of Jung's strange experience after his mother's death, when his deep sorrow, as he traveled back from the Tessin to Zürich, was constantly interrupted by "dance music, laughter and jollity, as though a wedding were being celebrated." (*MDR*, p. 314.)

conception in the chapter "On Life after Death,"[23] he evidently felt that to think of his ecstasy as the *usual* condition of life in the Beyond would be too much "wishful thinking." He summed up his conclusion:

To follow out the thought that involuntarily comes to me: the world, I feel, is far too unitary for there to be a hereafter in which the rule of opposites is completely absent. There, too, is nature, which after its fashion is also God's. The world into which we enter after death will be grand and terrible, like God and like all of nature that we know. Nor can I conceive that suffering should entirely cease. Granted that what I experienced in my 1944 visions—liberation from the burden of the body, and perception of meaning—gave me the deepest bliss. Nevertheless, there was darkness too, and a strange cessation of human warmth. Remember the black rock to which I came! It was dark and of the hardest granite. What does that mean?[24]

He spoke afterward of that "strange cessation of human warmth" and said that, looking back, it seemed very strange to him that, on the point of entering the temple which he knew was death, he had not once thought of anyone on earth or felt any regret at leaving them. In fact, he told me later that the "world of Europe and all my life there had quite disappeared; that is, I remembered there had been some interlude of the kind but it was of no importance whatever." The only earthly thought that crossed his mind was that he hoped no one would disturb his pipes, as if somewhere he knew he was going to need them again. It was naturally very difficult and painful for his wife to endure his ardent longing for death and the temporary cessation of his usual human warmth. It is therefore interesting to remember that after her own death she evidently experienced exactly the same thing, judging by the dream-vision Jung had of her soon after she died.[25] He wrote that he saw her in the prime of her life, wearing the most beautiful dress she ever had. "Her expression was neither joyful nor sad, but, rather objectively wise and understanding, without the slightest emotional reaction, as though she were beyond the mist of affects." Jung commented on this dream and the result of his own visions:

The objectivity which I experienced in this dream and in the visions is part of a completed individuation. It signifies detachment from valuations and from what we call emotional ties. In general, emotional ties are very important to human beings. But they still contain projections, and it is essential to withdraw these projections in order to attain to oneself and to objectivity. Emotional relationships are relationships of desire, tainted by coercion and constraint; something is expected from the other person, and that makes him and ourselves unfree. Objective cognition lies hidden behind the attraction of the emotional relationship; it seems to be the central secret. Only through objective cognition is the real *coniunctio* possible.''[26]

This idea of "objective cognition" is very difficult to realize, for it is essentially beyond the experience of most people, including my own. But it most certainly changed and developed Jung to an incalculable extent. As I see it, however, it means seeing things from the mountain and being freed from all *identification* with the valley.[k] Before his illness one often felt he was on the mountain; one could say that the absolute knowledge in the unconscious was accessible to him, as it might be to an immortal; but he was also often completely in the valley. After his illness he seemed to be much more completely on the mountain, but at all times he could descend into the valley and speak and act in its terms.

Of course, I do not mean to assert that he was in any way freed from the general human ills that beset one in the valley, for, as he said, it might seem ''a vain illusion to deem oneself beyond what is human.'' He still had to go through a great deal of ill-health and was still liable to be annoyed, particularly by stupidity. Perhaps his attitude to annoyance can best be explained by an incident some years before during a discussion at the club. Jung said that when one lost one's temper, the battle was already lost. Emma Jung objected that in some situations anger was the only suitable reaction. He agreed with her but added: "Only if you could just as well react without anger; to be carried away by or possessed by anger is *always* a defeat." Jung said to me more than once that one was never beyond any human emotion, such as anger or jealousy, but one could always *know* it.

In his chapter on "Visions" he gave the most extraordinary description of his experience, which shows us the difference in standpoint between "mountain and valley" very closely. He said:

We shy away from the word "eternal" but I can describe the experience only as the ecstasy of a non-temporal state in which present, past, and future are one. Everything that happens in time had been brought together into a concrete whole. Nothing was distributed over time, nothing could be measured by temporal concepts. The experience might best be defined as a state of feeling, but one which cannot be produced by imagination. How can I imagine that I exist simultaneously the day before yesterday, today, and the day after tomorrow? There would be things which would not yet have begun, other things which would be indubitably present, and others again which would already be finished—and yet all this would be one. The

[k] See above, page 267.

only thing that feeling could grasp would be a sum, an iridescent whole, containing all at once expectation of a beginning, surprise at what is now happening, and satisfaction or disappointment with the result of what has happened. One is interwoven into an indescribable whole and yet observes it with complete objectivity.[27]

This presumably portrays the quintessence of what can be experienced on the mountain. While one is in the body, it would clearly be impossible to remain permanently outside time, for time is the condition, the essential limitation, of our earthly existence. Looking back on how Jung was in those seventeen years between his illness and his death, I realize that, though the mountain had been accessible to him for over a quarter of a century, since the "confrontation with the unconscious," its quintessence was first revealed to him during his 1944 illness, and that this gave him a far greater objectivity than he had ever attained before. Probably it was due to the accessibility of this timeless wholeness that he was able to go on living so completely after the blows of Toni Wolff's death in 1953 and that of his wife in 1955.

There was also a vision or experience—not mentioned in *Memories*—which he described to Emma Jung and myself very vividly, when I visited him in the hospital during his early convalescence. I never heard him speak of it later, but he told us then that as he was recovering from the very worst of his illness, he felt that his body had been dismembered and cut up into small pieces. Then, over quite a long period, it was slowly collected and put together again with the greatest care. This is a very interesting parallel to the widespread primitive rituals that were experienced by shamans or medicine men. There are innumerable such examples all over the world, described by Mircea Eliade in his interesting book on shamanism.[28] For example, both in Siberia and Australia the candidate for shamanism "is subjected to an operation by semi-divine beings or ancestors, in which his body is dismembered and his internal organs and bones are renewed."[29] In South America, as in Australia or Siberia, "both spontaneous vocation and the quest for initiation involve either a mysterious illness or a more or less symbolic ritual of mystical death, sometimes suggested by a dismemberment of the body and renewal of organs."[30] Very frequently crystals or other symbolic stones are introduced into the renewed body. I remember Jung saying that day that he had been obliged to do most of or all the reassembling himself, so it is interesting that Eliade wrote: "The primitive magician, the medicine man or shaman is not only a sick man, he is above all, a sick man who has been cured, *who has succeeded in curing himself*."[31] The idea always is that the body is put together better than it had been before.

I do not know if Jung remembered any of these parallels. I think he was too ill to do so at the time, and he did not mention anything of the kind. He spoke mainly of the physical side and of what an almost intolerable effort it had been in his weakened state to reassemble the whole body.

We mentioned this parallel to becoming a medicine man and how much it changed Jung, when speaking of his "confrontation with the unconscious." Although as a rule there is only one initiation, yet sometimes in an emergency, for example, when a great disaster threatens the tribe, the medicine man also goes through a second. One should remember in this connection that the first of Jung's initiations—to use that word—took place during the First World War and the second during the Second. We simply do not know if this had to be. Synchronistically—exactly as the end of the "confrontation with the unconscious" coincided with peace coming to the world—D-Day, which was the beginning of the end of the Second World War, took place while Jung was still in Hirslanden hospital, but after he had overcome his illness and was well on the road to convalescence.

When his body was once more assembled, Jung must have still been in the depths of the unconscious, for he told Marie-Louise von Franz that he first reexperienced his body as that of a big fish. This was such a realistic experience that for some time, whenever he was fed with spoonfuls of soup, he felt anxious about whether it would not flow out again at his gills!

In early July, about five months after his accident, Jung was at last pronounced well enough to go home. He stayed for some hours on the first floor—his own rooms were on the second floor—and he told me afterward that he wandered around their large room, picking up all the objects on the shelves and tables. He said it was as if he had to assure himself that everything was as it had been before his illness, for it seemed to him that he had been so far away and for so long that it was hardly possible that everything in his home could have remained unchanged.

It was not until the spring of 1945 that he was again allowed to live a very modified version of what his life had been before. In the meantime, he led a life that seemed to him very strange,[1] a period in which he had more time for himself than ever before. He worked on the *Mysterium Coniunctionis* with great enthusiasm, but was not strong enough to do more than at most two hours a day. Marie-Louise von Franz saw a great deal of him during those months, for she collaborated with him on that book both before and after his illness, and had continued her research work without interruption during the time he was in the hospital. She therefore had a great deal of the greatest interest to show him. At that time, he intended to go straight on with his *opus magnum* but this plan was interrupted, and he was to publish several other books before he was able to finish the *Mysterium Coniunctionis*. At the time we are considering, however, he was still working direct on the *Mysterium,* and since he could work only for a short time every day he had a great deal of leisure. He formed the habit at that time of

[1] I see in my notes that he described it as living right out of the twentieth century.

seeing one person every afternoon, not for analysis but for a friendly talk. This was the time we heard about the visions, which he afterward published more briefly in *Memories*. He remained from July, 1944, until the spring of 1945 in Küsnacht, for although he was longing for Bollingen it was not a suitable place for convalescence. The life there was intentionally primitive, with no modern conveniences, and it was not until April that his doctor allowed him to go, fourteen months after his accident.

Naïvely we all thought that going back to Bollingen would be a great pleasure for him. But I vividly remember a walk with him, just after his return to Küsnacht, when my illusions were rudely shattered. On being asked how he had enjoyed it, he replied: "It was hell." He then explained that he had not realized, in the comfortable life at Küsnacht, how little physical effort he could make, but at Bollingen he was reminded of that at every touch and turn. He did not stay very long those Easter holidays, for he realized he would have to change his whole attitude to the place before he could be happy there again. He had always done everything himself there—cut wood, draw water, manage his sailing boat, and so on—and of course for several years after such a bad heart attack he could do none of these things for himself. It was not the primitive life he minded; right to the end he steadfastly refused his friends' entreaties to have at least one room with modern conveniences. It was the helplessness of seeing jobs that needed doing and not being able to do them. He faced the whole thing squarely, and by the summer holidays could once more be perfectly happy at Bollingen. But this had required a very painful readaptation. Like so many things that are sacrificed, all those things eventually returned to him, at least to some extent.

Soon after he got back from Bollingen in the spring of 1945, Jung took up a very modified form of his former life. He no longer had lectures or a seminar at the E.T.H. and, although Basel University had given him a full professorship in 1943, he was regretfully unable to take up any work there. In fact, he tried to give up his professorship immediately after his illness, since he felt sure he would never be able to do the work attached, but the university insisted on his retaining it.[m] It certainly meant something to him that he had been given a chair at his grandfather's university, where he had done the whole of his own medical training. But he seldom gave a lecture after his illness and the added fatigue of the journey to Basel made it, of course, impossible.

The war meanwhile was slowly drawing to a close. After D-Day the Allies never looked back, and on May 7, 1945, the war in Europe came to an end. This was naturally a great relief to Jung, who so hated war, but it was

---

[m] When Jung died in 1961, he was still on the faculty at Basel University as a professor, although he was no longer active.

not such a well-marked event as it had been in 1918, for the war in the Pacific, which involved a great many Europeans, dragged on until later in the summer.

During this interregnum Jung celebrated his seventieth birthday, on July 26, 1945. Since no foreigners had yet come to Zürich, he was still able to keep it on a more or less private scale. It was not until his seventy-fifth, eightieth, and eighty-fifth birthdays that he could no longer prevent large celebrations. He enjoyed small celebrations as much as he disliked them on a big scale. His immediate family circle had become so large—all his children were married by this time and all of them had several children who were then growing up—so that family dinner parties were always quite as large gatherings as he really liked, especially after his 1944 illness. Therefore, the chief celebration for his seventieth birthday was a family dinner. However, he also had a tea party in his garden on the day itself, to which he invited all his nearest pupils and friends. There was a marvelous atmosphere at that party, for we were all so deeply thankful, after the fright of the year before, that he was still with us to celebrate the day.

By this time his health had greatly improved; in fact, visitors were inclined to think he seemed as well as before his illness. But his heart was always a cause for anxiety, and he had to have frequent electrocardiograms to check on its condition. Nevertheless, he was well enough to lecture at the Psychological Club to a small audience on June 9, 1945.

The Psychological Club resisted any celebration of Jung's birthday. This was mainly because Toni Wolff was still on the committee and, knowing how Jung disliked any larger fuss being made of his birthday, she was able to restrain the club from doing more than giving him a present she thought he would like. Incidentally, after the war Toni felt it was time there was a change in the presidency of the club, and she retired in favor of C. A. Meier. But when there was great difficulty in finding a club secretary, she immediately undertook this arduous and rather thankless post and worked even harder than she had as president. This was characteristic of Toni; she always did what she thought was best for the club and never bothered about her own prestige or power.

Emma Jung told me some weeks before the birthday that Dr. Jolande Jacobi had been eager to found an institute as a seventieth birthday present and a surprise for Jung. Emma had been quite sure, and I fully agreed, that it would be a most unwelcome surprise, and had managed to dissuade Dr. Jacobi. At that time Jung had entertained no idea of an institute, and in fact felt it would not suit his psychology. When he heard about it after his birthday, he was grateful to his wife for discouraging the idea.

On August 6, 1945, the atom bomb was dropped on Hiroshima and at last put an end to the war in the Pacific. Jung, like almost everybody else, was aghast at the suffering involved, but I think would probably have welcomed

Colonel Laurens van der Post's book, *The Night of the New Moon,*[32] which proves to me *how* necessary it was. At all events, 1945 saw the end of the worldwide clash of the opposites and left Jung much freer to devote his main attention to their union in his *Mysterium Coniunctionis.*

Jung much enjoyed his contact with Laurens van der Post, which began a few years after the war ended. Laurens was one of the rare people with whom Jung could communicate concerning his living experience of Africa, its beauty, and the problems of its primitive world. Although Jung often mentioned his loneliness in *Memories,* he once told me that though there was no one person with whom he could communicate all "the things that seemed important" to him, there was yet usually someone available for each of these things. Laurens filled this role to perfection regarding the deeper side of his experience in Africa.

Like Zimmer, he became a friend not only of Jung but of many of us. On June 6, 1972, he gave the speech at the memorial meeting which is held by the C. G. Jung Institute every year on the day Jung died, and everyone agreed it was one of the best speeches, if not *the* best, that had ever been given.

# 15

# Reaping the Harvest
## 1945–1952

The year of convalescence, after Jung's severe illness in 1944, when he was strictly rationed as to the amount of time he might work, expired almost simultaneously with the end of the war in Europe. Jung then entered on the most creative period of his life, during which the most important of his books were written. From that time on, for the first time in his life, his writing took precedence over his other work, though by the early summer of 1945 he had resumed some of his analytical work and, to a very limited extent, his lecturing; he also wrote short articles, as the need for them arose. He said of this creative period:

> After the illness a fruitful period of work began for me. A good many of my principal works were written only then. The insight I had had, or the vision of the end of all things, gave me the courage to undertake new formulations. I no longer attempted to put across my own opinion, but surrendered myself to the current of my thoughts. Thus one problem after the other revealed itself to me and took shape.[1]

It was these problems that "revealed" themselves to him and insisted on "taking shape" that prevented him for some years from continuing and finishing the *Mysterium Coniunctionis*, as he had intended. This last long book of his is comparable to *Faust* in the life of Goethe who used to call it his "main business" to which he always returned.

In order to give precedence to his writing, Jung enormously reduced his analytical work. With very rare exceptions he no longer took new cases, but he gave many single interviews to people who came to him from afar, and he made his regular pupils, who were still in analysis, stand much more on their own feet, seeing them only when they were really unable to find

288

their way for themselves. He thus succeeded in drastically cutting down the hours he gave to analytical work. After his illness, I do not think he ever did more than four hours[a] of analysis in a day. He tried to reduce this to two, one hour before lunch, after taking a walk and then writing; and one hour before dinner in the evening, after he had finished his writing for the day.

One of the first short articles he wrote after the war was entitled "After the Catastrophe" and was published in a Swiss magazine[2] in 1945. This was the first time since "Wotan" in 1936 that Jung had written on contemporary events. He did so in response to a persistent general request for some enlightenment as to what had really happened during the upheaval. As a rule he avoided such subjects, for he thought: "The great events of world history, are, at bottom, profoundly unimportant. In the last analysis, the essential thing is the life of the individual." But the suffering caused to innumerable individuals, by just such "great events" as the Second World War, was by no means unimportant to him. Knowing as he did that the German people could find peace in their all-important souls only if they faced up to what Germany had done, he wrote "After the Catastrophe" primarily as an attempt to help them to do so. It did enormously help a few individuals, but alas there were very few; for the most part Jung received only denials and protests for his pains. Even the appalling suffering that the war had brought to Germany itself was not enough to open German eyes to the paramount value of self-knowledge. In common fairness, however, I must add that Germans are by no means alone in their blindness in this respect. It is a lamentably common, almost universal, form of blindness in *all* nations.[b]

During these years I saw Jung most frequently on walks, and rereading my notes of our conversations on these walks, I see that he often emphasized, perhaps even more than before his illness, the necessity of always looking for the opposite to everything. He applied this one day even to his conviction that the individual is the only thing that matters. He pointed out, in reference to the period we are considering, that we in the West were justified in laying such exclusive stress on the individual only because of the tremendous tendency to collectivism in our age. The Nazis tried and now the Communists are trying to blot out consciousness, *which can be*

[a] I see in my notes for this period that one day, when he was unusually tired, he attributed it to having for once seen five people the day before.

[b] The committee of the Psychological Club decided that it must expel any member or statutory guest who had been a Nazi during the war. As far as I recall, there were only two: Dr. G. R. Heyer of Munich, who was a member; and a statutory guest, Dr. O. Curtius (who, I believe, had arranged the interview with Goebbels—see above, page 211 ff). It was a distasteful task, for it seemed like kicking a man when he was already down. But Jung agreed with the committee that it must be done, since the individuals in question had proved themselves entirely lacking in any understanding of Jungian psychology. Dr. Gerda Bertram of Bremen told me that at the end of his life Heyer most bitterly regretted not having remained loyal to Jung.

*attained only by the free individual*, and we must do all we can to compensate for this disastrous fact. Jung said that we do not fully live in the opposites: individual—collective. We live, rather, he said, "only on the fringe of collectivism and avoid the mainstream of events as much as possible. I am very conscious indeed that in this we are one-sided."

It is very difficult, if not impossible, to live right in the mainstream of events and keep one's consciousness. All too easily the individual is seized by the stream of events and swept into *participation mystique* with the crowd. Jung was deeply shocked when he saw how unconscious many of his earlier pupils had become as they slowly returned after the war from their war-torn countries. It was fortunate that Jung belonged to Switzerland, a nation which, for centuries, has been able to preserve its neutrality, for some distance was necessary in order to see what had really happened, as he did.

Although the individual tries to avoid the mainstream of events, Jung not only discharged all his own duties to collectivity extremely conscientiously, but also was very disapproving if any of his pupils tried to shirk this side of their lives. "You cannot individuate on Everest," he often said, pointing out that our relationships to other individuals and to collectivity are just as important as the work on ourselves. In fact, one belongs to the other, for there is certainly something wrong within ourselves if we cannot function in our environment.

Jung gave his first lecture after his illness at the Psychological Club on June 9, 1945, and in August he went to lecture to a much larger audience at the Eranos Tagung in Ascona. He thus missed only one Tagung on account of his 1944 illness. Marie-Louise von Franz and I had been to the 1944 Tagung and, quite apart from missing Jung's lecture, were very much struck by how much the whole atmosphere changed when his dynamic personality was not there to act as a center for the group. This was noticed by everybody present, not just by us. As Ernest O. Hauser began his article on Jung in the *Saturday Evening Post* (May, 1958): "It is impossible, on meeting Dr. Jung, not to be struck by the tremendous force that emanates from him."

In 1945, although the war was over, we all still went down to Ascona by train, for we did not get any gasoline until the following year. The Jungs stayed, as was now usual, in the flat over the lecture hall, and had their meals at Frau Fröbe's.

The general subject of the 1945 Tagung was "The Spirit." Jung's lecture that year is reproduced in *Papers from the Eranos Yearbooks* as "The Phenomenology of the Spirit in Fairy Tales,"[3] which describes its content very well, though at the time he called it *"Zur Psychologie des Geistes"* (Concerning the Psychology of the Spirit). There was also an extra volume of the Eranos Yearbook that year, in honor of Jung's seventieth birthday, to which most of the regular lecturers at Eranos contributed a paper. It forms the twelfth volume of the German series.

As Jung began to realize that "the current of his thought"—to which after his illness he was able to surrender fully—was not going straight on with the absorbingly interesting subject of the union of the opposites, he realized that something must be done to meet the constant demands on him to say something about the transference, a subject he had so far mentioned very little in his writings. Therefore, he took a section of the original *Mysterium Coniunctionis* that was complete in itself and published it as a separate volume called *The Psychology of Transference*.[1] I do not think he altered it at all, or only very slightly. He submitted it for publication in 1945 and it appeared in 1946.

In this work, Jung took a series of pictures from the *Rosarium Philosophorum* and used them as a thread of Ariadne to guide him in the difficult task of showing the reader how the process of individuation develops in a really deep analysis and how the relationship between analyst and analysand gradually finds its right form as the impersonal—one could say divine—elements are recognized and freed, so that they no longer obscure the situation by projection in the so-called transference. Just as the alchemist and his *soror mystica* learned that they were the earthly exponents of an impersonal or divine pair of opposites, so the pair in analysis have to learn that the most important task is furthering the relationship of the impersonal figures *within them*, represented by animus and anima. At the same time, this quaternity—analyst and analysand, anima and animus—represents the totality, which is often the first opportunity the analysand has of seeing his own totality: the Self.

Rereading my notes on our walks at the time, I see that Jung constantly talked to me about this theme. He told me, for instance, that the great difficulty for the analysand in seeing the reality of his or her analyst is the projection of the Self. Then, Jung pointed out, the analyst is really indispensable, because he has, or seems to have, the kernel of the analysand's whole personality: the Self. This naturally leads to all sorts of unreasonable demands on the analyst, demands which are not the least unreasonable as regards the Self itself. It is clear, therefore, how important it is to learn to distinguish between the impersonal (divine) elements and the personal (human) element.

*The Psychology of Transference* is probably difficult for the general reader to understand; indeed, it cannot be understood by the intellect alone for the quaternity described is also highly irrational and beyond our comprehension. The book is, however, a most profound description of the transference, and could be called an exposition of the practical application of the *mysterium coniunctionis* by which the warring opposites, which are causing so much strife and suffering in our days, can be seen and can be helped to relate to each other. Jung said of this aspect of the problem:

> Looked at in this light, the bond established by the transference—however hard to bear and however incomprehensible it may seem—is vitally important not only for the individual but also for society, and indeed for the moral and spiritual progress of mankind. So, when the psychotherapist has to struggle with difficult transference problems, he can at least take comfort in these reflections. He is not just working for this particular patient, who may be quite insignificant, but for himself as well and his own soul, and in so doing he is perhaps laying an infinitesimal grain in the scales of humanity's soul. Small and invisible as this contribution may be, it is yet an *opus magnum*, for it is accomplished in a sphere but lately visited by the numen, where the whole weight of mankind's problems has settled. The ultimate questions of psychotherapy are not a private matter—they represent a supreme responsibility.[5]

The publication of this book was an important step in preparing the way for Jung's longest work and masterpiece, the *Mysterium Coniunctionis*, which came out nine years later. He mentioned at the beginning of *The Psychology of Transference* that what he was going to say about transference and the whole development of the individuation process applied only to those few cases who are destined to go through with that process. By far the majority of the people who came to him for analysis never experienced anything of the kind, for—as he always emphasized to his pupils who were beginning to be analysts themselves—most people come to analysis to have some hindrance removed; then they can and should go on with their lives in their own way.

Jung's health continued to improve steadily, although after such a severe infarct his heart did not allow any liberties. High altitudes, for instance, were forbidden, and this kept him for two or three years from his beloved mountains. He did slowly drive over passes again, even staying on the Rigi in the autumn of 1947. When I say he drove over passes, I mean he was driven over them, for he did not drive a car after the Second World War. This was a great deprivation for him; but, much as he wanted the freedom that driving his own car gave him, he felt it would not be a reasonable thing to do, considering his age—he was a year over seventy before we were given any gasoline—and the condition of his heart.

The subject of the Eranos Tagung of 1946 was "Spirit and Nature," and Jung gave one of his best lectures, "The Spirit of Psychology."[6] The discussions on the terrace outside the lecture hall after the lectures had by this time become a feature of Eranos. Although in the years to come Jung lectured on only two occasions (in 1948 and 1951), he still attended the Tagung for several more years and used to sit after almost every lecture on the broad terrace and allow himself to be asked any questions. At first it was mainly his own pupils who took advantage of this, but gradually more and more of the audience joined in.

In the autumn of 1946 Winston Churchill paid a visit to Switzerland. He was enthusiastically received by the Swiss, who looked upon him as the saviour of Europe. There were cheering crowds wherever he drove and several official receptions. He also spoke at Zürich University, a fact that is recorded in the Aula (the largest auditorium) by a large plaque on the wall. There was a curious unconscious bond between Churchill and Jung: the latter used to dream of the former every time Churchill approached the Swiss border during the war, although of course Jung never knew Churchill had been there until it was announced in the papers later. They were indeed the two most *whole* men of their time, although their fates and their psychologies were totally different.[c]

While Churchill was in Switzerland, Jung met him socially twice: at a luncheon garden party near Berne, and at a big evening banquet near Zürich. On the first occasion Jung found himself escorting Mary Churchill, whom he admired and enjoyed very much. He said that she had a most rare, almost royal quality and something of the greatness of her father. He was therefore almost disappointed at the subsequent banquet to find that he was to sit next to Churchill that time instead of his daughter. He also found the meal a little difficult, when Churchill refused to talk while he was eating. Now Jung himself always did the same, so nothing could have pleased him more, but he found the disappointed glances of his hosts unpleasant, for they evidently felt he was not entertaining the guest of honor at all as they had hoped. (Sitting beside Jung at meals one always encountered the same glances, so I must admit to having been highly amused that on that occasion he had, so to speak, experienced what it was like to sit by Jung!) Once dinner was over, however, he had a very interesting talk with Churchill, who spoke of his experiences in the war in a surprising but delightfully open way. I have already mentioned how moved Jung was that the arrangement of the tables was exactly as in his Liverpool dream in 1926.[d]

Altogether, Jung's health seemed to be particularly good in the autumn of 1946. It was during that year that he encouraged Marie-Louise von Franz and myself to take a flat together. He always tried to encourage his pupils *not* to live alone and, if they were not married, to share a house or flat with someone of the same sex. As a rule, he was not very successful with this suggestion, so he was extremely pleased when we found a flat by the lake and moved into it. That very afternoon—November 2, 1946—he took a discussion group of his closest pupils. Tired though we were with the move

[c] Jung told me these dreams were also subjective, Churchill representing the extravert in Jung.

[d] See above, page 186.

in the morning, we drove Jung to this discussion, and I still remember how particularly well he seemed during the drive and in the discussion itself. It was, therefore, a completely unexpected shock to hear two days later that he had had another heart attack the night before and was again very ill. This time, refusing to go to the hospital, he had to have two nurses to look after him, day and night, in his own house.

This illness was even more unexpected, especially to Jung himself, than the one in 1944. He had had the feeling then that "there was something wrong with my attitude"[7] and at first had felt in some way responsible for having broken his leg. But this time it was a real bolt from the blue. He had spoken most confidently to both Marie-Louise and myself about being always there to help us, when each of us complained that we thought the other would be difficult. As it was, we had to fight out our own battles as best we could for the first months, which was probably a blessing in disguise.

Jung remained ill for about three months. About December 16 he sent me a message that he was still suspended over the abyss and warning me against optimism; he added that the real trouble was in the sympathicus. After his illness he told me that he was doubtful if he had really had a heart infarct. At all events, it was mainly a disturbance of the vegetative nervous system that had the effect of giving him attacks of tachycardia (racing of the pulse). He again found himself confronted, like medicine men all over the world, with curing himself. The doctors insisted that it was another heart infarct; and he was thus forced to find out for himself what was really the matter and how it should be met. Once again he said that he had an illness because he was faced with the mysterious problem of the *hieros gamos* (the *mysterium coniunctionis*). As late as October 15, 1957 (eleven years after this illness), he wrote in a letter:[8]

> As some alchemists had to admit, that they never succeeded in producing the gold or the Stone, I cannot confess to have solved the riddle of the *coniunctio* mystery. On the contrary, I am darkly aware of things lurking in the background of the problem—things too big for horizons.

It was his effort to write about these "things too big for horizons" and to solve their riddle that brought about Jung's further illness.

These illnesses were really the direct result of what Jung always called "the only unbearable torture of not understanding." He had taught himself long before—at Basel University and Burghölzli—to face up to this torture, but, since the *hieros gamos* is so infinitely more incomprehensible than anything he was ever faced with in his life, it required at least two actual physical illnesses and the near neighborhood of death before he could understand it enough to go on with his book. Even then, he felt that there were things lurking in its background too big to be even seen on the horizon two years after the book was completed.

This time, however, Jung fortunately did not lose his wish to live. Impossible though he knew the task was, he remained determined to face it to the best of his ability, if a further lease of life could only be granted him. Nor was there any "strange cessation of human warmth."[e] On the contrary, directly he found he was so ill, he sent for his secretary, Marie-Jeanne Schmid. He gave her the strictest injunctions to provide absolutely truthful news of how he was, and as soon as he possibly could he wrote letters or sent messages to those of his friends whom he thought would be most anxious.

Although this 1946 illness was probably quite as dangerous as his far longer illness in 1944—as we have seen, he himself reckoned with the possibility, if not the likelihood, of death—it had a much shorter convalescence. By the early summer of 1947 he was as active as he had been before this second severe illness, and, although his whole wish was to get back to his writing, something quite unexpected came up from outside that cost him a great deal of time and energy.

By this time, a good many English and Americans were coming to Zürich to study and there was every prospect of more and more coming in the following years. But they found themselves in a much less favorable position than before the war: there was no English seminar and Jung was very much less accessible. The committee of the Club, especially Toni Wolff and C. A. Meier, felt it was absolutely necessary to offer them something more nourishing, and decided to start a small bureau to arrange lectures, especially lectures in English, and to offer some social life. But they wanted this bureau to be run by someone who, though highly intelligent, was not trusted by the members of the club. The proposal was sprung as a surprise on the general meeting and was all decided too quickly. The members consequently raised a petition for a further meeting, to reconsider the situation.

We knew that Jung had thought that the bureau plan would not meet the needs of the situation and that he was very glad when he heard that the members had protested. He said nothing to anyone, however, not even to his wife or to Toni Wolff, before the evening of the second meeting. Everybody was therefore amazed by his totally unexpected proposal for the foundation of an institute on quite a large scale. Knowing how very much against this idea he had been only two years earlier, after his seventieth birthday, I asked him on the way home (I usually drove the Jungs to the club meetings) why on earth he had changed his mind. He replied that he had seen it was impossible to prevent something of the kind from being started, for too many people were determined to do so. "They

[e] See above, page 281.

would start one between my death and my funeral in any case," he said, "so I think it is better to do so while I can still have some influence on its form and perhaps stop some of the worst mistakes." This was typical of Jung. He would say "no" once—as he had after his seventieth birthday— then, if people insisted, he practically always gave in. He used to advise his pupils: "Say what you think *once* and, if no one listens, retire to your estates."[f]

Another reason Jung himself started the C. G. Jung Institute can probably be found in a Mandaean text. It contains a conversation between John the Baptist and Christ, in which the former wants to keep the mysteries secret for, he maintains, people will not understand them and will thus destroy them. Christ, on the other hand, thinks they should be given to everybody, on behalf of those who will understand and profit by them. Jung used to point out that this represented the introverted and extraverted points of view and, just as the Mandaean conversation came to no conclusion, neither can the argument between introversion and extraversion, because both are right and valid points of view. It seems to me that his was the reason behind Jung's changing his mind. As an introvert he himself greatly preferred, like John the Baptist, to keep the process of individuation only for those individuals whose fate would compel them to *seek* it, but he fully recognized the validity of the extraverted point of view which longs to put values on the map.

We can see the same conflict, which that time he allowed a dream to decide, when at the very end of his life, after a firm refusal he decided to give the process of individuation to a much wider public and arranged for the publication of *Man and His Symbols*.[9] John Freeman, general editor of that volume, described the events which led to this decision very vividly in his Introduction.

In the autumn of 1947, Jung was extremely exhausted, as the result of all he had done toward the founding of the institute and other activities, so he went for the first of several holidays he took on the Rigi at about this time. This shows us how well he had recovered from his heart trouble of three years before, when all heights had been forbidden, for the hotel on the Rigi (Berghaus, Rigi-Staffel) was nearly five thousand feet above sea level. Since Bollingen was becoming very bad for Toni's arthritis, he joined her and some other friends[g] on the Rigi, of which she was very fond. They walked farther every day, and he came back proudly saying that they had even managed one three-hour walk to the hotel at Scheidegg, where they lunched and rested in the sun, and back.

Jung returned to Küsnacht looking brilliantly well, but there was a great deal of stored-up work awaiting him. It was not all connected with the

[f] An old Chinese saying.
[g] I remember that Esther Harding and Eleanor Bertine were there for one weekend.

founding of the institute; there were also many appeals for help, both by consultation or by letter, appeals to which, as he said, he knew only he could respond and therefore wanted to do so. It was now proved that his heart was perfectly all right again, as long as he lived a simple, quiet life, but directly he was in Küsnacht he felt besieged by more appeals than he could possibly meet.

Rereading my notes for this autumn of 1947, I marvel at the amount of work he achieved, for he was already seventy-two and had had two dangerous illnesses, the latter less than a year before. Without giving up any of his time for writing, he yet saw about four people a day, wrote an endless number of letters, and went to many meetings concerning the founding of the C. G. Jung Institute. He consented to draw up the statutes for the institute, with the help of C. A. Meier and Toni Wolff. This was the only administrative activity which Jung allowed Toni to take. He refused to let her go on the curatorium, to the great surprise of many of her admirers and indeed of herself, though she admitted to me that the institute was not "her cup of tea!" Jung told me he did not want people who were too introverted on that board; they would not know how to deal with the world, and it would also be a great pity for very creative people to be on it since it would take far too much of their time and energy and give their thoughts a wrong direction. He still hoped that Toni might return to her writing toward the end of her life. She did indeed give many excellent courses of lectures in the institute, but, as mentioned earlier never got around to the book she would have been so well fitted to write.

Jung gave a lot of time and thought to those who should go on the curatorium. At last he decided on the people he thought most suited to the work, and laid his proposal before the club, which had to give its casting vote. He unwillingly took the presidency himself, just to give the organization a start, but kept it only for two years; nor did he interfere afterward in the executive side at all. He chose two medical doctors, C. A. Meier and Kurt Binswanger, and two extraverted women, Jolande Jacobi and Liliane Frey, for the other four members. He did not get his proposal accepted without considerable opposition from the club, for the highly extraverted Dr. Jacobi had not made herself particularly popular in the club. The first vote went against her, but as she was the one person Jung was quite sure *should* be on the curatorium, he made a speech asking for a second vote. He explained that he understood why her extreme extraversion was so unpopular in the introverted club and admitted that she had an unfortunate gift for making herself unpopular. But, he contended, she was far more gifted at dealing with the world than any of the rest of us and would therefore be a most valuable asset. As a rule, the members were willing to bow to Jung's greater knowledge and wisdom, but even after his speech only two changed sides. It made the difference, however, and instead of being defeated Dr. Jacobi was elected. It would indeed have been wrong to exclude her, for the idea of the institute had been originally hers, and it was she who had convinced Jung that an institute would eventually be founded, whether he gave his support or not.

Jung gave the most time and energy, however, to the drawing up of the statutes. The statutes gave power over the institute entirely into the hands of the curatorium, something that was opposed at the time by the club and has been bitterly attacked by a few of the patrons in recent years. But Jung remained firm on this point, for he saw that the *people who did the work must have the power*, that anything else would lead to abuse of power, which was the great danger he feared in allowing his psychology to be given a worldly form like the institute. The statutes are a very wise document; they have steered the institute safely through almost thirty years, already far longer than Jung expected it to last. Of course, power has sometimes been used—and worse, a lot of projection of power motives onto others—but work is the great antidote to power, and although there have been many changes in the members of the curatorium since the foundation of the C. G. Jung Institute in 1948, they have all worked extremely hard, with barely an exception. Moreover, the occasional exception has never remained on the curatorium for very long.

In January, 1950, Jung began to find the work as president too tiring. He also felt he could no longer attend the meetings of the curatorium, so he arranged that his wife should represent him. This representation lasted for three months, but on April 28, 1950, after two years of holding the presidency, Jung retired altogether from all active participation. C. A. Meier became president, Emma Jung was elected in her own right as a member of the curatorium and as vice-president, and Jung became honorary president. Since Emma felt very much drawn to accepting this post —although all her life she had been reluctant to take on work of such an extraverted nature—Jung warmly encouraged her to do so. But a few months later he told me that in some ways he was convinced that, at all events for himself, this had been a mistake: he felt now that he had given it a start he might retire entirely from the work of running the institute, but with his wife on the curatorium he still had to hear a great deal about it at home. Moreover, he had been very happy about Emma's long study of the Grail, and hoped that she would spend the evening of her life writing her book about it, whereas actually she cut it up more and more into material for seminars at the institute, and much, if not most, of her energy went into the affairs of the curatorium.

I have often wondered whether it was a good plan for Emma to spend the last few years of her life on the curatorium. On the one hand, it developed a side of her that she had lived very little before; on the other hand, it took her away from breaking any more new ground in her studies on the Grail. She gave just as much energy as before to her husband—I never heard him utter a word of complaint, except to say that he heard rather too much about the institute—but she certainly, to my great regret, had much less time than before for her friends. If I tried to remonstrate, she would admit it was a great pity, but add that she regretfully found she also had much less time even for her own family.

The curatorium at that time was very dynamic, and emotional differences of opinion often arose. Emma was always on the side of peace and spent a lot of energy trying to reconcile different points of view. She was certainly an irreplaceable value to the curatorium itself, and also to the institute. After her death, Franz Riklin Jr. never tired of saying how much he missed her at their meetings.

Jung felt that since the institute was now a going concern he could withdraw from its management completely. He occasionally gave a word of advice, but if it was not taken he immediately "retired to his estates." He was once asked why he intervened so little, even when he disapproved of something that was being done. He replied that he was not doing the work, and any old man who went on interfering became a power fiend, a fate he meant to avoid at all costs.

I remember him intervening only twice during the eleven years that elapsed before his death. Once, when the students complained that there were too many courses on myths and fairy tales and too few on case material, he called a meeting of all lecturers and students and explained why he thought it was so important for them to understand myths and fairy tales. These all come from the collective unconscious and reflect the structure of the deeper layers which would be common to *everyone they would analyze later*. It was vitally important to know this foundation. Case material, on the contrary, differs in every case, and they would usually only do harm by applying what they learned about one case to another. The students found this difficult to understand; it is still a point on which there is a great deal of misunderstanding, not only in the institute, where presumably it is now at least partly understood, for Marie-Louise von Franz's courses on myths and fairy tales attract *by far* the largest audiences of any institute lectures, but in many other Jungian centers.

The other point on which I remember Jung intervening was when a proposal was made to abolish, or greatly reduce, the examinations. He strongly recommended then that they should *all* be retained. "That is one thing we can do for our students," he said, "we can see they all really know something when they leave." Fortunately, everyone saw the importance of this, and the examinations still stand as Jung originally arranged them.

Although he knew it was far better to leave all management questions to the curatorium, he did lend a helping hand to both lecturers and students insofar as his health and his own creative work allowed. He had discussions with the former, at least once every semester, at which time they could bring him any questions they liked. He also from time to time saw groups of students, but after the first two years nothing to do with the institute was allowed to interfere with his writing, for in all the seventeen years between his 1944 illness and his death his writing took precedence over everything else.

Jung's time was also diverted from continuing with the *Mysterium Coniunctionis*, during the founding and beginning of the institute, by the fact that in 1947 and 1948 he prepared three new German volumes, which consisted of Eranos lectures and various other essays, many of them considerably revised and enlarged from their original form. All this took a lot of time, not only in rewriting but also in proofreading. Jung always read proofs himself, although he also had them checked by several of his pupils, because he used to say it was quite remarkable how the devil could interfere with even the best printers and slip in a tiny misprint (fatally easy to read over) which changed or even reversed the whole meaning.

In 1948 Jung also gave a lecture at the Eranos Tagung: "Concerning the Self." This appears, very little changed, except for the omission of the end of the lecture, in Chapter 4 of *Aion*.

The first weighty problem that "insisted on taking shape" before he went on with his *opus magnum* was the *"Auseinandersetzung"* with the Christian era in *Aion*.[10] He could not deal adequately with the problem of the union of opposites until he had fully considered their history over the last two thousand years. This was a tremendous undertaking, entailing a great deal of research, some of which was undertaken by his pupils, but most of it by himself. Marie-Louise von Franz especially was his collaborator on this book, as she contributed a paper to it on Perpetua.[11] This paper, as Jung said in his Preface, analyzes the psychological transition from antiquity to Christianity, whereas his own part of the book deals with the Christian era and tries to illuminate it by Christian, Gnostic, and alchemistic symbols of the Self. He pointed out that even Christian tradition, most particularly the Revelation, takes the probability of an enantiodromia into account, by which he refers to the dilemma Christ–Anti-Christ. This precedes the Marriage of the Lamb, a symbol *par excellence* for the *mysterium coniunctionis*, so one sees why the problem of the last two thousand years "insisted on taking shape" before he could write his *opus magnum*.

The first four chapters of the book were written or at least completely rewritten last. After he had completed the rest of the book, Jung realized that the reader who was not well acquainted with Jungian psychology would be unable to follow him. Therefore he wrote a very clear description of the concepts that were most necessary for an understanding of the volume: ego, shadow, anima and animus, and Self. These descriptions are the clearest and most illuminating he ever wrote on the subject. They were written, as he told his collaborator, with special care, to represent the subject from the side of feeling and experience, not from that of thinking and intellect.[h]

Jung had already touched on the main theme of *Aion* in *Psychology and Alchemy*, in the chapter on "The Lapis-Christus Parallel."[12] There he mainly wanted to show how alchemy compensated and completed Christianity; in *Aion* he is concerned with the history of the opposites during the whole Christian era. Christ is still the great symbol of the Self in the West, and there is a long chapter entirely on this subject. But although Christ represented exactly those aspects of the Self which were required at the time, he was so much on the light side that the New Testament itself reckoned with an enantiodromia. Jung pointed out how many symbols Christ shares with the Devil:[13] lion, serpent, bird, raven, eagle, and fish. He also pointed out that the morning star symbolizes both Christ and the Devil. Astrologically, as is well known, the Christian era coincides exactly with "The Sign of the Fishes," so the fish as the common symbol of Christ and the Devil is an image that Jung went into in great detail in many chapters.

The fact that the fish is a symbol of Christ and the astrological designation of our era seems to point to a relationship between Christian symbolism and time. Thereafter Jung devoted the last part of *Aion* to "The Structure and Dynamics of the Self" and showed that the images of the quaternities in the Self seem to represent a circular, or rather a spiral, movement. It remains forever itself, but simultaneously it produces a higher level of consciousness. One could describe this movement as a spiral-shaped chain of quaternities which circumambulate an unchanging center, at the same time rising each time to a higher level.

Jung had hardly finished *Aion* before he began to develop the same subject still further and wrote *Answer to Job*. Before we leave *Aion*, I should say that Jung told me that, from the reactions he had received, he thought *Aion* was the least understood of his books that had so far been published. It was some time before an English version appeared. Those in Zürich who could not read German were impatient for it, so I gave a course of lectures on it at the institute. Jung was pleased to hear this and encouraged me to repeat the course, even after the English translation appeared, because, he said, people really needed more explanation than he himself had given. Feeling always runs very high at these courses for what Jung said about the *privatio boni*,[14] in particular, seems to act as a red rag to a bull, particularly to theologians. I have never experienced such lively discussions and passionate participation in any of my other courses.

*Answer to Job* is totally different from all of Jung's other books, in that he

---

[h] This must have been completely rewritten, for curiously enough Jung wrote to Victor White that he had been forced to write "some of the finer points about anima, animus, shadow and last, but not least, the Self." This led him on to the conviction that Christ as the divine being (the God-man) was his "secret goal." This must refer to the first conception of *Aion*.—C. G. Jung, *Letters*, 19 December 1947, pp. 480 ff.

did not write as usual in "a coolly objective manner" but gave a free rein for once to his "emotional subjectivity."[15] He had been deeply moved from his earliest childhood, as we have seen, by the dark side of God. He had even been puzzled by the contradictory sides of Jesus at Laufen, and still more by the vision when he was eleven of God defecating on Basel Cathedral. Right through his life, as we have seen, he was deeply preoccupied by the piling up of evidence that evil must be regarded as part of God and *not* as something extraneous, for which man is wholly responsible. When, after the war, we heard the full horror of what had been done in the concentration camps, for example, almost everyone in Jung's environment was at last also deeply moved by the same problem, and he felt the time had come to write openly about it, for, as he ended his preface, "What I am expressing is first of all my own personal view, but I know that I also speak in the name of many who have had similar experiences."[16]

It is not surprising that *Answer to Job* followed directly after *Aion*. Jung had been considering the history of the opposites throughout the whole Christian era in "a coolly objective manner," particularly the history of the *privatio boni*. This interpretation of evil as merely the absence of good, which so many people still try passionately to believe, roused emotions in him which he never allowed to reach the surface in *Aion*. A reaction from that side was due and inevitable, for he had to know "the way in which a modern man with a Christian education and background comes to terms with the divine darkness which is unveiled in the Book of Job and what effect it has on him."[17]

*Answer to Job* is a passionate attempt to answer this question, which one might say culminates in the realization that God needs man in order to become conscious. This is really the underlying meaning of the Christian belief that God became man. He had to become man in order to know man's reality. As Jung said nearly ten years later in the chapter "On Life after Death" in *Memories,* speaking of the eternal Self:[i]

> . . . it assumes human shape in order to enter three-dimensional existence, as if someone were putting on a diver's suit in order to dive into the sea. . . . In earthly form it can pass through the experiences of the three-dimensional world, and by greater awareness take a further step toward realization.[18]

We come back to Jung's realization of the myth of modern man on the Athi Plains in East Africa, nearly thirty years before.

One could say that *Answer to Job* shows us how all through the ages God has suffered from His own unconsciousness and, because He did not realize this, made man suffer for it still more. What else but unconscious-

---

[i] Used in this sense, the terms "God" and "Self" are practically synonymous.

ness of what He was doing would explain or excuse God's listening to the libels of His dark son, Satan, against Job, and delivering the latter entirely into the former's hand to torment in any way he chose, with the single condition that he not be killed?

After considering the Book of Job, Jung turned to God's determination to become man, indicating all the precautions taken to prevent this incarnation from being corrupted by the dark side. Though fully agreeing that this was the necessity of the time, he showed how certain this was to be followed by an enantiodromia. He illustrated this by demonstrating how likely it is psychologically that the John of the Epistles is also the John who wrote the Revelation, with its unparalleled prophecies of the cruelest destruction. The Epistles are full of the Christian virtues, particularly of love, emphasizing God as a loving father who can be blindly loved and trusted. But a too one-sided emphasis on love is psychologically certain to constellate its opposite: hate; and too great a reliance on salvation by an all-loving father must constellate its opposite: wholesale destruction.

Jung went into the Apocalypse in almost as much detail as the Book of Job itself. He said, for example:

> Ever since John the apocalyptist experienced for the first time (perhaps unconsciously) that conflict into which Christianity inevitably leads, mankind has groaned under this burden: *God wanted to become man, and still wants to*. That is probably why John experienced in his vision a second birth of a son from the mother Sophia, a divine birth which was characterized by a *conjunctio oppositorum* and which anticipated the *filius sapientiae*, the essence of the individuation process. This was the effect of Christianity on a Christian of early times, who had lived long and resolutely enough to be able to cast a glance into the distant future.[19]

Jung pointed out how accurately John prophesied our present age, which may even come to surpass the horrors in the Revelation if the atom bomb, for example, is used; and that the only answer to such dangers lies in doing all we can to assist God to become man, and thus more conscious. He saw a ray of light in the then very recently announced "dogma of the Assumptio Mariae." He said:

> This dogma is in every respect timely. In the first place it is a symbolical fulfilment of John's vision. Secondly, it contains an allusion to the marriage of the Lamb at the end of time, and, thirdly, it repeats the Old Testament anamnesis of Sophia. These three references foretell the incarnation of God. The second and third foretell the Incarnation in Christ, but the first foretells the Incarnation in creaturely man.[20]

Jung pointed out the danger inherent in the last fact:

Everything now depends on man: immense power of destruction is given into his hand, and the question is whether he can resist the will to use it, and can temper his will with the spirit of love and wisdom. He will hardly be capable of doing so on his own unaided resources. He needs the help of an "advocate" in heaven, that is, of the child that is caught up to God[j] and who brings the "healing" and making whole of the hitherto fragmentary man.[21]

The last chapter is devoted to pointing out the difference between "creaturely man" and the archetype that works through him. The behavior of the latter, infinitely the more powerful factor,

. . .cannot be investigated at all without the interaction of the observing consciousness. Therefore the question as to whether the process is initiated by consciousness or by the archetype can never be answered; unless, in contradiction to experience, one either robbed the archetype of its autonomy or degraded consciousness to a mere machine. We find ourselves in best agreement with psychological experience if we concede to the archetype a definite measure of independence, and to consciousness a degree of creative freedom proportionate to its scope.[22]

A reciprocal action then develops between these two relatively autonomous factors, in which sometimes one and sometimes the other is the acting subject. However much the archetype may dwell in us we can never change our human limitations, any more than Saint Paul, although he felt himself to be directly called and enlightened by God, could ever rid himself of the "thorn in the flesh" or of the Satanic angel who plagued him. Jung therefore ends the book with the words:

That is to say, even the enlightened person remains what he is, and is never more than his own limited ego before the One who dwells within him, whose form has no knowable boundaries, who encompasses him on all sides, fathomless as the abysms of the earth and vast as the sky.[23]

Probably no book of Jung's has attracted more attention than *Answer to Job*. In the paperback edition, it has been a bestseller in the United States, so that the close of his preface, in which he said that, although he was primarily expressing his own personal views, he knew that he was also

---

[j] Revelation 12:5. This is, of course, the "second birth of a son" alluded to above.

speaking "in the name of many others who have had similar experiences," turned out to be true on a far larger scale than he ever expected. As a matter of fact, he hesitated for a considerable time before publishing the book at all. Therefore, though both *Answer to Job* and "Synchronicity" were published in the same year (1952), the former had been completed some time before the latter was begun.

Jung gave a short lecture on synchronicity[24] at the Eranos Tagung in 1951, the last time he lectured there. It appears as it was given in the English *Papers from the Eranos Yearbook*.[25] Immediately afterward he revised and enlarged it for its final form. It was then published, together with an article by the physicist Wolfgang Pauli, under the title *The Interpretation of Nature and the Psyche*.[26] Although in a totally different way from *Answer to Job,* it also broke new ground and caused a good deal of excitement, this time in scientific circles. The minds of most people are so steeped in the idea of cause and effect that it is quite remarkably difficult for them to view things synchronistically. To illustrate how difficult it is, I remember a meeting of the lecturers and analysts of the C. G. Jung Institute at Jung's house for a discussion of his article, which had just appeared. There was a lively discussion but, when it was drawing to an end, Jung remarked: "Well, every one of you has discussed synchronicity from the standpoint of cause and effect. Not one of you has thought synchronistically!"

I still find thinking synchronistically so difficult that I prefer not to venture a summary of this article. Marie-Louise von Franz has an excellent account of synchronicity in her book *Number and Time*[27] and was kind enough to condense what she said there as follows:

> Since he experimented in the early twenties with the *I Ching*, Jung was acquainted with the phenomena that he afterward called "synchronistic events." He had felt for a long time that the deficient and only statistically valid principle of causality needed a complementary, explanatory principle in science. But he waited for many years before he published anything fundamental about it because he wanted to convey the idea to scientists which seemed specially difficult because of their rational outlook. The chance to combine his paper on synchronicity with Wolfgang Pauli's work on Kepler was therefore exceedingly welcome as he hoped it would make scientists take this new idea more seriously.
>
> Jung defined a synchronistic event as the coincidence between an inner image or hunch breaking into one's mind, and the occurrence of an outer event conveying the same meaning at approximately the same time. He mentions as an example one of his patients who, at a critical moment in her analysis, was telling him a dream of a golden scarab, a symbol of a deep renewal of consciousness. At that moment a scarabaeid beetle, the common rose-chafer (*cetonia aurata*) tapped at

the window. Jung caught it as it flew into the room. This beetle is the nearest analogy to a scarab found in our latitudes and at that particular moment it seemed to feel an urge, contrary to its usual habits, to get into a darkened room.[28] [k]

Encouraged by Rhine's experiments at Duke University, Jung tried at first to find a way in which such events could be made probable by statistics. He searched for proof that undeniable inner psychological symbols coincided regularly with equally undeniable outer events. He chose the marriage constellations in astrology (which are images of psychological facts) for the former and the corresponding actual marriages for the latter.[29] At first this statistical experiment yielded an incredibly positive result but, repeating the experiment later in greater numbers, proved the first positive result to be in itself a synchronistic event, and that nothing could be proved by statistics.

Jung therefore returned to his basic argument: synchronistic events only take place when the experimenter has a strong emotional participation with his experiment. The emotion is usually due to an archetype being activated, that is constellated, in the unconscious of the experimenter.[30] Jung went on to show that synchronistic events seem to be only a particular instance of a much wider natural principle which he termed "acausal orderedness,"[31] a just-so modality without a cause, such as we can find in the case of the discontinuities of physics (e.g. the orderedness of energy quanta, or radium decay, etc.) or the properties of natural numbers.[32] Such modes of acausal orderedness occur regularly and have always existed, whereas synchronistic events are *acts of creation in time*.

Jung said:

It is only the ingrained belief in the sovereign power of causality that creates intellectual difficulties and makes it appear unthinkable that causeless events exist or could ever occur. But if they do, then we must regard them as *creative acts*, as the continuous creation of a pattern that exists from all eternity, repeats itself sporadically, and is not derivable from any known antecedents. We must of course guard against thinking of every event whose cause is unknown as "causeless." This, as I have already stressed, is admissible only when a cause is not even thinkable. . . . This is necessarily the case when space and time lose their meaning or have become relative, for under those circumstances a causality which presupposes space and time for its

---

[k] Jung said later: "Synchronistic events rest on the *simultaneous occurrence of two different psychic states*. One of them is the normal, probable state (i.e. the one that is causally explicable), and the other, the critical experience, is the one that cannot be derived causally from the first."

continuance can no longer be said to exist and becomes altogether unthinkable.

For these reasons it seems to me necessary to introduce, alongside space, time, and causality, a category which not only enables us to understand synchronistic phenomena as a special class of natural events, but also takes the contingent partly as a universal factor existing from all eternity, and partly as the sum of countless individual acts of creation occurring in time.[33]

In the autumn of 1955 Marie-Louise received a letter from Korvin, Count of Krasinski, a Benedictine monk who had studied local medicine in Tibet, asking her for an explanation of synchronicity. She showed her reply to Jung before she sent it and was kind enough to let me quote[1] the relevant part of his reaction:

Küsnacht-Zürich. 27. Oct. 1955.

Dear Marie-Louise,

. . . Your answer to Krasinski is excellent. But I should have added the argument that, in so far as causality is only statistical probability, there *MUST* be *exceptions*. The more exceptions there are, the less they can be subjugated to a causal explanation. The exclusively causal viewpoint *(CAUSA efficiens, finalis, formalis, materialis)* claims absolute validity, through which indeterminism is eliminated and all events in nature become mechanical and nature itself becomes a machine. You have implied all this by the stress you lay on the *creatio continua*. . . . Krasinski, like all theologians, forgets on account of his Aristotelianism, that the most important cause of all things, i.e. God, Himself has no cause, and probably maintains a continuous creation with his eternal omnipresence. For this reason all acausal events appear to be numinous, that is, the naïve mind regards them as *numina*. It is marvelous that it is just theological causality which does not allow God any free play. God not only must be exclusively good, over and above this He must also obey his own laws in His own creation. God is thus subordinated to the Church's apotropaeic tendency toward limiting His freedom.

I do not think negatively of synchronicity as a mere absence of cause but, as may be concluded from the above (symbolic) conclusions, I also see it positively as a creative act which comes from the ultimate acausal, from a *proton anaition*. This lies closer to us than we think, for the generally recognized psychical relativity of space and time, which becomes manifest in the E.S.P. experiments, points to an

---

[1] The original letter is in German.

empirical condition becoming visible in which the (temporal) succession of cause and effect becomes completely impossible on account of the relative absence of space.

With the most cordial greetings,

Yours,<br>C. G. Jung

While Jung was writing his paper on synchronicity, he also carved the face of the laughing trickster in the west wall of the original Tower.[34] It was almost as if the images lay dormant in the stones themselves, asking to be brought into existence. Sometimes, before he touched the stone, he would ask someone present if he also saw anything there.

In 1950, some months before Jung carved the laughing trickster, he had completed the "monument out of stone to express what the Tower" meant to him, as he wrote in *Memories*.[35] Some time before, a large square block of stone had been delivered by mistake, instead of the triangular stone that had been ordered for a wall he was having built. The stonemason refused it indignantly, but Jung knew at once that, although useless for the wall, it was nevertheless *his* stone and that he wanted it for an as yet unknown purpose. As far as I remember, he had it for some time, even perhaps for some years, before he knew what this purpose was. Then, as he wrote:

The first thing that occurred to me was a Latin verse by the alchemist Arnaldus de Villanova (died 1313). I chiseled this into the stone; in translation it goes:

> Here stands the mean, uncomely stone,
> 'Tis very cheap in price!
> The more it is despised by fools,
> The more loved by the wise.

This verse refers to the alchemist's stone, the *lapis*, which is despised and rejected.

Soon something else emerged. I began to see on the front face, in the natural structure of the stone, a small circle, a sort of eye, which looked at me. I chiseled it into the stone, and in the center made a tiny homunculus. This corresponds to the "little doll" *(pupilla)*— yourself—which you see in the pupil of another's eye; a kind of Kabir, or the Telesphoros of Asklepios. Ancient statues show him wearing a hooded cloak and carrying a lantern. At the same time he is a pointer of the way. I dedicated a few words to him which came into my mind while I was working. The inscription is in Greek; the translation goes:

"Time is a child—playing like a child—playing a board game—the kingdom of the child. This is Telesphoros, who roams through the dark regions of the cosmos and glows like a star out of the depths. He points the way to the gates of the sun and to the land of dreams."

These words came to me—one after the other—while I worked on the stone.

On the third face, the one facing the lake, I let the stone itself speak, as it were, in a Latin inscription. These sayings are more or less quotations from alchemy. This is the translation:

"I am an orphan, alone; nevertheless I am found everywhere. I am one, but opposed to myself. I am youth and old man at one and the same time. I have known neither father nor mother, because I have had to be fetched out of the deep like a fish, or fell like a white stone from heaven. In woods and mountains I roam, but I am hidden in the innermost soul of man. I am mortal for everyone, yet I am not touched by the cycle of aeons."

In conclusion, under the saying of Arnaldus de Villanova, I set down in Latin the words "In remembrance of his seventy-fifth birthday C. G. Jung made and placed this here as a thanks offering, in the year 1950."

When the stone was finished, I looked at it again and again, wondering about it and asking myself what lay behind my impulse to carve it.

The stone stands outside the Tower, and is like an explanation of it. It is a manifestation of the occupant, but one which remains incomprehensible to others. Do you know what I wanted to chisel into the back face of the stone? *"Le cri de Merlin!"* For what the stone expressed reminded me of Merlin's life in the forest, after he had vanished from the world. Men still hear his cries, so the legend runs, but they cannot understand or interpret them.[36]

The manikin which Jung had carved when he was nine years old and which had made him feel secure, without "the tormenting sense of being at odds" with himself,[37] thus came back to him as the Telesphoros of Asklepios in his most important stone when he was seventy-five years old.

*Answer to Job* and the article on synchronicity were certainly "new formulations" that he could hardly have achieved before his 1944 illness. It was only then that he could fully surrender himself to "the current of his thoughts" as "one problem after another" revealed itself to him and took shape.[38] As regards "Synchronicity," it must have been the experience outside time, when he felt himself to "exist simultaneously the day before yesterday, today and the day after tomorrow," that rendered him capable of freeing himself from our ingrained habit of thinking in terms of cause and effect, liberating him to think synchronistically and to formulate a whole article entirely from that point of view.

The reactions to these two works, although many were positive, must sometimes have been rather trying. Theologians were in part rendered quite angry by *Answer to Job*, and scientists by "Synchronicity." Jung was always ready to accept intelligent criticism—it could even please him much more than unintelligent praise—but he hated stupid criticism, based on a total misunderstanding of what he had meant. Both these works met with an unusual number of criticisms of the latter kind. Jung often used to say that if our civilization perished it would be more due to stupidity than to evil.

Nevertheless, this period of his life—in spite of its many illnesses and his increasing age—was on the whole not only fruitful but also, I think, a happy time. Not that Jung found aging an easy process. He used to say: "I have never been old before so I don't know how one grows old!" But he faced the problem with his usual courage and patience, and by the end of 1951 had certainly found the answer.

# 16

# The Mysterium Coniunctionis
# 1952–1955

After *Aion*, *Answer to Job*, and the long article on synchronicity had been written, the decks were clear for Jung to devote himself to his *opus magnum*, his goal ever since he had finished *Psychology and Alchemy*. It was only after he had completed the preliminary books that he wrote the sixth and last part on the *coniunctio* itself, the section which contains the essence of the book. As mentioned before, he wrote the greater part of the earlier five sections before his illness in 1944. He did add to and deepen the thought in some places, but the "new formulation" of the union of opposites "took shape" only in the sixth and final part.

In 1952, however, he sustained a great loss in the sphere of his work. Marie-Jeanne Schmid, who had been his secretary for over twenty years, left him in the autumn in order to get married. In the nine subsequent years that passed before his death, Jung had three other secretaries, but none of them was able to settle into his work and life as Marie-Jeanne had done. This was not the fault of the subsequent secretaries; they simply did not have the advantages which Marie-Jeanne possessed.[a] Another difficulty—especially for the first—was that whereas Marie-Jeanne had always stayed all day and had consequently done full-time work, Jung decided when she left that, as he was now doing so little analytical work, it was not necessary for him to have more than a half-day secretary. It was quite true, of course, that there was much less work than before, but it must have been very difficult, if not impossible, for the new secretaries to keep up Marie-Jeanne's standards with only half the time at their disposal. And though Marie-Jeanne, as an old family friend, fitted in very well at lunch every day, it would not have been so easy for a

[a] See above, page 205 ff.

comparative stranger to do the same; Jung therefore did not attempt it, which was another reason for limiting the secretary's work to a half-day.

Fate had a much worse blow in store for him before he could finish the *Mysterium Coninuctionis*. In the early spring of 1953 he suffered a most unexpected and poignant sorrow: Toni Wolff died as suddenly as her father had done over forty years earlier,[b] on March 21. As Jung said to me later: "Toni was thirteen years younger than I am and I never seriously considered the possibility that she could die before me." He had, it is true, been seriously disturbed by one dream of hers and two of his own concerning her, which occurred seven years before her death, in the spring of 1946 but since the dreams could just as well have pointed to rebirth as to actual death, and since he had done everything he could in interpreting them to her, his alarm had subsided. Therefore her sudden death was a most unexpected shock and blow to him.

Jung had been seriously unwell for a few weeks, but was up and about before the blow fell. Curiously enough, a short time *before* Toni died he had told me a dream which had made him decide to give up smoking. Now, Jung had smoked a great deal all his life, although usually a pipe and never to the extent that Freud had smoked, but to give it up entirely so suddenly must have been exceedingly difficult. Toni, on the other hand, did undoubtedly smoke too much—about thirty to forty cigarettes a day—and she told me that half of the doctors she had seen had told her it was aggravating her condition and ordered her to give it up, whereas the others said there was no connection. She preferred to believe the latter. Jung had urged her for years to reduce it at least, but this was one of the very few pieces of advice she refused to listen to, and she smoked incessantly until the day of her death. This was not in any way due to weakness of will. She used to say: "We must have a vice and I have chosen smoking as mine." I believe her to have been completely convinced that her smoking (which seemed excessive to us but not to her) was right for her, whatever it might be for other people. At all events, I have never seen anyone look more peaceful and fulfilled or so strangely alive than Toni did after death. I found myself asking her old maid, Lena, if she could really be dead, was the doctor *sure* she was not asleep?

Toni had apparently been in good health that spring of 1953, except for her terrible arthritis, and though it was the Easter holidays, she had two analysts from England analyzing with her every day. One of these told me afterward that she had been very disquieted by Toni the day before her death, although Toni had insisted there was nothing wrong. Toni did, however, walk around to see her doctor after tea. He apparently found nothing to alarm him. Lena, who had faithfully been with her for well over

[b] See above, page 103 and page 117.

twenty years, told me that she ate hardly any supper that night and went to bed directly afterward, a thing Lena had *never* once known her to do before. She absolutely refused any attention in the night; when Lena went to call her in the morning she found her dead.

The shock caused a relapse in Jung's own health; his tachycardia returned, he kept an unusually high pulse for several weeks, and was not well enough to go to the funeral. Outwardly he kept extremely calm, so that both his wife and his secretary told me they thought he had overcome the shock after a few days, but from my notes for April, 1953, I see that he said himself that his pulse was still between 80 and 120; moreover, this trouble continued for some time. He had been helped, it is true, by seeing Toni in a dream, which he dreamed on Easter Eve, looking much taller and younger than she had been when she died, and exceedingly beautiful. She was wearing a frock of all the colors of a bird of paradise, with the wonderful blue of the kingfisher as the most emphasized color. He saw just her image, there was no action in the dream, and he was especially impressed by having dreamed it on the night of the Resurrection.

Although it took Jung a long time to overcome the shock physically, he was able much sooner to find a psychological attitude to Toni's death and to accept the pain it gave him.

The strain of not smoking must have been especially hard just then but Jung was sure the craving must be overcome, so he went on doing without for about two months. Then his doctor remonstrated and said that, since he had smoked all his life, it would be much better for him to smoke *in moderation* than to give it up altogether. This is well known to be much more difficult, but from then on until his death, about eight years later, Jung smoked his pipe again, and an occasional cigar, but in strict moderation.

It is an impossible task to give any idea of the essence of the *Mysterium Coniunctionis* in a few pages. The earlier chapters are concerned with the components of the *coniunctio,* and with the endless paradoxes, symbols, and personifications in which the opposites have appeared. One marvels how Jung ever found the time, even with the assistance of his collaborator, to do the immense research necessary for this work, for it is founded solidly on the texts and there is not one word of speculation in the entire book.

Jung began the last and culminating chapter by crediting Herbert Silberer with having been the first to realize that the *coniunctio* was the "central idea" of the alchemical procedure. Alchemy separated the opposites before it tried to unite them, and Jung often pointed to the historical necessity of the Christian religion to put its whole stress on the light and spiritual opposite in order to preserve it at all in the dark state of the world at the time it arose. He said in this book that "the division into two was necessary in order to *bring the 'one' world out of the state of potentiality into reality.*" [1] The dark opposite, including matter, was so increasingly rejected by the Church that alchemy, which was always the current beneath the surface and the inner compensation of the outer teaching, was inevitably forced to turn its full attention to saving the dark opposite from oblivion and to uniting it with the light opposite.

The alchemists' preoccupation with and incessant work on matter in their retorts was, of course, mainly a projection of the then entirely unrecognized unconscious, a fact which a few particularly intelligent alchemists, such as Gerard Dorn, suspected. As they labored passionately in their retorts, they called up much the same symbols as are produced spontaneously today by the dreams of modern people. The parallel is so striking that Jung followed the three stages, as they were described by the sixteenth-century Dorn, and was able to show exactly the same stages in the individuation process today, for it was this that Dorn found projected into his work in the retort.

The first stage is called the *unio mentalis* and can be more or less completed by the *mind* of the alchemist. He thinks over the whole situation, more or less what we should call intellectually, although his intellect was nothing like as one-sided as ours has become. Medieval man could easily *think* of the same *veritas* being found in God, in man, and in matter. It was his task to liberate this *veritas*, sometimes spoken of as a subtle substance, or as the soul, from matter, where it was imprisoned. Some alchemists, even in very early alchemy, realized that it must first be liberated in themselves before they could achieve it with their substances in the retort. This first stage of the *unio mentalis* is really a separation of the spirit from matter and has mainly to be accomplished by the mind, or as we should call it, by becoming conscious of the situation.

Jung pointed out that we go through exactly the same stage in analysis. We call it "becoming conscious of the shadow," or you could also describe it as becoming conscious of all the turbulent emotions by which we are caught and then learning to separate ourselves from them by *knowing* them. As *The Secret of the Golden Flower* said all those centuries ago: "Indolence which a man knows and indolence he does not know are a thousand miles apart."[c] Therefore both in alchemy and analytical psychology the first stage can be achieved primarily by the mind.

The alchemists, however, fully realized that this separation of the soul by intellectual effort was not enough. Jung emphasized that, although Dorn expressed this more clearly, he did not discover it, it was known right through the tradition of alchemy.[2] The objective standpoint that has been gained or, as one could call it, the liberated spirit, must then be reunited with the body, with matter. This stage was represented in alchemy by many symbols, of which perhaps the best known is the "chemical marriage." But the alchemists were not satisfied with representing it as a marriage between

[c] See above, page 189.

man and woman. It was too far-reaching and mysterious for that. They used many other symbols, such as the dragon embracing a woman in her grave, two fighting animals, or the king dissolving in water. They also described this stage as opening a window on eternity. They tried by repeated distillation to produce an actual sky-blue fluid of the subtlest consistency, which they called their *caelum* (their heaven).

In analytical psychology this stage consists of making the knowledge we have gained *actual* by applying it in our daily lives. Clearly it is no use learning to know our shadow, for instance, if we are not going to draw the conclusions and *act* upon them. The goal of this stage could also be called *uniting the highest and the lowest in oneself*, a gap which was left wide open by Christianity and which alchemy constantly tried to fill. Jung said:

> The second stage of conjunction therefore consists in making a reality of the man who has acquired some knowledge of his paradoxical wholeness. The great difficulty here, however, is that no one knows how the paradoxical wholeness of man can ever be realized. That is the crux of individuation.[3]

Jung went on to say that in this dilemma it is especially worthwhile "to see how the more unencumbered symbolical thinking of a medieval 'philosopher' tackled this problem." Jung pointed out that no alchemist ever laid claim to having gone beyond the second stage, but he emphasized that how far the alchemist succeeded in his endeavors is really much less important than the fact that he was gripped by the numinous archetype behind his effort, so that he went on trying without interruption throughout his whole life. Dorn was an exception in that he tried to reach a third stage, which he called the union with the *unus mundus*. Dorn did not, however, regard this as the outer world but as the potential *one* world from which everything was created, and his highest aim was to reunite mankind with this *unus mundus*, this potential world of the first day of creation when everything was still one. This is possible only after the soul has been reunited with the body, or the spirit with matter, in the second stage and man, or the content of the retort, has thus become strong and whole enough to stand the impact. This potential world is the foundation of everything, just as the Self is the basis of the individual and includes its past, present, and future.

Jung said: "The thought Dorn expresses by the third degree of conjunction is universal: it is the relation or identity of the personal with the suprapersonal atman, and of the individual tao with the universal tao."[4] Western man thinks this a mystical idea because he has no experience of any world except the outer visible world, and he cannot therefore see that the Self enters three-dimensional reality when the ego touches the potential world, the *unus mundus*.

Jung had just such an experience—as we have seen and often recalled—
on the Athi Plains near Nairobi when he saw:

> . . . the world as it had always been in the state of non-being. . . .
> There I was now, the first human being to recognize that this was the
> world, but who did not know that in this moment he had first really
> created it.
>
> There the cosmic meaning of consciousness became overwhelm-
> ingly clear to me. "What nature leaves imperfect, the art perfects,"
> say the alchemists. Man, I, in an invisible act of creation put the stamp
> of perfection on the world by giving it objective existence. This act we
> usually ascribe to the Creator alone, without considering that in so
> doing we view life as a machine calculated down to the last detail,
> which, along with the human psyche, runs on senselessly, obeying
> foreknown and predetermined rules.

Then Jung thought of his old Pueblo Indian friend and how he had envied
his meaningful certainty that he had to help his father the sun to cross the
sky each day; and in that moment Jung realized the longed-for myth of our
own: "Human consciousness created objective existence and meaning,
and man found his indispensable place in the great process of being."[5]
This was such a moment when the Self came into reality by the ego
entering "into relationship with the world of the first day of creation," for it
was naturally the Self and not the ego that put "the stamp of perfection on
the world by giving it objective existence." Or, in the language we used
when considering this experience of Jung's before, it was his No. 2 personality, although the experience had to be registered by No. 1. The No. 2
personality was called forth and made intensely real by the glimpse Jung
had of the world as it was first created, the potential world of the beginning.
The *unus mundus* showed itself to Jung as he stood there by himself.

Although Dorn saw that man himself had to become one in order to be
capable of facing this third stage, he, like all the other alchemists, labored
incessantly to produce in his retort the sky-blue fluid, and his hope was that
he could bring about a union between this subtle substance and the *unus
mundus* and thus complete the third stage.

Jung remarked at the beginning of his chapter on the third stage, "The
Unus Mundus," that Dorn was a "significant exception," for he realized
that the production of the stone, or sky-blue fluid, marked only "the
completion of the second stage of conjunction." He pointed out that this
agrees with psychological experience, and continued:

> For us the representation of the idea of the self in actual and visible
> form is a mere *rite d'entrée*, as it were a propaedeutic action and mere
> anticipation of its realization. The existence of a sense of inner

security by no means proves that the product will be stable enough to withstand the disturbing or hostile influences of the environment. The adept had to experience again and again how unfavorable circumstances or a technical blunder or—as it seemed to him—some devilish accident hindered the completion of his work, so that he was forced to start all over again from the very beginning. Anyone who submits his sense of inner security to analogous psychic tests will have similar experiences. More than once everything he has built will fall to pieces under the impact of reality, and he must not let this discourage him from examining, again and again, where it is that his attitude is still defective, and what are the blind spots in his psychic field of vision. Just as a lapis Philosophorum, with its miraculous powers, was never produced, so psychic wholeness will never be attained empirically, as consciousness is too narrow and too one-sided to comprehend the full inventory of the psyche. Always we shall have to begin again from the beginning. From ancient times the adept knew that he was concerned with the "res simplex," and the modern man too will find by experience that the work does not prosper without the greatest simplicity. But simple things are always the most difficult.

"The One and Simple" is what Dorn called the *unus mundus*. This "one world" was the *res simplex*.[6]

It was just this simplicity that was so evident in Jung himself. He could always reduce the most complicated situation to simplicity, and the same gift was the secret of his unrivaled dream interpretation. One was constantly reminded of Columbus and the egg! But unfortunately, as he said, "simple things are always the most difficult," and I have never seen anyone else attain the simplicity which was the essence of Jung.

He pointed out that, in spite of the projection, the alchemists had an advantage over us in that they were constantly engaged with matter in their retorts, whereas in psychology we tend to "pale abstractions." The alchemist, on the contrary, felt his work to be "a magically effective action which, like the substance itself, imparted magical qualities."[7] It is often evident in modern dreams that the trend in the collective unconscious itself is toward a better balance between spirit and matter, a balance that was maintained throughout the Middle Ages, when Christianity became more and more spiritual, by the undercurrent of the alchemists working passionately in their retorts. When the alchemistic current ceased, the archetype itself seems to have moved Pope Piux XII, impressed by the many dreams and visions of simple people, to produce a new blossom on the Christian surface which even raises a symbol of matter—Mother Mary's body—to the level of the Godhead. Jung never tired of pointing out the vital importance of the new dogma, and in *Mysterium Coniunctionis* he went into it particularly deeply. For example, he said that for more than a thousand years, the alchemists prepared the ground for the dogma of the Assumption, which is

> . . . really a wedding feast, the Christian version of the hierosgamos, whose originally incestuous nature played a great role in alchemy. The traditional incest always indicated that the supreme union of opposites expressed a combination of things which are related but of unlike nature. . . . Alchemy throws a bright light on the background of the dogma, for the new article of faith expressed in symbolic form exactly what the adepts recognized as being the secret of their conjunctio. The correspondence is indeed so great that the old Masters could legitimately have declared that the new dogma has written the Hermetic secret in the skies.[8]

Later Jung said:

> The archetype is a living idea that constantly produces new interpretations through which that idea unfolds. . . . It is naturally not only the archetypes mentioned in the canonical writing of the New Testament that develop, but also their near relatives, of which we previously knew only the pagan forerunners. An example of this is the newest dogma concerning the Virgin; it refers unquestionably to the mother goddess who was constantly associated with the young dying son. She is not even purely pagan, since she was very distinctly prefigured in the Sophia of the Old Testament.[9]

It is strange that so many Catholics—to say nothing of Protestant theologians—have failed to see the vital importance of the new dogma. Father Victor White (author of *God and the Unconscious*), a friend of Jung who stayed with him more than once at Bollingen, used to say he heard far more about it in Zürich than in Rome, but then, Victor White had an excellent sense of humor and was not at all narrow-minded. He was an authority on Thomas Aquinas and I have never forgotten how he said to Marie-Louise von Franz with a delighted grin: "Oh, how marvelous it would be if you could bring irrefutable proof that it was certainly Thomas who wrote the *Aurora Consurgens*." [d]

Just as Jung brought alchemy vividly into the present by his description of its connection with the new dogma, he also provided the modern reader with a technique by means of which he can labor with the same fervor and

---

[d] The third volume of the *Mysterium Coniunctionis* is devoted to this text which is ascribed to Thomas of Aquinas. Marie-Louise von Franz has made out a very convincing case in this volume for Thomas being the real author, and Jung thoroughly agreed with her on this point. As the original manuscript of the *Aurora* has long since disappeared, Rome can of course claim there is no *irrefutable* proof, as both the authors admit.

industry that the alchemists devoted to their retorts. We have seen the beginning of active imagination when we were considering Jung's own "confrontation with the unconscious," a technique he always recommended to those of his pupils who were destined to experience the same confrontation, and which he mentioned often in his writings. But his latest and perhaps his most profound description of it is to be found in the volume we are considering. Space prevents more than a very few short excerpts, and all that he says about it here should be read in full.[10]

> The production of the *caelum* is a symbolic rite performed in the laboratory. Its purpose was to create, in the form of a substance, that "truth," the celestial balsam or life principle, which is identical with the God-image. Psychologically, it was a representation of the individuation process by means of chemical substances and procedures, or what we today call active imagination. This is a method which is used spontaneously by nature herself or can be taught to the patient by the analyst. As a rule it occurs when the analysis has constellated the opposites so powerfully that a union or synthesis of the personality becomes an imperative necessity.[11]

Later he explained more clearly how this could be done. For example, he said:

> Take the unconscious in one of its handiest forms, say a spontaneous fantasy, a dream, an irrational mood, an affect, or something of the kind, and operate with it. Give it your special attention, concentrate on it, and observe its alterations objectively. Spare no effort to devote yourself to this task, follow the subsequent transformations of the spontaneous fantasy attentively and carefully. Above all, don't let anything from outside, that does not belong, get into it, for the fantasy-image has "everything it needs."[e] In this way one is certain of not interfering by conscious caprice and of giving the unconscious a free hand. In short, the alchemical operation seems to us the equivalent of the psychological process of active imagination.[12]

Jung also illustrated how the opposites can unite:

> In nature the resolution of opposites is always an energetic process: she acts *symbolically* in the truest sense of the word, doing something that expresses both sides, just as a waterfall visibly mediates between above and below. The waterfall itself is then the incommensurable third. In an open and unresolved conflict dreams and fantasies occur which, like the waterfall, illustrate the tension and nature of the opposites, and thus prepare the synthesis.[13]

[e] The German runs: " . . . everything it needs *in itself.*" Italics added.

Jung went on to explain the way fantasies can develop and unite conscious and unconscious, as the water unites above and below. But, he emphasized, this process will remain fruitless unless the patient learns "to take part in the play and, instead of just sitting in a theatre, really have it out with his alter ego," in order to fix its actuality and to do so whatever it costs him. "Only in this painful way is it possible to gain insight into the complex nature of one's own personality." [14]

These few excerpts are scarcely sufficient to give the unprepared reader an idea of the value and use of active imagination. The whole misunderstanding of Jungian psychology begins right here: that many people do not seem able to understand "the complex nature of one's own personality" or that they can have an "*alter ego*" real and powerful enough to justify treating it with the same concentration and labor the alchemists gave to their retorts. The unconscious and its content, the *alter ego*, seem to them something fantastic, even mystical, whereas even a little *experience* would convince them that the contents of the unconscious are just as real and unalterable as the chemical substances of the alchemists. Both are symbols for something beyond human comprehension, which nevertheless gives life its meaning and value.

The epilogue[15] with which Jung closed his *opus magnum* presents the whole picture so vividly in two pages that I cannot resist quoting it almost in full:

> Alchemy with its wealth of symbols gives us an insight into an endeavour of the human mind which could be compared with a religious rite, an *opus divinum*. The difference between them is that the alchemical opus was not a collective activity rigorously defined as to its form and content, but rather, despite the similarity of their fundamental principles, an individual undertaking on which the adept staked his whole soul for the transcendental purpose of producing a *unity*. It was a work of reconciliation between apparently incompatible opposites, which, characteristically, were understood not merely as the natural hostility of the physical elements but at the same time as a moral conflict. Since the object of this endeavour was seen outside as well as inside, as both physical and psychic, the work extended as it were through the whole of nature, and its goal consisted in a symbol which had an empirical and at the same time a transcendental aspect.

Jung then pointed out that alchemy groped its way through an endless maze and that in the nineteenth century the psychology of the unconscious took up the trail that was lost at the end of alchemy. Just as alchemy was always searching in the darkness of cheap substances thrown out into the street, so psychology searches in the rejected darkness of the human soul, which has meanwhile become accessible to clinical observation. He continued:

> . . . There alone could be found all those contradictions, those grotesque phantasms and scurrilous symbols which had fascinated the mind of the alchemists and confused them as much as illuminated them. And the same problem presented itself to the psychologist that had kept the alchemists in suspense for seventeen hundred years. What was he to do with these antagonistic forces? Could he throw them out and get rid of them? Or had he to admit their existence, and is it our task to bring them into harmony and, out of the multitude of contradictions, produce a unity, which naturally will not come of itself, though it may—*Deo concedente*—with human effort? . . . To-day we can see how effectively alchemy prepared the ground for the psychology of the unconscious, firstly by leaving behind, in its treasury of symbols, illustrative material of the utmost value for modern interpretations in this field, and secondly by indicating symbolical procedures for synthesis which we can rediscover in the dreams of our patients. We can see today that the entire alchemical procedure for uniting the opposites, which I have described in the foregoing, could just as well represent the individuation process of a single individual, though with the not unimportant difference that no single individual ever attains to the richness and scope of the alchemical symbolism. This has the advantage of having been built up through the centuries, whereas the individual in his short life has at its disposal only a limited amount of experience and limited powers of portrayal. It is therefore a difficult and thankless task to try to describe the nature of the individuation process from case-material. . . . No case in my experience is comprehensive enough to show all the aspects in such detail that it could be regarded as paradigmatic. Anyone who attempted to describe the individuation process with the help of case-material would have to remain content with a mosaic of bits and pieces without beginning or end, and if he wanted to be understood he would have to count on a reader whose experience in the same field was equal to his own. Alchemy, therefore, has performed for me the great and invaluable service of providing material in which my experience could find sufficient room, and has thereby made it possible for me to describe the individuation process at least in its essential aspects.

Jung finished his *opus magnum* in all its essential aspects before the beginning of the fateful year 1955. He always continued to improve and correct his writing up to the stage of page proofs. In fact, he had an arrangement with his publisher, Rascher Verlag of Zürich, by which he gave the latter various advantages in exchange for permission to change his text right up to the last proofs. Not that he made extensive use of this privilege, but he hated to have to read his work for printing errors and then discover passages in which he might have expressed himself better without being able to alter them.

We have lost sight of Ruth Bailey since the return from Africa in the spring of 1926. Up until now there has been no special occasion to mention her, although she frequently stayed with the Jungs; in fact, I think she did so every year except during World War II. But from 1955 on, she became of vital importance in Jung's life. As early as the summer of 1926, Emma had invited Ruth to stay with the Jungs at Küsnacht, and she became a firm friend of the whole family. All the Jung children stayed with her at the Bailey family home, Lawton Mere in Cheshire, during their various (exceedingly successful) attempts to learn English, and Jung and his wife each managed to visit her there also. The third daughter, Marianne, even stayed for many of her holidays from her English school.

Ruth had promised Jung and his wife (after her own mother had died, during the war) that she would live with and look after the survivor, whichever it might be, and even before 1955 her visits became longer and more essential every year. Emma Jung's health had given cause for mild anxiety ever since her seventieth birthday in 1952, and she was in the hospital for some time with trouble in her back. While there, to Emma's great relief, Ruth came and kept house for Jung. Bollingen became more and more difficult for Emma, but when Ruth stayed there with them and undertook most of the work, she could still enjoy the place very much. It worried Jung a great deal, however, that while Bollingen remained his greatest pleasure and source of health, it was beginning to be too rough a life for his wife. He could never bear people doing things *for him* if they did not enjoy it themselves, and he began to feel that Emma was going to Bollingen for his sake.

Although she seemed to be aging more rapidly than her husband, in spite of being nine years younger, and although she sometimes did not seem very well, there was no cause for real anxiety until the spring of 1955, when she got really ill and had to go for a time to the hospital. To her great relief, Ruth immediately came from England, so that she was spared any anxiety about her husband. As a matter of fact, Jung was himself very well just then and quite all right up at Bollingen with Hans Kuhn[f] to help him, but ever since his illness in 1944, when she had had such a sudden shock, Emma was almost overanxious about him. Jung returned immediately to Küsnacht and remained there all the while his wife was in the hospital. The operation

[f] See above, page 233.

went very well. We all hoped it had been undertaken in time and that we should keep Emma Jung for a number of years. She was out of the hospital after a short time and Ruth returned to England, under promise, however, to return for the summer holidays in order to make the Bollingen life suitable for them both. Emma could not speak too highly of how much Ruth's help meant to her in her last two years.

In July, 1955, Jung celebrated his eightieth birthday. Any hope for quiet, small celebrations had already disappeared by his seventy-fifth birthday,[g] and for his eightieth the club had a large afternoon celebration, and the C. G. Jung Institute had two, one morning and one evening, all three at the Dolder Grand Hotel.[h] The morning event, open to anyone who had attended any lectures at the institute, was on a very large scale, so we expected it to be accordingly dismal. But the opposite was true, for it had one of the most meaningful and healing atmospheres I have ever experienced. Jung stayed for an unusually long time and seemed to drag himself unwillingly away.

The same evening there was a small dinner party, consisting of all the "high ups" from the many Jungian groups all over the world and from the curatorium and lecturers of the Zürich institute. The atmosphere was the reverse of the morning. Jung was very pleased to receive a bound advance copy of the first volume of the *Mysterium Coniunctionis,*[i] but on the whole he looked anything but happy and left as early as he could.

This contrast struck me so deeply that I asked Jung about it a few days later. I vividly remember that we were sitting by the lake in Bollingen while he was engaged in his favorite occupation of chopping wood. He agreed immediately and said the same thing had struck him very forcibly. He added: "I am sure there must have been a great many good spirits there that morning, and I think they mostly belonged to people we did not even know. But you know, those are the people who will carry on my psychology— people who read my books and let me silently change their lives. It will not be carried on by the people on top, for they mostly give up Jungian psychology and take to prestige psychology instead."

This made the difference very clear to me: in the morning no one had been trying to get anything; it was too large a gathering to hope for special contacts with Jung and by far the majority were satisfied to see him looking so well and happy. Many of them had probably never seen him before. There were tables and refreshments, but there was no seating order; everyone sat where and with whom he liked. But in the evening there was a

g From age seventy on, the five-year anniversaries are always very special occasions in Switzerland.
h This hotel and the Baur au Lac are Zürich's largest and best hotels. The Dolder Grand is situated in the woods, high above Zürich, with a magnificent view of the lake and mountains.
i In German this book is printed in two volumes, which makes it much lighter and easier to handle than the one English volume.

rigid seating order and the majority of the guests were occupied with such questions as to whether they had been given a good enough place, how much they could manage to talk to Jung, whether he had been nice to them or not, and so on, naturally producing a most disagreeable atmosphere. This experience taught me a lot; it was the only time I ever knew Jung more pleased with a very large group than with a comparatively small one.

That summer of 1955 was a particularly happy summer for the Jungs. Emma felt well enough to enjoy the eightieth birthday celebrations and the great appreciation that was shown to her husband. She was also well enough to spend most of the rest of the summer at Bollingen, with Ruth Bailey's indefatigable care and the family paying visits. Jung was very happy too, for he felt—at any rate for the present—that a solution had been found for the Bollingen dilemma, and he very much enjoyed his wife's evident pleasure at being there.

Linda Fierz, who was so long on the committee of the club and a pupil and friend of Jung, died in the spring of 1955, having survived her husband only for a year or two. As mentioned before,[j] she left a *Gastrecht* of her house at Bollingen to Marie-Louise von Franz and myself, so that we now had the great privilege of being near neighbors of the Jungs. They had lent their car[k] to a daughter and son-in-law that summer, so Jung asked if they could depend on mine. Naturally, I was delighted and thus saw a lot of them those holidays. Not that they used a car much at Bollingen—they were too happy at home—but one or the other of them quite often had to go to see the doctor, or on some other essential errand, so it was necessary to be able to use a car whenever they needed one. Emma was usually very introverted at Bollingen, but that summer she was hospitable and friendly, and always seemed pleased to see either or both Marie-Louise and myself whenever we went over.

Even when she returned to Küsnacht in the autumn, her good health apparently continued, but in early November, to everyone's surprise and horror, she became seriously ill again. She went to the hospital for a short time, but evidently there was nothing they could do, for she was soon home again, where she died peacefully, at the last very unexpectedly, on November 30, 1955. Jung told me afterward that the surgeon had warned him in the spring that there might be more trouble later, but, he added: "I thought we might reckon on a few years."

Emma's death was the worst relationship loss that Jung ever experienced. Nothing is worse than losing your congenial daily companion and, after fifty-two years of very meaningful and deeply related marriage, it must have been almost more than most old men of eighty could have

[j] See above, page 155.
[k] The Jungs had only one car after the war.

recovered from. Indeed, at first it seemed to be an almost mortal blow to Jung.

In all my eighty years, I have never seen a marriage for which I felt such a spontaneous and profound respect. Emma Jung was a most remarkable woman, a sensation type who compensated and completed her husband in many respects. I also esteemed her very highly and loved her as a friend.

Jung led his now very large family into Küsnacht Church for the funeral service. The way he did this, evidently tortured but erect and composed, struck the large congregation to the heart. I still often hear from comparative strangers: "When I think of Jung, I always see him as he came in that morning." He also attended the luncheon that was held at his house later, and though he made it very clear to his near friends that he wanted to be let alone, he was calm, friendly, and very related to all the people he knew less well.

It had been a great comfort to Emma, when she realized the end was nearing, to know that Jung's health and daily comfort would be safe in Ruth Bailey's hands. Any or all of his daughters would have gladly looked after him, but as he said to me: "They all have their own full lives with their families and I could not bear to be a disturbance." It was a great comfort to him that Ruth had, at the time of Emma's death, no vital obligations. The brother with whom she had lived since her mother's death had died a few years earlier, and a long visit to South Africa, where her youngest sister and husband had moved from East Africa, had ended a year or two before. She had, it is true, a house—Lawton House—of which she was very fond, close to her old family home—Lawton Mere—but Ruth was the born companion (and, if necessary, nurse) to someone she valued, so that coming to live in Switzerland with Jung just at that time, for the five and a half years until his death, was also a godsend to her. Jung often told me what a blessing it was to him to feel that the natural dependency of his old age was interrupting no one's life.

After learning of Emma's death, Ruth came as quickly as she could, but was only able to make it a day or two after the funeral. On our Saturday drive Jung spoke to me about the attitude he wanted me to take toward Ruth, insofar as psychology was concerned. She was the only one of his friends, of whom he saw a great deal in the last years of his life, who had never been analyzed or made a deep study of his psychology, a state of things that had its advantages and drawbacks. He said that morning: "You are sure to see a lot of Ruth and I want you to answer any questions about psychology she may ask you to the best of your ability, but *never* to begin the subject yourself or in any way to rub in *anything* about it."

That drive lives with particular vividness in my memory, for Jung's courage had never struck me more forcibly. He was evidently stricken to the heart by the loss of his wife, yet he quietly faced the necessity of going on. Although he had finished his *opus magnum,* the *Mysterium Con-iunctionis,* there was apparently more he still had to do before his own appointed time. During these weeks after his wife's death, he wrote in a letter that it helped him most *not* to dwell on the past, but to concentrate on *why* he had to be the survivor, and to give his whole energy to finding the purpose he still had to fulfill.

# 17

## Late Years
## 1955–1959

Jung reported in *Memories* that he could hardly have survived the first months after his wife's death if he had not constantly worked at carving his stone tablets.[1][a] He worked on them all winter in his garden room at Küsnacht, and had them transported to Bollingen in the spring, where he finished them. There were three of these tablets and on them he carved the names of his paternal ancestors. This fact entirely refutes the theory that he believed as an *outer fact*, that his grandfather was the illegitimate son of Goethe,[b] for in that case the Jung family line would have broken off with his grandfather and been replaced by Goethe's family tree. As it is, he reported:

> When I was working on the stone tablets, I became aware of the fateful links between me and my ancestors. I feel very strongly that I am under the influence of things or questions which were left incomplete and unanswered by my parents and grandparents and more distant ancestors. It often seems as if there were an impersonal karma within a family, which is passed on from parents to children. It has always seemed to me that I had to answer questions which fate had posed to my forefathers, and which had not yet been answered, or as if I had to complete, or perhaps continue, things which previous ages had left unfinished.[2]

[a] He wrote in 1957: "Everything that I have written this year and last year, *The Undiscovered Self, Flying Saucers: A Modern Myth, A Psychological View of Conscience,* has grown out of the stone sculptures I did after my wife's death. The close of her life, the end, and what it made me realize, wrenched me violently out of myself. It cost me a great deal to regain my footing and contact with stone helped me."

[b] See above, page 22.

The garden room at Küsnacht has a great many windows and almost gives one the feeling of being out of doors. It is, however, part of the house, with a door and short staircase from the large room, and can be heated like the rest of the house; not that Jung ever wanted his rooms really warm, he was perfectly happy in a temperature considerably below 60 degrees Fahrenheit. When he was younger, his room was often so cold visitors needed a fur coat to keep from shivering. Now the Swiss usually keep their houses very warm, so in this—as in many other things—Jung was an exception. Yet—as emphasized in the first chapter—Jung was Swiss through and through.

At this time, whenever Jung did not go for a drive on Saturday mornings, I used to join him for an hour or so in his garden room, while he worked on his stones. Some of the best conversations I ever had with him took place while he was engaged in carving stone or cutting wood. Whenever he needed to give his full mind to what he was doing, he would ask for silence, but on the whole the work seemed to free his mind, so that he thought particularly deeply and always seemed glad to talk of the thoughts with which he was occupied at the time. One could indeed always speak to him of *inner* things and ask questions. But in those last years, Marie-Louise and I (and probably others of his pupils) learned that it was not at all a good plan to speak to him of *outer* difficulties. He was so conscientious that if one of us was in a fix, he would give his full attention to it, but one realized more and more that it went terribly against the grain, for his interest had left everyday *outer* life. There were exceptions, but they were all outer expressions of an inner importance. Therefore his interest in building not only his own house but also in that of his friends increased rather than decreased.[c]

Ruth had arrived from England within a week of Emma Jung's death and had taken the household, and all the arrangements for Jung's external well-being, into her capable hands. He said to me with great gratitude: "I don't have to bother my head about anything of that kind. Ruth sees to it all." But mere efficiency would not have been enough. Ruth had almost a genius for giving daily companionship and for spreading a good and peaceful atmosphere. In those first months, she revealed herself as being able to leave him alone while giving him that complete security on the physical side which is one of the chief needs of old age. It must be remembered that Jung was over eighty when Ruth first came to live in Switzerland. Moreover—and this was perhaps the most important quality of all in contact with Jung—Ruth was always willing to listen when she did anything Jung did not like, and what is more, to profit by listening and to make every effort to change accordingly.

Nevertheless, the first months after Emma's death were naturally a very dark time for Jung. He was quite willing to face the fact that it was in a way a merciful fate that had forced him to survive both Toni and Emma, because, as he proved in the five and a half years that elapsed before his own death, he was able to go on *creatively* with his life and his individuation process after losing them. I think it is doubtful whether either of them could have done this. I saw a good deal of Emma while Jung was in India and witnessed how terribly she missed him and how much she depended upon him. Toni, moreover, had openly declared, from the beginning of my friendship with her, that on no account did she want to survive Jung, but they were both very courageous women, and would certainly have faced life without him, each to the best of her ability. Of course, his children also helped him very much and surrounded him with human warmth. Marianne Niehus, especially, looked after him devotedly whenever Ruth had to go to England.

Jung went down to the Tessin with Ruth Bailey in February. It was a very hard winter, with intense cold coming late; since the sap was already up in the trees, this led to the loss of many of them. Jung lost one of the two box bushes by his front door, much of his bamboo, and the clematis which grew so luxuriantly in the courtyard at Bollingen. The temperature was far below freezing. The vine over the front door at the Tower produced a curious red sap which ran down over Jung's crest. He felt this was a strange synchronicity, so soon after Emma's death, as if the vine were weeping tears of blood.

Jung was glad to seek the south. The evening before they went, Jung, Ruth, Dr. and Mrs. Konrad Lorenz, Franz Riklin, Marie-Louise, and myself had a very interesting time at a dinner in a Zürich restaurant. Jung and Lorenz discovered that each of them had originally wanted to follow the profession of the other, and a most fascinating exchange of experiences ensued. After Lorenz had described his work, Jung said, "Ah, I see: the *religio animalis*," which seemed to impress Lorenz deeply. Discussing it afterward, we understood that Jung meant Lorenz was unconsciously seeking a new orientation for man by studying the behavior of animals.[d]

The weather—repenting of its arctic cold—soon turned warmer, and Jung and Ruth were able to go to Bollingen not long after their return from the Tessin. Jung gave himself once more to his ancestral tablets. But before these were finished and put into their places, he carved a stone in memory of his wife, which was placed in front of the covered loggia at his Tower. This stone is one of the most beautiful that Jung ever carved.

Jung had not added to or changed the Tower since 1935. But when he was at Bollingen this spring, he began to feel something more was needed. He said:

---

[d] This of course was long before Lorenz published *On Aggression*.

> After my wife's death in 1955, I felt an inner obligation to become what I myself am. To put it in the language of the Bollingen house, I suddenly realized that the small central section which crouched so low, so hidden, was myself! I could no longer hide myself behind the "maternal" and the "spiritual" towers. So, in that same year, I added an upper story to this section, which represents myself, or my ego-personality. Earlier, I would not have been able to do this, I would have regarded it as presumptuous self-emphasis. Now it signified an extension of consciousness achieved in old age. With that the building was complete.[3]

He worked out the plans with his son during the spring holidays and began with the building early in the summer holidays. This 1956 building was *primarily* undertaken for an *inner* obligation, and only secondarily for the "concrete needs of the moment." In the earlier additions the latter were the impetus, so to speak, and only later did Jung realize that "a meaningful form had resulted: a symbol of psychic wholeness."[4] Now Jung realized that there was something lacking in the psychic wholeness, himself or his ego personality, which now signified "an extension of ego consciousness achieved in old age." And one could say that was also the task that kept him on earth after his wife's death, a task he punctually fulfilled up to the day of his own death. There were secondary concrete advantages also: he usually did his writing afterward in the new room, which could be well heated and which was very much more spacious and airy than the small study below it, where he had heretofore always worked when in the house since it was built in 1927.

The fact that the view no longer distracted him when he was working indicates how enormously his concentration had developed. He always had unusual powers of concentration, but earlier he needed small windows to reinforce it against the powerful magnet of nature and the lake; now they were just a pleasant background to his work. He could also work undisturbed, in the summer of 1956, when the building noise would have upset almost anyone else. The new building also had another concrete advantage: there were two small bedrooms that were very useful for visiting children and grandchildren.

Staying at Bollingen now became very easy, for Ruth liked the life there almost as much as Jung did, so he no longer felt any compunction in going there as much as was right for himself. He spent all his holidays there, as he had done in earlier days, and he also often went for a week or so during the term. One cannot feel too grateful to Ruth Bailey for her courage in this respect, for she was often there alone with him, when it would have been very difficult for her to get help should he have been ill. She even stayed with him there sometimes in the winter when they were snowed in. Since he always had said he would like to die at Bollingen, she was determined to make it possible for him to follow his own instinct and to do just what he liked in this respect, whether they were at Bollingen or Küsnacht.

Another way in which Ruth showed extraordinary courage was in letting him sail his boat, often going out alone with him on the lake, leaving him to manage the boat. It was a great pleasure to him to be able to do this, for it was one of the many things he had had to sacrifice after his illness in 1944, though he resumed several of these activities in old age. He was, of course, very reasonable and did not abuse his regained freedom. Ruth did all this so gallantly that, though I knew her well, I did not realize for a long time how afraid she had been sometimes in the depth of her own soul. Once when we came back to the nearby Fierz house, she suddenly said to me that it was a relief to have someone so nearby whom she could call in an emergency.

Hans Kuhn was also there a good deal and, though Ruth sometimes complained that he was not much help to her with her work, he could always have been sent to telephone from his parents' house in any emergency. Still, he was by no means a permanency. His employer, Mrs. Crowley, was very generous in lending Hans to Jung, but he always disliked inconveniencing anyone, especially when she grew more and more dependent on Hans. He subsequently looked after her with great devotion until her death, when she was nearly ninety on January 6, 1972.

The three tablets with the names of Jung's ancestors and his descendants in the direct male line until his son's sons had meanwhile been completed and erected in the covered loggia by the spring of 1957. The first tablet begins with the Delphic oracle, "Called or not called, God will be present," that Jung also carved over his front door at Küsnacht and near the door of the original Tower in 1923.

These tablets represent innumerable hours of work over many months, for every word is carved in stone. But when they were in place, Jung felt the task was not yet completed. He turned his attention to the ceiling, which he had decided to decorate with paintings of his own crest and those of his wife and his sons-in-law. He designed this himself and carried it out with the help of Ruth Bailey, Marie-Louise von Franz, and Hans Kuhn.

Being able to help in such work was always the greatest pleasure to Marie-Louise, but she had always longed for some ground of her own, on which she could build the house of her dreams. Although very grateful to Linda Fierz for leaving us the *Gastrecht* of her house and mindful of the privilege of being so close to Jung's Tower, this longing did not leave her. She had been looking for a suitable site since the Second World War, but it proved elusive. Then in the autumn of 1957, Jung's son, Franz, told her of some ground for sale in Bollingen, which he thought would be suitable, on the hill about a mile from Jung's Tower. We went up to see it that same evening and went to ask Jung's opinion the next morning. He immediately expressed his wish to see it, and he, Ruth Bailey, Marie-Louise, and myself drove up to it there and then. He walked about it, then stood still, looking at the beautiful view, and said to Marie-Louise: "Go and buy it at once." As we drove down the hill, he added: "But you must not build an ordinary house there, it must be a Tower." Had the suggestion not come from him, she would never have dared use this form, since she would have been afraid of imitation and presumption. Even so, she built her tower square, whereas Jung's original Tower and subsequent additions are round. As it is, we are often asked by strangers if her Tower is not very old, so well does it fit the landscape.

Marie-Louise gave herself at once to designing her Tower, professionally supported by Franz Jung, who was its architect. But at first, as the whole enterprise would take the last penny she had, she thought she must wait a few years before building. Jung would hear nothing of such procrastination, and told her she would regret every moment she waited. So she started building in the summer of 1958. It was completed that autumn. Jung took the greatest interest in this building, discussing every detail with his son and Marie-Louise, and frequently driving up to watch its progress. He even did this when Marie-Louise was not there, showing that his interest was in the building itself, not just in encouraging her.

At first Marie-Louise built her Tower as a hermitage. I also did not feel at all ready to give up staying at the Fierz house, which had one disadvantage, however: Jung refused to let me stay there alone (on account of possible breaking in) unless I could shoot. Since I had never touched a gun, I therefore always had to have someone stay with me, though Marie-Louise herself came down from time to time. But as her wish for solitude slowly decreased, and as I found I could get down to Jung's Tower easily to help Ruth, we gradually stayed there more and more, especially since Jung was rarely at Bollingen during the last year of his life.

It was in these years that Jung took to going on long drives, all over Switzerland, and sometimes into Austria or Italy. He told me once that being unable to go for long walks in the mountains was one of the greatest trials of his old age. He added that when he found his health would stand long expeditions, including going over even the highest passes in Fowler McCormick's large, comfortable American car, he felt that the mountains had been unexpectedly given back to him. The only restriction that his health and age put on these expeditions was that they never spend the night, or even stop for lunch or supper, in a very high place. There was little that would tempt Jung away from his beloved Bollingen, but in his last years these drives often made him leave it, for as much as a week or even longer. He always came back from them very much refreshed, full of his interest in the places he had seen.

His companions on these drives were Ruth Bailey and of course Fowler McCormick. Fowler and Ruth got on very well indeed; although they met for the first time only in 1952, they rapidly became great friends. They had known of each other since 1925, when Ruth took Fowler's place and had the benefit of his equipment on the East African trip[e] but they never happened to be in Switzerland at the same time in subsequent years. Although Fowler was often in Switzerland as a boy and had traveled with Jung to the American Indians and to India, he did not make a habit of spending part of each year in Switzerland until the 1950s, a habit he then kept up every summer.[f] But during Jung's last years, he also used to come sometimes in the winter, so that he could give Jung the benefit of long drives during his almost annual winter stay in the Tessin.

Ruth had never been analyzed and Jung once told me that this was very restful to him. "I do not have to worry about making her more conscious," he once said, "as I always have before with everybody round me." Fowler had some analysis and had made efforts to read all of Jung's books, still Jung also felt under no obligation to make him more conscious, since he had not analyzed him himself for many years. This made a very restful background. Jung had all the companionship and care that he needed on those drives, yet was completely free to be alone in "God's world" [5] just as he had been alone on the Athi Plains, over forty years before.[g] As a boy he had recognized "God's world" most particularly in the mountains, a world behind which one feels the presence of the *unus mundus*.

Of course, the fact that Ruth had never been analyzed or gone deeply into Jung's psychology had its disadvantages. Jung used to speak occasionally of her amazing naïveté concerning his psychology, and she was sometimes quite especially naïve in her judgments of people. This used to amuse him at times, but I am sure there was no one else who could have made his last years so amazingly happy, in spite of the fact that he had to put up with a great many of the physical drawbacks of old age. This was mainly due to the fact that his well-being was her chief concern and that she was always willing to accept people and things because he wanted them, even though I think his taste was occasionally surprising to her. Moreover, as Jung testified in his account of his African journey, the "experience she had acquired as a nurse during the First World War" was a great blessing to them when a member (George Beckwith) of their "party came down with a bad case of tropical malaria." [6] It was even more of a blessing to Jung during these last years. She did any nursing he required without—and this was very important to him—ever fussing over him or curtailing his liberty.

When Jung wrote the preface to the *Mysterium Coniunctionis* in October, 1954, he began it by expressly stating that it was his last book.[7] It was indeed his last *long* book, but the creative daimon that had driven him all his life[8] did not grant him the peace and rest that his old age seemed

[e] See above, page 167.

[f] He was there for the last time in 1971, before his death in January, 1973.

[g] At that time, he withdrew physically from his companions, but as he got older this was not always feasible and he learned to withdraw just as effectually psychologically.

richly to have earned. On the contrary, until shortly before his death, it spurred him on to one more creative effort after another. In fact in the nearly six years after his eightieth birthday he produced a great deal of his most interesting work, though much of it is too little known.

The first of these creative efforts was called *Gegenwart und Zukunft* (*Present and Future*) and first appeared as a supplement to the *Schweizer Monatshefte* in March, 1957. Jung's publisher, Rascher Verlag, produced it as a paperback later in the same year. It came as the result of many questions concerning the future which had been asked him, especially by Carleton Smith, who drew it to the attention of the Atlantic Monthly Press.[9]

There was more trouble over the translation of this work than with any other book or paper by Jung that I remember.[h] I must place on record the fact that though, as is expressly stated in more than one of the volumes, I am sure that Jung did authorize all the larger changes that were made, they were mostly made in the way I have already described: Jung very seldom wholeheartedly *liked* these changes (at least I always had that impression when we discussed them), but if they were persisted in he just "retired to his estates" sometimes explaining it by saying that he supposed if the translator, Richard Hull, did not understand neither would the public. Jung's correspondence was always overwhelmingly large and was almost—at times quite—beyond what he could cope with. This was sometimes much increased by letters from his translator, also from the editors, but much less as they restricted themselves for the most part to one long meeting a year. Richard Hull proposed such far-reaching changes in *Present and Future,* that Jung's almost inexhaustible patience gave out. He asked me to go down to the Tessin (where the Hulls were then living) to remonstrate.[i] Hull accepted Jung's remonstrances willingly[j] and the work now follows the German much more exactly. I do not know when and why the title was changed from the German *Present and Future* to the English *The Undiscovered Self.*[k] Both titles describe the content well.

It was, it seems to me, very touching that most of what Jung wrote in

[h] In the early years of Richard Hull's translation of the *Collected Works,* I was associated with him and he could ask me any questions he liked.

[i] I remember Richard Hull explained his unusually drastic changes by saying that since the article was to be published first in a magazine it was sure to be changed a lot, so he had thought it better to forestall this. Hull is the most competent translator I know. I doubt if anyone else could have translated Jung's *whole Collected Works* as quickly or in many ways as well, certainly no one but a thinking type. But this last has the inevitable disadvantage that the irrational and feeling often come too short and the "double floor" has been lost. This "double floor," as Jung himself called it, came about because he always allowed the unconscious to express itself, side by side with his rational conscious contribution, in order to allow the irrational and feeling side to have its just share in his writing.

[j] He was even generous enough to write in the copy of *The Undiscovered Self* which he sent me: "To Barbara with warmest thanks, Richard."

[k] *Present and Future* is used as a subtitle in the English.

these last five years was full of anxious concern for the future of the world. Most people are inclined to think that what happens after their death will no longer concern them but, though he knew he had only a short time to live, Jung had a love of humanity which made him more, rather than less, concerned with its fate after his death. We can find this anxious concern in all he wrote in these last years, though only *The Undiscovered Self* is directly devoted to this theme and even begins with the question "What will the future bring?"

This short book of Jung's,[10] which goes deeply and most constructively into our most urgent problems, is far too little known. He asked, for instance, the meaning of our living "in an age filled with apocalyptic images of universal destruction," and inquired into the significance of the split in humanity "symbolized by the iron curtain." He further asked: "What will become of our civilization, and of man himself, if the hydrogen bombs begin to go off, or if the spiritual and moral darkness of State absolutism should spread over Europe?"[11]

It is this spiritual and moral darkness, in other words, the unconsciousness of man, that is by far our greatest danger. It is utterly useless to project this darkness onto the other side of the "iron curtain," for it is only the individual who *can* become conscious. It is true that he has lost his freedom far more disastrously in the countries where religion has been repressed and his faith demanded for the fiction called the "state," but, as Jung pointed out, the idea that the individual human being is the central problem is "enough to arouse the most violent doubts and resistances on all sides, and one could almost go so far as to assert that the valuelessness of the individual in comparison with large numbers is the one belief that meets with universal and unanimous assent."[12] The non-Communist world is just as bad in this respect as the people on the other side of the curtain. Our churches also proclaim the valuelessness of the individual, in comparison with the congregation, and organize and believe "in the sovereign remedy of mass action."[13] They do not realize that the "individual becomes morally and spiritually inferior in the mass," and have apparently entirely forgotten that the process of individuation is the central theme of original Christianity. Jung asked: "Are not Jesus and Paul prototypes of those who, trusting their inner experience, have gone their individual way in defiance of the world?"[14][1]

This distrust of the individual comes from the widespread error that the individual is identical with the ego and with its conscious fiction of what it is. But Jung was speaking of an individual who knows the eternal being in himself and who—like Jesus and Paul—sacrifices his egotistical desires to his *inner* experience of this being. Jung even said: "*Resistance to the*

---

[1] In the small edition Hull translated the German sentence: "*der Welt die Stirne geboten haben*" as "disregarding public opinion" instead of "in defiance of the world."

*organized mass can be effected only by the man who is as well organized in his individuality as the mass itself.*" [15] And this is the crux of the matter: this organization of oneself can be reached only by self-knowledge, by enormous effort and willingness to take the full responsibility for oneself. Unfortunately, most people prefer to be infantile in this respect, and to leave the responsibility to others. But they are thus "already on the road to State slavery and, without knowing it or wanting it, have become its proselyte." [16]

This short book is perhaps Jung's most vivid exposition of the myth of modern man that revealed itself to him on the Athi Plains over thirty years earlier. It really leaves the reader with the choice between becoming conscious enough to create "objective existence and meaning," or becoming unconsciously the slave of the state and those who know how to manipulate it, [17] and thus going down to his unknown end "in the profoundest night of non-being." [18]

Very shortly after finishing *The Undiscovered Self*, Jung turned his attention to writing *A Modern Myth of Things Seen in the Sky*. [19] [m] Flying saucers had interested Jung for several years before this; in fact, the very early reports of this phenomenon had caught his attention. At first he regarded flying saucers as purely visionary in character, though nonetheless real and interesting for that. He very often spoke of them in private conversations, but only once—in 1954—did anything by him appear in print. At that time he was interviewed on the subject by the *Weltwoche*, which subsequently published the interview. [20] The world press discovered this interview in 1958 and circulated the rumor that Jung was a believer in the objective reality of flying saucers. Since Jung had actually expressed skepticism in the interview as to the physical existence of the saucers, he wrote a correcting statement to the United Press; but this time, as he expressed it, "the wire went dead."

This reaction interested him very much: evidently it was welcome "news" when someone well known testified to the physical existence of saucers, and the reverse when he merely stated that something was certainly seen but no one knew what it was. The public evidently wanted saucers to be *real*. Actually he himself was much less interested in whether they existed physically than in the undeniable *fact* that many people, all over the world, were *seeing* round objects in the sky. Roundness is the symbol *par excellence* for the Self, the totality; and this fact, in our skeptical, rational modern world, is of overwhelming interest in and for itself. Moreover, most of these people seemed to expect something fateful from these round objects, ranging from salvation to destruction.

Jung's skepticism concerning their possible physical reality became

---

[m] The words "Flying Saucers" were added to the title in the English edition.

much less marked as more and more reliable testimonies appeared, but as he said in his introduction: "As a psychologist, I am not qualified to contribute anything useful to the question of the physical reality of Ufos. I can concern myself only with their undoubted psychic aspect." And this aspect is quite interesting enough. Just as events in National Socialist Germany had showed Jung that an archetype was stirring in the unconscious, and he felt compelled to write his article "Wotan" as a warning that "events were brewing of fateful consequence for Europe," so now again he felt compelled to warn his readers that an archetype was again stirring in a way that was even characteristic for "the end of an era." History has taught us to expect exceedingly fateful events at the end of each Platonic month (approximately two thousand years) as the Spring sign leaves one astrological sign and enters another. Jung had already spoken at some length in a seminar in 1929 of the great changes and upheavals that were to be expected as the age of the Fishes ended and as the Spring sign entered the sign of Aquarius, the water carrier. Since very few people heeded the warning in "Wotan," he had little or no hope that he would be heard again. Nevertheless, he felt so concerned that those who would listen should not be "caught unprepared by the events in question and disconcerted by their incomprehensible nature" that he wrote his warning at the risk of jeopardizing his "hard-won reputation for truthfulness, trustworthiness, and scientific judgment." He realized fully that this warning would not only be "exceedingly unpopular but come perilously close to those turbid fantasies which becloud the minds of world-improvers and other interpreters of 'signs and portents.' " But just as Jung, the undergraduate, would not allow himself to be discouraged by the unpopularity of "the despised realm of occultism,"[n] so now, sixty years later as a famous old man of over eighty, he would not be discouraged by any consideration from exploring the subject of flying saucers with the same conscientiousness that had won the skeptical Oeri's admiration in the discussion on occultism in the Zofingia fraternity.

Jung carefully explored all the evidence, first as rumors, then in dreams and in modern painting, and also went into the saucers' previous history. Finally, in an epilogue, he dealt with two very different books which had come into his hands *after* he had finished his manuscript. The first[21] was a very naïve document in which the author, Orfeo Angelucci, described his first encounter with "two balls of green fire" that had been released from an oval-shaped object and that explained to him in many interviews how infinitely more intelligent and conscious they were, how beneficent they felt toward their friends, the inhabitants of the earth, and how they intended nothing but their salvation. He was even taken to another planet by something that looked like a "huge misty soap bubble" and saw the

[n] See above, page 66 ff.

earth at a distance of about a thousand miles.[22, o] After this he preached his experiences as a kind of gospel.

The second book, titled *The Black Cloud,* intrigued Jung by being a kind of science-fiction story by a well-known authority on astrophysics, Fred Hoyle, two of whose "impressive" volumes Jung already knew: *The Nature of the Universe* and *Frontiers of Astronomy.*[23] The Black Cloud (also circular in shape) threatens the whole earth with extinction. A physicist and a mathematician of genius then get into communication with the cloud. Neither survives the experiment, though the latter is able to leave a record of what the cloud told him. The cloud eventually decides to quit our solar system and leaves, having destroyed about half the life on our planet. Its intelligence, however, has proved itself unendurably high for human beings.

Angelucci saw these beings from outer space as our salvation, Hoyle as our destruction, but *both* attribute a superhuman intelligence to them. Even the skeptical Hoyle, as Jung said "comes perilously near" to endowing them "with a divine or angel like nature. Here the great astronomer joins hands with the naïve Angelucci."[24]

It seems to me that far too few people have read this paper of Jung's and have thus missed his "warning." Yet, the worldwide perception of these round symbols of the archetype of the Self does give a meaning to the catastrophic days we live in, which would at least save us from what Jung thought was the only intolerable suffering: the "torment of not understanding." Moreover, the fact, which history teaches us, that similar phenomena appear at the end of every astrological age links us with the past in a reassuring way.

In the winter of 1957–58 the C. G. Jung Institute organized one of its lecture series for a wider public. The general theme of this series was "Conscience" and the lectures were given, from the standpoint of their subject, by several well-known professors. Jung was persuaded to write a paper called "A Psychological View of Conscience."[25] He agreed to write it—and the writing of it gave him a great deal of trouble—but he stipulated that someone else should read it. Knowing his custom of often good-naturedly giving in to outer pressure, certain members of the curatorium, convinced that he would do so again in this case, hired the Auditorium Maximum at the E.T.H. and said nothing in their newspaper advertisements about Jung himself not appearing. But Jung was already eighty-two at the time and knew that such an effort was far beyond his physical strength, so he remained firm. The pressure was so persistent, however, that he remained at Bollingen much later into January than usual in order to keep himself beyond reach. "They just don't realize what an effort I have

o Cf. Jung's own vision in his 1944 illness in which he also saw the earth from the distance of about a thousand miles.

already made for them in writing the lecture," he said to me at the time.

Marie-Louise von Franz and I attended the lecture and found the unwieldy Maximum full to capacity. There was a great deal of disappointment at first that Jung was not there, but Franz Riklin[p] rose magnificently to the occasion and, undismayed by the reproaches (not even earned by himself, as he had had no part in putting pressure on Jung), read the paper so well that the huge audience listened in complete silence and applauded almost as if Jung himself had been there. It is indeed one of the most interesting of Jung's shorter papers and, like *The Undiscovered Self* and *Flying Saucers*, too little known.

In his masterly description of what the word "conscience" really means, Jung drew a very clear distinction between conscience and the moral code. If we allow our "conscience" to make every decision in accordance with the traditional standards of right and wrong, we include only one opposite and avoid real ethos, which—in earlier days—meant obeying the *vox Dei*. Jung had known since he was eleven years old that God (whether one calls this supreme inner voice God or the Self here makes no difference) often asks much more of us than mere obedience to the moral code. The reader will remember the agony the boy Jung went through in trying to avoid the blasphemous thought.[q] Yet it was just this thought that he had regarded as "the sin against the Holy Ghost, which cannot be forgiven,"[26] which was followed by his first experience of the miracle of grace. That experience had been decisive for his whole life, and he knew ever afterward that the vital necessity was fulfilling the will of this divine power.

His lecture on conscience was written over seventy years after that childhood experience, yet it is clearly a blossom that comes from that root, a very complete and beautiful flower, as the hushed silence with which it was received that night at the E.T.H. bore witness. But the kind of conscience that Jung described does not make for popular reading, because putting in into practice demands the utmost integrity and willingness to suffer. So the lecture has never been much read.

All this while Jung had been considering two major projects, either of which would involve him in a great deal of work. The first, which he gave up only very regretfully, had been in his mind ever since he finished his long paper on synchronicity. He saw clearly that the investigation of numbers would carry on and illuminate the concept of synchronicity. From 1956 onward, however, a great deal of pressure from outside was brought to bear on him to give his attention to an autobiography. This was by no means a welcome idea to him,[27] and if he had followed his own inclination he would undoubtedly have decided for the work on numbers. But he felt the research on the latter would take more time and energy than he had at his

p Franz Riklin had been made president of the C. G. Jung Institute in 1957.
q See above, p. 45 ff.

disposal and that he should give it over into younger hands. Since he knew that Marie-Louise von Franz would be capable of the task (I even heard him say, after listening to a lecture of hers, that she was the only one of his pupils who fully understood his ideas), he handed over to her the notes he had made on the subject, with the request that she undertake the research and eventually write the book.[28]

Aniela Jaffé was his secretary at the time, and he thought it would be most practical to dictate the necessary material for the autobiography to her. Since she had already proved her excellence as a writer,[29] he intended to leave the writing entirely to her, for he very much distrusted autobiographies. He said:

> An autobiography is so difficult to write because we possess no standards, no objective foundation, from which to judge ourselves. There are really no proper bases for comparison. I know that in many things I am not like others, but I do not know what I really am like. Man cannot compare himself with any other creature; he is not a monkey, not a cow, not a tree. I am a man. But what is it to be that? Like every other being, I am a splinter of the infinite deity, but I cannot contrast myself with any animal, any plant or any stone. Only a mythical being has a range greater than man's. How then can a man form any definite opinions about himself?[30]

Later Jung found, however, that it was impossible for *anyone* to write his "personal myth," so he wrote the first three chapters of *Memories, Dreams, Reflections* himself. These and Chapter 12, "Late Thoughts" and "Retrospect," were, as far as I know, all of his autobiography that he wrote entirely himself, but he told me that he went through, added to, and corrected all the rest of the manuscript very carefully, so that the book forms a most meaningful whole. Sometimes he became quite interested and would discuss it with considerable enthusiasm; at other times he felt it was taking more energy and time than he could afford.

In 1959 the British Broadcasting Corporation began to put pressure on Jung to allow himself to be interviewed by John Freeman for its series of famous living people called "Face to Face." He had less resistance to overcome in this instance than he had in the matter of an autobiography; he was even rather intrigued by the idea. The B.B.C. took endless trouble in the matter. Not only did John Freeman come to Zürich to make Jung's acquaintance in the spring, but a representative—Mrs. Branch—was sent during the Whitsun holidays to interview all the people whom the B.B.C. knew were intimate with Jung. She made a great many suggestions for the subjects to be discussed, and wherever one could one answered. But if in any doubt I, at all events, asked to be allowed to inquire and to write to Mrs. Branch later; so it was done that way. As I suspected, Jung did not want any planned program, preferring to let the conversation develop spontaneously.

Although John Freeman and everyone else concerned were as considerate as possible, it was nevertheless a tiring ordeal for Jung at eighty-four. The actual filming took the whole morning and they were not finished until about 2 P.M. But he went through it remarkably well, showing no sign of any strain on the television. When I asked him beforehand if he would not find it too tiring, he said he felt it must be done; there would be so many conflicting reports about him after his death that people must have the chance to see him, in order to judge for themselves. Indeed, the whole film is Jung *exactly* as he always was: natural, simple, and spontaneous.

Although I heard him make the above remark only in connection with the television interview, I think the same reason really led to his decision to consent to the autobiography. Indeed, above all, the "Face to Face" television interview and *Memories, Dreams, Reflections* give people who did not know him personally the best chance to "judge for themselves."

Jung went to Bollingen very often during these years to recover from all these efforts. In fact, he still did a great deal of his writing while he was there, and he still carved images and chiseled inscriptions. As late as 1958 he carved, on the west outer wall of the original Tower, the figure of a woman extending her hands toward the udder of a mare. Behind her, a bear (also a female) is rolling a round sphere toward her back. Over the woman, he chiseled the words: "May the light I carried in my womb arise. 1958." Over the horse: "Pegasus, living spring, the water poured out by the water carrier (Aquarius)." Over the bear: "The bear who moves the mass." [31]

This was one of the images revealed to him, so to speak, by the stone itself. Astrologically, as Jung often pointed out, we are entering the age of Aquarius and, dark as our times seem, a new light and living water may yet arise from them.

# 18

# Back to the Rhizome
# 1960 –1961

Although he was eighty-five in July, 1960, fate that year demanded yet another great effort from Jung. I do not remember hearing him speak of his original refusal to become involved in a popular exposition of his psychology.[a] The first time I remember hearing him mention the subject was one spring evening when Ruth Bailey and he came to supper with us in Marie-Louise von Franz's Tower. By that time he had become quite enthusiastic about the idea of producing a popular volume to be called *Man and His Symbols*, and he asked for Marie-Louise's collaboration. He wanted to write only one of the articles himself, asked her to do the very important one on individuation, then discussed the formation of the whole book with her and who would be the best person to ask to write on each subject he wanted to include. Only later did he ask her to undertake the editing of the whole book from the psychological point of view in the event of his death or ill health. He did not actually begin to write his own article until some months later.

Jung seemed very well in the early summer of 1960 and was a great deal at Bollingen, including most of July, until just before his eighty-fifth birthday on July 26. He even fulfilled a long-planned invitation to the members of the Psychological Club to spend an afternoon with him there. Ruth willingly undertook the considerable work involved and, assisted by Jung's daughters and daughter-in-law, made it a very successful party indeed. It was especially enjoyed by those members of the club who had never been to Bollingen before.

Nevertheless, when I went down the next morning to help Ruth—as I

---

[a] Cf. *Man and His Symbols*, page 9, where John Freeman explains that Jung refused the idea "with great firmness."

usually did during those last years—I found Jung very thoughtful and sad. I do not know, however, whether this was because he had not fully realized before how much the club had changed, since Toni Wolff was no longer there in her role of "club tiger,"[b] and how many familiar faces were missing, or whether it was a foreboding that this would be his last really happy visit to his beloved Tower. At all events, he left for Küsnacht shortly after the club party, to return to his Tower only once again, in the early spring of 1961.

Jung's eighty-fifth birthday was much more of a strain than his eightieth had been, and it soon became sadly evident that he was indeed five years older. Nevertheless, he went through it all without showing that it was tiring him so much. In addition to the same two C. G. Jung Institute parties at the Dolder Hotel, he was made an *Ehrenbürger*[c] of his own village, Küsnacht, which, though he appreciated it very much indeed, involved him in yet another official dinner at the Hotel Sonne. By that time he was so tired he had serious misgivings as to whether he would be able to get through the evening. As usual, though, he rose to the occasion, and in no way disappointed his hosts, the *Gemeindepräsident,* Edward Guggenbühl, and the *Gemeinderat.*[d]

When the birthday celebrations were over, Jung felt a great need to get right away, in order to be completely quiet for a time. He decided to go with Fowler McCormick and Ruth Bailey to a favorite small hotel at Onnens in West Switzerland, which they had often made their headquarters before, for drives around its lovely and interesting environs. When I went to help Ruth with her last-minute preparations, she told me she felt Jung was really badly overtired, but he seemed so glad to be getting away that she could only acquiesce in his wish. Later she told me that at lunch, about half way to Onnens, he had seemed so seriously unwell that both she and Fowler had tried to persuade him to return home. But Küsnacht just then was associated with too much effort, so he insisted in going on to Onnens.

That night, however, he was taken seriously ill. The local doctor, who spent the night in the hotel, was very much afraid it would be the end but, largely thanks to this doctor's efforts and the excellent nursing of Ruth Bailey, Jung pulled through his collapse. Naturally, the family had been notified that he was dangerously ill. They could not bear the idea of their father dying in a distant hotel, so Marianne Niehus and her husband went to Onnens immediately, determined to bring him back in a helicopter. This he absolutely refused, but since he was by this time considerably better, he did consent to return home in an ambulance.

[b] See above page 198 ff.
[c] This is comparable to being given the freedom of the city.
[d] The Mayor and Corporation of Küsnacht.

Jung stood the journey very well, and was glad to be home again, especially since he was still too ill to have any obligation to meet demands. Not long after his return, he told the same dream to both Marie-Louise and myself (separately). We both had the feeling that he still thought he would probably die and wanted the dream to be recorded. He dreamed:

> He saw the "other Bollingen" bathed in a glow of light, and a voice told him that it was now completed and ready for habitation. Then far below he saw a mother wolverine teaching her child to dive and swim in a stretch of water.

This was obviously a death dream, for he had often dreamed of this "other Bollingen" before, in various stages of construction, and he had always spoken of it as being in the unconscious, in the Beyond. The end of the dream has the same meaning: the dreamer must soon pass into another element (usually called another world) and learn as different a way of adaptation as the young wolverine, who was already at home on dry ground, had to learn in the water. Evidently Mother Nature was ready for the change and prepared to give him her full support.

This dream made both Marie-Louise and me very sad, for it was clear that Jung would soon be leaving us to go to "the other Bollingen." In fact, it may have been this dream that loosened his strong tie to his earthly Bollingen. Once again, as had happened so often before, Jung's complete acceptance of death gave him a new lease of life, to his own great surprise. He recovered quickly and was pretty well all winter, but I do not think quite as well as before his eighty-fifth birthday. At all events, contrary to his earlier practice, he made no attempt to go to Bollingen and also abstained from his usual winter visit to the Tessin. Although he was undoubtedly declining physically, his mind and psychic understanding steadily increased, right up to the end. If he forgot the slightest thing (actually he did so less than when he was younger!), he immediately said: "There, I told you I was getting senile!" *If* he believed this himself, it was the only illusion I ever knew him to harbor.

Although he remained steadily in Küsnacht until the early spring, he was very active. He gave himself fully to writing his article for *Man and His Symbols*—which he wrote in English, since the book first appeared in that language—and to reading and criticizing the other articles as they were submitted to him. He was especially pleased with Marie-Louise's article and made no changes in it.

Jung wrote his article—"Approaching the Unconscious"—for *Man and His Symbols* in a different way from anything he had written for many years. He was not pressed into writing it by his creative daimon, but was *consciously* obeying his dream. He had dreamed that "instead of sitting in his study and talking to the great doctors and psychiatrists who used to call on him from all over the world, he was standing in a public place and addressing a multitude of people who were listening to him with rapt attention and understanding what he said. . . ."[1]

Explaining his psychology to people who knew *nothing* about it had long been most difficult and uncongenial to Jung. I remember when I first came to Zürich, he told me he had to send those people who knew little or nothing of his psychology to his assistants first, because he no longer had sufficient patience to teach them the ABCs. When he was asked to give three lectures during the war to the inhabitants of Küsnacht (who knew nothing of his psychology) he told me they gave him more trouble to prepare than all his other lectures put together. Yet once having realized from his dream that there was "a multitude of people" who *could* understand his psychology, he never hesitated, but put himself to endless trouble to explain its most fundamental points as simply as possible.

His eightieth birthday experience and the many letters he received from simple people who had read his books or seen and heard him on television must have helped, for he was fully convinced that it was such people who could carry on his psychology. At all events, there is no doubt that he gave his last months to unremitting effort in carrying out this task. Perhaps it was the reason he had so unexpectedly been granted a new lease of life after Onnens. In any case, if he had died then, about nine months earlier, this final article would never have been written.

Jung's great concern with the future of mankind is evident throughout the paper. He constantly alluded to the danger we are running of destroying ourselves and to the impotence of our conscious efforts to avert this disaster. In fact, this article might be called his last appeal to man to realize the reality of the unconscious and above all to take his own soul seriously, for Jung saw that this was his sole hope. Since *Man and His Symbols* has had a very wide circulation, and has been translated into several languages, this article has certainly been read by a far wider public than anything else he wrote in his last five years. In fact, we may hope it has reached the people of whom Jung had the most hope: the people who read his books and let them silently change their lives.

Jung no longer had time to edit the book from the psychological point of view, as the publishers had hoped, but foreseeing this, he had arranged for Marie-Louise von Franz to do it for him. John Freeman has already testified to her success in this endeavor.[2] Jung indeed read through all that was written of the book before his death, and finished his own article. He also went steadily on seeing one or two people every day, and kept up his drives and short walks. He even found the energy to attend the annual Christmas dinner of the Psychological Club, though it evidently tired him and he left soon after dining. It meant a great deal to the members to meet him at this annual event, and I do not think he ever missed it, except for the years he was away in Africa and India, and in 1946 when he was very ill.

In March he again went to Bollingen with Ruth. Hans Kuhn was also there, as often as he could be spared from his other duties. Superficially, Jung seemed much as usual at Bollingen, but one felt it was no longer all important to him to be there. Presumably, though he never said so, the attachment he had always had was now being transferred to the "other Bollingen," in the Beyond. But he was well enough to come up to lunch at Marie-Louise's Tower on a day so lovely that we were able to have coffee outside.[e] He also could sit most days at his "water works" where the little stream ran into the lake.

He did not stay nearly as long at Bollingen as he usually did at that time of year. As far as I remember, he was there only about three weeks. Very soon after he got back to Küsnacht he had to go for a short time to the Red Cross Hospital in Zürich for a minor checkup. He had not been in the hospital since 1944—when he was at Hirslanden for five months—and since he had then taken a dislike to hospitals, it was fortunate that this time he had to stay only two or three days.

Although we had been through the English of his article for *Man and His Symbols* while he was at Bollingen,[f] he went on working at minor alterations for some weeks. It soon became evident, however, that his physical health was really giving out. He still saw a few people and went for drives, but on the last drive we took together (on May 6, exactly a month before his death) he did not walk at all, as had been his invariable habit up until then. He also did not feel like talking, though he seemed anxious to see his favorite roads[g] again, and we drove longer than usual. One strange thing happened on this last drive: we met and were held up *three* times by weddings.[h] Even at the time, I was reminded of the *"Todeshochzeit"* and Jung's experience on the way back from the Tessin just after his mother's death.[3] I do not know if Jung noticed it himself. I have the feeling he did, but he did not say anything.

Jung was out only once after this, for a drive the next day in his own car. Although he was out a great deal on his large balcony, he no longer came downstairs. About three weeks before his death, he had a slight stroke which blurred his speech a little, but did not otherwise lame him in any way.

---

[e] Her loggia was not built until several years after Jung's death, so we still had to sit in the open before the house. This long postponement of a loggia was the result of Jung's experience and advice.

[f] Since Jung had given permission to Freeman to popularize his, and all the other articles, it was less important than usual to get the English correct.

[g] We very often drove on the roads around Pfannenstiel, which Jung knew by heart from bicycling long ago.

[h] The Swiss often go for drives, with several cars following, as part of wedding festivities.

Although he was still about, and even saw people occasionally, it was getting clear that his exceptionally strong body was at last giving out. He had so often been on the brink of death, however, and been granted a new lease of life, that it was very difficult for us all not to hope that this would happen yet again. But he was not deceived in this way himself. He said, several days before his death: "Do the people know I am dying?" It was evidently still important to him that there should be no repetition of the 1944 dearth of news.[i]

He moved about on the second floor (his library, his bedroom, and a large balcony were on the same floor) until Tuesday May 30, exactly a week before he died, and even did some writing. Then he had another slight stroke and had to leave his library for good. He was just one week in bed and remained conscious to the end. His last visions were largely concerned with the future of the world after his death. He told Marie-Louise, the last time she saw him, eight days before his death, that he had had a vision in which a large part of the world was destroyed, but, he added, "Thank God, not all of it."

His last recorded dream which he dreamed a few nights before his death, we owe to Ruth Bailey. She kindly wrote it out for me at the time:[4]

1) He saw a big, round block of stone in a high bare place and on it was inscribed: "This shall be a sign unto you of wholeness and oneness."

2) A lot of vessels, pottery vases, on the right side of a square place.

3) A square of trees, all fibrous roots, coming up from the ground and surrounding him. There were gold threads gleaming among the roots.

This is a very beautiful last dream, in which Jung's unity and wholeness are confirmed and shown to him in the symbol of a round stone. The pots in the square to the right are also full of meaning, when we remember that in ancient Egypt some parts of the dismembered corpse of the god Osiris were kept in pots, because it was from these that the resurrection was expected to take place. Moreover, the old Greeks kept pots in their houses full of wheat seeds. The pots and the soil represented the underworld and the seed the dead waiting for resurrection. About the time of All Souls' Day, the pots were opened and the dead were supposed to join the living.[j] Christ's saying: "Verily, verily, I say unto you, Except a corn of wheat fall into the ground and die, it abideth alone: but if it die, it bringeth forth much fruit" (John 12:24) belongs in the same connection.[5]

[i] See above, page 279 ff.

[j] It is interesting to remember that sometimes when Jung spoke of his reasons for taking someone to be his pupil or patient, he said: "Oh, I thought he or she was a good pot, and therefore I would invest in it."

As to the roots, Jung said in *Memories:*

> Life has always seemed to me like a plant that lives on its rhizome. Its true life is invisible, hidden in the rhizome. The part that appears above ground lasts only a single summer. Then it withers away—an ephemeral apparition. When we think of the unending growth and decay of life and civilizations, we cannot escape the impression of absolute nullity. Yet I have never lost a sense of something that lives and endures underneath the eternal flux. What we see is the blossom, which passes. The rhizome remains.[6]

Now that the "blossom was passing away and proving itself, like all mortal life, to be "an ephemeral apparition," the eternal roots, that were also C. G. Jung, appeared above the surface and spread themselves protectingly over him. This dream tells us with the greatest clearness that Jung was dying at the right time, and was about to be received by that rhizome which he had always known was there as his "true invisible life."Or, to use the language he used in *Memories,* his No. 1 personality was dying, but his No. 2 remained unchanged.

Jung died at a quarter to four on Tuesday afternoon, June 6. There were again some synchronistic events, as there had been in 1944.[k] I remember most vividly that when I went to fetch my car, just before he died, I found the battery, which was not old and had never given the slightest trouble before, completely run down. This puzzled me very much at the time; when Ruth telephoned about half an hour later, it seemed quite natural and as if the car had known.

There was, however, no thunderstorm at the time Jung died (as has been reported from time to time). That came an hour or two *later*, at which time lightning struck a tall poplar tree in his garden at the edge of the lake. This is most unusual, for the water attracts the lightning and therefore trees and houses on its banks are usually immune. The tree was not destroyed, only a geat deal of its bark was stripped off. In fact, it was discovered by the family when they found the lawn covered with bits of bark when they went into the garden after the storm was over.

Jung himself said of death in *Memories*:

> . . . death is indeed a fearful piece of brutality; there is no sense in pretending otherwise. It is brutal not only as a physical event but far more so psychically: a human being is torn away from us, and what remains is the icy stillness of death.[7]

---

[k] See above, page 278 ff.

Everyone who had known Jung well was hit amidships by this fact, for his warm, genial physical presence had indeed been replaced by the icy stillness of death. I remember Franz Riklin, for instance, breaking down when he heard the news and crying like a child, although in our long friendship I never knew him shed another tear. He was president of the C. G. Jung Institute at the time and, although no president could have bothered Jung less with outer problems, he had always felt Jung's presence behind him, giving him security and strength.

Jung had died so exactly at the right time, and his death was such a natural event, that we were able to pull ourselves together, to go on with our own lives and the life of the institute by the next morning. Ever since Jung had so nearly died in India, I had been wondering how far his pupils would endure his death and be able to stand on their own feet. The answer in 1938 was catastrophic, and not much better during his worst illness in 1944. During every serious illness I asked myself the same question, and each time the answer became slightly more hopeful. Had Jung died on one of the earlier occasions of illness, I am sure we should have felt his death to be a far more brutal catastrophe. As it was, it was more a terribly painful natural event, that we must, could, and did accept. I realized vividly how mercifully the unconscious had prepared us and how well Jung himself had taught us to stand on our own feet.

The C. G. Jung Institute carried on as Jung would have wished. It shut its doors only for one day: Friday, June 9, the day of the funeral. A good deal of pressure was brought to bear on the family to hold the service in Zürich, in the cathedral or the Fraumünster. I am glad to say they remained firm and held it in their own village church. Many people came from great distances, such as Fowler McCormick from Chicago, but Küsnacht church is exceptionally large and, although there were crowds of people, everyone found a seat. Curiously enough, there was another thunderstorm during the service and afterward a downpour of rain.

As time went on and Jung continued to appear in dreams and active imagination, just as he had done in his lifetime, one did indeed realize that the rhizome—or No. 2 personality—seemed completely unchanged by death. Death is indeed a paradox, as Jung himself had realized so vividly on his way back from the Tessin after his mother's death. Not that there is anything parapsychological or spiritualistic concerned; we simply cannot tell how much the individual Jung is involved, for, in his present No. 2 personality, he is utterly beyond our experience or comprehension. Perhaps the help comes from an archetype that Jung's whole life and teaching has constellated so strongly that in dreams it often appears in his form or speaks with his voice. I do not know. When I stood by his infinitely peaceful and yet very remote dead body, I could only say "Thank you" again and again. And that is how I still feel toward this life which was lived so fully and that we were privileged to know: a profound and boundless gratitude.

# Reference Notes

Abbreviations: *MDR* = *Memories, Dreams, Reflections,* recorded and edited by
Aniela Jaffé (New York: Pantheon Books, 1962)
*CW* = The Collected Works of C. G. Jung

## CHAPTER 1

1 Henry T. Ellenberger, *Die Entdek-kung des Unbewussten* (Bern, Stuttgart, Vienna: Verlag Hans Huber, 1973), II, 913.
2 *MDR,* p. 170 ff. All references to this volume are to the Pantheon Books edition. The pagination is the same in the paperback edition, but unfortunately it is quite different in the edition published in England.
3 This broadcast was published as an Introduction to *Essays on Contemporary Events* (London: Kegan Paul, 1947), p. xv *ff.*
4 *MDR,* p. 7.

## CHAPTER 2

1 German edition of *MDR,* p. 404.
2 *Ibid.,* p. 404.
3 *MDR,* p. 233.
4 *Ibid.,* p. 233.
5 *Ibid.,* p. 60 *ff.* and p. 87.
6 *Ibid.,* p. 7.
7 *Ibid.,* pp. 6-15.
8 *Ibid.,* pp. 11-15.
9 *Ibid.,* p. 356 *ff.*
10 *Ibid.,* p. 15.
11 *Ibid.,* p. 9 *ff.* Italics added.
12 *Answer to Job* was first published in German in 1952. *CW,* Vol. 11, par. 553-758.
13 *MDR,* p. 9.
14 *Ibid.,* p. 7 *ff.*
15 *Ibid.,* p. 90.
16 *Ibid.,* p. 8.
17 *Ibid.,* p. 18.
18 *Ibid.,* p. 91 *ff.*
19 *Ibid.,* p. 315.
20 *Ibid.,* p. 48.

[21] *Ibid.*, p. 19.
[22] *Ibid.*, p. 90.
[23] *Ibid.*, p. 91.
[24] *Ibid.*, p. 18.
[25] *Ibid.*, p. 90.
[26] *Ibid.*, p. 17 *ff.*
[27] Oeri's reminiscences were printed in *Die kulturelle Bedetung der komplexen Psychologie* (Berlin: Springer Verlag, 1935), p. 524 *ff.*
[28] *MDR*, p. 19.
[29] *Ibid.*, p. 18.
[30] *Ibid.*, pp. 20-23.
[31] *Ibid.*, p. 23.

[32] *Ibid.*, p. 356. Italics added.
[33] *Ibid.*, p. 20.
[34] *Ibid.*, p. 322 *ff.*
[35] *Ibid.*, p. 325.
[36] *Ibid.*, p. 21.
[37] *Ibid.*, p. 21.
[38] *CW*, Vol. 5.
[39] *MDR*, p. 23.
[40] *Ibid.*, p. 22.
[41] *Ibid.*, p. 356.
[42] *Ibid.*, p. 9.
[43] *Ibid.*, p. 26.
[44] *Ibid.*, p. 100.

CHAPTER 3

[1] *MDR*, p. 24.
[2] *Ibid.*, p. 29.
[3] Ernst Jung, *Extracts from the Diary of My Father,* quoted by Albert Oeri, *op. cit.*, p. 525.
[4] *MDR*, p. 31.
[5] *Ibid.*, p. 30 *ff.*
[6] *Ibid.*, p. 32 *ff.*
[7] *Ibid.*, p. 22.
[8] *Ibid.*, p. 39.
[9] *Ibid.*, pp. 36-41.
[10] *Ibid.*, p. 40.
[11] *Ibid.*, p. 33 *ff.*
[12] F. Max Müller. Trans., *The Upanishads*. This forms Volume I of *The Sacred Books of the East,* edited by F. Max Müller (Oxford University Press), p. 136.
[13] *MDR*, p. 34.
[14] *Ibid.*, p. 319.
[15] *Ibid.*, p. 42.
[16] *Ibid.*, p. 91.
[17] *Ibid.*, p. 66.
[18] *Ibid.*, p. 35.
[19] *Ibid.*, p. 87 *ff.*
[20] *Ibid.*, page 64 *ff.*
[21] Albert Oeri, *op. cit.*, p. 525.
[22] *MDR*, p. 66.
[23] *Ibid.*, p. 43.
[24] *Ibid.*, p. 67.
[25] *Ibid.*, p. 41.

[26] *Ibid.*, p. 52 *ff.*
[27] *Ibid.*, p. 56.
[28] *Ibid.*, p. 56 *ff.*
[29] *Ibid.*, p. 60 *ff.*
[30] *Ibid.*, p. 61.
[31] *Ibid.*, p. 68.
[32] *Ibid.*, p. 69 *ff.*
[33] *Ibid.*, p. 55.
[34] *Ibid.*, p. 91 *ff.*
[35] *Ibid.*, p. 43.
[36] *Ibid.*, p. 93.
[37] *Ibid.*, p. 84.
[38] *Ibid.*, p. 75.
[39] *Ibid.*, p. 73.
[40] *Ibid.*, pp. 87-90.
[40] *Ibid.*, p. 85.
[41] *Ibid.*, pp. 87-90.
[42] *Ibid.*, pp. 84-90.
[43] *Ibid.*, p. 86.
[44] *CW*, Vol. 12, p. 208.
[45] *MDR*, p. 291 *ff.*
[46] *Ibid.*, p. 86.
[47] *Ibid.*, p. 84. Italics added.
[48] *Ibid.*, p. 95.
[49] *Ibid.*, p. 42.
[50] *Ibid.*, p. 100.
[51] *Ibid.*, p. 66.
[52] *Ibid.*, p. 67.
[53] *Ibid.*, p. 83.
[54] *Ibid.*, p. 77 *ff.*
[55] *Ibid.*, p. 79 *ff.*

CHAPTER 4

¹ *MDR*, p. 95.
² Albert Oeri, *op. cit.*, p. 526.
³ *MDR*, p. 104 *ff.*
⁴ *Ibid.*, p. 99.
⁵ *Ibid.*, p. 180.
⁶ *On the Psychology and Pathology of So-Called Occult Phenomena* (*CW*, Vol. 1, par. 1-150).
⁷ *Ibid.*, par. 134.
⁸ *Synchronicity: An Acausal Connecting Principle* (*CW*, Vol. 8, par. 816 *ff*).
⁹ *MDR*, p. 107.
¹⁰ *Ibid.*
¹¹ *Lehrbuch der Psychiatrie*, fourth edition, 1890.
¹² *Ibid.*, p. 108 *ff.*
¹³ It appears in English in *CW*, Vol. 9, Part 2, par. 20 ff.
¹⁴ *MDR*, p. 111.
¹⁵ *Ibid.*, p. 109.

CHAPTER 5

¹ *CW*, Vol. 14, footnote to par. 129.
² *MDR*, p. 112.
³ Albert Oeri, *op. cit.*, p. 528.
⁴ Jung, *Analytical Psychology: Its Theory and Practice*. Multigraphed at the time, these lectures were first published in 1968 by Pantheon Books, New York; pp. 52-61, 78-86.
⁵ *Analytical Psychology*, pp. 58-61; *MDR*, pp. 115-17.
⁶ *MDR*, p. 114.
⁷ *Ibid.*, p. 9.
⁸ *Ibid.*, p. 193.
⁹ This is found in an appendix by Aniela Jaffé about Jung's ancestors and family, which appears only in the German edition of *MDR*, p. 407.
¹⁰ *MDR*, pp. 117-19.
¹¹ Cf. *The Freud/Jung Letters* (Princeton University Press, 1974).
¹² *MDR*, p. 148.
¹³ See, for instance, *Ibid.*, p. 163.
¹⁴ *Ibid.*, p. 158 ff.
¹⁵ *CW*, Vol. 5. First published in 1912 in German as *Wandlungen und Symbole der Libido*. A rather unfortunate English translation appeared in 1916 as *The Psychology of the Unconscious*. Jung revised it in German and published it as *Symbole der Wandlung* in 1952. The translation in the English *Collected Works* is from this edition.
¹⁶ *MDR*, p. 158 *ff.*
¹⁷ *Man and His Symbols*, p. 56.
¹⁸ *MDR*, p. 158.
¹⁹ *Man and His Symbols*, p. 57.
²⁰ Ernest Jones, *The Life and Work of Sigmund Freud* (London: The Hogarth Press, 1958, and New York: Basic Books, 1955), II, 65.
²¹ *Ibid.*, III, 20 *ff.* Italics added.
²² *MDR*, p. 150.
²³ *Ibid.*, p. 151.
²⁴ *Ibid.*, p. 151 *ff.*
²⁵ Ernest Jones, *op. cit.*, II, 171.
²⁶ *Ibid.*, III, 81.
²⁷ *Ibid.*, I, 159.
²⁸ Cf. *The Freud/Jung Letters*, p. 456.
²⁹ *MDR*, pp. 355-359.
³⁰ Ernest Jones, *op. cit.*, I, 68, 175 ff, 202.
³¹ Extracts from these letters were published as Appendix II of *MDR*, pp. 365-70.
³² *MDR*, p. 117.
³³ *Ibid.*, p. 114.

CHAPTER 6

[1] *MDR*, p. 158 *ff.*
[2] *Erinnerungen, Träume, Gedanken von C. G. Jung*, pp. 378-79.
[3] *MDR*, p. 167.
[4] *Ibid.*, p. 168.
[5] Ernest Jones, *op. cit.*, II, 160 *ff.*
[6] *Ibid.*, II, 155.
[7] *Ibid.*, II, 161 *ff.*
[8] *MDR*, p. 171.
[9] *Ibid.*, p. 171 *ff.*
[10] *Ibid.*, p. 173.
[11] Cf. Marie-Louise von Franz, *Number and Time* (Evanston, Illinois: Northwestern University Press, 1974), p. 293 *ff.*
[12] *MDR*, p. 175.
[13] *Ibid.*, p. 175.
[14] *Ibid.*, p. 175 *ff.*
[15] *Ibid.*, p. 179.
[16] This dream and its dramatic sequel can be found in *Ibid.*, p. 180.
[17] Cf. *The Freud/Jung Letters*, p. 301 *ff.*
[18] *MDR*, p. 193.
[19] *Ibid.*, p. 176.

CHAPTER 7

[1] *MDR*, p. 176. Italics added.
[2] *Paracelsus as a Spiritual Phenomenon* (*CW*, Vol. 13, par. 210).
[3] Homer, *The Odyssey*, translated by E. V. Rieu. (Penguin edition, pp. 72-79).
[4] *MDR*, p. 189.
[5] *Ibid.*, p. 137.
[6] *Ibid.*, p. 189 *ff.*
[7] *Ibid.*, p. 191.
[8] *Ibid.*, p. 149.
[9] *Ibid.*, p. 153.
[10] *Ibid.*, p. 183.
[11] *Ibid.*, p. 185 *ff.*
[12] *Ibid.*, p. 185.
[13] *Ibid.*, p. 195.
[14] *Ibid.*, p. 296 *ff.*
[15] *Ibid.*, p. 195 *ff.*
[16] Goethe's *Faust*, Part II (Penguin Books, Ltd., 1959, p. 79).
[17] *MDR*, p. 196 *ff.*
[18] *Ibid.*, p. 199.
[19] C. G. Jung, *Synchronicity: An Acausal Connecting Principle*, *CW*, Vol. 8, par. 816 *ff.*
[20] *MDR*, p. 179.
[21] *Psychological Types* (London: Kegan Paul, 1923), p. 7; *CW*, Vol. 6.
[22] Ernest Jones, *op. cit.*, II, 148 *ff.*
[23] Translated from the text in *Die Victoriner: Mystische Schriften* (Jakob Hener in Vienna), p. 179 *ff.*
[24] *MDR*, p. 328 *ff.*

CHAPTER 8

[1] *MDR*, p. 223.
[2] *Ibid.*, p. 238 *ff.*
[3] *Ibid.*, p. 371 *ff.*
[4] *CW*, Vol. 14, par. 226.
[5] *Ibid.*, par. 223.
[6] I owe this reference to the kindness of Esther Harding.
[7] *MDR*, p. 242 *ff.* There is a misprint in the English-language edition which might confuse the reader: "embarked from Marseilles" should read "for Marseilles." It is correct in the German edition, p. 246.
[8] Although this paper was originally written about 1945, it was revised and expanded only in 1954 for inclusion in *Von den Wurzeln des Bewusstseins*. English translation in *CW*, Vol. 13, p. 248 *ff.*

9 *The Philosophical Tree, CW,* Vol. 13, par. 424.
10 "Allegoriae Sapientum" in *Theatrum Chemicum* (1622) V, 67. In *The Philosophical Tree, CW,* Vol. 13, par. 426.
11 *MDR,* p. 223 *ff.*
12 A volume of these lectures and papers is in preparation at the C. G. Jung Foundation, New York.
13 *CW,* Vol. 7, par. 206-20.
14 M. R. James, translator, *The Apocryphal New Testament,* p. 27. Italics added.
15 *Ibid.,* p. 26.

16 *MDR,* p. 225.
17 Cf. *Ibid.,* p. 235.
18 Cf. Aniela Jaffé's footnote, *Ibid.,* p. 235.
19 *Ibid.,* p. 225.
20 *Ibid.,* pp. 228-31.
21 *Serma Suppositus,* 120, 8; for further examples see M. L. von Franz, *Aurora Consurgens* (New York: Bollingen Series LXXVII, Pantheon Books, 1966), p. 428 *ff.* This book is the third volume of Jung's *Mysterium Coniunctionis* in the German edition.
22 *MDR,* p. 315 *ff.*

CHAPTER 9

1 *MDR,* p. 246 *ff.*
2 *Ibid.,* p. 251 *ff.*
3 *Ibid.,* p. 325.
4 *Ibid.,* p. 248.
5 *Ibid.,* p. 251.
6 First published in *Wirklichkeit der Seele* (Zürich, 1931). This lecture appears in English in Vol. 10 of *CW,* par. 49-103, as *Mind and Earth.*
7 Cf., for example, Part II of *Psychology and Alchemy.*
8 *MDR,* p. 253.
9 *Ibid.,* p. 373.
10 *Ibid.,* p. 260.

11 *Ibid.,* p. 260 *ff.*
12 *Ibid.,* p. 264.
13 *Ibid.,* p. 254.
14 *Ibid.,* p. 256.
15 *Ibid.,* p. 324.
16 *Ibid.,* p. 267.
17 "Der altaegyptische, der christliche und der moderne Mythos" (The ancient Egyptian, Christian and Modern Myth). *Eranos Jahrbuch,* XXXVII, 1968.
18 *MDR,* pp. 270-72.
19 *Ibid.,* p. 271.
20 *Ibid.,* p. 273.
21 *Ibid.,* p. 273.

CHAPTER 10

1 *MDR,* pp. 197-99.
2 Figure 3 in *The Secret of the Golden Flower* (London, 1931); *CW,* Vol. 13, Plate A.3.
3 *MDR,* p. 198.
4 It is reproduced as Figure 10 in *The Secret of the Golden Flower, CW,* Vol. 13, Plate A.10.
5 *The Secret of the Golden Flower,* p. xiii *ff.* Retranslated in *CW,* Vol. 13, par. 1 *ff.*

6 *MDR,* p. 189.
7 *The Secret of the Golden Flower,* p. 91. *CW,* Vol. 13, par. 17.
8 *MDR,* p. 255 *ff.*
9 *Ibid.,* p. 197.
10 *CW,* Vol. 13, par. 20-26.
11 Cf. G. R. S. Mead in his article on "Ceremonial Game-Playing and Dancing in Mediaeval Churches," first printed in October, 1912, in *The Quest: A Quarterly Review* and re-

printed (together with two other articles by the same author on "The Sacred Dance of Jesus" and "Ceremonial Dances and Symbolic Banquets in Mediaeval Churches") in *The Quest Reprint Series*, No. 11, in 1926.

[12] *Ibid.*, p. 110 *ff.*

[13] *Psychology and Alchemy, CW*, Vol. 12, par. 182.

[14] G. R. S. Mead, *The Hymn of Jesus*, Vol. IV of *Echoes from the Gnosis*. Cf. also M. R. James, *The Apochryphal New Testament* in *The Acts of John*, p. 258 *ff.*

[15] Cf. B. Hannah, *Striving Toward Wholeness* (New York, The C. G. Jung Foundation and G. P. Putnam's Sons, 1971).

[16] *MDR*, p. 224.

[17] *C. G. Jung, sein Mythos in unserer Zeit* (Frauenfeld, Huber Verlag, 1972), p. 69 *ff.* It was published in English as *C. G. Jung: His Myth in Our Time* (New York: C. G. Jung Foundation and G. P. Putnam's Sons, 1975).

CHAPTER 11

[1] "Wotan" first appeared in the *Neue Schweizer Rundschau* in March, 1936. It appeared in English in *Essays on Contemporary Events* in 1947. It is now in *Civilization in Transition, CW*, Vol. 10, par. 371 ff.

[2] From the Epilogue to *Essays on Contemporary Events* (1947), *CW*, Vol. 10, par. 472-75.

[3] *CW*, Vol. 9, Part 1, par. 617.

[4] *CW*, Vol. 10, par. 315.

[5] *CW*, Vol. 9, Part 1, par. 525 *ff.*

[6] From "A Rejoinder to Dr. Bally," *CW*, Vol. 10, par. 1016 *ff.*

[7] *CW*, Vol. 10, par. 1022.

[8] *CW*, Vol. 10, par. 1060.

[9] *Neue Zürcher Zeitung*, No. 343 of February 27, 1934.

[10] *Ibid.*, No. 437 of March 13, 1934 and No. 443 of March 14, 1934. English translation in *CW*, Vol. 10, pp. 535-44.

[11] Lewis Mumford, *The New Yorker*, May, 1964, p. 174.

[12] It can be read in full in *CW*, Vol. 10, par. 1016-34.

[13] This can also be read in full in *CW*, Vol. 10, par. 1014 *ff.*

[14] Quoted in full, with Jung's reply, in *CW*, Vol. 10, p. 543 *ff.*, note 5.

[15] *The Role of the Unconscious, CW*, Vol. 10, par. 17 *ff.*

[16] *CW*, Vol. 7, par. 240.

[17] *CW*, Vol. 10, par. 1024.

[18] *Ibid.*, par. 1028.

[19] *Ibid.*, par. 1029.

[20] *Ibid.*, par. 1031 *ff.*

[21] *Ibid.*, par. 1034.

[22] *CW*, Vol. 9, Part I, par. 1-86.

[23] *MDR*, p. 202 *ff.*

[24] The series of pictures that forms the thread of Ariadne in *The Psychology of Transference* also comes from the "Rosarium." *CW*, Vol. 16.

[25] *MDR*, p. 205.

[26] In the Swiss edition. Since the English *Collected Works* includes only Jung's own writings, Part III of the *Mysterium Coniunctionis* was published separately as *The Aurora Consurgens* in the Bollingen Series (New York: Pantheon Books, 1966).

[27] This is in the text of the Swiss edition, but appears only as a footnote in the English edition. *CW*, Vol. 14, p. xvi.

[28] Cf. Marie-Louise von Franz, *C. G. Jung: His Myth in Our Time* (New York: The C. G. Jung Foundation and G. P. Putnam's Sons, 1975), especially chapters 11 and 12.

[29] *MDR*, p. 325.
[30] First American Edition, Pantheon Books, New York, 1968.
[31] *CW*, Vol. 12.
[32] In *The Mystic Vision, Papers from the Eranos Yearbooks* (New York: The Bollingen Foundation, and London: Routledge), Vol. 6, p. 247 *ff*.
[33] This lecture was published at the time in a symposium, *Factors Determining Human Behavior*. In 1942 it was republished as *Human Behavior* in yet another symposium edited by Ruth Nanda Anshen. It now appears in *CW*, Vol. 8, par. 232-62. Both of the later versions underwent "slight alterations."
[34] These lectures were published by the Yale University Press in 1938 under the title *Psychology and Religion*. They were published in German in 1940, when Jung revised and augmented them. This is the version that appears in *CW*, Vol. 11, par. 1-168.

## CHAPTER 12

[1] *MDR*, p. 273.
[2] *Ibid.*, p. 274 *ff*.
[3] *Ibid.*, p. 275.
[4] *Ibid.*, p. 280.
[5] *CW*, Vol. 10, par. 993 *ff*.
[6] *Ibid.*, par. 999.
[7] *Ibid.*, par. 236-75.
[8] *Ibid.*, par. 260.
[9] *MDR*, p. 279.
[10] *Ibid.*, p. 278 *ff*.
[11] *CW*, Vol. 10, par. 991-92.
[12] *MDR*, p. 279.
[13] *MDR*, p. 278.
[14] *CW*, Vol. 10, p. 525 *ff*.
[15] *CW*, Vol. 10, par. 1006. Italics added.
[16] *Ibid.*, par. 1005.
[17] *MDR*, p. 329.
[18] *Ibid.*, p. 276.
[19] *Ibid.*, p. 192.
[20] *Ibid.*, p. 323.
[21] *CW*, Vol. 12, end of par. 37.
[22] *CW*, Vol. 16, par. 353 *ff*.
[23] *CW*, Vol. 10, par. 1013.
[24] *MDR*, p. 277 *ff*.
[25] *Ibid.*, p. 280 *ff*.
[26] *Ibid.*, p. 282 *ff*.
[27] *Good and Evil in Analytical Psychology*, in *CW*, Vol 10, par. 877.
[28] *MDR*, p. 283 *ff*.
[29] *Ibid.*, p. 322 *ff*.

## CHAPTER 13

[1] Jung's "Presidential Address" can be read in *CW*, Vol. 10, par. 1069 *ff*.
[2] Ditto, par. 1064 *ff*.
[3] *CW*, Vol. 10, par. 998.
[4] It is this version that appears in *CW*, Vol. 9, Part 1, par. 148 *ff*.
[5] *The Dreamlike World of India* and *What India Can Teach Us, CW*, Vol. 10, par. 981-1013. Both were originally in *Asia*, XXXIX, 1939.
[6] Vol. VII, *Tantric Texts*, edited by Arthur Avalon (Sir John Woodroffe) and published by Luzac and Co., London.
[7] *MDR*, p. 275. The lectures referred to were preserved in multigraphed form.
[8] *On the Psychogenesis of Schizophrenia, CW*, Vol. 3, par. 504 *ff*.
[9] *The Therapeutic Value of Abreaction, CW*, Vol. 16, par. 289.
[10] Emma Jung and Marie-Louise von Franz, *The Grail Legend* (London:

Hodder and Stoughton, 1971; New York: C. G. Jung Foundation and G. P. Putnam's Sons, 1972).
[11] Rascher Verlag, Zürich, 1960.
[12] *CW*, Vol. 9, Part 1, par. 199 *ff.*
[13] *Eranos Jahrbuch*, 1939, pp. 399-447.
[14] *CW*, Vol. 9, Part 1, par. 199-239.
[15] Rascher Verlag, Zürich, 1950.
[16] This lecture, then called *Die Stimme des Innern* (The Voice from Within) is now revised and published in English as *The Development of Personality* in *CW*, Vol. 17, par. 284 *ff.*

CHAPTER 14

[1] Cf. *MDR*, p. 225.
[2] *The Secret of the Golden Flower* (1962 edition), p. 42; *CW*, Vol. 13, par. 17.
[3] *Ibid.*, p. 91; *CW*, Vol. 13, par. 17.
[4] *MDR*, p. 256.
[5] *CW*, Vol. 11, par. 169 *ff.*
[6] *CW*, Vol. 15, par. 18 *ff.*
[7] *CW*, Vol. 13, par. 145 *ff.*
[8] *CW*, Vol. 11, par. 296 *ff.*
[9] *CW*, Vol. 13, par. 239 *ff.*
[10] *CW*, Vol. 12.
[11] *MDR*, p. 292 *ff.*
[12] *Ibid.*, p. 293.
[13] *Ibid.*, p. 289 *ff.*
[14] *Ibid.*, p. 155 *ff.*
[15] *Ibid.*, p. 295.
[16] *Ibid.*, p. 36 *ff.*
[17] *Ibid.*, p. 10 *ff.*
[18] *Ibid.*, pp. 293-96.
[19] *Ibid.*, p. 293.
[20] *Hamlet*, Act III, scene i.
[21] *MDR*, p. 295.
[22] *Ibid.*, p. 302.
[23] *Ibid.*, pp. 299-326.
[24] *Ibid.*, p. 321.
[25] *Ibid.*, p. 296.
[26] *Ibid.*, p. 296 *ff.*
[27] *Ibid.*, p. 295 *ff.*
[28] Mircea Eliade, *Shamanism, Archaic Techniques of Ecstasy*. Originally published in French in 1951, it was translated into English by Willard R. Trash and published in the Bollingen Series LXXVI (New York: Pantheon Books, 1964).
[29] *Ibid.*, p. 50.
[30] *Ibid.*, p. 53.
[31] *Ibid.*, p. 27. Italics added.
[32] The Hogarth Press, London, 1970. Published in the United States by W. W. Norton & Co., 1972, under the title *The Prisoner and the Bomb*.

CHAPTER 15

[1] *MDR*, p. 297.
[2] *Neue Schweizer Rundschau*, Zürich, n.S. XIII.
[3] Bollingen Series XXX, Vol. 1, pp. 3-48. Revised longer version in *CW*, Vol. 9. Jung had changed the title himself when he revised the lecture in 1947 for *Symbolik des Geistes*.
[4] *CW*, Vol. 16, par. 402 *ff.*
[5] *Ibid.*, par. 449.
[6] This lecture appears in the first volume of the *Papers from the Eranos Yearbooks*, p. 371 *ff.* Jung enlarged and revised it, and published it in *Von den Wurzeln des Bewusstseins* (Rascher Verlag, Zürich, 1954). The translation which appears in *CW* —*On the Nature of the Psyche*, Vol. 8, par. 343 *ff.*—is from this later version.
[7] *MDR*, p. 297.
[8] Printed as a preface to John Trinick,

*The Fire-Tried Stone* (London: John Watkins, 1967).

⁹ Aldus Books Limited, London, 1964; Doubleday and Company, New York, 1964.

¹⁰ *CW*, Vol. 9, Part 2.

¹¹ Unfortunately omitted in the English edition, although like the later *Aurora Consurgens,* it is an intrinsic part of Jung's book.

¹² *CW*, Vol. 12, par. 447-515.

¹³ *CW*, Vol. 9, Part 2, par. 127.

¹⁴ *Aion, Ibid.,* par. 74 *ff.* The subject continues for many pages and recurs later.

¹⁵ *CW*, Vol. 11, par. 559.

¹⁶ *Ibid.*

¹⁷ *Ibid.,* par. 561.

¹⁸ *MDR*, p. 323 *ff.*

¹⁹ *CW*, Vol. 11, par. 739.

²⁰ *Ibid.,* par. 744.

²¹ *Ibid.,* par. 745.

²² *Ibid.,* par. 758.

²³ *Ibid.*

²⁴ *Synchronicity: An Acausal Connecting Principle.*

²⁵ Vol. 3, p. 201 *ff.*

²⁶ First published in English in 1955 (Routledge, London, and Pantheon Books, New York, Bollingen Series LI). Jung's part of this book is in *CW,* Vol. 8, par. 816-997.

²⁷ Northwestern University Press, 1974, p. 6 *ff.*

²⁸ *CW*, Vol. 8, par. 840-55.

²⁹ *Ibid.,* par. 869 and par. 872 *ff.*

³⁰ *Ibid.,* par. 902 *ff.*

³¹ *Ibid.,* par. 965 *ff.*

³² *Ibid.,* par. 966.

³³ *Ibid.,* par. 967 and 968.

³⁴ Cf. Marie-Louise von Franz, *C. G. Jung: His Myth in Our Time* (New York: C. G. Jung Foundation and G. P. Putnam's Sons, 1975).

³⁵ *MDR*, p. 226 *ff.*

³⁶ *Ibid.,* pp. 226-28.

³⁷ *Ibid.,* p. 21.

³⁸ *Ibid.,* p. 297.

CHAPTER 16

¹ *CW*, Vol. 14, par. 659. The italics come from the German edition.

² *CW*, Vol. 14, par. 664.

³ *Ibid.,* par. 679 and 680.

⁴ *Ibid.,* par. 762.

⁵ *MDR*, p. 255 *ff.*

⁶ *CW*, Vol. 14, par. 759 *ff.*

⁷ *Ibid.,* par. 758.

⁸ *Ibid.,* par. 664.

⁹ *Ibid.,* par. 744.

¹⁰ *Ibid.,* par. 705 *ff.* and par. 749-58.

¹¹ *Ibid.,* par. 705.

¹² *Ibid.,* par. 749.

¹³ *Ibid.,* end of par. 705.

¹⁴ *Ibid.,* par. 706.

¹⁵ *Ibid.,* par. 790-92.

CHAPTER 17

¹ Cf. *MDR*, p. 175.

² *Ibid.,* p. 233.

³ *Ibid.,* p. 225.

⁴ *Ibid.*

⁵ Cf. *Ibid.,* p. 78.

⁶ *Ibid.,* p. 261.

⁷ *CW*, Vol. 14, p. xiii.

⁸ Cf. *MDR*, p. 356 *ff.*

⁹ *CW*, Vol. 10, par. 488-588.

¹⁰ It appears in a small volume published by Routledge and Kegan, Paul, London, and by Little, Brown, Boston in 1958, as well as in *CW*, Vol. 10, par. 488 *ff.*

¹¹ *CW*, par. 488.

¹² *Ibid.,* par. 524.

[13] *Ibid.*, par. 535.

[14] *Ibid.*, par. 536.

[15] *Ibid.*, par. 540.

[16] *Ibid.*, par. 503.

[17] *Ibid.*, par. 504.

[18] *MDR*, p. 256.

[19] This small book appeared in German late in 1957 and in an English version in 1959. It eventually appeared in *CW*, Vol. 10, par. 589-824.

[20] *Weltwoche*, Zürich, 22 Jahrgang, No. 1078, July 9, 1954, p. 7.

[21] Orfeo M. Angelucci, *The Secret of the Saucers* (Amherst Press, 1955).

[22] *MDR*, p. 289 *ff.*

[23] All three books were published by Heinemann in London and Harper & Row in New York.

[24] *CW*, Vol. 10, par. 816.

[25] *Ibid.*, par. 825-86.

[26] *MDR*, p. 36.

[27] Cf. *MDR*, Aniela Jaffé's Introduction, p. v.

[28] This book appeared in 1970 as *Zahl und Zeit* (now translated as *Number and Time*), and fully justified Jung's choice. It was published in German by Ernst Klett Verlag, Stuttgart, and in English by Northwestern University Press.

[29] For example, in "Der Goldene Topf" which Jung had printed in his *Gestaltungen des Unbewussten* (Rascher Verlag, Zürich, 1950).

[30] *MDR*, p. 3 *ff.*

[31] There is a good photograph of these carvings and their inscriptions in G. Wehr, *C. G. Jung* (Hamburg: Rowohlt Monographien, 1969, 1970, 1972), p. 53.

CHAPTER 18

[1] *Man and His Symbols*, p. 10.

[2] *Ibid.*, p. 13 *ff.*

[3] *MDR*, p. 314.

[4] Cf. Miguel Serrano, *C. G. Jung and Hermann Hesse: A Record of Two Friendships* (New York: Schocken Books, 1966), p. 105 *ff.*

[5] I owe these references to Marie-Louise von Franz.

[6] *MDR*, p. 4.

[7] *Ibid.*, p. 314.

# Bibliography

*Allegoriae Sapientum* . . . in *Theatrum Chemicum* . . . Strasbourg, 1660, Vol. 5

Angelucci, Orfeo M., *The Secret of the Saucers,* Amherst Press, 1955.

The Apocryphal New Testament, see James.

*Artis Auriferae* . . . . Basel, 1552, 2 vols.

Aschaffenburg, Gustav, "Experimentelle Studien über Associationen" in Kraepelin, Psychol. Arb., I (1896) 209-99; II (1899), 1-85; IV (1904), 235-374.

St. Augustine, "Sermo Suppositus" CXX (in *Natali Domini* IV), in Migne, *P.L.,* vol. 39, cols. 1984-87.

——, "The Serpent Power," *Tantrik Texts,* Vol. II.

Avalon, Arthur (Sir John Woodroffe), "Shri Sembhara Chakra," *Tantrik Texts,* Vol. VII, Luzac & Co., London, 1919.

*Basler Stadtbuch,* 1965, see G. Steiner.

——, *Germany Possessed, Jonathon Cape, London, 1941.*

*Baynes, Godwin, The Mythology of the Soul, Ryder and, Co., 1969.*

——, *La Chimie au moyen âge,* Paris, 1893.

Berthelot, M., *Collection des anciens alchemistes Grecs,* Paris, 1887-88.

Bertine, Eleanor, *Human Relationships,* Longmans, Green & Co., New York, 1958.

——, *Jung's Contribution to our Time,* C. G. Jung Foundation and G. P. Putman's Sons, New York, 1967.

Biedermann, Alois. *Christliche Dogmatik,* Forell Füssli, Zürich, 1869.

Dorn, Gerard, Principal Writings in *Theatrum Chemicum,* Vol. I.

Eckhart, Meister, translated by C. de B. Evans, John M. Watkins, London, 1924.

Eliade, Mircea, *Shamanism, Archaic Techniques of Ecstasy,* Pantheon Books, New York, 1964.

Ellenberger, Henry F., *The Discovery of the Unconscious,* Basic Books Inc., New York, 1970.

*Encyclopaedia Britannica,* 1911.

Flournoy, Théodore, *From India to the Planet Mars,* translated by D. B. Vermilye, New York and London, 1900.

Franz, Marie-Louise von, *Aurora Consurgens,* Bollingen Series XXVII, New York, Pantheon Books, 1966.

———, *C. G. Jung: Sein Mythos in unserer Zeit,* Verlag Huber, Frauenfeld and Stuttgart, 1972. English edition, *C. G. Jung: His Myth in Our Time,* C. G. Jung Foundation and G. P. Putnam's Sons, New York, 1975.

———, *Number and Time,* Northwestern University Press, Evanston, 1974.

Frey-Rohn, Liliane, *From Freud to Jung, A Comparative Study of the Psychology of the Unconscious,* C. G. Jung Foundation and G. P. Putnam's Sons, New York, 1974.

*The Freud/Jung Letters,* Routledge and Kegan, Paul, London, 1974; Bollingen Series XCV, Princeton University Press, Princeton, 1973.

Goethe, Johann Wolfgang von, *Faust,* translated by Philip Wayne, Penguin Books, Limited, Harmondsworth, 1959.

Gower, John, *Confessio amantis,* II, in the complete works of John Gower; edited by G. C. Macaulay, Oxford, 1899-1902, 4 vols.

Harding, Esther, *The I and the Not I,* Pantheon (Bollingen Foundation), New York, 1965; Princeton University Press, Princeton, 1970.

———, *Journey into Self,* Longman's, Green & Co., New York, 1956; Vision, London, 1958; David McKay, New York, 1963.

———, *The Parental Image,* C. G. Jung Foundation and G. P. Putnam's Sons, New York, 1965.

———, *Psychic Energy,* Pantheon Books, (Bollingen Foundation), New York, 1963.

———, *The Way of All Women,* Longmans, Green & Co., London, New York, 1933; C. G. Jung Foundation and G. P. Putnam's Sons, New York, 1970.

———, *Woman's Mysteries,* Longmans, Green & Co., London, New York, 1935; C. G. Jung Foundation and G. P. Putnam's Sons, New York, 1972.

Homer, *The Odyssey,* translated by E. V. Rieu, Penguin edition.

Hoyle, Fred, *The Black Cloud,* Heinemann, London and Harper & Row, New York, 1957.

———, *Frontiers of Astronomy,* Heinemann, London and Harper & Row, New York, 1955.

———, *The Nature of the Universe,* Heinemann, London and Harper & Row, New York, 1960.

*The I Ching or Book of Changes,* the Richard Wilhelm translation rendered into English by Cary F. Baynes, Routledge and Kegan Paul, London, 1951. Also Bollingen Series XIX, Princeton University Press, 1960.

St. Ignatius Loyola, *The Spiritual Exercises,* edited and translated by Joseph Rickaby S. J., 2nd Edition, London, 1923.

Izquierdus, Introduction to the *Spiritual Exercises* of St. Ignatius Loyola.

Jaffé, Aniela, "Bilder und Symbole aus E.T.A. Hoffmann's Märchen 'Der Goldne Topf,'" printed in C. G. Jung's *Gestaltungen des Unbewussten,* Rascher Verlag, Zürich, 1950.

James, Montague Rhodes, *The Apocryphal New Testament,* Clarendon Press, Oxford, 1924.

Jones, Ernest, *The Life and Work of Sigmund Freud,* The Hogarth Press, London, 1958, and Basic Books, New York (3 vols.), 1953-57.

Jung, C. G., *After the Catastrophe*, Collected Works, Vol. 10, par. 400-43.

———, *Aion*, Collected Works, Vol. 9, Part 2.

———, *Analytical Psychology: Its Theory and Practice*, Pantheon Books, New York, 1968.

———, *Answer to Job*, Collected Works, Vol. 2, par. 553-758.

———, *Archetypes of the Collective Unconscious*, Collected Works, Vol. 9, par. 1-86.

———, *Collected Papers on Analytical Psychology*, edited by Constance Long, Ballière, Tindall and Cox, London, 1917, 2nd edition.

———, *Contributions on Analytical Psychology*, translated by Godwin Baynes, Kegan, Paul Ltd., London, 1928.

———, *The Dreamlike World of India*, Collected Works, Vol. 10, par. 981-1001.

———, *Erinnerungen, Träume, Gedanken*, edited by Aniela Jaffé, Rascher Verlag, Zürich, 1962.

———, *Essays on Contemporary Events*, Kegan, Paul Ltd., London, 1947.

———, *Experimental* Researchs, Collected Works, Vol. 11.

———, *The Fight with the Shadow* (originally entitled *Individual and Mass Psychology*), Collected Works, Vol. 10, par. 444-457.

———, *Gestaltungen des Unbewussten*, Rascher Verlag, Zurich, 1950.

———, *Good and Evil in Analytical Psychology*, Collected Works, Vol. 10, par. 877-86.

———, *Individual Dream Symbolism in Relation to Alchemy*, in *Psychology and Alchemy*, Collected Works, Vol. 12, par. 44-331.

———, "Individual and Mass Psychology," B.B.C., Nov. 3, 1946, printed as Introduction to *Essays on Contemporary Events*, Kegan Paul Ltd., London, 1947.

———, *Letters*, Vol. 1, Routledge and Kegan Paul, London, 1973. Bollingen Series XCV:I, Princeton University Press, Princeton, 1973.

———, *Memories, Dreams, Reflections*, edited by Aniela Jaffé, Pantheon Books, New York, 1961.

———, *Mind and Earth*, Collected Works, Vol. 10, par. 49-103.

———, *Mysterium Coniunctionis*, Collected Works, Vol. 14.

———, *On the Nature of the Psyche*, Collected Works, Vol. 8, par. 343-442.

———, *On the Psychology and Pathology of So-called Occult Phenomena*, Collected Works, Vol. 1, par. 1-150.

———, *Paracelsica*, Rascher Verlag, Zürich, 1942.

———, *Paracelsus as a Spiritual Phenomenon*, Collected Works, Vol. 13, par. 145-238.

———, *Paracelsus, the Physician*, Collected Works, Vol. 15, par. 18-43.

———, *The Phenomenology of the Spirit in Fairy Tales*, Collected Works, Vol. 9, Part 1, par. 384-455.

———, *The Philosophical Tree*, Collected Works, Vol. 13, par. 304-482.

———, *A Psychological Approach to the Dogma of the Trinity*, Collected Works, Vol. 11, par. 169-295.

———, *Psychological Aspects of the Mother Archetype*, Collected Works, Vol. 9, Part 1, par. 148-98.

———, *Psychological Factors Determining Human Behavior*, Collected Works, Vol. 8, par. 232-62.

———, *Psychology of Transference*, Collected Works, Vol. 16, par. 353-539.

———, *Psychological Types*, translated by Godwin Baynes with the assistance of the author, Kegan Paul, London, 1923.

———, *Psychological Types*, translated by Richard Hull, Collected Works, Vol. 6.

———, *Psychology and Alchemy*, Collected Works, Vol. 12.

———. *Psychology and Religion*, Collected Works, Vol. 11, par. 1-168.

———, *A Rejoinder to Dr. Bally*, Collected Works, Vol. 10, par. 1016-34.

———, "The Relation between the Ego and the Unconscious," in *Two Essays on Analytical Psychology*, translated by H. G. and C. F. Baynes, Baillière, Tindall and Cox, London, 1928.

———, *The Relations between the Ego and the Unconscious*, translated by Richard Hull, Collected Works, Vol. 7, par. 202-507.

———, "Religious Ideas in Alchemy," in *Psychology and Alchemy*, Collected Works, Vol. 12, par. 332-565.

———, *The Role of the Unconscious*, Collected Works, Vol. 10, par. 1-48.

———, *Seelenprobleme der Gegenwart*, Rascher Verlag, Zürich, 1931.

———, *The Spirit Mercurius*, Collected Works, Vol. 13, par. 239-303.

———, *A Study in the Process of Individuation*, Collected Works, Vol. 9, Part 1, par. 525-626.

———, *Symbolik des Geistes*, Rascher Verlag, Zürich, 1948.

———, *Symbols of Transformation*, Collected Works, Vol. 5.

———, *Synchronicity: An Acausal Connecting Principle*, Collected Works, Vol. 8, par. 816-997.

———, *The Therapeutic Value of Abreaction*, Collected Works, Vol. 16, par. 255-93.

———, *Transformation Symbolism in the Mass*, Collected Works, Vol. 11, par. 296-448.

———, *Von den Wurzeln des Bewusstseins*, Rascher Verlag, Zürich, 1954.

———, *What India Can Teach Us*, Collected Works, Vol. 10, par. 1002-13.

———, *Wirklichkeit der Seele*, Rascher Verlag, Zürich, 1934.

———, *Woman in Europe*, Collected Works, Vol. 10, par. 236-75.

———, *Wotan*, Collected Works, Vol. 10, par. 371-99.

Jung, C. G., and Pauli, Wolfgang, *The Interpretation of Nature and the Psyche*, Routledge, London and Pantheon Books, New York, Bollingen Series LI, 1955.

Jung, C. G., and Wilhelm, Richard, *The Secret of the Golden Flower*, Kegan Paul, London, 1931; Commentary on "Secret of the Golden Flower," Collected Works, Vol. 13, par. 1-84.

Jung, Emma and Franz, Marie-Louise von, *The Grail Legend*, Hodder and Stoughton, London, 1971; C. G. Jung Foundation and G. P. Putnam's Sons, New York, 1972.

Jung, Ernst, "*Aus den Tagebüchern meines Vaters*, Winterthur, 1910.

Kant, Immanuel, *Critique of Pure Reason*, Everyman's Library, 1934.

Krug, W. T., *General Dictionary of the Philosophical Sciences*, 2nd edition, 1832.

*Die kulturelle Bedeutung der komplexen Psychologie*, Springer Verlag, Berlin, 1935. "Festschrift" for Jung's sixtieth birthday.

Lorenz, Konrad, *On Agression*, Methuen & Co., London, and Harcourt, Brace, Jovanovich, New York, 1966.

Mead, G.R.S., "Ceremonial Game-Playing and Dancing in Mediaeval Churches," in *The Quest*, a Quarterly Review, No. II, Watkins, London, 1926.

———, "The Hymn of Jesus," of *Echoes from the Gnosis*, Theosophical Publishing Society, London, 1906, Vol. IV.

Nietzsche, Friedrich, *Thus Spake Zarathustra*, translated by Thomas Common, Modern Library, New York.

Oeri, Albert, "Ein paar Jugenderinnerungen," in *Die kulturelle Bedeutung der komplexen Psychologie*, Springer Verlag, Berlin, 1935.

Ostanes, Arabic Book of, in Berthelot, M., *La Chimie au moyen âge*, 1893.

*Papers from the Eranos Yearbook*, Bollingen Series XXX, Princeton University Press and Routledge and Kegan Paul, London, 6 vols.

Puech, H. G., "Concept of Redemption in Manichaeism," in *Papers from the Eranos Yearbook*, Vol. 6, 1968, pp. 247-314.

*The Quest Quarterly Review Reprint Series*, Series No. II, Watkins, London, 1926.

Richard de St. Victor, see Victor.

"Rosarium Philosophorum," in *Artis Auriferae*, 1553.

Schopenhauer, Arthur, *The World as Will and Idea*, translated by Haldone and Kemp, English and Foreign Philosophical Library, 3 vols., 1883–1886.

Steiner, Gustav, "Erinnerungen an Carl Gustav Jung," in *Basler Stadtbuch*, 1965, pp. 117–63.

*Teutsches Liederbuch.*

Trinick, John, *The Fire-Tried Stone*, John Watkins, London, 1967.

"The Upanishads," *The Sacred Books of the East*, Vol. 1, Oxford University Press, Reprint, London, 1926.

*"Die Victoriner": Mystiche Schriften*, edited by Paul Wolff, Thomas-Verlag, Jacob Hegner in Wien, 1936.

Victor, Richard de St., "Benjamin Minor," printed in *Die Victoriner*, pp. 131-92.

White, Victor, *God and the Unconscious, Harwill, London, 1952.*

Wilhelm, Richard, *I Ging, das Buch der Wandlungen*, Jena, 1924.

———, *I Ching*, translated by Cary Baynes, Kegan Paul, London, 1951.

Woodroffe, Sir John, see Avalon.

Wordsworth, William, *Intimations of Immortality from Recollection of Early Childhood*, Everyman's Library, No. 203 Vol. 1, 1955.

Wundt, Wilhelm, *Philosophische Studien*, 20 vols., Leipzig, 1883-1902.

Yates, Frances, *Giordano Bruno and the Hermetic Traditions*, Routledge and Kegon, London, 1964.

Zumstein-Preiswerk, Stefanie, *C. G. Jung's Medium. Die Geschichte der Helly Preiswerk*, Kindler, Munich, 1975.

# INDEX

Abegg, Emil, 130
Acausal orderedness, 306
Active imagination, 108, 115, 116, 119, 190, 191, 202, 267–68, 319–20. *See also* Passive imagination
*Adhista,* 175
Adler, Alfred, 16, 69, 80, 94, 132
Adler, Gerhard, 226
Aesculapius, 33, 57, 277
"After the Catastrophe" (Jung), 289
*Aion* (Jung), 72, 300–1, 302, 311
Alchemy, 114, 139, 146, 229–31, 234–35, 236, 238, 240, 242, 253, 257, 258, 271–72, 275, 277, 291, 294, 308–9, 313 ff.; and analytical psychology, 314 ff., 319 ff.; and Christianity, 229–30, 301, 313–15, 317–18; and Sexuality, 102; Symbolism in, 102, 230, 31, 314
Alleluia game, 194-95
Allemann, Fritz, 197 n.
*Allgemeine Zeitschrift für Psychiatrie,* 78
Alter ego, 320
American Indian. *See* Pueblo Indians
American Negro, 163–64
Ammann, Anni, 194, 196 n.
Analytical psychology, and alchemy, 314 ff., 319 ff. *See also* Jungian psychology
Analytical Psychology Club (London), 259, 276
Analytical Psychology Club (New York), 164
*Analytical Psychology, Its Theory and Practice* (Jung), 234

Angelucci, Orfeo, 337–38
Angulo Baynes, Cary de. *See* De Angulo, Cary
Anima, 60–61, 64, 71, 118, 122–25, 146, 258, 291, 300, 301 n.
"Anima possession," 125
Anima types, 118
Animal ancestors, 16, 190
Animus, 71, 125, 291, 300, 301 n.
Animus thinking, 64
*Answer to Job* (Jung), 25, 301, 302–5, 309–10, 311
Anthropos, 114
Anti-Christ, 265, 300
Anti-Semitism, 222–26
Apocalypse, 303
"Approaching the Unconscious" (Jung), 344
*Arabic Book of Ostanes,* 146
"Arbor Philosophica" (Jung), 146
Archaic symbol, 212
Archaic vestiges, 101
Archetypal content, 81
Archetypal experience, 146
Archetypal images, 17, 149
Archetype(s), 114, 123, 213, 304, 306, 318, 337; of the totality, 127; of the triad, 169
"Archetypes of the Collective Unconscious" (Jung), 228
Aristotle, 135, 136
*Artis Auriferae,* 229
Aschaffenburg, Gustav, 80
*Asia,* 257
Association test, 80, 82–85
Atlantic Monthly Press, 334
Atman, 114, 315
Augustine, Saint, 156